Underground LONDON

TRAVELS BENEATH THE CITY STREETS

Underground LONDON

TRAVELS BENEATH THE CITY STREETS

STEPHEN SMITH

LITTLE, BROWN

A *Little, Brown* Book

First published in Great Britain in 2004 by Little, Brown

A CIP catalogue record for this book is available from the British Library.

ISBN 0 316 86134 0

Illustrations by Fred van Deelen

Typeset in Sabon by M Rules
Printed and bound in Great Britain
by Clays Ltd, St Ives plc

Little, Brown
An imprint of
Time Warner Book Group UK
Brettenham House
Lancaster Place
London WC2E 7EN

www.TimeWarnerBooks.co.uk

CONTENTS

Acknowledgements *vii*

MINE OF INFORMATION *1*
The Vertical City

MONSTER SOUP *27*
London's Lost Waters

WITHIN THE STONES *61*
Roman London

THE CANTERBURY TOLLS *83*
Anglo-Saxon London

VOYAGE TO THE BOTTOM OF THE SEE *101*
Medieval London

THE LOVE GAMES OF HENRY VIII *131*
Tudor London

HIGH TREASON *159*
The Gunpowder Plot

LIFTING PEOPLE *175*
The Plague

SPOILS *201*
London's Treasures

GOING OUT WITH A BANG *231*
Victorian London

EUSTON, WE HAVE A PROBLEM *253*
London Underground

POSTE RESTANTE *293*
London's Lost Railway

BUNKER MENTALITY *309*
Cold War London

POOL OF LONDON *341*
The Essential City

Select Bibliography *369*
Index *373*

ACKNOWLEDGEMENTS

With many thanks to Rosemary Smith, Zaiba Malik, Bill Dunlop, Dom Young, Luke Jacobson, Yvette Edwards, Sophie Orr, Alex Thomson, Jim Gray, Cat Ledger, Richard Beswick, Steve Guise, Fred van Deelen, David Atkinson, Ian Crane, Frances Stonor Saunders, Cristina Odone, Charmaine Colvin, Mick Murphy, Ian McCrory and Billy McKeown at London Underground, Phil Reed, John Hawks, Jonathan Foyle, Jeremy Ashby, Headley Swain, John Schofield and the Museum of London, Geoffrey Knowles, Simon Berry and Berry Brothers & Rudd, John Scholey, Peter Jewell and David Whittaker at Halliburton, Murray Craig, Brigadier Mike Keun and the City of London Corporation, Louise Donkin at Skanska, Steve East, Ben Nithsdale, Hilary Bennett and Ade Hartland at Thames Water, Friends of Kensal Green Cemetery, Subterranea Britannica. In memory of Gaby Rado and James Miller.

This author's endeavour should be to make the Past, the sense of all the dead Londons that have gone to the producing of this child of all the ages, like a constant ground-bass beneath the higher notes of the Present.

Ford Madox Ford, *The Soul of London*

MINE OF INFORMATION

The Vertical City

Of all the men and women who live and work in London, all the diverse castes of Londoners, none is more extraordinary than the miners. These unlikely city-dwellers make good money, and have been known to report to the pithead on a Monday morning still wearing the same good suits in which they've enjoyed a full weekend. Their tailors hear from them again when pay day comes around. In extremis, the problem of what to wear for a night on the town after clocking-off time is solved by taking a work shirt and rubbing chalk on the soiled collar and cuffs.

After a long and wearying shift below ground, nothing rounds off the day better than a fight of lump-removing ferocity. The miners I know found themselves tangling with a Romany crew. With the indulgent air of a man fending off his kid sister with one arm behind his back, they were languidly disputing precedence at a pub which happened to be handy for both the pit and the campsite. 'One of them reckoned he had a gun,' said Pete, a miner and an ex-marine. 'I nearly laughed my cock off.' For their part, the tunnellers declined to make the odds more favourable by going equipped to the scrap with their 'banjos', their shovels. Perhaps for this reason, they weren't having everything their own way. The morning after the scrap before, an engineer was in hospital as a result of the bar stool which had been broken over his back, another man had had his head cracked against a bus stop and the driver of an underground loco was marked with a rosebud on his forearm where he had been bitten. The driver was immediately, and inevitably, nicknamed Buffy.

The miners spend their nights under the roofs of landladies and make round trips of migratory proportions to be reunited with the families whom they raised at the scenes of earlier contracts, bygone jobs. Incredibly, I ran into these men not in South Wales or south Yorkshire but in Cricklewood, north-west London. Unbeknown to home owners in West Hampstead and St John's Wood, the miners were digging a shaft deep beneath their desirable foundations. Before I trigger a rush of prospectors in search of black gold and Cricklewood Broadway echoes to the song of canaries in cages, I should add that the miners were not extracting coal. Instead, they were excavating air, quarrying a pristine space below ground. Their skills, acquired in traditional but now redundant pits, were being employed in the service of the latest technology. To supply Londoners with all their foreseeable electricity demands, they were creating a £100 million subterranean corridor twenty kilometres long, from the old Elstree aerodrome in the north to Lord's cricket ground in the south. The National Grid had dubbed its mighty power line the London Connection.

'It's weird down here when it's dark,' said Pete, the old soldier. 'It's not like outside, where you can always make something out. You can't see anything here. Your eyes don't adjust.' Of all the strange experiences of spending time underground, the absence of light is the most easily overlooked but also the most profoundly unnatural. In total darkness, Pete and I were hunched over inside a metal box a hundred feet below ground and three miles from the nearest way out. Three miles; or, to put it in terms of the travelling time of our box, the bone-jarring carriage of a locomotive and our only means of transport, the best part of two hours. Not that the loco was going anywhere; not while the lights were off, at least. I tried to remember what the tunnel had looked like before it went dark. It had only been a few moments earlier but already it was hard to picture our surroundings clearly, so completely is sight, is light, taken for granted. The tunnel hadn't been brilliantly lit to begin with. It had to meet safety standards, of course, but why blow money on it over and above that? After all, once it was finished, nobody would ever see it again. The way the light had struck the concrete tunnel lining, I remembered, had made it look like photographs of the surface of the moon. Pete said that the sparkies, the electricians, had turned the power off. It was for safety reasons. They were rigging a transformer so that they could pay out a cable to extend the reach of the power, the light, further below ground. The tunnel was cold and damp and we were trapped, but I wasn't panicking. It was just as well, because there was nothing anyone could have done for me even if I had been. This thought in itself was almost enough to make me panic. Perhaps Pete could have knocked me out cold until the sparkies had the current back on, but short of that, there was nothing for it but to sit and wait.

I wasn't panicking, but even a comparatively short period earlier, I would have been. The underground – specifically, the Underground – made me short of breath with anxiety. I was back in London after living in the country and I couldn't face travelling by Tube, which was incomparably more comfortable than the railroad I was on with Pete, whatever disgruntled commuters might think. I would do anything to avoid making a journey under the city. And if there was no way around it, I would only attempt the trip once I was kitted out with my portable ju-ju of smelling salts, battered rosary, a ring that my girlfriend had given me and a phial of tonic made to a fortifying homoeopathic recipe, i.e. practically neat alcohol. These were my prophylactics against the terrors of going by Underground. Even armed with them, a journey on the Tube was no joyride. The sight of a crowded platform was enough to send me heading for the doors – back up the escalators and into the fresh air again. It was the same with a full train. It didn't matter how late I was, I was always prepared to let a busy Tube pull away from the platform without me. On those occasions when I managed to board a carriage, I drew the line well short of actually taking a seat, of committing myself to installing myself for the duration of a journey. Instead, I stood. To give myself credit, I didn't stand by the doors, as if I was so nervous about the ride that I reserved the option of getting off at the very next stop, although I did in fact reserve this option, and quite often exercised it. No, I stood by the open window. If it wasn't open, I insisted on opening it. It had to be the one at the end of the carriage which was closest to the driver's cab, because this had the benefit of the draught created by the motion of the train. When the train was moving, you could feel the currents against your skin. The dirt in the tunnels might turn your white shirt spotty, and the noise of the rushing air might drown out the sound of your Discman in your ears – another prophylactic against Tube terrors – but on the other hand, you experienced the illusion of being buffeted by the wind, of being out in the open air. Standing by the window at the other end of the carriage was no good, by contrast, because by the time the airflow had travelled the full length of the compartment, its effects were imperceptible.

What was I so scared of? As a reporter, I'd had to cover a number of transport disasters including the King's Cross fire, and I had learnt from them that the chances of anything happening to you on the Tube were thankfully rare. On the other hand, the first tragedy of this kind that really made an impression on me had happened in the Underground. In 1975, forty-three people were killed and seventy-four were injured at Moorgate station after a Northern Line train ran into a concrete wall at forty miles an hour. At the age of thirteen, what stuck with me about the Moorgate disaster was the length of time it took for the emergency services to reach the people who were trapped in the wreckage. It was four days before they removed the last casualty, who was the driver, Leslie Newson. The railway inspector could find no fault with the train or the track and drew the conclusion that driver error must be to blame. But Newson was experienced and had a good record. An inquest heard there was no evidence that he had been drinking. Two railwaymen who were on the platform as the train arrived at Moorgate recognised Newson and said that he had seemed calm, his usual self, with his hands at the controls. The jury returned a verdict of accidental death on all the victims. To the coroner, this meant that there was no evidence to bear out 'wicked, reckless behaviour or suicide'. The railway inquiry found that 'no previous incident in the whole history of London Transport Railways can be regarded as in any way comparable with the Moorgate accident'. The cause of the disaster is still a mystery.

Did I have Moorgate at the back of my mind whenever I flinched before boarding the Tube? What had stayed with me from the tragedy was the idea that people got trapped in the Underground. I was afraid of the train stopping in a tunnel, stranding me there with my fellow commuters and none of us knowing how long we would have to wait. It was an irrational fear, of course – even if the train stopped, no harm was likely to befall us – but at the same time, it wasn't an irrational fear, not entirely. Trains *did* stop. I knew because it had happened to me. And passengers were stranded, sometimes for hours. You read with alarm about their feats of shirtsleeved endurance.

I suffered from a kind of claustrophobia. It didn't only apply to being in a confined space like a compartment on the Underground, although it was there that I was most aware of it, or rather, it was there that it made most sense. I found that I also suffered from it above ground, out in the open air, at home. I'd returned from the wide-open spaces of the north of England to a cramped flat in a cramped street. It was my daily commute which demonstrated this change most vividly. Instead of going to work through green fields, my journey now took me through the less than verdant environs of the Jubilee and Central lines. But I was ill at ease even after the rush hour had ended. This reaction came as a shock to me. London was a city where I had lived and worked before I had moved up north. And even earlier, I'd had a connection to it through the school I'd attended. 'London' was in its name even though its address was outside the city limits. A highlight of the school year was the visit to the city, the trip to the big smoke. So why was I feeling like this? It wasn't perhaps so unusual. Le Corbusier, whose name will forever be linked with urban design, thought that cities were dystopian, 'so antagonistic to the fundamental needs of the human heart that the one idea of everybody is to escape . . . To live where there are trees and to look out on grass. To escape forever from the noise and racket of the city.' It was some comfort to register that I wasn't alone, and this was particularly true of travelling by Tube. Even before a fear of terrorist attacks made people think twice about the Underground, this was something that many of them were doing for themselves.

Then a strange and paradoxical thing happened. That makes it seem as though it happened with a bang, when really it was more of a slow-dawning realisation. As unlikely as it sounds, I found that the Tube was a good place to go if you were looking for peace. That would sound absurd to the commuter who is unfortunate enough to know the Underground only at its worst, in its heaving peak-time form. Then it's a kind of purgatory, no doubt about it, the very thing that I used to flee from – and still do, for that matter. But despite the crowds, or perhaps because of them, the Tube isn't really a social place. It's more like a private place. I realised that I hardly ever found myself sharing a Tube journey – as opposed to a walk in the park or a taxi ride or even a trip on the bus – with someone I knew. A rendezvous on the Underground never seems to happen and my impression is that we travel by Tube singly. Marc Auge, a French author who wrote a book on the Metro, Paris's answer to the Tube, said, 'only individual itineraries give it a reality . . . Solitude: this would probably be the keyword of the description an impartial observer might be tempted to make of the social phenomenon of the Metro.'

You could descend into the Underground and be gone for hours. It was true that, compared to the citizens of other great capitals, you were charged a lot of money to travel from A to B. But you could go to B via any number of intermediate places, if you wished. Provided you didn't surrender your ticket into the maw of the gateline at B, you could in theory go back to A and do the whole trip again. Believe it or not, there are people who actually enjoy taking the Tube. 'I like travelling by Underground,' wrote Doris Lessing, a happy strap-hanger.

> This is a defiant admission. I am always hearing, reading, I hate the Underground. In a book I have just picked up the author says he seldom uses it, but when he did have to go a few stops, he found it disgusting. A strong word. If people have to travel in the rush hour, then all is understood, but you may hear people who know nothing about rush hours say how terrible the Underground is. This is the Jubilee Line and I use it all the time. Fifteen minutes at the most to get into the centre. The carriages are bright and new – well, almost.

You could sit on the Circle Line and go round and round all day in a reverie, like the teenagers Imogen and Tony in Rose Macaulay's novel *Told by an Idiot*: 'past King's Cross and Farringdon Street, towards the wild, romantic stations of the east: Liverpool Street, Aldgate, and so round the bend, sweeping west like the sun. Blackfriars, Temple, Charing Cross, Westminster, St James's Park, Victoria, SLOANE SQUARE! O joy! Sing for the circle completed, the new circle begun.'

The reader who has read the above extract with his mouth ajar – I'm thinking particularly of the reader from London – who is not convinced even by the great Lessing, is urged to try the following simple experiment. If you start a conversation about what's under London with a group of friends who know the city, I guarantee that within moments they'll be vying to cap each other's tall tales of secret tunnels, government shelters, abandoned Underground stations. It can't just be the hysteria of still-fresh Tube nightmares that makes them so garrulous.

You could take the weight off your feet on an Underground platform, read a book, people-watch, look at the advertisement hoardings. In one of these, a blonde waitress served champagne to a packed Tube carriage. The joke was that, while the building society behind the poster could offer its customers advantageous terms, it had to keep what it could do for them within the bounds of possibility. But I looked at the billboard and thought, 'Champagne on the Tube? Why not?' It didn't have to be hellish. There were escalator halls like staircases from MGM musicals. Southwark station, with its hall wittily faced in blue pinstripe, was a Royal Fine Art Commission building of the year. True, the Underground could be hot and crowded and smelly but it wasn't impossible to find cool, deserted stations. Is it because they're all so posh in St John's Wood that no one ever takes the Tube?

Another thing I discovered was that my mobile phone didn't work on the Underground. Nor did my pager. An example of what makes the Tube so exasperating to some, this communications blackout was entirely welcome to me. So long as I was in the Tube, this radio silence meant that I was beyond the reach of my newsdesk, or alternatively, that I was spared the resentment of whoever I was keeping waiting at the pub or restaurant. You were untouchable in the Underground. You could get away from people, even as you were surrounded by them. And it was only a short step from knowing that you couldn't be reached on your mobile in the Tube to knowing that the Tube was an excellent excuse to have up your sleeve, as a reason why you couldn't be reached on your mobile. After I had made these discoveries, one of the comparatively few moments of distress I suffered in an Underground compartment came when I read in a newspaper about plans to extend the reach of mobile phones to Tube trains: as I write, it hasn't happened yet, thank God.

I began to see that the Underground could be a kind of haven or refuge, which would have struck me as ridiculous only a matter of months earlier. Looking for something to cheer up a wall of my London flat, I chose a poster of Simon Patterson's *The Great Bear*, in which the artist has taken Harry Beck's famous and much imitated map of the Tube, one of the most recognisable symbols of the city, and playfully replaced the familiar lines – the Victoria, the Piccadilly and so on – with his own outlandish routes: 'Film Actors', 'Saints', 'Italian Artists'. In *The Great Bear*, you find stations named after footballers or planets or even journalists. Kilburn, where I used to board the Tube for work, was 'Pele', according to Patterson, a huge improvement. Westbourne Park, the nearest stop to me now, was rechristened 'John Simpson'.

In July 2002, a new record was set for visiting all 272 stations in the Underground. Jack Welsby, a 24-year-old sub-editor from Nottingham, got round them in 19 hours, 18 minutes and 45 seconds, slashing forty minutes off the previous best time. A man on the radio described this challenge, which he too had attempted, by saying, 'There's an element of the last great adventure about it.' Even I, as well disposed to the Underground as I was becoming, found this a bit of a stretch. But I thought that the intrepid traveller had a point. It all depended on how you looked at the Tube experience. You could concentrate on all the things about it that very reasonably upset you, all the things that made the front page of the London *Evening Standard* – the crowds, the filth, the sweltering summertime commute. Or you could take a step back and appraise it as a staggering project of civic works, albeit one which was showing its age, as a bold conceit, even as a strange, self-contained inverted world. I came across something written by the architect and Londonphile Professor Maxwell Hutchinson which expressed this dichotomy.

'It is sad indeed, at the beginning of the third millennium,' he wrote, 'that this awe-inspiring concoction of engineering achievements has become such a vile object of hatred.' Prof. Hutchinson recalled coming to London as a boy and making his first journey by Tube, 'a ride that was far better than anything I had experienced at a fairground'. Now that he mentioned it, wasn't that my childhood experience, too? Wasn't it everybody's? I never forgot the smell of the Underground – the singed smell of an electrical retailer's – or the knife-grinding noise of the wheels on the track, or the darkness rushing to swallow me as the train shot into a tunnel. It wasn't impossible to recover something of this sense of wonder. I haven't told anyone this before but, when I alighted for work at Chancery Lane station, I got into the habit of watching the Central Line train disappearing into the tunnel on its way to the next stop at St Paul's, imagining that its tail-lights were really the thrumming afterburners of a spaceship or a crust-scraping mole-craft.

A short time ago, I was in an Underground train when a group of teenagers boarded the carriage. A few of them came and stood in the slipstream of the open window, my preferred position. 'There must be twenty carriages on this,' one of them told his mates. He was a blond boy with a Lancashire accent.

'More like seven or eight,' I said.

'Oh, I see,' he said, suddenly bashful. 'I've never been on the Tube before.' The youngsters had come down from Lancaster on a school trip. The train picked up speed and the lads were grinning as the wind buffeted them. To look at their faces, you would have thought they were in a speedboat rather than an old Tube train. 'We're flying!' exclaimed the blond boy.

I don't want to be an apologist for London Underground or Transport for London, who are responsible for the present condition of the Tube. But there is a way of using the thing other than with gritted teeth, with fear. When I was travelling on the Underground, I liked to look at Beck's map on the wall of the compartment: I would crane towards it from my spot beside the open window. As well as all the working stations, there were many disused stations, too. It was said that you could glimpse some of them, if you knew where to look and pressed your face to the glass as they flashed past. Perhaps you'd be lucky enough to see a panel of marble tiles, or a poster dating back to the Second World War, when the Underground was used as a vast air-raid shelter.

When you heard anyone talking about Beck's map, it was always to praise his reinvention of London's geography. 'That brilliant design turns an intricate web of lines strewn randomly across London into a coherent network depicted in those basic colours that resemble those on the equally comforting and familiar representation of the capital, the Monopoly board,' said the journalist and rail-head Christian Wolmar. Beck had taken liberties with scale, making extra room for the busiest stations in the middle of town by squeezing the other stops on the outskirts closer together. It wasn't really a map at all but an artist's impression. When people spoke about Beck's reinvention of London, his recalibration of the city, they meant the surface, what was out in the open. Hence the odd unavoidable drawback: a tourist who relied on Beck's map could set off from Leicester Square to go to Piccadilly Circus without appreciating that the two stations were a hundred yards apart.

I wasn't so curious about what Beck's map told you about the face of London, or even what it failed to tell you. I was more interested in what it told you about London beneath the surface. It said that it was vast, that there was a development under the city which was as big as the city itself, or at least, that it was as extensive. To someone who was looking for a getaway from the city above ground, this was good news. Beck's map was a join-the-dots picture of this hidden London. For all that it revealed, it only hinted at so much more. 'While it makes the Tube into a closed system, the map also retains the possibility of an infinite journey through an alternate London space,' writes David L. Pike in a book called *Imagined Londons*. With his commission uppermost on his mind, Beck the conscientious draughtsman had only included the barest of ancillary detail, to help the map-reader get his bearings. Beck's Tube lines were pivoted about London's constant, the Thames, though even the river's signature curves were straightened. What lay on every side of the lines – those familiar browns and reds and blues – one could only guess at.

And that's what I found myself doing. As I travelled on the Underground, I began to think about the London which lay to either side of the railway. There was more water and clay than anything else, of course, but there had to be all sorts of other things, too – entirely unfamiliar things, fantastic in their own way. What was there to see underground? The writer Andrew O'Hagan had a good stab at this in a bravura passage of his 2002 novel, *Personality*.

> The life underground. Caverns and chambers filled with darkness – arches, corridors, greasy pipes carrying gas to the metropolis, cracked sewers, bad air, ancient bones, mud, layers of broken plaster, former shelters, night-gloop, the remnants of the Great Fire, dust, soil and the mash of brick, passageways, vaults, lost merchandise, skin cells, a labyrinth of vanished facts, paving stones, Victorian whispers, telephone cables, a Saxon cross of powdered sandstone, down there, in London.

> There were rivers, streams, creeks, buried wharves, conduits, culverts, cellars, shelters, basements, eaves, lower ground floors, walk-downs, disappearing staircases, grottoes, dungeons, graves, tombs, crypts, a disused morgue at the foot of Tower Bridge, catafalques, sepulchres, catacombs, brick arches at Waterloo station where cabbies sat and chatted in each other's taxis, tunnels, subways, lost terraces, warrens, mazes, kitchens,

lock-ups where supermarkets stored their goods, shunting yards and railway turntables, wrecks, ruins, dregs, the Elephant Man's hat in the archives of the Royal London Hospital, precious relics, forgotten booty, buried treasure. I wanted to know more about this subterranean landscape. It was going to be an escape from the city above, but an escape in another sense, too, an adventure to make me forget my inner-city blues.

What would it be like to discover a new part of London? I'm not using the verb in the sense favoured by people who tell you that they've found a dear little delicatessen, or an unlicensed eyrie from which to watch football matches for nothing. I'm using it in the sense that a prospector or explorer might, a man who had staked his claim or planted his pennant. But of course the idea is laughable in a place like London. Has there ever been a more thoroughly explored city? Leaving aside Beck's contribution, the footsore Phyllis Pearsall tramped the streets of London to compile the first *A–Z*, thereby inaugurating a worldwide industry. London is a place which prizes cartographical nous so highly that it's referred to simply as 'the knowledge', notwithstanding the fact that the taxi drivers who acquire it famously discard everything they've learnt about the southern half of the patch the instant they're badged up. Moreover, the city is surveyed, informally but very thoroughly, day after day by the seven million people who inhabit it. But I doubt whether it's any more graspable, comprehensible, than it was a hundred years ago when Ford Madox Ford wrote, 'One may easily sail around England, or circumnavigate the globe. But not the most enthusiastic geographer . . . ever memorised a map of London. Certainly no one ever walks round it. For England is a small island, the world is infinitesimal amongst the planets. But London is illimitable.' And this was the city of the street, of the surface. I began to discover that London was like an iceberg, with only a portion of it visible above the tarmac.

Imagine looking at the city through a pair of X-ray spectacles, a dubious invention that used to be advertised in the back pages of comics with the titillating promise that the goggles would make women's tops transparent to you. By training your powerful lenses on London streets instead, you'd be rewarded with results which were similarly impressive, and less actionable. Dating as far back as Roman times, the London underneath our feet acts as the foundations of the modern capital, and not just in the winsome sense of an early draft of an evolving world-city, a work in progress. The original town lies up to thirty feet below the existing one, covered by two millennia of development and rubbish. You only have to look at the London of the surface, the revealed city, to appreciate that it is the sum of its historical parts. Elegant terraces of Georgian homes share a postcode with no-nonsense Victorian brick. The venerable premises of livery companies are book-ended by brand new banks. The same is true of subterranean London. The difference is that the landscape we are accustomed to encountering can literally be read like a book – perhaps I should say *laterally*: its story unfolds from side to side, from left to right. By contrast, the chronology of what's underground unfolds vertically. This is J. G. Ballard's 'vertical city'.

The architectural journalist Jonathan Glancey writes, 'The London we experience today is essentially a heavy-duty and enduring Victorian overlay on pretty, if flimsy, Georgian foundations stretched over a medieval street pattern settled on Roman foundations.' An archaeologist told me that doing his job was like reading a book backwards. Suppose that he was to study one of London's old churches. He might find that a piece of stone left behind by a Roman broke up the pattern of a medieval tiled floor in the Tudor crypt, and sedimentary layers of crispy carbon just beneath the flagstones indicated that the building was razed in the Great Fire and then, three centuries later, by the Luftwaffe. Sneaking into midnight mass in just such a church on Millennium Eve, Iain Sinclair admits that he's a non-believer. But

the church is a place where 'the vertical view of history holds . . .
the important dead are given their alcoves. Nothing disappears
without trace.'

It was layer upon layer, history upon history. The remnants
of past centuries hadn't been sloughed off, they weren't a kind
of discarded skin. Instead, they were part of London's warp and
weft. Sigmund Freud, a fine name for a man to be dropping
in an account of his interest in subterranean passages, said that
an ancient city like Rome could be thought of not only as a
place but also as 'a physical entity with a similarly long and
copious past – an entity, that is to say, in which nothing that has
once come into existence will have passed away and all the
earlier phases of development continue to exist alongside the
latest one'. Where the Colosseum now stands, for example, 'we
could at the same time admire Nero's vanished Golden House'
and anything else that was ever there. Freud's argument was
surely true of London, which was almost as old as the Eternal
City.

At first sight, Freud's approach to urban orienteering couldn't
have been more different to Beck's. But in fact the two men had
a lot in common. Modernism brought us Beck's map – it's now
part of heritage London, true, reprinted on everything from tea
towels to knickers, but it was boldly modernist in conceit,
corralling the abstract space of the subterranean metropolis
within the frame of a wallchart – and modernism also gave us
Freud's exploration of dream space. 'This, too, was an urban
space,' says Pike, 'from Freud's Vienna to the surrealists' Paris.'
Freud and his followers interpreted dreams while Beck allowed
commuters the 'plausible if unlikely daydream' of riding each line
of the Underground through every one of its stations. More
recently, the outstanding British conqueror of this dream space
has been Sinclair, the self-styled 'psychogeographer', who
observes the way that history leaches into the ground like a dye.
Contemplating the M25 in his most recent book, he turns the

great blue line which marks London's city limits into a kind of Rorschach test.

To the explorer of a dream space like the subterranean, paintings are as reliable a guide as any map. In *Pool of London*, the artist Tod Hanson makes Freud's point about cities more locally. This is a vast panorama of London, consciously reproducing the broad sweep of canvases such as Wenceslaus Hollar's seventeenth-century overview, except that it's rendered with the faux-blandness of an architectural drawing, to which Hanson has applied day-glo colours – salmon, verdigris, camel. In Hanson's perspective, all of London's history coexists within the same hectic frame. At first sight, his London Bridge is the Tudor model. There are turreted dwellings on Hanson's pontoon and a water wheel below. But the window of one building glows with the caloricity of artificial light, and the roof is a pincushion of aerials. Beneath the blazing corona of Hanson's Monument, flame-shaped decals suggest that a real inferno is consuming a line of buildings. This could be a snapshot of 1666 or, given the deep, star-shaped hole embedded in the pavement, of 1941. Hanson has taken the history of London, her vertical story, and expressed it laterally. On a good day, the capital gives you the refreshing sensation that you're seeing it all for the first time, that it's reborn just for you, but *Pool of London* is a reminder of its serried continuity. Eyeing the work in a gallery on that storied London highway, the Harrow Road, I felt that Hanson's way of looking at the city – Freud's way – was the way to see it. I concurred with the sentiments of the poet Sue Hubbard, whose verse could be seen undulating over the walls of a foot tunnel outside Waterloo station. 'Ruby shards of Roman glass and wolf-bone mummified in mud . . . in hidden rooms filled with dust and sour night-breath the hidden city is sleeping.' I wanted to find the oldest parts of this hidden city and read the book of London backwards to the present day.

All very interesting, the complacent metropolis might

yawningly allow from on high, but so what? What's down in the cold earth, it might add, is there for a good reason. As well as the charming history alluded to earlier, we've got a lot of workaday and frankly unpleasant stuff down there. We don't want it out in the open, where it will only block the traffic and frighten the horses, offend the eye and wrinkle the nostrils. We keep all the prosaic bits and pieces out of sight for a good reason. The London that we're familiar with doesn't care to be reminded of the Cinderella city below stairs, the one which does all the work. And you can't get much more quotidian, more earthbound, than the functions of drains and sewers and graveyards. But can it be right to describe them as prosaic? We're so insulated from the workings that service the workings of our own bodies that I doubt whether this can be meaningfully claimed.

But there's more to the underground than the past and the soberingly practical. To those who are inclined to notice these things, what's down in the earth is not just cold, it's also cool. Fashionable tailor Paul Smith showed one of his collections in disused railway arches, while his fellow ragtrader Hamish Morrow installed a catwalk in the underground car park at Marble Arch. Far beneath the West End is one of those disused Underground stations I mentioned, a 'dead station' in the plangent shorthand of Tube workers. It's looked after by a man named Barry. Although 'cool' might not be the first word you would use to describe Barry, he is the next best thing: a law unto himself. As well he might be, you might think, when you learn that the last scheduled service called at his station more than a decade ago. Indeed, there are platforms at Barry's station, the Aldwych, which haven't seen a working train since 1917. But this Kurtz of commuter-land is indulged, even fêted, by his bosses, for no other reason than that his is the most profitable halt on the system. How is this possible? Well, it doesn't hurt the bottom line that Barry is the only member of staff at his station. There's no need for anyone else. There is no one to sell a ticket to, or to warn about the defunct lift. The day-to-day tasks, which Barry seems to discharge perfectly well by himself, entail making sure that the bulbs haven't gone in the deep stairwells and that the rat traps are baited. On a surprisingly regular basis, however, Barry also makes an effort to be civil to the advertising types who want to see what their posters would look like on the walls of his abandoned platforms, and to the actors and directors who are desperate to shoot in his station. 'We had that James Bowlam down here,' Barry told me. 'He was a very nice man. I let him change in my office.' In the recent James Bond movie *Die Another Day*, Barry's basement was the place where the secret agent learnt from 'M' that he was to be cashiered.

For a further fee, Barry will even take visiting creatives for a spin in his very own Tube train, which is berthed at the closed but far from redundant stop. I like to imagine him rattling like a revenant through the Underground in his personal train, selecting his route on a whim – the *real* reason that the trains the rest of us patronise are delayed and stations shut – and the inspectors unable to lay a glove on him, because of his unexampled profitability.

You don't have to be Dr Freud to have an inkling about what makes the subterranean so fascinating. It's the repository of what's precious to us, and also what we fear and abhor. It's where we bury our treasure – and before that's dismissed as the stuff of pirate yarns, it's worth noting that the Tower of London prefers to curate the crown-jewels in a bunker below ground, and similar measures are favoured by managers of London's less well known lock-ups. The lore of the London criminal would be incomplete without the stash of moody money, to be dug up and divvied out as soon as the gang is back together again. Secrets are a form of treasure, and the underground is synonymous with secrecy. As the director of the Cabinet War Rooms told me, 'The thing about secret buildings is, they go down as far as they go up.'

London's stockroom in the ground doubles as a charnel house.

The city is notoriously full of plague pits, long since hygienically landfilled, but a curiosity to the ghoulish and those who'll pay good money to have their flesh crept. In Charterhouse Square, an urchin called John is said to have slipped and fallen into a deep seventeenth-century pit. He couldn't get out again, and in his desperation gnawed on a human limb in a futile attempt to postpone starvation. Escorted walks of London's notable quarters, which often wind their way through shadowy places, include the square in their itineraries. At Hallowe'en, you may be lucky enough to see a wild-haired man in a gore-flecked nightshirt running through the appalled and giggling walkers, brandishing a prosthetic limb resembling poor John's last meal and crying, ''Ere! Have a bit of this! It's lovely!'

My adventures under the capital would have meant less without the people I met there. Sewermen told me tall tales of coming across people who dwelt in the culverts of London, men and women who passed their time below ground like the well documented inhabitants of the New York subway. These apocryphal stories reminded me of the cult British thriller *Death Line*. The plot, which exploited the fears of those of us who had ever imagined being trapped in the Underground, concerned a group of people who had been walled up at Russell Square station and turned feral, attacking hapless commuters. That said, I did meet a real-life denizen of the underworld, an old man who had been tunnelling in north London. Unlike the miners of Cricklewood, he wasn't getting paid for his pains. Indeed, his excavations were likely to cost him dear, if the council ever penetrated his ramshackle garden and ramshackle house in order to serve a writ on him. Holes had begun appearing without warning in surrounding roads. The same thing was happening on a larger scale at Blackheath, where stretches of the A2 had been falling into the pits left by seventeenth-century chalk workings – and nineteenth-century drinking dens. But the old man who had literally undermined the streets where he lived had done the whole thing by himself. I could never fathom the motives of this eccentric character. My favourite explanation was the one offered by a neighbour, who reckoned that the tunneller had a grudge against his bank. 'Yes, I think he was planning to come up through the floor of the branch and rob it. Unfortunately, it shut down before he finished the tunnel. Now he can't get out of the habit of digging.'

The old boy belonged to a stripe of men – and they *were* predominantly men – who had a fascination with what was underground. This fascination was just this side of obsession, as outsiders might see it: their wives, for instance. Possibly the other side of obsession, too, if we're being brutally honest. Another man I met who had a thing about the Underground told me with an apologetic expression that his other half saw it in the most starkly Freudian terms. The members of a group called Subterranea Britannica were engrossed in studying the built environment beneath our feet. As membership secretary Nick Catford put it, 'If it's man-made and underground, we're interested.' The founder members got together in the 1970s to investigate mines, tunnels, drains and suchlike, and it all developed from there. I came across them in my earliest forays into the hidden capital; I would make sightings of these moles on the Internet – their website was well produced and regularly refreshed – and take soundings of them in conversations I had with people who knew the capital upside-down. One of Subterranea Britannica's experts kindly gave me an itinerary of secret London places, broken down according to the degree of difficulty of getting into them. I'm pleased to say that I've since managed to cross off destinations not only from the 'easy' and 'moderate' categories but also to bag sites from the list headed 'Difficult (But therefore unusual and never been done before)'.

My friend from Subterranea Britannica didn't even know about the Cricklewood mine where I got myself trapped with Pete, in a broken-down railway in a dark tunnel with no chance of getting anywhere near fresh air for hours, a pretty good working description of my worst nightmare, or so I would have said not many moons earlier. But I wasn't panicking. On the contrary, I was exhilarated. I felt as though I was back in love with the city at last. The tunnel had led me to something new about London, this ancient, overcrowded place. Until that moment, I would have said that the old town was established, settled, mature. Yes, estates might rise up here and there to nibble at the green belt. But from the no doubt comfortable vantage point of someone whose own backyard wasn't under threat – someone who didn't have a backyard, in fact – these encroachments felt marginal. Sure, from time to time old buildings came down and new ones went up in their place. There was turnover and makeover. But this was London marching on the spot, presenting first one profile to the world and then a different one, perhaps, but occupying the same space all the while. In the jargon of the builder and the town planner, it was brownfield development. But surely London's colonising days were over. The city which had reclaimed marsh and river in order to grow had lost its taste for expansion. Or so I'd thought. But I saw a sight to change my opinion. Deep in the London clay, there was another kind of brownfield development, one which proved that the city was growing in the most unanticipated way.

In William Blake's *Jerusalem*, 'the fields from Islington to Marybone, / To Primrose Hill and Saint John's Wood, / Were builded over with pillars of gold; / And there Jerusalem's pillars stood.' To London Electricity, the Jerusalem of a great, inexhaustible supply of power to the capital under the streets of St John's Wood rested not on pillars of gold but rings of concrete. The life of the London Connection tunnel was measured in rings, fat concrete hoops a metre and a half wide. They were transforming a hole in the ground into a giant electricity cable. Each shift was expected to move the face of the dig forward by twenty rings. Anything on top of that was worth bonuses. Distances into the tunnels were expressed in numbers of rings:

tens and hundreds and thousands of rings. At the foot of the pit
was a metal panel which was scored with chalk marks like
notches on a prison wall. There were eight strokes, one for each
ring installed so far by the early shift. Gerry and John, miners of
the old school, had looked me up and down and pretended that
I had the makings of a tunneller. 'There's a few rings in you,' said
Gerry. 'Aye, we'll have to give you a banjo,' said John. To the
north-west of us, another group of miners was also digging out
clay and replacing it with rings. If all went according to plan,
their dig and the one at Cricklewood would meet and then the
miners would celebrate with a breakthrough party, a fearful piss-
up. 'Better bring your boxing gloves,' said Gerry.

The wet and mud underfoot made you think that you were in
a real mine, a coal mine, and so did Mark from Newport. Mark
had worked at the Marine Colliery in South Wales until it closed
down. His friends had invested their redundancy money in
becoming pit owners. 'Now the power people will buy everything
they can dig,' said Mark. 'They've got a job for life.' This was the
grail, the good life. Mark was going on holiday to Benidorm, he
said. 'We're taking my boy away with his mum and dad for one
last time.' Mark turned his face towards the mouth of the pit and
spread his arms. The thought of exchanging a hole in the ground
for the sizzling beaches of Benidorm! Mark's son wanted to
follow his old man into mining. 'But he's never done a day's work
in his life. He doesn't even cut the grass.'

It was Mark's job to supervise the amazingly ticklish process
of taking fresh rings as they were lowered by a crane from the
top of the pit, and jockeying them onto the open wagons of the
trains bound for the face of the dig. Signalling to the driver of a
loco, who sat in the cab of his khaki-coloured iron-horse, Mark
ordered the leading wagon back and forth until he was satisfied
that the rings were in the right position. Then he released the
harnesses which held them and they thumped into place.

Working conditions could scarcely have been more

rudimentary. You'll get a sense of this, I think, when I say that the carriage in which Pete and I became stranded was known as a 'man-rider'. It did exactly what it said on the tin. You sat bent double in a clanging, unupholstered can for the duration of your journey, which could last anything up to two hours each way. When the tunnel lamps were working, light entered the man-rider through wire mesh over the bare windows. It was like a Black Maria. But if it was unrestful, the diabolical tunnelling machine itself was patently life-threatening, if operated inexpertly. The machine weighed eighty tons. It had a diameter of 3.5 metres but it was sixty metres long, trailing conveyor belts of spoor. In front of the cab where the driver sat, blades clawed and ripped the earth. Behind the cab, a clanking, slithering chain dragged concrete rings within the reach of a claw-hammer grab. This robot arm clasped the rings and swung them into place to line the tunnel.

By jinking through the chicane of this flailing machinery, I reached the cab. Ahead of the driver's console, the great drill bits were cleaving the earth. I put my hand on the tunnel wall behind the cab and felt the clay. It was cool, damp, smooth, like the best-quality sculpting or potting material. Though the tunnelling machine left an immaculate, even finish on the walls, just here and there were the slightest ridges and pleats. I broke one of them off. And in that moment I realised that I was holding in my hand a new part of London. The immutable old place was changing in front of my eyes. The city was colonising its inhospitable element. To see the column of dully lustrous clay emerging was to watch London grow.

MONSTER SOUP

London's Waters

On another day when I was deep below London, down where it's dark and cold and wet, I was puzzling over this unfathomable side of the city when a jellyfish went past my head like a think-bubble. Of course! This was what London was like, even before there was a London at all. Far above me was the surface of the modern metropolis. It rests on its cold, wet base as negligently as a fat old man on a waterbed. But the mighty River Thames once inundated the very spot where I was standing, where I was easefully breathing. Today, it's the sunken chamber of an aquarium beneath the former Greater London Council building on the South Bank. Oh sure, it's the South Bank *now*, but the aquarium had been an entirely natural water feature in the days when the river was broader and shallower than it is in the twenty-first century. Schools of eel and salmon had made their piscine living where the tame jellyfish was now moving away from me as lazily as a smoke-ring.

Water was the reason that there was a London at all. Many citizens are unaware that their home is really a sea port. Father Thames, as seen in his bust in the courtyard of Somerset House, is a genial old cove poised to tip out a cornucopia in front of his fortunate riverine people. The Thames is still so dominant in the image of London, the river of life in the title sequence of the nation's favourite soap opera about cockney types, that we tend to forget that it is really a city of many rivers. Virile Father Thames had progeny: Stamford Brook, the Wandle, Counter's Creek, the Falcon, the Westbourne, the Tyburn, the Effra, the Fleet, the Walbrook, Neckinger and the Earl's Sluice, the Peck and the Ravensbourne. These tributaries were well known to Londoners until just a few generations ago. In their fledgling way, they brought the city as many boons as their more celebrated parent: water from London's hills; a means of transport; an outflow for their waste. If you gave them any consideration at all, you could be forgiven for thinking that these rivers had dried up and only survived in the street names of the arid topography to the north and south of the Thames. But they are overlooked only because they can no longer be seen. Very reasonably, it seldom occurs to commuters at Sloane Square station that the black, round-bottomed pipe which shoots the rapids of the east- and westbound platforms is in fact a conduit for the Westbourne. It adds a bucolic touch, a river – a *stream*, really – gurgling through this dropping-off point for those twin but very contrasting bastions of London living, Peter Jones department store, where well brought-up gels have their bridal books, and the Royal Court Theatre, a cradle of agit-prop.

The Westbourne and other waterways remain the capillary system of a sunken city. The rivers of London run for more than a hundred miles, all told. Even deeper than the rivers are 1.5 billion litres of groundwater, trapped beneath the London clay. Here was where my adventures in subterranean London properly began, I felt, with the water which moved and pooled under the city. I started with that most colourful of London's buried waterways, the River Fleet. The Fleet was a historic stretch of water, with connections to some of the city's outstanding personalities and events. It was also associated with some of the old trades of London. It had been the whiffy helpmeet of cutlers and tanners and butchers. At the beginning of the sixteenth century, the spendidly handled Wynkyn de Worde set up shop on Fleet Street with the printing press which had belonged to the late William Caxton, the first man in England to build such a thing. Wynkyn's old haunt became journalism's spiritual home, in so far as this was possible. The Fleet, through this connection, had been what drew me to London to make my living.

The river first appears in the history books during the reign of King John, when the Knights Hospitallers had a wharf at Fleet Lane. They allowed St Bartholomew's Hospital to share it. Patients who were too ill to travel by foot were put off at the quayside. The river was then the reeking backyard of men who dealt in hides and flesh. More and more rubbish was dumped in it as the population grew. In his *Survey of London* of 1598, John Stow lists five bridges over the Fleet. But 'it was impassable for boats, by reason of the many encroachments thereon made, by the throwing of offal and other garbage by butchers, saucemen and others and by reason of the many houses of office standing over upon it'. The Fleet was a boundary between the City and royal Westminster. In 1643, it became the natural barrier around which London's revolutionary militia set about resisting the royalist army, when earthworks were built on both banks to keep out Prince Rupert's men. In the Great Fire of 1666, flames sprang from one bank of the river to the other, consuming wharves and houses on either side. Wren redesigned the watercourse, deepening and widening it and constructing docks thirty feet wide on both banks. But shipping still preferred to steer clear and the river continued to fill with waste. As London has grown, so the Fleet has disappeared. It has been landscaped out of sight. This trend, affecting not only the Fleet but other lost rivers too, has had very little to do with sanitation and everything to do with the demand for land in central London. Broadly speaking, the covering of the Fleet has proceeded in the opposite direction to the flow of the river, beginning close to the point where it discharges into the Thames and retracing its route back towards its source. In 1733, the stretch from Fleet Bridge as far north as Holborn Bridge was arched over. Six years later, City fathers approved the demolition of the most famous market in London, the Stocks Market, to allow for the construction of Mansion House, and the market was rebuilt over a specially covered stretch of the Fleet. By the end of the eighteenth century, the remainder of the river from Fleet Bridge to the Thames was channelled underground. The sewerising of the Fleet led to rumours about a gross swine living underground. Perhaps this had something to do with the popular saying about where a pig is happiest. 'A fatter boar was hardly ever seen than one taken up this day, coming out of the Fleet ditch into the Thames,' reported the *Gentleman's Magazine* in August 1736. 'It proved to be a butcher's near Smithfield Bars, who had missed him five months, all which time he had been in the common sewer, and was improved in price from ten shillings to two guineas.'

With the excavation of the Regent's Canal in 1812, the next stretch of the Fleet to be enclosed was from King's Cross north towards the emerging suburb of Camden Town. The uppermost reaches of the river were the last to be concealed. As Hampstead grew in the nineteenth century, the river was built over from Camden to Hampstead and Highgate Ponds. As London expanded, so did the demands on its sewers. In 1846, the pressure of trapped gases became too much for the Fleet and a section of it spectacularly blew up. Traffic couldn't move for effluent at King's Cross, three poorhouses in Clerkenwell were swept away in a tidal stream of sewage, and a Thames steamboat rammed into Blackfriars Bridge on a bow wave of crap.

If you've been leafing through this book in the hope that subterranean London will be a respite from the vulgarity of the world above, I'm afraid I can only apologise. Dear reader, it gets worse.

'*Cuntis* is Latin,' said Jane. '*Cunte* with an 'e' on the end is Anglo-Saxon. *Cunena* was the goddess of children.'

I wouldn't have minded but this was supposed to be a Saturday afternoon stroll through the Fleet valley.

'Cuntipotent.' Jane went on, 'What do you think cuntipotent means? All-powerful. Cuniculate is a tunnelled passage open at one end.'

Yes, Jane had a mouth on her, all right. She had an almost Tourettic fixation with the c-word. In addition to being a distaff version of the foul-mouthed but otherwise charming Hugh Grant character in *Four Weddings and a Funeral*, Jane was a guide. She was our guide to the Fleet, and to so much more besides. Jane was warming to her theme, which she had embarked upon some time ago now, concerning the derivation of the name Kenditch, another of London's lost rivers. If Jane was to be believed, then the 'Ken' in 'Kenditch' meant, well, not to put too fine a point on it—

'—I don't think there's much doubt that "Ken" comes from cunt,' said Jane. 'Rivers are symbols of fertility. Just think about the one we're exploring, the Fleet. Cunt-shaped pools, water the colour of menstrual blood.'

Jane had a point. The water *was* red. While she was dilating on the bawdy origins of London place names, one of her fellow guides was passing round a beaker of Fleet water so that we could all have a swig. The metallic-tasting Fleet was the colour of a dentist's mouthwash, pinkly tinted by the minerals through which it drained. We were taking a breather at Mount Pleasant, perhaps for no better reason than the pungent etymology of the place. Jane said, 'Mount Pleasant was originally an ironic name for a really disgusting tip. Next to it was Laystool Street. *Stool* as in your turd, yeah? Lovely name for a block of flats: *Laystool Court*, everybody!'

'You see, *fleet* is Anglo-Saxon for tidal inlet,' Jane continued. 'The fleet would carry off your urine and your turds, essentially. In the late thirteenth century, the Whitefriar monks complained that they couldn't smell their own frankincense because of the stench of the Fleet. There was the most *extraordinary* cocktail of effluents.' I looked at the beaker of Fleet water and saw that the dregs had begun to turn green.

I might have seen this coming. As early as the first half-hour of the walk, when we were craning for a sight of the dribbling river in a gully on a hill, Jane had said, 'And we have a flow, ladies and gentlemen! We have a flow!' We were on Hampstead Heath. You might think that one of the highest natural locations in London was a strange choice of stepping-off point for an exploration of the subterranean city. I had come across a listing for a guided walk of the Fleet valley. Admittedly, the ramble would be overground, but it would orient me, I hoped. The heath was the source of the Fleet, as well as three other tributaries of the Thames. 'The heath is positively *flowing* with springs,' said Jane.

We visited Flask Walk in Hampstead, where wells had been set into the wall. It wasn't only the village's splendid views and leafy purlieus which had made it desirable but also its potable springs. To this day, the well-to-do still lived within walking distance of prized pools, such as the Vale of Hampstead pond. One of the party asked a question about plants, about species native to the heath, but Jane wasn't happy about the idea of *native* species. 'Some people have raised the whole question of race,' she said. This got approving nods from a pair of blondes in dressy trainers. A black boy sitting on a bench with a can of Stella and his girlfriend looked at us pityingly. Jane explained that people used to follow the Fleet and other tributaries of the Thames, accompanying them all the way into the city. She mimicked these wayfarers who rode beside the water. She was tensely holding reins, taking the heath at a gentle trot. But now waters like the Fleet were disguised, underground, putting an end, it seemed, to a tradition of river-following. 'On a cultural level,' she said, 'you've removed a way of being.' The black boy was agog that anyone would choose to spend a Saturday lunchtime doing what we were doing.

Like advanced water-dowsers who had dispensed with their hazel sprigs, we followed the river's lost bed past the Fleet

Primary School on Fleet Road. We stalked the hidden watercourse beside the Goddess beauty salon on Mansfield Road, where old dears sat under hairdryers like motorcycle crash helmets. We tracked the river into Cressfield Close, a road named after the paddy-fields of salad which the river had irrigated in Victorian times.

'Baron! *BARON!* Slow down!' A short, stocky man was taking a short, stocky dog for a walk on a chain you could have raised a drawbridge with. 'Socialist Alliance!' said a voice through the PA of an idling van. It was a left-wing candidate canvassing for votes, but ironically his loud-hailer technique was from the come-out-with-your-hands-up school of a Scotland Yard armed response unit. The amplified voice of the Socialist Alliance man trained his fire on New Labour. 'They've put people . . . they've put *profit* before people,' he said.

From Kentish Town Road, a place with a bacchanalian address in Jane's eyes, we turned onto the towpath of the Regent's Canal. White-green water boiled into the canal. The foam looked like an old duvet snagged underwater. Another of our guides, James, told us that in some cultures, bodies of water were credited with teaching man to speak, hence references to *babbling* brooks and *whispering* rushes. 'These societies believe that if you remove all the reeds from a river, you cut out the river's tongue,' said James, to rush-like nodding from some of our party. The noise of the streets, including the PA of the circling Socialist Alliance, faded away beneath a canal bridge.

The Fleet has often been hymned by the poets, although hymned might not be quite the word for it. For the balladeers, a favourite trope was that the river's turgid waters were the last resting place of Londoners' unwanted pets. In 'A Description of a City Shower', Jonathan Swift drew attention to the Fleet's freight of 'drown'd Puppies'. In a similar vein, Pope's *Dunciad* tells us,

This labour past, by Bridewell all descend,
(As morning pray'r and flagellation end)
To where Fleet-Ditch with disemboguing streams
Rolls the large tribute of dead dogs to the Thames.

The connection between the river and the city's unfortunate
strays, this shaggy dog story, has persisted into the present day.
There's a creek on the Regent's Canal, not far from its junction
with the Fleet, known as Dead Dog Basin. It's regularly visited by
a dog who is very much alive, a mutt called Timmy. With his
masters Mick and Peter, Timmy inspects Dead Dog Basin as he
makes the rounds of the canal on a flat-bottomed barque, *The
Pride of London*, a British Waterways vessel. The mission of
the *Pride* and her crew is to keep the canal navigable by removing
the rubbish from it. The *Pride* looks a bit like the craft in which
Martin Sheen goes upriver in *Apocalypse Now*, though not even
in the director's cut do I recall seeing shopping trolleys in the
prow of Sheen's river patrol boat.

I was aboard when the *Pride* made a routine check of the
basin. It's a watery hollow underneath an old warehouse by
Camden Market. The grotto got its name in the same way as
Houndsditch, now a suit-thronged street in the heart of the City
but once an insalubrious trench between the Fleet and the Tower
into which Londoners tipped all their rubbish, their late best
friends included. Happily, there were no dogs in the water but
dozens of bobbing bottles, as if every SOS ever sent from a desert
island had washed up there.

Mick said that he once fished a drunk out of Dead Dog Basin.
'Pissed as a parrot, he was.' The drunk had been showing off on
a footbridge and fell in. When Mick approached him, he was
thrashing and struggling. He said, 'You lie still or I'll do you.' He
thought that he might have broken the drunk's ankle in saving
him. 'Did he ever get in touch and say thanks? No.' Drug dealers
also ended up in the canal – one had been pulled from a lock only

a few days earlier – and the bodies of Asian women were removed from the westerly reaches at Southall. Mick and Peter speculated that the girls had dared to fall in love with men of whom their families didn't approve. It was no pleasure cruise, the canal. Another British Waterways man had ticked off some boys for fishing. 'He wasn't very tactful,' said Peter.

'Not him. It was "Stop so-and-so fishing and bugger off,"' said Mick. The boys returned with a dad – or perhaps more than one – and pushed the Waterways man into the canal.

From Kentish Town lock, the Fleet wound its invisible way towards St Pancras Old Church. Jane, James and the rest of our walking party went in pursuit. To the south of the church, where Victorian railway arches rise, St Pancras Wells had been a popular place of resort in the seventeenth century, boasting pump rooms, entertainments and pleasure gardens. The thought of water, its buried presence, moved James to animadvert on a watery theme. 'The nurse washes the blood off you immediately you're born,' he said in a meaning voice. 'You're in touch with water. Within minutes of birth, you're connected to a hydrology. And when we die, we turn back into ooze. We just leak! So if you look at the bodies here, they're part of the Fleet. Millions of people have been connected with this river.' Iain Sinclair also saw St Pancras Old Church as a watery tomb, 'an island shaded in torpor, heavy with melancholy, the drowned dead'. To mention but two of the departed: Sir John Soane, who gave his name to an exquisite miscellany of a museum in Lincoln's Inn Fields, and the early feminist Mary Wollstonecraft. There was an astonishing rockery of tombstones behind a tree. The tablets and lozenges were as dense as stones on a beach. This was 'The Hardy Tree'. Thomas Hardy had worked in the graveyard as a sexton.

At the back of King's Cross station, work was well under way on the Channel Tunnel rail link. Gasometers carved up, divided, the sky, framing it with their bare ribs. As if that wasn't a pretentious enough conceit, one of the walkers weighed in at this point with 'I live near here so the gasometers are my wallpaper.' He redeemed himself with a story about the rusty old girdles. He said that a woman who lived a few doors from him had once set her fiancé a courtly challenge. If he really loved her, she said, he should prove it by painting the gasometers black and red for her. Which he did!

We passed King's Cross station, where legend insists that Queen Boudicca lies entombed beneath platform 10; past the strip of shops in the red-light district near the terminus. *All* the shops were like porn shops, shameful, surrounded by litter. The Fleet runs between King's Cross Road and Gray's Inn Road in the channel now occupied by the Metropolitan Line. St Chad's Place, to our right, used to be Chad*well*, said James. Sadlers Wells was supplied by the Fleet. 'You feel you really are in a major river valley at this point,' said Jane.

The Fleet popped up, most unexpectedly, in one of the most densely developed parts of the Smoke, almost within sight of its final destination, the Thames. You could descend a metal staircase in a shopfront on Farringdon Lane for a glimpse of the churning flow. It swept beneath a wooden panel resembling a door which had fallen over. It was really a duckboard over a well, the reservoir which had given its name to Clerkenwell.

Under the guidance of Jane and James, the last leg of our journey, from Holborn Viaduct to Blackfriars, was revealed as a walk through a humid delta. The mouth of the Fleet had once been six hundred feet wide. Turnagain Lane, on our left, sounded as though it owed something to the legend of Dick Whittington. In fact, it had marked the riverbank of the Fleet, the point at which you had to turn around and retrace your steps to avoid falling in. Next to it was Newcastle Close, so called because of the shipments of coal which began arriving in London from the north-east of England in the twelfth century. In the same period, stones destined for the original St Paul's Cathedral had been transported upstream on the Fleet. You began to see connections to the lost river all around you.

At Blackfriars, where the Fleet spills into the Thames from a drain set into the embankment wall, James sent us on our footsore way by reading a short story by John Berger called 'King'. It included a reference to 'the voice of the Fleet'. James's own message was that you couldn't keep a good river down. 'The Fleet will win,' he said, with a throb in his voice. 'The tunnels under here, including the Tube lines, pierce the aquifer of the Fleet, disturbing it. Perhaps more than any aquifer in the world! But the tubes and tunnels are only kept dry by pumps, and one day we'll run out of energy to run the pumps.' During storms, the Fleet still percolated through the hidden layers of London to gather in pools on the roadway, and building works on its course had to be evacuated of river water. The poet Alan Brownjohn wrote,

> I like to think
> – or fear to think it – that one day my city will
> Disclose itself, its faces reclaim their focus,
> Its culverted rivers flood the hypermarkets.

James didn't fear this: he was damp-eyed at the thought of a wringing London, reconquered by old Father Thames and his watery offspring. I was grateful to Jane and James for my introduction to the underground waterways of London. Now it was time to explore them for myself. Like so many of London's lost rivers, the Fleet had become a sewer; I wanted to get into a sewer, to splash about in London's buried waters.

There was a man who worked in London's sewers who could kill rats with his hat. Admittedly, it was a hard hat – in fact, it was a helmet – but it was still a rare and recherché thing that this man could do. His name was Jack. Jack's knack was his patience. He had ineffable patience. That's what sewers teach you. There will never be an end to rats. There will never be an end to sewage. It must have been someone who knew the sewers well who first coined the usage 'What goes around, comes around'.

Jack was a flusher. That's the title given to the workers who inspect and maintain the hundreds of miles of sewers underneath the capital. Like undertakers, flushers perform a vital public service but don't bask in the same unalloyed admiration as nurses and lollipop ladies. They're the worldly successors of men like Richard the Raker, who fell into a London cesspit in 1326 and drowned 'monstrously in his own excrement'.

I heard about Jack from the flushers of Wick Lane in east London. Naturally, they like to tell tall stories to outsiders. Before I went into the sewers with them, I asked them about rats, and one of them said, 'The rats are this size,' describing with his hands the proportions of a small horse. But it was different when they were talking about Jack. An awed look came into their eyes. They told me that when Jack's gang of flushers came upon a nest of rats, a squirming ratking, perhaps in a stretch of sewer directly beneath a dirty fast-food restaurant – a filthy takeaway signifying rats as surely as a buoy signifies rocks – Jack's nonplussing response was to stand perfectly still. Sometimes he would sit on a ledge, or the rung of a metal ladder underneath a manhole cover. Jack would fix his eyes on one of the rats in the gloom. He would wait. He would carry on waiting. Just when the rest of the gang were losing patience and giving up on old Jack, he'd snatch his hat off and bring it down on the rat in a blur of moulded plastic. Jack was to the water board what Oddjob was to Goldfinger.

I met the flushers when they were playing host to Thames Water's Sewer Week; by anybody's standards, a highlight of the cloacal calendar. Sewer Week is an event run by the utility to familiarise Londoners with the less obvious of its two principal functions (the other being to put the wet stuff *into* our homes and schools and businesses in the first place). The dropping-off point for Sewer Week was Pudding Mill Lane, a stop on the Docklands

Light Railway. I was the only living soul at Pudding Mill Lane station. A dollop of offal was once known as a pudding: butchers had their scalding houses in Pudding Mill Lane as early as the twelfth century, as they did on the banks of the Fleet. The station was surrounded by wasteland and, a little beyond that, by breakers' yards and lock-ups and paint shops, businesses which belonged to the legal but unremarked commercial sector. Not the black economy or even the grey economy, but the brown economy. Even the air, full of beige spores, was brown, as it was in the days when the saucemen made their high-smelling living in Pudding Mill Lane. The ventilation unit of an unknown concern was putting out zephyrs of warm air and a man was cutting a paving slab to size on the pavement in a mist of brown dust. Under a bridge on Wick Lane itself was a burnt-out Golf and a tan settee with a career-ending hernia.

Thames Water have a depot at Wick Lane because it's at the end of the northern outfall sewer, one of the city's great culverts, which receives waste from north of the Euston Road. There was a banner up at the depot saying 'Welcome to Wick Lane Sewer Week', and directions to a marquee. The programme was that visitors listened to a presentation before being gifted a finger buffet and then, with uncomplicated literal-mindedness on the part of the utility, saw where it all went.

Inside the marquee, we were like a crowd at a timeshare presentation: thirty or more of us, mainly retired people, our numbers swollen by a party from the Victorian Society. Next to me was a man in his fifties with a straggly beard, the sort who wears a thick jumper all year round. Another gentleman sat in a cirrus of white hair. One of the grannies in the row in front of us said to her neighbour, 'Some people look at you slightly askance when you say you're going dashing down a sewer.' Her friend agreed. 'It's not everybody's idea of a fun day out,' she said.

The introductory remarks were made by Ben Nithsdale, a man whom I would come to think of as the Pied Piper of Thames

Water, after he had led me like a compliant rodent through London's sewers. His talk did the job as an appetiser for the humming culverts directly beneath our seats, with lip-smacking euphemisms such as 'foul drainage' and 'midden', and the sobering intelligence that the water supply Londoners now take for granted was until not so long ago a comparative trickle, brought to your home, if you were among the prosperous, by five hundred wheezing men with buckets.

We went down into the sewers half a dozen or so at a time. While you waited your turn, a brick shaft afforded a sneak preview of the northern outfall, perhaps twenty feet below. You could see a slow-moving sludge at the bottom of this teak-stained column, and hear a man's voice, as if from far, far away, crying 'Mind the doors!'A favourite flushers' joke, it transpired. You won't be surprised to learn that there was a head-clearing smell, though it wasn't the one that you have every reason to expect. It was a sudsy odour instead, and the effect of it was to take me back to my grandparents' backyard and to long-ago kickabouts there with my brother. It was like inhaling an unstoppered phial of gases gathered from the sunken drain to which our football naturally gravitated. I suppose it was the smell of washday, of Monday morning.

Like any trade or profession thrust into contact with members of the public, the flushers were keeping to themselves. In their jumpsuit-style overalls, complemented by harnesses and waders, they might have been parachutists; parachutists expecting an extremely soft landing. Which wasn't terribly wide of the mark, I suppose. If they weren't entirely convincing as skydivers, then perhaps they looked like Sylvester Stallone did when he was costumed as a bomb-disposal expert for the action film *The Specialist*. In a word, they looked hard. Perhaps they *were* hard, too, but it was an unfortunate feature of their work that under no imaginable circumstances was it the stuff of tough-guy myths.

Before my group could take our turn in the sewers, we were issued with flushers' fatigues in a locker room. This enclave of tattoo and snap tin was concealed inside a quaint igloo of yellow brick which looked as if it had been at Wick Lane since the northern outfall was built in the nineteenth century. I changed beneath a brace of lockers respectively tagged CHAS and FAT CHAS.

'Young gentleman there, what shoe size do you take?' This was a flusher in overall trousers and a straining white T-shirt. He was one of the men who had been detailed to dole out the kit. He was talking to me but he could have been addressing any of his guests in the locker room. He spoke to us all with the same archaic courtliness. 'Young man there,' he said to a greybeard from the Victorian Society, 'have I given you your gloves yet?' When you did as you were told, you were rewarded by the flusher saying 'Top man!' He was nimble, even dainty, in his actions, as big men often are. Was there something about working out of sight that encouraged people to grow stout?

The full sewer-going wardrobe consisted of hard hat with Davy lamp; disposable paper boiler suit; high-visibility body-warmer; germ-proof gauntlets; and crofter's socks twinned with buttock-brushing waders, which had some kind of metal sole or toecap. I climbed into the stirrups which went with my day-glo bodkin. They fitted snugly around the crotch. 'People'll pay good money for that in the West End,' said the flusher.

'A bloke asked me once if he could borrow it to wear to a party,' said one of his colleagues, in tones of bewilderment and suspicion.

'Madame Jo-Jo's. That's the place for that. Cor, dear!' said Flusher 1. Had they spent so long in the Victorian world, the frankly unerotic sewers, that they were as out of touch as this? There was a kind of cosy, thank-God-we're-all-blokes-together aspect to the life of the flusher. Is it one of the secret attractions of manual work for men that there are no women to frown at our beloved puerile jokes and make dreamworld demands for self-improvement?

A man in a Prince of Wales double-breasted put his head around the door of the locker room. 'Who's doing the chat down there?' he asked.

'Westy,' said Flusher 1.

'I've just seen him in the car park.'

'Who, Lee?'

In the event, the chat wouldn't be done by anyone called Westy or Lee but by a large man called Keith. Keith's gut was buttressed by his harness to the north, east and west, and to the south by a broad belt. Around his neck was a green gadget which emitted a beeping noise every few moments. It was a device for monitoring the accumulation of any hazardous gases in the sewers. Keith's tie was a pennant of his senior status. He was a man with the ungainsayable air of a Tammany Hall politician. 'If there was a flash flood in north London now,' Keith began as we regrouped outside in our kit, 'it would show up here – what? – a couple of minutes later. No more than that. And you're talking about a lot of water down there.' Keith indicated with a tap of his wader where he meant: down *there*, down in the sewer. 'You're not talking about inches. You're talking about feet.' He made it sound like the deluge in Dante's *Divine Comedy*.

> I am now in the Third Circle: that of rain –
> One ceaseless, heavy, cold, accursed quench,
> Whose law and nature vary never a grain;
>
> Huge hailstones, sleet and snow, and turbid drench
> Of water sluice down through the darkened air,
> And the soaked earth gives off a putrid stench.

It was time for me to enter the Third Circle. Bulky in my Sellafield scrubs, I cumbersomely addressed the open manhole, fringed with orange rust, which was the hatch to the northern outfall. I squatted beneath what appeared to be the poles of a small tepee – actually, the winding platform or derrick of the winch which would take the strain as I lowered myself into the sewer. By way of hand luggage, I was allowed only a small going-away case, a goodie-bag which contained my turtle, the perhaps unfortunately named chemical breathing apparatus, resembling an infantryman's canteen, that is a must for all sojourns in the sewers. The survival sack containing my turtle was coupled up to the hoist and sent down ahead of me. Then the jaws of the winch were attached to an eyelet at the back of my over-jacket, in the place where you would otherwise expect to find a label. The hoist had been rigged up in order to stop you from falling, in the event of your losing your footing on the greasy ladder which dropped away directly beneath the manhole. It was also there to haul out anyone who sprained an ankle or banged his head in the sewer. Without it, the task of evacuating a casualty became a much more formidable one. As he paid out the slack to me, the flusher operating this lifeline remarked that it had a third and last function, less well advertised than the others. 'It's to get you out of there if you start going funny,' he said.

Down I went, from rung to rung of the ladder, the hawser looped through the top of my jacket giving me a strange sensation of buoyancy, of weightlessness; but at the same time, impeding my progress: holding me up in two meanings of that phrase. In my downward climb, I might as well have been descending through strata of time, to the origins of the unchanged brick sewer which was opening up around me.

In the nineteenth century, the Thames had become so squalid that the *Journal of Public Health and Sanitary Review* was reporting 'stories of men struck down with the stench, and of all kinds of fatal diseases, upspringing on the river's banks'. The private water companies retained scientists and other salaried apologists to praise the river water for its 'liveliness'. But the public and press were sceptical. A cartoon of 1827 entitled 'Monster Soup' showed a horrified harridan looking through a microscope at a slide of tentacled nasties. Water quality had been a scandal for years but nothing was done until 1858. In that year, another cartoon, 'The Silent Highwayman', depicted a skeleton in a skiff rowing through a flotsam of dead creatures with the silhouette of St Paul's behind him. In the long, hot summer, the Thames blew the Houses of Parliament a ripe and lingering kiss. The river had stagnated. At the waterside legislature, the smell was so bad that rags drenched in chloroform of lime were hung at the windows in an attempt to mask it. But not even this industrial-strength pot-pourri could prevent Benjamin Disraeli himself from bolting from the chamber with a handkerchief clamped to his nostrils, and cursing the Thames as a 'Stygian pool'. An attempt has been made to recreate this stench for latter-day Londoners at the visitor centre attached to the Thames Barrier. There is a model of Big Ben and you lift a flap. It's the same idea as releasing the scent from a perfume-impregnated page of a glossy magazine, except that at the barrier, you are regaled with *eau de Thames*. Or at least that's the idea. The pong reminded me of the ersatz pine you inhale in minicabs. There's no smell of rotten eggs, or piss.

If they did but know it, the Victorians had less to fear from the gases given off by the river than from the Thames itself. It was by now an oily bouillabaisse of raw effluent. 'Since much of the capital's drinking water was drawn from the river the citizens of the metropolis were literally drinking one another's sewage', in the succinct but lunch-losing summation of Stephen Halliday in his account of that steamy season, *The Great Stink of London*. The city's rapidly expanding population, and the demands made on water supplies by new industrial processes, only brought to the surface a problem which had long been a noxious feature of underground London. The flushers I met at Wick Lane were in the long and whiffy tradition of the 'gong-fermors' or rakers, who were making brass out of muck as early as the Middle Ages. There were occupational hazards. In addition to the tragic loss of Richard the Raker, two men were asphyxiated as they tried to retrieve a barrel of wine that had fallen into a cesspit.

Not until the reign of Henry III did an English sovereign turn the kingly attention to questions of hygiene. He commissioned the first public conveniences since the Romans, and installed an underground drainage system at his palace in Westminster. In terms of derivation, 'privy' doffs its cap to the French word for private. But on the basis of London's history, you could be forgiven for thinking that privy was on the end of a linguistic chain beginning with 'privilege'. The house of easement enjoyed the implausible status of a rich man's plaything. To erect a latrine on London Bridge in 1383 cost £11, the equivalent of a year's wages for a skilled man. Accordingly, entrepreneurs of easement expected to make a return, and were prepared to pay lavatory attendants as much as seven pence a night to tend their investments.

So much for fashionable London. The common or garden Londoner had to make do with the common or the garden. In a complaint registered at the Assizes of Nuisance in 1328, a man called William Sprott objected that his neighbours, William and Adam Mere, had allowed their 'cloaca' to overflow his wall. In 1347, two men were up before the beak for siphoning their 'odours' into next door's property, a misdemeanour which came spectacularly to light when their neighbour's cellar overflowed. Basements of slipper-swamping odiousness were still a hazard of London life as late as the seventeenth century. In an entry in his diary on 20 October 1660, Samuel Pepys records, 'Going down to my cellar . . . I put my foot into a great heap of turds, by which I find that Mr Turner's house of office is full and comes into my cellar, which doth trouble me, but I will have it helped.'

The predecessors of the Parliament of the Great Stink took
their sweet time over cleaning up the city. The first sanitary act
was passed in 1357. It required the chancellor of London's
university to 'remove from the streets and lanes of the town all
swine and all dirt, dung, filth . . . and cause the streets and lanes
to be kept clean'. Subsequent acts ordered those who had latrines
over the Walbrook to pay the Lord Chamberlain two shillings a
year towards keeping the river clean, and made it illegal to
'corrupt or pollute ditches, rivers, water and the air of London
or elsewhere'.

The reign of Elizabeth I saw the invention of a prototype water
closet. Its day would come, but in Tudor London it was strictly
a minority interest compared to the ongoing success story that
was the cesspit. This amenity became even more popular after the
boffins discovered that nitrogen from nightsoil could be used to
make gunpowder. The government licensed characters called
saltpetremen to enter houses at will and dig up the waste. To
Parliament, this carried the whiff of oppression. One MP
grumbled in 1601, 'They digge in doves cotes when the doves are
nesting; cast up malting floor when the malt be green, in
bedchambers, in sick rooms, not even sparing women in
childbirth, yea even in God's house, the Church.'

Acts passed in the seventeenth century outlawed 'withdrawes'
in public at pain of a twenty-shilling fine and made it illegal to
build latrines over drains and sewers without a licence from the
Commissioners of Sewers. This august body included the diarist
and pamphleteer John Evelyn, who got the job despite, or perhaps
because of, an overheated account he had nibbed of the infernal
waters bubbling under London during the Great Fire. 'The ground
under my feet,' he wrote of a journey he made from Whitehall to
Fleet Street, 'was so hot as made me not only sweat, but even
burnt the soles of my shoes and put me all over in a sweat.' The
vista that Evelyn claimed to see was 'the lead ironworks, plate and
melted – the fountains dried up and ruined, whilst the very waters

remained boiling; the viragos of subterranean cellars, wells and dungeons formerly warehouses still burning in stench and dark clouds of smoke like Hell ... the City of London resembles the face rather of Mount Etna than an assembly of Rational Creatures.'

The silver lining of the great pall of smoke which hung over the city was an opportunity to rebuild along enlightened lines. Evelyn lobbied Wren to the effect that the reborn London couldn't truly become the envy of the world without a new underground city to service it. This would entail the preparatory spadework of compiling a 'subterranean plan of all the vaults, cellars and arched Meanders yet remaining, thereby to consider how they may fall out, and accommodate to new erection, what were fit to be filled and dammed up, and what to be reserved'. But like the master plan that Wren himself had hatched for the resurrected city, Evelyn's modest proposal got lost in a labyrinth of land ownership: over the years, the Great Wen had been parcelled out and cheese-pared. A civic project of any size was faced with the insuperable obstacle of tracing all the landlords concerned, never mind persuading them to agree on anything. The reconstructed London was soon as filthy as the old one, despite the innovations of enclosing the Fleet and building the London Bridge sewer around the Walbrook. In 1810, most of London's one million inhabitants were still regular customers of the city's 200,000 cesspits.

Then came two great shocks, which would unseat the familiar latrine as surely as a saltpetreman's careless pipe. The explosion of the industrial revolution was answered by the thunderclap of a population boom, as more and more people made their way to the city to meet the labour-intensive demands of the new sector. In the first fifty years of the nineteenth century, London doubled in size, growing to more than two million inhabitants. To make matters worse, old plans for the WC were dusted off and the unsuccessful Tudor invention became a popular piece of London sanitaryware. 'The arrival of the water closet was a giant step forward for personal hygiene and two steps backward for public sanitation,' write Richard Trench and Ellis Hillman in *London Under London*. 'The snag was that its water and waste went straight into existing cesspits, which overflowed into the street sewers (originally designed for rainwater) and contaminated the city before emptying themselves into the Thames.'

This turn of excretory events created opportunities for a stripe of men who went by an unusual and resonant name, but were in fact familiar features of the subterranean landscape. Toshers, who prospected and panned the noisome nineteenth-century sewers for lost jewellery and dropped change, and bequeathed us such usages as 'a load of tosh', were a reincarnation of the gong-fermors; in due course, the flushers of today would follow in the toshers' slurping footsteps. 'Many persons enter the sewer openings on the banks of the Thames at low tide, armed with sticks to defend themselves from rats . . . and carry a lantern to light the dreary passages, they wander for miles under the crowded streets, in search of such waifs as are carried there from above. A more dismal pursuit can scarcely be conceived,' wrote a man called Archer about the lot of the toshers, in his *Vestiges of Old London*. 'Many venturers have been struck down in such a dismal pilgrimage, to be heard no more; many have fallen suddenly choked, sunk bodily in the treacherous slime, become a prey of swarms of vicious rats, or being overwhelmed by a sudden increase of the polluted stream.'

Ah, yes, the rats. The toshers put the wind up the early anthropologist Henry Mayhew with their rats' tales. This is what one of them told him, lent a chilling *noir* quality, I think you'll agree, by the dirty realism of Mayhew's phonetic transcription.

I've often seed as many as a hundred rats at once, and they're woppers in the sewers, I can tell you; them there water rats, too, is far more ferociouser than any other rats, and they'd think nothing of taking a man, if they found that then couldn't get away no how, but if they can why they runs by and gits out o' the road. I knows a chap as the rats tackled in the sewers; they bit him hawfully: you must ha' heard on it; it was him as the water-men went in arter when they heard him a shouting as they was a rowin' by. Only for the watermen the rats would ha' done for him, safe enough. Do you recollect hearing on the man as was found in the sewers about twelve years ago? – oh you must – the rats eat every bit of him, and left nothing but bones.

Despite their tradition of outlandish stories, toshers – now flushers – don't dread rats the way that you and I do. Familiarity drives out fear. Orwell's Room 101 would have been a piece of cake for Winston Smith if he'd only done a few shifts in the sewers first. The flushers have a wary respect for rats, a man like Jack, the rat-killer of the modern sewers, appreciating them the way a matador might a pen of prize bulls. The sewermen instinctively understand that the rat is London's true mascot. Londoners honour Dick Whittington's cat, but it's no coincidence that she was a first-rate mouser – and indeed, ratter. In the 1850s, while the toshers were telling Mayhew that they went in fear of their lives in the rat-loud sewers, London's drinkers were enjoying rat fights. A landlord called Jimmy Shaw claimed to buy 26,000 rats a year, at 3d each, from farm labourers in Enfield and Essex. Never likely to attract the Marquess of Queensberry's seal of approval, these bouts were bloodbaths involving dogs and scores of rats at a time. As part of the Queen's golden jubilee celebrations of 2002, Goldsmiths' Hall exhibited the plate which is habitually burnished by the regal Brasso, including a canteen of spoons featuring the royal beasts: unicorns, lions, that sort of thing. London's Sunday-best cutlery, by the same token, would be embossed with heraldic rodents. A brewery drayhorse or a greyhound would be a more touchy-feely familiar, it's true, but then it might be asked why anyone would expect London to have a cuddly creature for a pet. Before the reader nominates pigeons, it's worth recalling that their scientific name is 'rats-with-wings'. And, let's face it, rats were responsible for the biggest event in London's history. The Penguin Classic edition of Daniel Defoe's *Journal of the Plague Year* includes a 'clinical summary' by Anthony Burgess, in which the late polymath concedes that the fleas who piggybacked on the rats were the vector of the Great Plague before going on in the following strong-stomached fashion: 'The spread of the epidemic was due to its spread among rats, this being assisted by rat-cannibalism, infected food and even human faeces.'

Speaking of which: under the manhole cover in Wick Lane, I stepped off the last rung of the ladder and the northern outfall sewer splashed up over my thighs. I wasn't ready for the press of the water through my waders. It was like the experience of the fifth Duke of Portland as he explored the tunnels under his Nottinghamshire estate in *The Underground Man*, by the mole-eyed novelist Mick Jackson. 'The coldness of the tunnels first introduced itself at my ankles then crept slowly up me, in the same way that a bather's body is coldly embraced by the sea.' The water that I encountered was very far from being a tide, in truth; it was nothing compared to the pulse of a river. All the same, I was almost caught out by the kittenish undertow, nearly wrong-footed and humiliatingly up-ended into the far from appetising drink. For a moment, I pitched and swayed on the spot, my feet seeking equilibrium.

How to describe the waters which eddied and swirled playfully about me? In the half-light, it was easier to identify them by texture rather than by colour. The consistency was of a solution of mud, with a denser sediment of grit underneath my flailing feet. As I found my balance and grew accustomed to the gloom, I could make out wisps of white in the water – like anemones or jellyfish, or alternatively like flakes of cuttlefish in a reeking gumbo – which I was obliged to catalogue as sheets of loo paper.

I followed the flushers and my fellow visitors in single file through one bore of the northern outfall. It was known on their charts and plans as 'barrel five'. We were making for a source of artificial light, which dimly illuminated the sweating brick of the egg-shaped tunnel. For a time, all you could hear was the sloshing of waders and the muffled roar of the far Niagaras of the sewer delta and the faint sonar ping of Keith's gas-monitoring device, like the alarm clock tick-tocking in the stomach of the croc in *Peter Pan*. I was chagrined by the realisation that the water was only about a foot and a half deep. For the duration of Sewer Week, Thames Water had closed sluices or floodgates upstream of Wick Lane; or up-sewer, rather. This had turned the twin pipes of the northern outfall, normally brimming cataracts, into docile paddling pools. One of the flushers said that he and his colleagues thought nothing of navigating the sewers with the water lapping at their chests. But my near-capsize in ideal sanitation conditions was mitigated by my ignorance of the walk of the flushers. This sounds like the title of a challenging ballet but in fact it's what separates professional sewermen from landlubbers like myself. The flushers understood that a sewer was a capricious mistress, to be taken for granted at your peril. She could indulge you, but she could also bring you to your knees in a heartbeat. Not for the flushers the diffident and uncertain steps of the novice. They knew that the only hope a man had of dominating a sewer was to proceed with a sure and steady tread. Accordingly, they didn't lift their heavy waders as they moved but slid them over the shingly sewer-bed with the stiff-legged gait of deep-sea divers.

After inhaling a lungful of sewer vapour at the mouth of the ventilation shaft on the surface, I was primed that the air in the northern outfall would be perfumed with detergent. Less expectedly, the atmosphere was close. The notes I took down immediately after wading through the sewer, in my skidmarked pad, tell me that there was a 'moist gamminess' in the air. If there is any virtue in this neologism, it must be that it conflates the sewer's empirical qualities of a gamy smell and a clammy environment with a sense of the word 'gammy', the schoolboy's umbrella term for bacteria and nostril-offending decomposition.

We emerged from the tunnel into a vaulted chamber which was the seat of the electric light. The flushers had put up a floodlight. By its comparatively stellar wattage, I couldn't fail to notice a pair of great wooden hatches. They were like portcullises or drawbridges, drawn up to seal off the chamber from another length of sewer, which joined it at right angles. These mighty sluices were closed, now, but there was a clue to their strenuous function in the strands of toilet roll which clung to them like seaweed.

The flushers had also rigged up a rope to serve as a handrail. I held on to it and craned my neck to look at the brick nave which rose above us. As promised, Keith appeared, to do the talk. 'That goes all the way up to Dalston,' was all that he felt inclined to say for the time being. But that was quite enough to be going on with. There was something tremendously satisfying about the idea of a secret causeway running beneath the gridlocked city, with its own problems of congestion, no doubt, but without clamorous traffic and an incessant crush of people. If this could only be your own private way of getting around the place, then a little brackish water, the odd rat, half the housekeeping going on dry-cleaning bills: these were surely a small price to pay. If Keith had no further observations worth hearing just now, there was plenty for the other senses to be processing. Here, where branches of sewers met, the smell was unmistakably high. And you began to see that there were extraordinary sights, tricks of the light, which might recompense the flushers for the *longueurs* of their rounds. The floodlight picked out ripples on the water; in turn, their reflections writhed across the brick ceiling. In the long pipe ahead of us, these serpentine shapes seemed to merge with a thin cloud layer of fumes, where these gathered at the apex of the oval column. Or was I imagining things? Had I been thinking too much about the diabolical 'miasmas' of the nineteenth century? It struck me that a Victorian standing in my extruded shoes would very probably be having the same goggling thoughts that I was: the sights, and smells, of the northern outfall had been unchanged for more than a hundred years. Of how many other places in London could you say that?

The northern outfall had been emphatically buried. It was out of sight and out of mind. Another major culvert, the Ranelagh, is similarly well hidden. It is entered by means of a manhole in the grounds of the Royal Chelsea Hospital, where the strains of band practice carry from the nearby barracks. Passers-by on the Chelsea Embankment are occasionally startled by the sight of flushers in full fig, going about their business in this bagpipe-loud dell. For all its refinement, this part of town is steeped in London's filth. On the opposite bank of the river, 'bad air adheres' to Battersea Park, according to Will Self's *Dorian*. No amount of imperial land-scaping can cover up this malodorousness, the swamp that lies beneath the pleasure gardens and the miasma percolating up through the run-down ornamental terraces. Some sewers have an almost promiscuous intimacy with the Londoners they serve. The Tyburn sewer, for example lies just a few feet beneath the tarmacadam of a desirable Pimlico postcode. Under Tachbrook Street, SW1, is a chamber with a channel cut into the floor. The channel exits through the dainty arch of a much smaller tunnel, a tunnel within a tunnel, like a tunnel of love. Actually, that's exactly what it is: after a few days without rain, the floor of the sewer is dry and the flushers pick their way between pre-enjoyed condoms, which are parched and withered like sloughed-off snakeskin. It was under Tachbrook Street that I saw the only rat that I came across in the sewers. He was dead, a bloated but intact ratty carcass. 'You can't smell it,' I told the flusher next to me with relief.

'Not unless you tread on it,' he replied. 'Then it'll go off like a chicken Kiev.'

The Tyburn sewer runs directly beneath the American ambassador's residence in Regent's Park, MI5 HQ, and Buckingham Palace. A Thames Water manager once told me that it would be the ideal route for terrorists intending to strike at the royal family. It would be an audacious real-life re-enactment of an old Albert Finney caper movie called *Loophole*, in which a group of desperadoes emerge from the sewers to pull off a bank job.

The capital's culverts were an underground empire, founded by Sir Joseph Bazalgette. The historian Roy Porter has bracketed Bazalgette with Wren and Nash as 'London's noblest builders'. His achievements included many of London's best-known thoroughfares, embankments and major bridges, as well as parks and open spaces, but it is as the seer of sewerage that he deserves the thanks of every Londoner. Back in the Great Stink of 1858, when the prime ministerial palate was being tainted by the stench coming off the Thames, and toshers were still taking their chance with rats and vapours alike, an outbreak of cholera claimed 40,000 lives, and serious, structural reform was at long last ordered. The necessary powers were granted to a body called the Metropolitan Board of Works, whose chief engineer was Bazalgette. It was a growing, if minority, opinion among physicians that poor sanitation, especially the contamination of drinking water by sewage, was a health hazard. The year before the Great Stink, Dr John Snow had argued that cholera was carried in water. His hypothesis was confirmed some years later during an outbreak of the disease centred on Broadwick Street in Soho, when he was able to show that sufferers had all drawn water from the same pump. The good doctor is remembered in a more convivial Soho watering hole, a pub named after him.

Bazalgette's two overriding objectives were to put the sewers underground, and to stop them from flowing into the Thames in central London. He recalled,

The drains of London were pouring down their filth into the river at low water. There was no outflow from them at high water. The tide kept the sewage up the drains then; but when the tide had been running out for hours and the water in the river began to run low, then the drains began to pour out their sewage and of course when the tide came in again it was all swept up by the stream. When the tide ebbed it all came down and so it kept oscillating up and down the river, while more filth was continuously adding to it until the Thames became absolutely pestilential.

Bazalgette commissioned more than eighty miles of intercept sewers. As their name indicates, they were to connect with the existing sewers, at right angles. Three were sunk north of the river. The so-called high-level sewer ran from Hampstead through Hackney to Stratford, where it met the middle-level sewer from Kensal Green. The low-level sewer began at Chiswick. It didn't have gravity working in its favour to the same extent as the other two, so it was given a boost by a pumping station at Pimlico. The low-level intercept in particular demonstrated the brilliant simplicity of Bazalgette's conceit. Just as foaming gouts of waste and water were about to be disgorged into the river, in the way they always had been, they were swept away instead by the great culvert, running west to east beneath the engineer's newly constructed Thames Embankment. The contents of the three intercepting sewers all arrived at Abbey Mills pumping station in east London. From there they flowed to the northern outfall works at Barking Creek, very near where we were wading at Wick Lane. The sewage was discharged well downstream of London's main centres of population and their water supplies. South of the river, two further intercepting sewers were constructed: a high-level one from Balham and a low-level one beginning at Putney. They met at Deptford, where their contents were pumped to the southern outfall works at Crossness

on the Erith Marshes. At both outfalls, north and south of the
Thames, discharge only took place at high water, ensuring that
the untreated waste was carried downstream on the ebb tide.

By the time Bazalgette was finished, in 1875, he had spent
£6.5 million building or revamping 1,300 miles of sewers. In the
Victoria and Chelsea Embankments, he had also fashioned three
and a half miles of stunning earthworks, in the process
reclaiming more than thirty acres of riverbed. The under-
appreciated Bazalgette is memorialised by a mural in a public
convenience on the Embankment – not inappropriately, when
you think about it – and by a bust a short distance away, a little
to the west of Hungerford Bridge. The sculptor has chiselled a
laurel for Bazalgette's neck, giving him the aspect of a forgotten
Olympian, which to some extent is what he is. The system he
bequeathed is showing signs of wear and tear. Up to a quarter of
London's sewers are leaking. Despite the best efforts of Thames
Water, there are forty effluent 'overspills' per annum. If these
were all laid end to end, in what accuracy compels me to call a
time and motion study, it would be the equivalent of the sewers
flooding into the Thames around the clock for more than twenty
days a year.

But Bazalgette's work is done. His marmoreal ears hear 'the
city-licking sound of water moving slowly through the Thames
like years in thought', to borrow a line from the poet Glyn
Maxwell. At Bazalgette's back flows the river, the colour of shit –
but not smelling of shit, and indeed, *not* shit, thanks in large part
to his great works. To adapt the *pensée* of his contemporary
Oscar Wilde, we are all in the gutter but some of us are looking
at the sewers.

Inside the northern outfall sewer at Wick Lane, part of the
system that is another monument to Bazalgette, the flushers and
their guests reluctantly embarked on our return journey to the
surface. Leaving the vaulted chamber with its stinking
drawbridges, we set out along barrel four of the sewer, which

was parallel to the one by which we had entered. Padding towards the escape hatch of a raised manhole cover, I thought about the climax of *The Third Man* and what a brilliant stroke it had been of Graham Greene's to set the sequence in the Viennese sewers, a coup in no way hurt in the film by the fact that it was shot in black and white. As if it was an effect on a sound stage, a single spotlight appeared to be playing down the rungs of the ladder. I reached the foot of the metal staircase. The light was strong enough for me to observe, by gazing directly into the water between my thighs, a turd audaciously nutmegging me.

WITHIN THE STONES

Roman London

Scrabbling in the mud, my fingers snagged on something hard, cold and impossibly old. I recoiled at the touch, the touch of bone. Whatever it was and whatever it had belonged to – *whoever* it had belonged to, for that matter – it had been preserved undisturbed for centuries beneath London. The clods of mud surrounding it had acted like the ice packs in which paramedics wrap severed limbs on their journeys from shopfloors and semi-ploughed fields to A&E. To come across remains of uncertain animal origin as my untrained hands fumbled through the London substrata – was this really what I'd bargained for? I'm not sure everyone would have had the presence of mind to stay calm in the circumstances. In fact, I suspect a lot of people would have been so grossed out, they would have thrown their nailbrushes into their trays of soil there and then, and told the Museum of London what they could do with their hands-on archaeology project.

The museum was holding open days at which wannabe Indiana Joneses could rummage through samples of earth which had been taken straight from digs in London. Remove the topsoil and the rest was history – that was the idea. This interactive event was being held to celebrate the opening of the museum's vast new repository of artefacts, the London Archaeological Archive and Research Centre. Placed in plastic trays lined with newspaper, the samples were bran tubs of historical curios. They might yield stones, nails, bits of pottery, the personal effects of the ages. Or perhaps a jawbone or a clump of teeth. Like other volunteers, I had been issued with a bowl of warm water, a scouring brush with a head of tightly woven nylon bristles, and a toothbrush. The drill was that you removed a dirt-encrusted item from your tray and scrubbed it up, while experts looked on. They were on hand to offer encouragement and historical pointers and, presumably, to stop you from trousering any antique coinage you might stumble across. When I'd dunked my first mystery object into the bowl – a bone; possibly horse – the smell of soil dissolving in warm water returned me to schoolhood chores of cleaning my football boots. A large knuckle, with what appeared to be a pair of perfectly symmetrical bobbins at one end, the bone hardly seemed like the remains of a creature. You might easily have mistaken it for a manufactured product, or for an implement which an ancestor had skilfully whittled.

I was in the centre's chilly lock-up. A large roll-up metal shutter gave access to vans which bore fascinating conversation pieces to their new home on Eagle Wharf Road, backing onto the Regent's Canal in Hackney. All around were diverting exhibits such as a piano on which Sir Arthur Sullivan, the don of operetta, had composed, and a stagecoach with destinations including Hampton Court Hotel and Dorchester painted on its flanks. Racks and racks of metal shelves held pieces of stone and marble. They looked like scenery for a stage set, so much so that the lock-up reminded me of going backstage, and indeed *beneath*-stage, at the National Theatre, where I'd come across a props trolley for *My Fair Lady* laden with a rubber Stilton, fake cakes, and a latex cauliflower. ('They had to make hundreds of those for the production,' my theatrical guide had said. 'Imagine being backstage with half a ton of real cauliflower going off!') Some of the articles which had been truffled from excavations had been wrapped in string and brown paper, like the chunky, unrefined soap that you find in overpriced toiletry boutiques. Elsewhere, secreted in the several storeys of the archive, were *objets* as various as a bottle dating from AD 200 and a piece of gold leaf from 1500 whose provenance had been established as Venetian.

Stuart bric-a-brac was sealed in freezer boxes, to prevent oxidation. Despite these riches, the new centre was really a great mausoleum. The remains of no fewer than 18,000 Londoners were tagged and bagged and stacked in little shoeboxes, a few hundred of them Roman and the remainder dating from between the Middle Ages and the nineteenth century. There were the bones of Grace Woolley who died on 29 September 1835 at the age of eighty, and a child-size iron coffin of about the same period which had been recovered from Nicholas Hawksmoor's Christ Church in Spitalfields. The Archaeological Archive and Research Centre could lay claim to being the most important institution of its kind in the world.

As I applied my muddy brush to a gnarled bone, an expert called Robin was standing by in a pink shirt. Robin's thing was Roman ceramics. He was interested by a shard – did he say *sherd*? – of pot which I'd buffed up earlier. Its granulated brown surface was like the nut-coated crust of a chocolate ice lolly. Robin said that he'd written a paper on this type of ceramic and he went off to fetch it. But my brushes weren't idle while he was away, and by the time Robin got back I'd completed my path-lab procedure on a darker piece of pot, which was notable for its cross-hatched diagonal black lines. 'Black burnish ware,' said Robin, identifying it. 'Now I'll have to go and get another paper.' There were at least two different types of Roman BBW, he told me. One was mass-produced, with up to 20,000 pieces at a time fired in massive kilns. The other type was thrown on a wheel. It was this less common variety that I had buffed up. The trained eye (i.e. Robin's) could detect 'bands' in a pot, rather like a woodman can count rings in a cross-section of a tree, and these bands gave away the home-made origins of my fragment. Robin explained that the striations on the surface had been made by the artisan dragging an instrument lightly across it.

'Fishnets!' I said. It seemed like a sexy, catchy description of the pattern on the pot. All at once, I saw Robin seizing delightedly on the term, and the pair of us popularising Roman ceramics together. There would be a book, a TV tie-in, a range of reproduction casseroles. But instead Robin laughed uncertainly and gave me a suspicious look.

You've got to be dazzled by the fact that lumps of the original London are still with us. No, not 'still with us': that makes them sound like parchment-brittle geriatrics. These relics may appear almost unimaginably old but they stoutly resist being condescended to. These remnants stand their ground in the modern city and they cry out to be noticed. Bulwarks, buttresses, bathhouses – weathered, yes, and abraded, but implacably dense, with plenty of wear in them yet – endure in a metropolis which constantly eddies and fluctuates around them. Roy Porter likened London to a coral reef, and the Roman remains are like columns of coral in a busy channel. The modern capital floats above the seabed of Roman Londinium. A few remnants break the surface, but others lurk jaggedly just out of sight. Seen in terms of the long, long arc of their time in London, the obscurity in which they presently lie is practically an overnight development. Until the nineteenth century, it was quite common to think of London as the city that the Romans had walled. 'Within the stones' meant the centre of town. As late as 1902, the East Enders who spoke to Jack London for his book *The People of the Abyss* referred to the streets beyond Aldgate as 'London over the Border'.

We're accustomed to peering through display cases at petrified scraps of shoe leather which look as though they'd powderise on contact with a curator's tweezers. There are frangible pots and impossibly unhardy glassware which have been salvered or velvet-cushioned into the hushed and humidified galleries of museums, or else chauffeured to Eagle Wharf Road in their coddling clay. On the other hand, there's an underground car park, of all places, where you can slap your palm or bark your shin on a slab of real Roman wall. That's right; this is a reminder of our history as substantial as a rock face. Some kind of natural mineral deposit is in fact what it resembles: a hillock of stone, with a ferric seam of red slate or tiling running through it. The wall is to be found in a Corporation of London underground car park, to be precise, beneath London Wall, EC2. The motorist can hardly miss it as he makes his descent of the ramp. Though he doesn't see the wall drawn up to its full height of twenty-five feet or so, the section which has broken through into the car park reaches almost to the ceiling, dwarfing a pair of Range Rovers drawn up beside it. The driver has to negotiate the wall immediately the ramp levels out. You wonder whether boozed-up City boys have pranged their rag-top convertibles on its craggy surface. The wall which you can see for the price of a parking ticket, or nothing at all if you're on foot, was built beginning in about AD 190, and took thirty years to complete. This was during the Romans' return to the land on the banks of the Thames, a comeback from the spectacular sacking that Queen Boudicca and her tribes had handed out, culminating in putting the settlement to the torch in AD 60. Coins found by London Bridge were smelted together in the inferno, the first of London's many terrible fires. As Porter noted, 'it is the only occasion London has ever been completely destroyed, ironically by a Briton.' According to the Roman scribe Tacitus, the rebels had 'hastened to murder, hang, burn and crucify . . . up to 70,000 citizens and loyal Romanized Britons in Colchester, London and St Albans'. He wrote up his account fifty years after the event and may have been guilty of a little licence, but even allowing for that, it's no wonder the Romans wanted a wall around the city on their return. That said, there are other theories about the edifice. After all, archaeologists have pointed out that it's far too well made to have been thrown up in a hurry, against the threat of returning raiders. It was built by soldiers, like the best of the Roman boundaries including Hadrian's Wall. Perhaps London's barrier was a status symbol. Even more likely, it was a tax cordon, built to swell the coffers of Rome. The Romans often levied a toll at gateways, and for gateways you need a wall. The gates of the Roman stockade have survived into the pages of my *A–Z*: Aldgate, Bishopsgate, Cripplegate, Aldersgate, Newgate, Ludgate.

The wall was some 2.4 metres thick, increasing to the best part of three metres at the base. It was almost three miles in circumference, enclosing more than three hundred acres, and stretched from the Tower of London in the east to Blackfriars in the west. It was made out of more than a million ragstone blocks, fetched by boat from quarries in Kent, as was established by the discovery of a wreck laden with a cargo of ragstone in the Thames mud at Blackfriars. The wall was faced in stone and bonded with those rust-coloured clay tiles through its full width. To these core materials was added anything useful that came to hand. The Romans had no scruple about recycling carved stone blocks from burial grounds, and helped themselves from shrines and religious monuments. In the Museum of London, about a quarter of a mile away from the piece of wall in the car park, is a stone figure of a Roman soldier dating from the first or second century. He once stood guard over a tomb but was eventually recovered from a tower in the wall in present-day Camomile Street. Part of the tomb of Classicus, Rome's procurator in the British Isles, was pressed into service to support another bastion, at Tower Hill.

Throughout London's history, this magpie approach to redevelopment has held sway. In the case of the stretch of wall in the underground car park, for example, a lot of the core and all of the original outer facing were broken into and carried off for parts during the building boom of the nineteenth century. So what the motorist sees, trousering his keys and walking away from his car, is really the inner face of the sturdy Roman monolith. 'The parts of the wall that stand today have defied the picks and shovels of eighteen centuries and still command respect,' wrote Nikolaus Pevsner. 'The great Wall of London is a very thorough and competent piece of engineering, and it is a matter for regret that it has been subjected for nearly a thousand years to continuous destruction.'

I asked the car-park watchman in his booth about visitors. He eventually tumbled to what I was on about and said that, no, they didn't get sightseers down there to admire their wall. Notices about it were there if you looked for them, but with the same ahistorical sense of priorities that once led the Victorians to loot this old wonder for their building aggregate, the signage burdened the newcomer with workaday considerations such as 'Way In' and 'No Smoking'. Walking around the wall, I discovered a red ceramic ashtray. Was the Roman wall the place for a crafty ciggy before – perhaps also *after* – the 'No Smoking' regime came in?

At such close quarters, the wall looked as though it had been formed from the cooled outpouring of a long-dead volcano. One notice connected the wall to London's subterranean past. 'This section of the town wall of London, part of a length which in the course of centuries since Roman occupation had become submerged, was exposed during construction of this road and car park. It has been preserved by the Corporation of London.' The inauguration of the road, London Wall, was performed in 1959 by the Duchess of Kent.

Yes, but *has* it been preserved, with all the skulking smokers and their fumes, not to mention the other sort of gases you can expect down there? As I was pondering this, a motorbike afterburner exploded into life. I decided I didn't care. I liked what the art critics might describe as the 'found' quality of the wall – or did I mean its 'lost' quality? I was glad that it hadn't been taken apart, brick by brick, labelled and painstakingly reassembled in a museum. In its incongruous surroundings, it had a presence, a brooding quality, as if that stalled lava outflow might at any moment become unstoppered again.

It's a version of the old saw about multiples of buses coming along at once: you could drive your car until it had been around the clock and never so much as glimpse a solid chunk of Roman

fortifications, then pop into an underground car-park and
stumble on two at the same time. Strictly speaking, the other relic
of the Roman city is not visible to the motorist. It's hidden in a
locked and unmarked room, which is at the far end of the car
park from the stretch of wall. This chamber is only opened on
special occasions, but when it is, it reveals the extraordinarily well
preserved foundations of the Roman fort which pre-dates the
wall. In turn, these relics mark a forgotten gateway to the city.
Unlike other bastions, the name of this portal does not appear on
the street map of the modern city. A medieval building, Neville's
Inn, was built on the site and the memory of the Roman gate was
conclusively erased. The fort and the gatehouse were only
rediscovered as recently as 1956. What happened was that
Professor William Grimes, a pioneer of Roman archaeology in
London, came to the conclusion that it simply must be there, and
prospected for it as lustily as an oilman with a whiff of crude in
his nostrils. After the Second World War, Grimes was among a
group of practitioners who realised that there was the smallest of
consolations in the levelling that the Luftwaffe had administered
to large parts of London. The laying waste of buildings of recent
provenance gave archaeologists a rare opportunity to study what
lay beneath. Grimes was putting into practice what Freud had
espoused. He might have been looking at Victorian rubble, but in
his mind's eye he saw the London of the first settlers. Grimes
discovered the south-western corner of the fort, including the
foundations of a rectangular corner tower. His find was in Noble
Street. Today, the Roman remains reverberate to the clang of
hammers on girders in a building site on the opposite side of the
road: the office block which is under construction is the work of
a company called Asticus, a near-namesake of the cartoon
character from Roman times, *Asterix*. Having found one gate,
Grimes was able to plot the position of the west gate, and a dig
confirmed his calculations. He found it where it stands today,
entombed at the rear of the underground car park.

I went to see the fort with a party from the Museum of London, whose premises on London Wall are practically on top of the unremarked room. There were perhaps forty of us on the visit, including an American whose braces announced 'Veni, Vidi, Vici'. We descended a winding concrete staircase from London Wall. At a weathered cream door, which might have been expressly commissioned and kept in disrepair in order to be overlooked by the scores of commuters who pass it every day, we stepped into a chamber with the musty odour of a storeroom. Even the lighting somehow recalled a warehouse rather than, say, the pinpoint illuminations of a gallery.

Immediately on our left, a length of low wall bristled with protruding edges like the spine of a perfectly preserved stegosaurus. I thought about the beginning of *Bleak House*, in which Dickens conjures a primeval scene just a short distance from London Wall.

> As much mud in the streets, as if the waters had but newly retired from the face of the earth, and it would not be wonderful to meet a Megalosaurus, forty feet long or so, waddling like an elephantine lizard up Holborn Hill.

The wall ran up to the beautifully squared-off blocks which marked the base of a watchtower. This had stood on the spot since the second century. At the foot of the structure had been a guardhouse where legionnaires kept warm between watches.

The fort had been about two hundred metres square and made of stone, in accordance with the classic Roman blueprint. Its twelve acres housed the governor's guard and a thousand other ranks, *singulares*, who were posted to London to act as civil servants. They were billeted in barrack blocks which in turn enclosed a central range of administrative buildings and stores. The Romans built their fort from AD 90 to AD 120. When the wall was added later, two sides of the fort were incorporated into the city's new defences. The flank of the fort was originally no more than fifteen feet high and about four feet thick. To bring it into line with the new city perimeter, it was raised, and bulked out to twice its girth.

The former guardhouse had been exited across a stone threshold which was deeply notched with wear. Another furrow on the stonework had been scored by a bolt which had secured the wooden door of the guardhouse, itself long since removed and decomposed. This doorway gave onto what was once a road passing beneath the watchtower and through the west gate of the fort, the gate which had been forgotten until Grimes sunk his archaeological boreholes. This rockery of masonry, the neatly rectangular set of foundations in their bed of gravel, suggested something in the process of construction rather than a ruin. We might have been looking at a half-completed car port. The impression that the fort's custodians had had the builders in was reinforced by a partial cover of polythene sheeting, which had been rigged up to shelter the stones from rainwater. This had been pouring through the ceiling during the resurfacing of London Wall. Lorries rumbled above us in our marigold bunker, and a drill could be heard, dully going through its repetitions.

The Museum of London was an excellent source of ideas and information. Not long after I began my researches, I was lucky enough to talk to the museum's Hedley Swain. As head of early London history and collections, he was an authority on the city's origins. Hedley Swain had the right sort of ring about it, I felt. If you were trying to imagine someone cutting a dash at an excavation site, with trowel and air-puffer and leather-patched sports jacket, then you'd be hard put to think of a better name for him. Hedley Swain had a suggestion of the wind in the hair about it; perhaps it was the echo of Heathcliffe. I rang Hedley up and told him the sort of thing I was looking for and he said, 'You know there's a hairdresser's with a lump of Roman basilica in the basement? It's in Leadenhall Market.' As improbable as it sounded, a salon off Gracechurch Street had one of the very few remaining pieces of the basilica in its lower ground floor studio. The basilica was London's first civic centre, built in AD 70 but greatly expanded in subsequent years. It had dominated the high eastern slope of Cornhill, one of central London's raised pieces of ground, making it clearly visible from every part of the city. By 150, the basilica was a very substantial edifice: at five hundred feet, it was as long as St Paul's Cathedral is today. In fact, it was the biggest building of its kind north of the Alps. The church of St Peter's Cornhill, said to be the oldest in the City, still rests on some of the foundations of the basilica. The bustle of important and prosperous citizens around this building had naturally attracted shopkeepers. Today, the compliment is returned, and a shop accommodates a surviving fragment of this historic administrative HQ.

When I went into Nicholson and Griffin's to ask about their lump of basilica, I felt incongruous myself: dubious, *rumbleable*, like the group of airplane spotters who were then in the news for getting themselves arrested on a holiday in Greece. Enquiring after a chunk of Roman stone in a hairdresser's – suppose it was the *wrong* hairdresser's? – was daft. Fortunately, I hadn't come to the wrong place. 'When people ask where the ancient monument is,' said a middle-aged stylist practisedly, removing her scissors from a man's hair to jab them in the direction of her smirking colleagues, 'this lot say me.' Her client had his hair damped down and his eyes shut. 'Yes, it's in our basement,' the woman said.

Sure enough, over the arch of the staircase, a sign advertised: 'Ten Hairdressing positions and shoeshine. Plus Ancient Monument Downstairs.' I descended the stairs to the accompaniment of a dance tune on the radio and hunted for the remnant of the 1,800-year-old basilica among the impedimenta of a modern boutique. A blonde hairdresser and her City-gent client were discussing a mutual friend who had an interest in racehorses. Behind a vacuum cleaner and something called a 'Rollerball', which appeared to be a mobile basketball hoop (for crimping? Bleaching? Curling?), was what I had come for. On the far side of a glass wall, and fringed by ferns growing from a bed of stones, was the great brick trunk of basilica. It looked like something you might build as a windbreak for a barbecue. It was actually the base of an arch in what had been one of the basilica's arcades. It was found when the present Leadenhall Market was being built in the late nineteenth century. On the other side of the glass, the historic monument flickered in and out of darkness. 'The light doesn't work properly,' said the blonde stylist. 'Nothing to do with us. It's the Corporation.' In what I felt was a game attempt to fit in with the fragment of basilica, the owners of the boutique had had the floor tiled in terracotta, and a bust of Caesar had been placed on a shelf so that he trained his proud gaze on a range of Just Men grooming products.

When I'd spoken to Hedley Swain on the phone, he'd offered to show me an extraordinary discovery which had been made beneath the Guildhall. For a hundred years or so, ever since the Victorians had made archaeology a pursuit to be taken seriously, historians had been looking in vain for the site of London's amphitheatre. It had always been assumed that a city of London's status must have had an arena for animal-baiting, wild-beast hunts and gladiatorial combat, but it had always proved elusive. Only circumstantial evidence had come to light. In Storey Street, Southwark, builders dug up an iron trident, its middle tine bent out of true, which had probably been wielded by a type of fighter called a *retiarius*. The bottoms of a leather bikini, which were tied at the hip with a lace, were recovered from Shadwell. They had perhaps been worn by one of the female acrobats who were warm-up acts at the games. Then, in February 1988, archaeologists were digging under the former Guildhall Art Gallery which had been demolished to make way for a new building. The team was surprised to find a series of Roman walls, set in the ground at unusual angles and all to the same depth. One of the archaeologists speculated that the walls had once been curved.

But how many Roman buildings had curved walls? Perhaps it had been a temple. No, it was too big. A theatre, then? No, it had to be an amphitheatre, the lost Roman amphitheatre of London.

As far as British archaeology was concerned, it was one of the most important discoveries of the last century. The amphitheatre had been overlooked for 1,500 years. Although only the eastern end of the elliptical arena had endured, researchers calculated that the whole thing was once the size of Wembley stadium. When I went to look at the remains with Hedley Swain, it was still a construction site; better say, a *re*-construction site. After the slow process of drying out masonry which had spent centuries under soil and the rubbish of ages, the amphitheatre was being spruced up for inclusion on the itinerary of the London visitor. It would become part of a conference centre belonging to the Corporation of London.

Hedley himself proved to be the model guide, though he wasn't quite as I – or Emily Brontë – might have imagined him. He was a slight man, nattily turned out in a suit and sporting an ear stud. Over cups of coffee in the museum café, Hedley introduced me to the idea of liminality, a term for the fuzzy area in which one thing overlaps another. 'Take the banks of the Thames. The riverbank is a good example of what I'm talking about. You can see the sequence of London's history in order, like a cross-section. A lot of our best discoveries are made in places where the river and the land connect. There's a history of Londoners depositing things in the Thames: bronzework and swords. They were offerings to the gods.'

I thought of a trove of curios which had been recovered from the river mud and put on show at the aquarium on the South Bank, beachcombings including a casino chip, an American Express card and a hypodermic. Souvenirs of private lives which had been transformed into something like courtroom exhibits, they were pieces of private wreckage which had been swept up in the great tide of London life. Liminality was shop talk to Hedley, but it put a name to something which was at the heart of my investigation, the relationship between the overground, overfamiliar city and what lurked underneath it, the liminality of London.

In Iain Sinclair's book about the M25, he refers to the capital's orbital motorway as 'London's liminal strip'. When I was at university, I worked on the construction of the motorway in the holidays. My job was in a makeshift laboratory. Buckets of concrete which had been siphoned off from the cement mixers were brought to the lab and turned into cubes the size of funerary urns. They were sunk in tanks of water. One by one, the cubes were dried off and crushed into a thousand pieces. I gathered that it was to test the strength of the materials used in the motorway. I couldn't see the point of checking a sample of concrete after the rest of the batch had set hard in the highway. But that was what I was paid for: it was a liminal living, working on the sandwich filling of the M25, the layer between the aggregate and the tarmac. Sinclair, feeling the vibes of the road and interpreting them with his occult seismology, would probably insist that I had been taking part in a heathen rite in that lab. What with the sudden violence on the fringes of the site, we might have been laying the foundations of a Hawksmoor church rather than the blacktop for the London orbital. My liminal job marked a transition in my life from growing up at the periphery of the city to working and living at the centre of it.

With Hedley Swain, I walked the short distance from the museum to the Guildhall, through a garden where sawn-off columns survived from the nave of a medieval church. We talked about what I was writing, and Hedley brought up the subject of dead Tube stations, mentioning an episode of *Thunderbirds* in which a raid on the Bank of England involved redundant Underground platforms. 'The producers set it in the future – come to think of it, it would probably have been about now – and they obviously assumed that the Tube wouldn't be in use any longer. You had these characters riding through the deserted tunnels on their jet-bikes.'

In the paved and pedestrianised precinct of Guildhall Yard, Hedley stopped to point out an arc, marked in dark flagging. It described the outline of the amphitheatre directly beneath us, he said. The arc had been incorporated into the design of the new courtyard when the paving slabs were laid. I marvelled that the amphitheatre hadn't come to light until as late as the 1980s, and only then in the fortuitous fashion of earthworks which were linked to the redevelopment of the Guildhall Art Gallery. 'Well, of course, until then, the building was a bomb site,' said Hedley, meaning it in the literal sense.

It would be going too far to say that this was a bombshell, in the figurative sense. But it was a moment when one of the switchbacks of chronology that I was beginning to associate with underground London – the snakes and ladders in time that allow a building contract in the late twentieth century to connect with events from almost two thousand years earlier – seemed to find my own personal history in loops and knots. The thing is, I had vivid childhood memories of visiting the Guildhall. I went to the City of London Freemen's School, which was founded in 1854 in Brixton to educate the orphans of freemen. During the Blitz, the school was evacuated to Surrey, but it still retained its links with the city when I was a pupil in the seventies. The Lord Mayor was guest of honour on prize day. School outings were always to one or other of London's celebrated institutions: St Paul's, the Monument, the Stock Exchange. These excursions were referred to as city visits and they always culminated in the ritual of tea with the Lord Mayor in Guildhall crypt. All in all, I must have seen the Guildhall many times and yet I couldn't recall any bomb damage. It was odd, too, as someone who would have insisted that the Second World War was well before his time, to think that my generation actually came along so soon after the conflict that damage caused by the Blitz, still unfixed when we were growing up, was only patched up after we'd started going out to work.

Hedley had arranged with a contractor to take us down into

the amphitheatre. A suite of rooms at the rear of the Guildhall Gallery had been pressed into service as a site office. Polythene covered the carpets and there was the smell of new-made toast. A couple of men were studying sets of plans at desks but it seemed that most of the workers were already at their stations. In a hard hat and gumboots, a man called John introduced himself as our guide. While we waited for one of John's men to fetch hats for Hedley and me, John wondered aloud in a friendly way about how much I might make from my book. I deftly deflected him from this humiliating line of inquiry by comparing my putative earnings unfavourably with the winnings of contestants on the game show *Who Wants to be a Millionaire?*, then at the zenith of its popularity.

'I've been trying to get on that,' said John. He discoursed wistfully on what he'd do if he succeeded in his ambition to face Chris Tarrant across the *Millionaire* set. He was a fan of motor racing and fast cars. 'I'd really love a Ferrari,' he said. But this wasn't the last throw of the dice of the wage-slave working man. It was clear that John was an enthusiast about the project of restoring the amphitheatre. He was also enthusiastic about my forages in London. As we were buckling on our headgear, John began offering me the derivations of well-known but antique sayings which, according to him, originated within a short distance of where we were standing. 'If you take "being on tenterhooks", do you know where that comes from? No? Smithfield market. It's from when they used to hang the meat out. On hooks. "Cut and dried" – that's another one from there.'

Roman Londoners had watched bouts in the amphitheatre from prototype bleachers, which were supported by a scaffolding of wood. Archaeologists had found deep holes left by the posts which had held the stands up. Those with a more urgent involvement in proceedings had entered the arena below the seating, from a passageway which had been cleared between rows of little rooms or pens where the gladiators and wild animals awaited the moment of truth. During the Corporation of London's refit of the amphitheatre, however, access was via the ground floor of the Guildhall Gallery, past a wooden shed like a bathing hut which housed a security guard, and then down a metal staircase.

In the first incarnation of this theatre of combat, not just the stands but the entire stadium was made of wood. The arena itself was surrounded by a wooden wall like the one which encloses a bull ring: what was left of the timber uprights shoring up the wall was found by the archaeologists. They identified axe marks where the struts had been chopped down during renovations. The wooden gateway at the eastern entrance to the arena had been a substantial affair, some sixteen feet wide. Several of the lower timbers were also found. It had been easier for the Romans to abandon them than to pull them out when they were upgrading the place. The last thing that the gladiators had had to pass before entering the field of battle was a horizontal wooden spar. It was so well preserved that researchers identified slots which must have represented fittings for the hinges and locks of a great gate.

At the foot of the metal staircase leading to the ruins of the amphitheatre, the first century was almost overwhelmed by the twenty-first. At first sight, we could have been in a school assembly hall or gymnasium, awaiting making good and topping out. Great modern beams which appeared to be supporting the Guildhall Gallery were wrapped in shiny metal foil. They crinklily returned the glow of neon strip lights, which had been set up on tripods to guide groups of workmen who were busy with electric tools. Noticing that Hedley and I were in our everyday footwear, John told us to beware of loose nails we might find underfoot. Everywhere was metal scaffolding, builders' debris, hosereels of cable. This was nothing new, of course. The amphitheatre had steadily filled with spoil and refuse for centuries before the conservationists and builders had come along and dug it all out again. Hedley said, 'Nowadays we have landfill sites out in Essex and what have you, well away from central London. That's only happened quite recently in London's history. Before that, you pretty much left things where you dropped them.'

Where we were walking was effectively underneath the Roman grandstand, in the passageway where fighters and beasts had been marshalled before the bouts. On either side of us, embankments and earthworks marked the layout of what were once, improbably enough, gladiators' changing rooms. Running underneath our feet and through the middle of the old arena was the former main drain. In the years since the amphitheatre had been unearthed, archaeologists had found out a fabulous store of detail about the stadium. Since it had been to all intents and purposes a hole dug in the ground, drainage had presented a formidable problem. The Romans had to worry about rising groundwater as well as the inclemency of the English climate. They had installed a system of culverts running around and beneath the arena. The plumbing had come in for a lot of attention in the early second century. This was when the land just outside the eastern entrance of the stadium apparently turned into swamp after the Walbrook flooded. There was evidence that the drains had been raised as the arena was built up. Thanks to the painstaking business of panning the contents of the drains, the archaeologists were able to conjecture plausibly about the patrons of the games. A pearl earring in a golden hasp, an enamel brooch, and hairpins delicately scrimshawed from bone had been lost by female spectators. Chroniclers of the period had noted the allure of well-built and successful gladiators to wealthy women.

Some of the glories of the Guildhall Gallery basement were screened by tarpaulins. But John led us under the eaves of these canopies to view substantial walls, built to the Roman formula of ragstone and tile. They had been put up in the early second century to prevent wild animals from vaulting out of the arena and into the laps of startled spectators. The barrier had once been as much as eight feet tall, and despite the pilferings of centuries, still reached a height of five feet in places. Based on extrapolations from the portions of the walls which have survived, archaeologists believe that the capacity of the amphitheatre could have been as many as six thousand fight fans.

John and his colleagues were grappling with a problem which had confronted the original impresarios of the arena: what kind of surface to go for? The Roman solution had been a bedding of gravel mixed with hard pink mortar and dusted with soft sand. The sand absorbed impact while the layers underneath afforded purchase to sandal and hoof alike. The producers of *Ben Hur* had experimented with various surfaces when they were shooting the film's famous chariot-racing scenes, but ended up settling for something very similar to the original Guildhall recipe. John's worry wasn't horseshoes and wheels scuffing up his floor but the impact of the millions of heels expected to traverse the amphitheatre once the attraction opened to the public. Musing aloud about a particularly shoe-resistant flooring option, John summarised its virtues as 'All the joy of pea-beach gravel, but without it being kicked around'.

You could hardly doubt that visitors would be coming in their coachloads. Like *Ben Hur* itself, Ridley Scott's *Gladiator* had excited a generation of cinema-goers with the thrills and carmine spills of the Roman games. I said, 'So what did you think of *Gladiator* then, John?'

'I thought it was brilliant,' he said.

'It was a bit, I don't know, melodramatic, didn't you think?'

'Well,' said John, looking at me, 'It *was* dramatic, wasn't it?'

The team at the Guildhall had found a skeleton behind a small fragment of wall at the southern entrance to the arena, and speculated tantalisingly about whether this could have been someone who died in battle. But the promoters of the amphitheatre had no need to embellish the passing of this bony local in order to bark up trade. They already had a genuine celebrity with links to the blood-sports circuit of Roman London, in the beguiling shape of a *female* gladiator: perhaps she had worn the side-fastening leather bikini, the kinky gladiatrix kit, which was unearthed at Shadwell. The gentle sex was introduced to the fight game to titillate jaded gore-seekers. The women were a kind of novelty act, slugging it out in the intermissions between the regular bouts. They became popular in the first and second centuries but fell out of favour and were eventually banned in AD 200. Granted, the years hadn't been especially kind to London's feisty Roman miss. Not to put too fine a point on it, she was now ashes. She had been cremated in a funeral pyre in Great Dover Street, Southwark, in the late first century or early second century. Her unusual status was inferred from the fact that her dusty remains were found well away from a walled Roman cemetery where her contemporaries were buried, and also from the grave gifts and the leftovers of a funeral feast which were discovered alongside her. A slap-up spread marked the funerary rites of a Roman VIP. Judging by the scraps, a dove and at least four chickens were on the menu for the gladiator's farewell meal, not to mention a fig, an almond and a date. But it was the gewgaws and knick-knacks which had accompanied the woman on her final journey that really aroused the curiosity of the historians. As well as vessels for burning incense, they found ceramic lamps bearing scenes and motifs from the gladiatorial life. This told them that the woman could have been a wealthy follower of the goddess Isis, or a Roman for whom gladiators were symbolic of the highest ideals of the republic. But it was most likely that she had been a gladiator herself. Inexplicably, London's distaff warrior, a star of the recovered amphitheatre beneath the Guildhall Art Gallery, had failed to attract the nickname 'Glad'.

THE CANTERBURY TOLLS

Anglo-Saxon London

'Pairs!' cried the schoolmaster to his charges. 'Pairs, children! Pairs!' He was red in the face. A breeze from the river rifled his black gown. He was like a large and angry cormorant. The youngsters, excited by a day away from the classroom and the prospect of a trip on the Thames, ignored him. 'In couples, children!' he tried again. The wind threatened to invert his robe over his face. 'Twos!' said the teacher finally. It sounded like a concession of some sort, but at a command they recognised, the pupils obeyed, as if in a dream or trance, each one linking hands with his playmate.

Young as they were, they perhaps sensed something of the extraordinary nature of what they were about to take part in. They had certainly heard all about its outlandish showpiece. In a few minutes, one of their peers, by tradition the smallest boy among them, would be dangled upside down over the river from a barge linked to no less a London personage than the Lord Mayor. The child would be lowered so that his head was within a foot or two of the water. From this precarious and tortuous position, he would then batter the river with a bamboo pole. This spectacle was a curtain-raiser to the annual rite of beating the bounds, the marking out of parish boundaries on Ascension Day. The church was one of London's most venerable places of worship, and located in one of the most famous parts of the city. The frontiers between one church's territory and the next have helped to orient the Londoner in his home town, and have been absorbed into its geography. But while it's readily understood that such and such a street or alley – a recognisable feature on the face of the city – comes within one parish as opposed to another, I for one didn't appreciate that the bounds mimic the ineffable reach of the Almighty Himself. They go where none of our more familiar boundaries and markings, no double yellow lines nor bus lanes, can follow, cleaving through what's on the surface to what lies beneath; yea, even through the very waters of the Thames. In time, the secular authorities learnt from the Church. If you look closely at the map of London, you'll see that the blue column of the river is not only broken up by its bridges, but that another man-made feature runs through the middle of the Thames as it winds through the city. In the west of the capital, the waters claimed by the borough of Kensington and Chelsea are marked off from those which represent the formal frontier of Wandsworth; to the east, the water margin separates Tower Hamlets from Southwark. The famous divide between north and south London doesn't begin at the water's edge but in midstream.

All Hallows by the Tower, as its name suggests, is to be found near the most notorious prison in British history. It follows that the church is also by the river. At first sight, it's eccentric that the church authorities trouble to claim any of the muddy Thames for their parish. What souls are to be saved out there? But the question is no sooner posed than answered. Until quite recently, the river was the principal source of traffic in the capital. London's Customs and Excise service has been based in the parish of All Hallows since the Middle Ages, when Geoffrey Chaucer worked there. The author of *The Canterbury Tales* had a day job as a taxman. All this commerce bobbing past the church doors meant a lot of what the clergy, too, thought of as passing trade. No doubt All Hallows' stake in the Thames also gave it a useful leverage in decisions affecting the administration of this mighty causeway, not to mention an interest in the occasional valuable cargo that might unaccountably disappear overboard or otherwise be listed as missing. V.S. Pritchett wrote about 'the politics of the river, its ancient jealousies, its obdurately defended rights'. 'The Thames is just as closely tied up in cliques, coteries, clubs and privacies as anything else in London,' he said. 'The interests of the river are jealous and vested.'

All Hallows was the kind of place I had in mind when I thought of parts of London where the history of the city could be peeled away layer by layer: the story of the church could be read backwards. Even before Roman times, Tower Hill was already drawing those of a religious cast of mind. It was an early meeting place for people of pre-Christian faith. To this day, the English Druidical Order is attracted to the spot by an 'energy line', a contour on the religious relief map of the area as significant to white witches as the parish bounds are to Anglicans. George Orwell found representatives of another denomination when he visited in the thirties. 'On Tower Hill two Mormons were trying to address a meeting,' he wrote in *Down and Out in Paris and London*. 'Round their platform struggled a mob of men, shouting and interrupting. Someone was denouncing them for polygamists. A lame, bearded man, evidently an atheist, had heard the word God and was heckling angrily. There was a confused uproar of voices.'

The Romans were the first to build on the site. They are remembered by a fragment of pavement underneath All Hallows: a dusty palette of poster paints, in earth and brick tones. A sandstone cross of Saxon origin was found with the inscription WERHERE. As Peter Ackroyd has noted, it strongly suggests the defiant message WE ARE HERE. The present church stands on the route of the main road into the city from what became known as the East Saxon lands; in time, this was corrupted into 'Essex'. In AD 675, the Roman building was blessed as All Hallows, making it one of the earliest Christian sites in the city and one of the most significant features of Saxon London. It appeared much earlier than its more famous neighbour, the Tower, for example: four hundred years earlier, to be precise. The

church was attached to the Abbey of Barking so its full style was
the chewy All Hallows Berkyngechirche.

Compared to the Roman city which preceded it, Saxon London
has been under-reported; you might even say, underimagined.
Admittedly, there's a good reason for this. Saxon London doesn't
appear to have been a patch on its predecessor. The ruins of the
Roman city were largely abandoned in the centuries that followed
the fall of the empire. When their successors gazed upon the
works of the Romans at all, it was with a mixture of awe and fear.
They referred to the first generations of Londoners as 'giants'. But
I was astonished to discover that the other principal reason for the
mystery surrounding Saxon London was the neglect in which it
has languished in academic circles. Not only Saxon London, come
to that, but later periods besides. This was nothing more than
fashion, unless it was snobbery. Ever since archaeology began to
interest the Victorians, the Roman period was the only one that
mattered. The layers of history uncovered in the process of
reaching Roman remains were literally cast aside. Amazingly, the
serious spadework on Saxon London did not begin until little
more than twenty years ago.

But the aversion to digging into London's past went deeper
than this. Archaeology was the province of gentleman amateurs
until the middle of the last century. It wasn't a full-time
profession until the 1970s. As late as 1979, one archaeologist
told me, his tweedy peers considered Henry VIII's dissolution of
the monasteries 'a fairly new topic'. Ironically, a turning point in
the excavation and preservation of London's past was the great
battering inflicted by Hitler's bombs. On the one hand, the air
raids posed an immediate challenge in terms of rebuilding the
city: on one particularly black night, 11 May 1941, air raids
killed 1,400 people and left five thousand roads blocked by
rubble. On the other hand, the wartime craters became happy
hunting grounds for researchers such as Professor Grimes. The
remains of a Roman temple dedicated to Mithras were uncovered

at Walbrook. The find generated great press interest and thousands queued to see it. Behind closed doors, however, the government was worried about the precedent that the temple set. If developers were going to work in kid gloves to avoid damaging the relics of antiquity, and to budget for letting tourists on site, the reconstruction of London would never be completed. Contractors had tacit approval for taking matters into their own hands. They let workers know that they could keep any discoveries to themselves, rather than have the job delayed. A cartoon of the fifties showed a gaffer telling his men that there was a fine for the first one to strike a temple with his pick. There was no law to force developers to permit interventions, as this kind of archaeological research is known. Indeed, they were entitled to compensation at the going rate for the delays incurred by interventions, which made them prohibitive for museums and universities. In practice, archaeologists often reached informal agreements to visit sites, generally after unwanted buildings had been torn down and before the new ones went up. But this was increasingly unsatisfactory. Whereas the great builders of the Victorian period had been kind to the legacy of the architects who came before them – nineteenth-century buildings had comparatively shallow foundations, which did minimal damage to the layers of history beneath – the same wasn't true of the towering office blocks of the post-war era. Whatever was under the piles of a new bank building was liable to be crushed.

The deregulation of the stock market in the eighties led to a building boom in the City, and archaeologists found themselves acting as the firemen of London's history, snatching remnants of bygone times from the jaws of JCBs. In 1980, the Corporation of London entertained plans to pull down Billingsgate Fish Market within the parish of All Hallows and redevelop it as a lorry park. It fell to a great friend of capitalism to put the mockers on this unlovely scheme. Early one morning, workers were surprised by a visit from Michael Heseltine MP, the Environment Secretary in

Margaret Thatcher's government, who declared, 'I will list this building.' His position gave him the authority to do this, though the Corporation was far from pleased. Thanks to Hezza, archaeologists had their day at the old fish market, where they uncovered well-preserved remains of the original Roman waterfront.

By 1991, the privileges of researchers to dig on building sites were enshrined in a statutory instrument. Under its bumf-ish title of PPG16, this revolutionary piece of paperwork insists that remains which are important to the nation must be investigated and preserved *in situ*, any costs being borne by the developer. It's no coincidence that rich archaeological pickings have followed. Under service pipes installed for the Jubilee Line extension at Borough, for example, archaeologists found the first evidence of the fire laid by Queen Boudicca in AD 60. On a building site at Spitalfields, they discovered the body of a Roman woman in a stone sarcophagus. Excavations at Cheapside, on land acquired by a well-known high-street grocer, revealed part of an extra-ordinary conduit dating from 1250 which brought water from Tyburn to the City, by way of present-day Oxford Street and Holborn. It was fed with water at Paddington and worked by gravity, with pipes made from hollowed-out elm trunks radiating from it north and south, and quills of lead running off to the houses of the wealthy. Archaeologist Peter Wilson of the Museum of London told me about the Great Conduit. 'It's been preserved at the site but you can't get into it because there's a supermarket on top of it.' This was the limitation of PPG16, Wilson said. 'Heritage is still treated like low-level nuclear waste. Everything interesting is pinned under three-foot-thick steel floors.'

It was as late as Heseltine's time in office that archaeologists at last found Saxon London. In the late 1980s, they finally cracked the riddle posed by the Venerable Bede, who had located the heart of the city around 'a great market'. Researchers now believe that this was a reference to present-day Covent Garden and the Strand, west of the old Roman city. They found an old blacksmith's shop and weights which were used as part of an eighth-century weaving-loom. Where the Royal Opera House now stands was once the very centre of the Saxon town. The nearby address of Aldwych takes its name from an old Danish word meaning port. The church of St Clement Danes, whose bells peal the refrain 'Oranges and Lemons', stands on the margin of the Roman and Saxon settlements. Dark Ages London was abandoned following raids by Vikings in the early ninth century, and when the city rose again it was in the east, back where the Romans had built it. The remains of a farm at Queenhithe, at the northern end of Southwark Bridge, date from the reign of King Alfred. Researchers have found waterside revetments from this period, and evidence of burial sites in the Fleet valley. In the City, a late Saxon well, carved from a single tree trunk, has been unearthed, as well as a dwelling of the same period, built in the ruins of an old Roman house.

The beating of the bounds of a Saxon parish church in the east of the City has become a cherished ritual, meriting a write-up in the newsletter devoted to the churches of the Square Mile, and drawing a good crowd to All Hallows on a bright, crisp May afternoon in midweek. Marking the bounds with wands at 'Rogationtide' was a supplication in favour of bountiful crops, of good fortune. Ackroyd called the rite 'an act of parish assertiveness which derives from the importance of beating the devil out of the locality'. It had also been a noisy form of advertising, reminding the pious and the heathen alike of the presence of the church, and warning off any priest-adventurers from neighbouring parishes. Men of the cloth were as jealous of their pitches as market traders. This rivalry survived into the twenty-first century in vestigial form, with a mock battle every three years between All Hallows and its neighbour church, St Philip's in the Tower. The office of the Lord Mayor had immemorial links with All Hallows. It was one of a designated handful of City churches which boasted ironwork sword-rests, in which the first citizen was allowed to park his blade.

The Lord Mayor and his party processed to the landing stage by the Tower, to take two barges out into midstream for the near-dunking of a schoolboy which inaugurated the event. The lad was drawn from the rolls of St Dunstan's College, which is now in Catford but was founded in the parish of St Dunstan-in-the-East. The parish is part of the Tower Ward of the City of London, as is All Hallows. Obviously, the place to be for the ceremonial inversion of the schoolboy was among the VIPs on the Lord Mayor's barge. Beadles in their furs were embarking on this vessel, the *Royal Noor*, which had once belonged to the Port of London Authority (the PLA could trace its lineage back to the parish of All Hallows). The beadles were attended by members of the Worshipful Company of Watermen, in their traditional garb of voluminous red skirts and tight caps worn with their brims sticking up, after the fashion of Norman Wisdom's screen persona. In my pushy reporter's way, I made for the *Royal Noor*, only to be turned back at the gangplank. 'I'm terribly sorry, all the space is taken,' said a man whose ermined and cockaded ensemble announced him as none other than the Lord Mayor himself.

As he and the remainder of the 'beating party' set off, the rest of us followed aboard the *Silver Barracuda*. The event had the atmosphere of a larky beano for the Quality. It was an Anglican Henley, an ecclesiastical regatta. Those of us on the *Barracuda* assembled on the main deck, which was enclosed against the elements. This was where day-trippers enjoyed views of the river by day, and partygoers cut a rug by night. A corrugated metal screen had been rung down in front of what was presumably the bar. I spotted His Grace David Jenkins, the former Bishop of Durham, among the celebrants of the ancient ceremony. He and a young vicar were wondering aloud about the licensing laws, perhaps intrigued to know whether they had the same reach over water as God's by-laws, and articulating a general query about whether the bar would open. It didn't: it was a very dry Henley. The skipper of the *Barracuda* was standing beside the boat's PA system, the speaker stacks which livened up evening cruises with dance music. On the other side of the deck, a prelate with a transatlantic accent welcomed everyone on board. Suddenly the PA struck up with a recording of a crooner singing, 'Somewhere Beyond the Sea'. 'No, no, no, no, no!' cried the mid-Atlantic curate. He slid across the deck towards the controls of the PA system, to suppress the themed easy listening.

On such a brilliant afternoon, the river to every side of us was a transparent bag of new pound coins. In a carrying, pulpit voice, the former Bishop of Durham was saying, 'I'm an old Dunstonian. I go right back to before the war. We were evacuated in the first place to Reigate in Surrey. I was head boy in school once upon a time . . .'

We admired the Watermen aboard the *Royal Noor*, who were striking poses of ceremonial lookout. 'The red ones look a bit like jockeys,' said a young woman from the Port of London Authority, who was on a skive. Betraying no trace of embarrassment following the PA episode, the skipper of the *Barracuda* began going through the boat's safety drill in a learnt, reflexive style. 'The life-raft will be launched by a crew member,' he said at dictation speed, adding after a substantial pause, 'and float freely.'

A big shaggy old boy – in fact, the type Kingsley Amis would have called a 'shag' – began banging on at me about something called Doggett's Race for which I was, hilariously, well briefed, having read about it only a few days earlier. Doggett's was an annual rowing event held between city bridges. 'They row like stink, with these two launches behind,' said the shag. 'Everyone on the launches jugging it.' He mimed 'jugging it'. It seemed to involve drinking. The shag announced himself as the former mayor of a

London borough. He said that he was looking for some media coverage of his scheme to give Doggett's competitors a drink.

'That shouldn't be too difficult,' I said.

'Ah, but you've got to observe the protocol,' said the ex-mayor with a wily look. He was pleased that the day's remarkable events had afforded him an entrée to the people who ran the race, not only the Watermen but the Worshipful Company of Fishmongers, who were also represented in the flotilla.

The vicar with the transatlantic accent said, 'You'll see the young lad is being prepared for sacrifice,' and we turned to see a boy hanging head first over the bows of the *Royal Noor*, suspended from his ankles by a clergyman in a billowing cassock. The child was wearing a life jacket but otherwise all he had to defend himself with was a rod of bamboo. Some of his schoolmates were watching from the wheelhouse of the *Royal Noor*, giggling. But their mirth turned to applause as their friend's stout belaying of the Thames set up a tiny pool of froth on the surface of the river. Aboard the *Barracuda*, this was the cue for the vicar to give a brief address. Then we sang a verse of 'Praise My Soul, the King of Heaven' and the vicar said, 'We're safe for another year.' The claims of God and All Hallows to this stretch of the Thames – not only to its childishly agitated meniscus but to everything that lay beneath it – had been energetically asserted once more, in the face of the unsleeping pretensions of Satan and rival parishes alike.

On Sugar Quay, the Lord Mayor's car was waiting to purr him back to Mansion House. It was a limo and its registration was LMO, which was presumably some sort of acronym for his office, although I preferred to think the mayor's plates were honouring the sheer size of his ride, bling-bling style. The guest of honour was leaving us but the ritual of beating the bounds wasn't over. It required that the entire perimeter of the parish was paced out and flogged at selected important sites. It brought to mind one of those dinner parties, popular a few years ago, in which neighbours ate a course in each other's houses in rotation. Now the other children of St Dunstan's would be joining in with the beating. At the command of 'Beaters, are you ready? Beaters, beat!' the boys and girls dished out a good hiding to the pavement slabs. One of them had already confessed to me that the object was to reduce their pieces of bamboo to ribbons.

I snatched a few words with the star of the show, 12-year-old Joel Lewis, whose CV will record that he lashed out at a river with a stick on an important day in the Christian calendar. Joel had a pageboy haircut and his blazer was too big for him. In response to my solicitous opening question, Joel assured me that he was now perfectly dry.

'Did you have any training?' I asked him.

'For what?'

'Doing that. Beating a river.'

'Oh. No,' said Joel.

'Did you feel safe out there?'

'Yes. They were holding on to me pretty tightly.'

For a moment, I considered the polite, quietly impressive but unarguably small fry in front of me. 'Maybe it's an advantage to be the littlest?' I offered.

'Maybe,' said Joel, to please me. He had played his proud but mystified part in a stunt organised by the grown-ups, and visibly enjoyed by them, but which seemed more hare-brained than anything that Joel and his friends were ever likely to dream up.

I became aware that I wasn't the only interloper at the ritual, tagging along with a notebook in hand. The capital's legendary blue guides, the people who lead walking tours of the city, were also represented in our party. I know this because one of them, in his zeal to share his knowledge of our surroundings, hit me on the arm. His name was Armand. He introduced me to another guide, Beryl. She was leading a walk beside the river the following morning, and had a 'Doctors, Disease and Death' stroll pencilled in for the afternoon. Armand and Beryl capped each other's stories, not in a competitive way but because they were both overflowing with enthusiasm. I was the Greek chorus: 'Is that underground?' I asked of anything which had the least hint of the subterranean about it.

Armand mentioned the bridges that Wren had designed for the Fleet. The River Wandle, he went on, once powered sixty-eight mills, over a distance of no more than seven miles. 'In its day, it was the hardest-working stretch of water anywhere in the world,' he said.

Beryl told us about Dr Johnson. Armand was surprised to learn from her that the great man had penned a medical dictionary in addition to his better-known reference work.

'Yes,' said Beryl, 'it covers everything up to the scientific revolution, too.'

Armand, twitching and slapping himself, said, 'Johnson had Tourette's, you know.'

I said, 'Did he swear as well, then?'

They both looked at me as if I had sworn. They seemed to think that Dr Johnson didn't blaspheme, in view of his well-advertised faith. In fact, Beryl insisted that he was no more Tourettic than Armand or I.

The cue that the beating party had reached an important point on the parish perimeter was that the clerk would hold a wooden staff in the air, a signal for the procession to halt. One resonant locus was Custom House on Lower Thames Street. The beaters began on the edge of the kerb outside the building, then advanced in line abreast towards it, all the time thrashing the pavement, as if in some disastrously low-tech mine-detecting operation. It was perhaps just as well that they couldn't get any more force into their childish pasting of the Custom House precincts, because deadly weapons were indeed lurking almost directly beneath our feet, along with other dangerous substances. Down below the street, where this former royal warehouse abuts the river, was a trove of outlandish smuggling accessories, and the lethal wherewithal which has been employed to ensure that the contraband reached its intended destination. Customs officers had such a collection of drug-running contrivances – *trompe l'œil* devices and illusionists' props – that their haul was a kind of black museum. Or, given what this kit has concealed, a white museum. I slipped away from the beating party and continued my underground journey of London through the cellars of the Custom House. If at first sight this was a departure from my chronological itinerary, a long way from the Dark Ages ritual of beating the bounds, in fact the antecedents of the Custom House are every bit as venerable. In one form or another, this factory of tax has stood on the river for two thousand years and there's been a customs service of sorts since AD 742. In 1203, King John levied an export tax on wool, which led to a system of national taxes at ports. By 1275, the customs service had been put on a regular footing by Edward I. The Great Custom on exported wool, the Tunnage on wine and the Poundage on other goods were a nice little earner for the royal coffers.

It wasn't only the enthusiastic bounds-beaters of the twenty-first century who had to exercise caution around Custom House. Everyone who has ever worked there has known that the building is in constant peril from flammable substances including gunpowder and alcohol held in the basement. Unfortunately, despite this care, all of the former Custom Houses have burnt to the ground. In 1666, the building was consumed by the Great Fire. Wren obliged with a new Custom House in 1671 but it caught fire again in 1715. Thomas Ripley designed its successor, which was completed in 1718. It lasted not quite a hundred years before going up in flames in 1814. Its replacement, erected in 1817, is the one which can be seen by the Thames to this day, children with bamboo poles permitting. The present Custom House is the only surviving Georgian frontage on the river.

The king's warehouse was established beside the wharf so that illegal goods could be hauled ashore by a winch, which can still be seen on the quayside, and placed under lock and key out of temptation's way. Custom House also retained some exceptional documents in its archives. There was a chitty which showed that Admiral Nelson drank champagne and hock: the old seadog had responsibly declared them. But during his extraordinary posthumous repatriation from Trafalgar, when his body was placed in a bath of brandy to preserve it, the makeshift embalming fluid was not declared. The reason for this was that Nelson's personal allowance, including what was clearly a very generous provision of cognac for the wardroom balloon, had been cleared through customs when he went off to war, on what proved to be the admiral's last outward-bound journey from these islands. Even if Nelson had come home in hooky VSOP, England expects that customs men would have looked the other way, and not treated the matter like a ghoulish forerunner of today's booze-cruises.

Among the more dubious items that officers have confiscated is a family-sized tin of gherkins. Not everyone's cup of tea, certainly, but not in themselves illegal. Filled with heroin, however, these appetisers had been turned into canapés to make the party swing. A rusty ship's boiler had been a vital piece of evidence in another customs bust, dubbed Operation Pugwash. In January 1996, a vessel called the MV *Craigmore* docked at Felixstowe after a long voyage from Pakistan via Iran, Dubai, Morocco and Spain. Boarding to make a routine examination, customs officers overheard complaints from the crew that they hadn't had a hot meal for two weeks. The gas in the galley had run out, they said. But when the gas canister was examined, a false bottom was discovered and found to contain 25 kilograms of heroin. The ship's company were all questioned and bailed while inquiries continued. The cook jumped ship and was never seen again. As an explanatory note from HM Customs couldn't resist adding, 'whether this was due to the quality of his porridge or his guilt we cannot prove'. Other exhibits include a New English Bible with a stash-shaped hollow in it, and a statue of one of the Seven Dwarfs which had been used as a whimsical container for hashish. Yes, you're ahead of me: it was Dopey.

When they're not busting illicit garden furniture or bent snacks, officers are on the lookout for products made from protected species. In a room so clinical-looking that it would lend itself to the most feared of all customs investigations, the full cavity search, a selection of banned animal goods was set out on a trestle table. As if in a ghoulish bring 'n' buy, there were stuffed lizards, an alligator's head worked as an ashtray, and a leopardskin vanity case. I couldn't help noticing that an impounded lion pelt was doing duty as a tablecloth. I studied a pair of snakeskin loafers, wondering at the dandified tassels on them, until I realised that these pom-poms were in fact the heads of the reptiles. Another exhibit was a valise lined with bird boxes. A nest-robber had tried to take rare species out of the country in his luggage.

'So how did you rumble him?' I asked a customs officer. 'Did he sound like the dawn chorus at check-in?'

'No, it was dark in the bag so the birds would have been asleep,' she said reasonably. 'If the case had been full of clothes or something, he would have thrown it about a bit. But we noticed that he was handling it very delicately.' The maximum penalty for a bird in the hold was seven years' imprisonment.

I couldn't see Geoffrey Chaucer confiscating wacky gherkins but a stiff line against the rustling of our feathered friends, on the other hand, struck me as something that the poet might have had in common with his modern counterparts. In the fourteenth century, snatched peacocks and ill-gotten gaming birds might well have fallen under Chaucer's quill, in his capacity as Comptroller of Customs and Subsidies of Wools, Skins and Hides in the Port of London.

Though we might grumble about Chaucer's successors as

party-poopers, and wince at their taxes, they deserve credit for
their vigilance. In one display case beneath Custom House, the
blameless timer of a washing machine resides alongside much
more sinister circuitry, including the gyroscope of a Saud B
missile, from which it was practically indistinguishable. A cabinet
of other weapons includes a natty pen gun, a souvenir of the
Cold War, which was found on the skipper of a Russian fishing
boat, perhaps in the breast pocket of his sou'wester. Customs
officer Nick Kerridge showed me a 9mm Uzi pistol. 'That was
discovered in fifty kilos of Class A drugs coming in on a lorry at
Dover: loaded, cocked, ready to use. Not good,' he said. Making
up a diabolical pair with this was an AK74, a later version of the
more familiar AK47. Kerridge said, 'It was part of a consignment
of many hundreds of weapons including Semtex which we seized
at Teesport ten years ago. It had come in from the eastern bloc
and it was going to Northern Ireland.' In comparison with these
shoot-'em-up exhibits, the low-tech weapons with which they
were arrayed seemed almost friendly. There was a samurai sword
and a blowpipe, a spring-loaded baton and a set of martial arts
throwing stars. There was even a raffish cane-sword which looked
as though it might have been seized from Burlington Bertie's
morning room.

VOYAGE TO THE BOTTOM OF THE SEE

Medieval London

My underground odyssey had already taken me close to the Guildhall, to the Roman amphitheatre beneath its art gallery. But I wanted to go to the hall itself, to go back to the crypt where my school trips to London had culminated in the treat of high tea in this antique grotto. But on the day when I returned to the Guildhall and negotiated its defences – the metal-sensitive door jamb and the X-ray-capable conveyor belt which were integral to twenty-first-century security – the doorman told me that the crypt was out of bounds. 'They're doing a freedom,' he added, in what I'm going to have to call a cryptic fashion.

Doing a freedom? What on earth was that? It seemed that it was a ceremony in which the Freedom of the City of London was conferred. The Freedom of the City of London! Of course! This was one of the most romantic baubles in the long and colourful inventory of titles and privileges. Wasn't this the very plum that Dick Whittington carried off after his tests and trials in panto-land, along with the mayoralty of London and the hand of Alice Fitzwarren? I was almost certain that the Freedom of the City carried with it arcane perks, perhaps involving animal husbandry in built-up areas and the portage of bales of straw by sedan chair. But I was also more than half sure that the Freedom had once been a status ardently to be desired, an important sanction and refuge for the honest man in his dealings with an often summary state. Did I know that they still dished this Freedom out? If I did, it felt at that moment as if I had found out all over again. Experience said that it would be a largely cosmetic investiture: lounge suits, barely suppressed grins of self-consciousness, a certificate garnished with a reproduction of the impression made by a signet ring in hot wax. The newly freed man could probably purchase a souvenir Polaroid. But imagination countered that there would be many a courtly oath and fanfare; there would be scrolls borne on cushions; a pair of mastiffs would stir at the report of faggots in a roaring hearth the size of an aircraft hangar. In short, this was something I had to see. I said as much to the guard. 'You'll have to speak to the Chamberlain's Court,' he said.

From Guildhall Yard, I was put through from my mobile to this magicky-sounding institution. I explained my business to the clerk, not failing to lay it on a bit thick about where I had been to school, where I now lived, the almost tangible proximity of my employer to Guildhall, etc., etc. I finished by telling the clerk, 'So I'd really like to see somebody getting a Freedom.'

The clerk said, 'Oh, I think we can do better than that.' Bearing in mind everything that I had told him, said the clerk, a good sport by the name of Murray – everything about my education, my current address, my place of work and so on – 'Why don't you become a Freeman yourself?' he said.

For a moment, I was dumbfounded. Had I applied one too many coats of gilt to the lily? Was Murray being serious? As I listened to him running on, instructing me in what I needed to do in order to gain my Freedom, I could hardly doubt that he was entirely serious. I would have to satisfy the City authorities that I was a suitable case for Freedom, said Murray. 'No criminal convictions, not bankrupt; that sort of thing,' said Murray. We laughed. *No criminal convictions!*

I would have to complete and sign a form, which Murray would be happy to send me. Then there was the matter of the fee. The Freedom wasn't free. On the other hand, it wasn't very expensive. It was £30, payable to someone called the Chamberlain of London. 'You'll be interested to know that the money goes to your old school, City Freemen's,' said Murray. He was right, I was interested. I was very interested. Murray said that I would have to bring my application to the Guildhall in person, and it would then go before the Court of Common Council, which has been the judicial branch of the City of London for centuries. Provided the Court was favourably disposed to my petition, I would be called back to the Guildhall to recite a loyal oath and gain my Freedom.

I told Murray that I'd be obliged if he sent me the application form directly. A passer-by who happened to glance in my direction as I rang off might have noted a wondering expression on my face. Perhaps if I had paid more attention in class I would have known that the purchase of the Freedom of the City of London financed my Alma Mater, but I didn't know it, and discovering it entirely by chance, as I felt I had, while trying to visit the Guildhall crypt during my subterranean journey through London – this struck me as so unlikely, and yet also so serendipitous, if I can put it like that, that Whittington himself couldn't have been more beguiled by the concept of civic liberty than I was at that moment. The Freedom was an absurdity, I told myself, a branch of the heritage industry, the sort of thing that appeals to men who re-enact key skirmishes from the Wars of the Roses in gauntlets and tights. But I began to imagine myself swanking about town with the suffix of Freeman of the City of London bringing up the rear in my title. Or could it be that a gentleman affected the decoration *before* his baptismal moniker? Like other aspects of my underground adventure, the protocols laid down in the ancient gazettes of the City required a little digging.

The Freedom dates back to the Middle Ages, to a time when craftsmen across Europe were organising themselves into trade guilds. The aims of the guilds were the lofty ones of protecting customers, employers and employees alike, by means of monitoring workmanship and the quality of goods, and standardising weights and measures. In the old hall which lends its name to the institution of the Guildhall, dully gleaming metal rulers are bolted to the wainscoting. These are the standards of length, the templates for everyday measurements such as the foot, two feet, the yard: the yardsticks which gave the world this popular usage. They were the final point of reference and arbiter in forgotten disputes over rolls of cloth and bales of twine. The standards were made by Troughton & Simms of London in the days when it was assumed that the sun would never set on imperial calibrations. Not far from these rules, another set have since been affixed to the superstructure of the Guildhall. With who knows what archly Eurofriendly send-off, these brass strips were introduced as a guarantee of metric lengths.

As well as seeing that customers didn't receive short measure, the guilds trained the young, and took care of their members in old age and disability. In the City of London, the guilds became known as livery companies, of which a hundred are still active in the twenty-first century. The Corporation of London liked to exert its influence over the livery companies, and did so by requiring that all liverymen became Freemen of the City. At first, the cost of Freedom was comparatively high. During the fourteenth century, the fees brought in a tidy income for the Corporation. In exchange, freemen were favoured with boons and indulgences including exemption from market and bridge tolls. Moreover, only freemen could vote or have a say in how the City was run: this was the sanction and refuge of the honest liveryman that I had been thinking of. To this day, a synonym for 'Freeman' in Corporation of London literature is 'citizen'. The word is a kind of historical footnote to an ancient power struggle between the City and the Crown, the commercial metropolis extending and cementing its rights in exchange for the funds required by an often spendthrift and warmongering sovereign. The work of left-leaning historians such as Roy Porter is salted with the irony that republicans have the fat cats of the City to thank for the tentative steps we have taken towards citizenship and away from subjecthood.

The Corporation – and through it, the City of London – continued to make use of the franchising of Freedoms until 1800. By then, the population was expanding so fast that the old ways of controlling trade were becoming outmoded. After reforms passed in the nineteenth century, the City's commerce and franchise restrictions were scrapped, and the ancient rights and privileges ceased to be relevant. The Freedom was retained for aspiring members of livery companies, though it was felt that it was no longer fair to charge a substantial premium for this as though it was still the commercial leg-up it had once been. From 1835, the Freedom was opened up to men and women who had no connection with the guilds but an interest in the City nonetheless. Perhaps because it no longer gave its beneficiaries a clear competitive advantage, take-up was modest until the end of the nineteenth century. But with a revival in the status of the Square Mile in the last century, and an explosion in its size – it now fills with more than a quarter of a million commuters every weekday, and is home to eight thousand Londoners – the Chamberlain's Court is as busy processing Freedoms as it was four hundred years ago. Murray and his colleagues handle in the region of 1,700 a year.

Although the philosophers have argued about freedom for centuries, the clear-eyed City Corporation distinguishes three different types of it, and can quote you a price for each. In addition, it disburses honorary Freedoms – the City was savvy to the complimentary gong business long before the universities – and beneficiaries have included Nelson, Wellington, Disraeli, Florence Nightingale and Churchill. More recently, discretionary Freedoms went to Margaret Thatcher and Nelson Mandela. Depending on your point of view, granting the Freedom of the City of London to the former long-term inmate of Robben Island was either a graceful gesture or a clunking afterthought. Of the three types of Freedom on the open market, the first is the servitude. The connection with the livery companies is preserved through the servitude, because it's granted as of right to anyone who has served an apprenticeship to a Freeman or a liveryman. These days, applicants affiliated to livery companies account for only half of the total. Like servitudes, patrimonies carry automatic rights to the fraternity of the free; in this case, the rights reside in the children of freemen. The third route to Freedom is by redemption. Here, the verb to redeem is understood not in religious terms but in its pawnshop sense, viz. to buy back. This was the Freedom that I was eligible for. My hopes rested with the men and women who met every month in the oldest surviving cockpit of law-making in London. I had to await the pleasure of the Court of Common Council . . .

But I didn't cool my heels. I went in search of one of London's most important medieval buildings. It lies almost forgotten underneath the concrete and tarmacadam of a busy A-road, in the shadow of its current landlord, a supermarket. Thomas Becket once studied in this suburban setting and early codifications of English law were composed there, in the purlieus of a lost place of worship the size of Westminster Abbey. Kings of England lay in state in what is now a car park, and treaties were signed with the French foe where the only negotiation done nowadays is with shopping trolleys the size of siege engines. Like most Londoners, I had never heard of Merton Abbey. Oh, I'd heard of *Merton Abbey*, all right: Merton Abbey the place, Merton Abbey the address. Fortunately for me, a historian who knew of my interest in the buried city helpfully pointed out that the stress in 'Merton Abbey' could just as tellingly fall on the second word as the first. In the Middle Ages, a Christian order really had raised a vaulting house of God in a corner of south-west London which is now at the further reaches of the Northern Line. Its remains now lay buried under a Sainsbury's Savacentre. In its time, though, it had been complete with ancillary buildings including an infirmary, cloisters and a chapter house.

In defence of people such as myself who had overlooked

Merton Abbey, it wasn't one of the sturdy ecclesiastical landmarks of the capital. Long since sacked and abandoned, it was more like those great ruins of temporal London that existed in the mind's eye rather than in any extant view of the city, such as the forgotten ducal piles which had once dominated the Strand, or Castle Baynard, William the Conqueror's base at Barking, which is now preserved only in the name of a wharf off Upper Thames Street. Certainly, it was left to the imagination to conjure up Merton Abbey from the neglect into which it had sunk. Its name was bracketed these days with a struggling shopping experience-cum-entertainment park. No, I'm not talking about the supermarket. I'm referring to Merton Abbey Mills. Merton Abbey Mills was a wagon train of shops and market stands drawn up in a circle on the far side of the A24 from the supermarket.

For the time being, Merton Abbey Mills fought its corner with the aid of farmers' markets, a pocket-sized theatre, a pottery workshop. You couldn't accuse the people behind the place of being indifferent to history. On the contrary, they actively traded in it. But it wasn't the history of medieval England and one of the most significant religious communities of its day. Merton Abbey Mills set out its historical stall a good seven hundred years later instead, with the life and works of William Morris. In 1881, the visionary haberdasher had moved his business out of central London to Merton, believing that the waters of the River Wandle, on which the suburb stands, were ideal for his business of dyeing textiles. A contemporary account, recording the beneficial effects that a visit to Merton Abbey had on Morris, suggests that the monks' gardens were still recognisable as late as the nineteenth century: 'the latter part of the journey through the fields, was soothing and then there was the short passage from the station through the garden of the Abbey and the prospect of being soon at work which together may have restored his equilibrium'. Armand the blue-badge guide, whom I had met during the beating of the bounds ceremony at All Hallows, told me about the sixty-eight mills operating on the River Wandle in its pomp. They had included one at Merton Abbey which powered looms for Liberty's: the West End department store had experimented with an early outsourcing scheme. Liberty's water wheel had been restored to perfect working order, and was the showpiece of Merton Abbey Mills. You could watch its paddles of local elm cleaving the Wandle.

The medieval history of Merton Abbey, by contrast, was like a guilty secret. You went to see the Abbey in the way you might once have trepidatiously looked up an unfortunate relative who had been confined to an institution. You knocked on an office door and waited while someone fetched the key and escorted you. These arrangements, perhaps lacking in the majesty you might expect of one of the great fountainheads of faith in this country, in no way reflected on the custodian of the keys, John Hawks. John, the general manager of Merton Abbey Mills, was himself a great booster of the Abbey and had done his best to look after it and bring it to the attention of as many people as possible. I went to meet him on a wintry Saturday morning. From Colliers Wood Underground station, it was a mile or so to Merton Abbey Mills. By the time I got there, I was soaked through. John, on the other hand, was sitting pretty in his snug nook of an office. This was located in a covered souk at the heart of the market. As John rose to shake my hand, a pair of dogs sprang from a basket at his feet.

'Come on, Wooster! Jeeves – this way!' We were striding across a rain-pooled car park now, John in his Barbour jacket and flat cap, his dogs roaming where their olfactory organs took them, until a word from John drew them back again. We were heading towards the Roman road of Merantum Way, now the A24. There was a pedestrian subway beneath the road, giving access to the Savacentre. As you walked through this underpass, you realised that one side of it was faced with windows and even a door. What you were looking at was a kind of bunker. No light came from it. The windows looked as though they had been blacked out, but this was a trick of the foul morning, the effect of the dark space massed behind the glass. A thoughtful shopper with time on his or her hands might have paused to read one of the small flyers in the window. Otherwise, you would have been hard put to guess that this strange chamber preserved one of the most important religious sites in the British Isles.

'People talk about atmosphere, but I think this place has really got it,' said John, turning the lock and opening the door. In the moment before he flicked the light switch, it was possible to make out low, dense silhouettes: then blocks of masonry bulked into visibility. Laid out on a bed of raked gravel, they were the foundations of the old chapter house. The chamber was damp and chilly, an ossuary of stones. The cars plying to and fro on the weekly shop were barely audible overhead, but you could still hear the wind outside. 'This is a good place to tell kids ghost stories,' said John wickedly.

No fewer than eight hundred bodies had been buried at Merton Abbey, more than thirty of them entombed in sarcophagi. They had been exhumed before the supermarket was developed, with Cardinal Basil Hume, the then head of the Roman Catholic Church in Great Britain, officiating. The most illustrious shade likely to put in an appearance at the chapter house belonged to Henry I. He had been accorded the privilege of lying in state at Merton in 1135, perhaps in recognition of his contribution to the founding of the religious community. Henry had granted 'the ville of Merton' to Gilbert, sheriff of Surrey. Gilbert was allowed to build a church and establish a monastery. The Augustinian canons of the monastery began to build a new church, close to Gilbert's, in 1117. Four years later, Henry handed over the manor of Merton to the canons. The priory's chapter house was built in the middle of the twelfth century. It was 17.5 metres long by 10 metres wide, rectangular in shape, facing east, with a crescent tip. In front elevation, it resembled the hull of a ship, but with a strange, blunt stern. John said, 'I like the incongruity of it, the fact that this place is under a main road and by a Savacentre. By atmosphere, I also mean all the space that you have in here.'

From time to time, chairs were brought down into the underpass and the chapter house became a playhouse. It sat as many as two hundred. John said, 'We've had *Richard III* in here; *Macbeth*; *Murder in the Cathedral*, of course. It's completely unheated. I think of it as an outdoor theatre indoors.'

The old place had seen its fair share of theatrics long, long ago. The chapter house had been used for hashing out monastic business and settling matters of discipline. 'It was the boardroom of the Abbey,' said John. Becket, whose life was recalled in the productions of *Murder in the Cathedral*, had received his schooling at Merton from 1130 to 1141. The Augustinians had shrewdly kept lodgings ready in case the monarch wanted to drop by. Henry III was certainly in residence in 1217, when a full-scale international peace conference took place between the Crown and the Dauphin. 'That was held right here, in the chapter house,' said John. 'You can just imagine them, with their courtiers and advisers—'

'—their beer and sandwiches,' I said.

'Exactly! Exactly!' cried John, forgivingly. It was presumably mead that had slaked the royal thirsts, and it would be several hundred years before the sandwich was even thought of. But John was reckless with his enthusiasm where the chapter house was concerned. In 1236, following disputes between King Henry III and his barons, an early draft of English law was committed to vellum there, in the form of the unlikely-sounding Statutes of Merton. In 1437, Henry VI was crowned not far from where John and I were standing.

Led by Jeeves and Wooster, we inspected piles of Reigate stone and Purbeck marble, linen folds and capitals: exquisite rubble.

Fondling one handsomely worked fragment, John exclaimed, 'Pretty, pretty thing! What was it doing there? *But so nice!*'

The dissolution of the monasteries had put paid to the priory and its chapter house. The masonry was torn down and most of it carted the few miles down the road to Nonsuch in Surrey, where it furnished Henry VIII's love-nest for Anne Boleyn, itself long since lost. Apart perhaps from the gardens, the last trace of the priory had disappeared by the time William Morris was coming to Merton to escape the bustle of the city. Credit for finding it again belongs partly to a local antiquary by the name of Colonel H. F. Bidder. He carried out limited excavations in the early 1920s. Sainsbury's paid for a major dig from 1986 to 1987, said John, before they moved in. But latterly the mighty retailer had become a kind of absentee landlord, for all that its commercial premises were only a few yards away. 'They're sublimely uninterested in making the most of this thing in their backyard,' said John. He was studying a slab at his feet. With effort, he raised it. In a hushed and stagy voice, he said, 'This stuff is unbelievably dense and heavy!'

John understood that talking about the Abbey was a way of preserving it, of outfacing the dereliction which threatened to overwhelm it. Talk, said Michael Moorcock in *King of the City*, is London's lifeblood. 'It pumps into every side street and alley, pounds down every Tube and drain, enriches the heart, stimulates the brain. It carries the silt of centuries in its undertow.'

Later, John and I sat over mugs of tea in the fat-reeking café at Merton Abbey Mills. A woman with a lion's-mane hairdo struggled through the door out of the wind, proud curls blowing into her eyes. 'I quite liked the idea of being a vicar,' John was telling me. 'I like the sound of my own voice, I like playing a part. The compassionate bit, the intellectual bit. There was just one problem,' he said. 'I don't believe in God.'

'Well, that's no handicap these days,' I said, quoting Alan Bennett without attribution.

But John went on, 'It was the same with advertising. I couldn't *stand* the ads. They seemed so pretentious to me.' John said that he hardly ever watched television – 'The men's singles finals, Diana's funeral: the really big things' – and for some time after Tony Blair was first returned to Downing Street in 1997, he had no idea what the prime minister looked like. John's friend Eric Reynolds had set him up in the job at Merton Abbey Mills. Eric had been the visionary behind the development of Camden Lock; his new thing was over at Bishopsgate railway arches. John said he would ring Nigel, who was Eric's man at Bishopsgate. 'Nige?' said John into the chin-guard of his mobile, 'I've got a charming man with me who's interested in the lower depths.'

An interest in the lower depths was something that John and I had in common. He told me about a tributary of the Wandle, the splendidly named Bunce's Ditch, and the drains which ran beneath it, in order to keep refuse and sewage away from the water supply. He told me about the Second World War bomb which had exploded in the street where he now lived, and the elderly neighbour who could remember peering into the crater and seeing the buried River Effra flowing through the bottom of the chasm.

John said, 'Merton Abbey was this vast building, dominating the Wandle valley. It wasn't just a church. It employed, I don't know, a thousand people. There was a school, a hospital—'

'—it provided charity,' I contributed.

'There were *all* these things going on,' said John, nodding, 'people came from all over.' He turned his full-wattage, Soho-brainstorming gaze on me. 'Now look at the Savacentre: it employs a thousand people; people come from all over . . .'

I told John that I liked his point. Of course, Sainsbury's had established themselves on the former Merantum Way for the same three reasons as the Romans: location, location, location. But it was a nice conceit that a pastoral role or civic function might have worked its way into the earth like a mulch and was fertilising the works of this latter-day cathedral of groceries. It chimed with Iain Sinclair's view that the history of London stains the soil like a dye.

John's immediate preoccupation was how to attract more of the well-to-do people from Wimbledon to Merton Abbey Mills. They only lived a mile away, he said. 'But it's another Hampstead up there. They can catch a train into the West End to see Michael Gambon in the flesh. Why go to that poky little theatre at Merton Abbey?' he said, imitating a snooty Wimbledonite. 'Besides, it's Colliers Wood! You get stabbed!'

On my way back to Colliers Wood Tube station, I thought about the walks that William Morris used to take on his sorties to Merton Abbey, the ones that had put a spring in his step. By now, the rain had filled the Wandle so that the river was almost overflowing its banks. The wind sucked through the railings beside the water, exerting a pull and making a noise, like one of the ghosts in John Hawks's chapter house.

The moment had arrived for the meeting of the Court of Common Council at which my Freedom would be yeaed or nayed, perhaps in those very words. In the Guildhall, great barley-sugar chandeliers hung from the wooden rafters. There was an imposing sculpture dedicated to Nelson in which Britannia, couchant on a lion, was looking dejectedly at what appeared to be a giant coin struck in memory of England's hero. Why had the sculptor depicted him as though his head was on a plate? Neptune was present at the memorial, as well as a figure like a celestial game-show hostess, who was checking the admiral's scores on a marble display board: 'Nile, Copenhagen, Trafalgar . . .'

It was a Thursday lunchtime. Around me, a good show of snowy hair and pinstripe announced City types who were getting on a bit – though I wondered if the court didn't sit at one o'clock precisely to allow unsidelineable ancients of the Square Mile to resume their bony grip on their businesses in the afternoons. I collected an agenda for the meeting, and a document entitled 'List of Applications for the Freedom'. I found myself on the list, not many names away from that of Sir John Stevens, the Commissioner of the Met. Other applicants included the Secretary-General of the Commonwealth and an MEP, a fire officer and a plumber, and a lady from Hampshire who gave her occupation as 'a Woman of Independent Means'. The would-be Freeman whose name was listed immediately beside mine had been able to call on 'a Maker of Playing Cards' as his sponsor.

A young clergyman introduced himself. He said his name was Taylor. Was I perhaps a new member of Common Council? the Rev. Taylor wanted to know.

'No,' I said. 'I've applied to be a Freeman. I thought I'd come and see if anyone heckled when my nomination came up.'

'Ah, I see. Well, congratulations on your Freedom.'

'I haven't got it yet,' I corrected the vicar.

An affable-seeming cove in a suit also wished to satisfy himself about my status. When I told him, he gently explained that I had 'crossed the bar' – he indicated a wooden barrier, no more substantial than a piece of gym apparatus that might have belonged to a struggling school – which separated members of the Court of Common Council from the hoi polloi. 'But congratulations on your Freedom, though,' he added.

'I'm not free yet. That's what I'm here for,' I explained.

There was a cry of 'The Right Honourable, the Lord Mayor!' and a diffident-looking man in furs was walking past the bar and towards the far end of the hall, the same fellow who had apologetically barred my way to the *Royal Noor* before the beating of the bounds. He was at the head of a robed retinue, the very crew who used to descend on my school on prize day. As one man, the rest of us in the court were standing and applauding. The Lord Mayor's party took their places underneath a great stained-glass window. A mace and a fur hat were placed on a long table in front of them.

There were three blows of the gavel from a periwigged official, who said, 'Would honourable members kindly rise in their places?' The official, the Chief Commoner of the Court – a combination of prime minister and Speaker – led the assembly in the Latin oath which I recognised from the breast pocket of my school blazer: '*Domine Dirige Nos*', Lord Direct Us.

The Lord Mayor reported on his recent travels to the Far East. Could this by any chance have been item number two on the agenda, which went under the ripely archaic heading of 'Docquets for the Hospital Seal'? When His Worship was done, and the gifts he had accepted on his journeys were all formally inventoried, the factotum figure who had spoken to me earlier, and other similarly attired flunkies, began shuffling around the Guildhall with queer-looking glass-sided receptacles. There was a deal of gossiping and milling around among the councillors, so I occupied myself by leafing through the agenda. It seemed that a vacancy had arisen 'in the room of Henry Derek Balls', who had resigned from the Association of Port Health Authorities. The room of Alison Gowman, a governor of the City of London School for Girls, was similarly undercrowded. I had just worked out that the phrase 'in the room of' was a delightfully quaint rendering of the more familiar 'in place of' when I was interrupted by the Rev. Taylor. He was standing over me, beaming and proffering his outstretched hand. 'Congratulations!' he said.

'What for?'

'Your Freedom.'

I laughed – I won't say uneasily. 'I don't have it yet,' I told the vicar for a second time. 'That's why I'm here. For the vote.'

'It's just gone through.'

'Has it?'

'Yes. On the nod.'

I climbed to my feet and Rev. Taylor pumped my hand. He told me how much he was looking forward to seeing me again in the future. Of course, the vote on applicants to the Freedom was a formality; I should have known. My name and those of my fellow prospective Freemen had gone through without a second glance. There was as much chance of an applicant being rejected as there was of a wedding guest piping up at the moment when the Rev. Taylor asked whether anyone knew of a reason why these two people, etc., etc. All the same, I had been admitted to the same brotherhood which also included Dick Whittington and Nelson Mandela. If it was good enough for them, it was good enough for me. And there was still the ceremony of the investiture itself to look forward to, in the surroundings of the Guildhall crypt.

The next stop on my underground tour of medieval London was a house of God as famous and popular as Merton was unregarded. Its queues and bustling souvenir shop were beyond even the wildest dreams of John Hawks. Westminster Abbey was everything that Merton might have been – literally, if John is to be believed, because according to him, Westminster was once no grander than its brother abbey in south-west London. But after the tumbledown stones of Merton, the soaring Gothic temple of SW1 made you feel like a pilgrim who has progressed from the humblest chapel to the heart of Christendom. Getting on for 3,500 souls are buried there. Inch for inch, it's the most densely packed tomb of my notable countrymen anywhere in the kingdom. Westminster Abbey was the inspiration of the greatest monarch of the Middle Ages, Edward the Confessor. It was through his piety that the Abbey was created, and it went on to become the most important shrine in the country once Edward was laid beneath the Westminster sod: it was rightfully on my itinerary of subterranean London. I didn't know it but my explorations there would also turn up one of the most outlandish and little known of the city's buried treasures.

Whereas the chapter house at Merton Abbey Mills was

unvisited by anybody, the dependably thronged Westminster Abbey was unvisited by anybody British. A wild claim, no doubt, but the Abbey enjoys the ambiguous status of certain London landmarks such as *The Phantom of the Opera* which are on the must-see list of tourists but seldom have their doors darkened by Londoners. Rather to my shame, I couldn't remember ever having crossed the Abbey's threshold before, which is why I signed up for something called a 'verger-guided tour' – that, and the pleasing echo it carried of 'heat-seeking missile'. To show that you had paid for the tour, and to distinguish you from other visitors who were less privileged, you pinned a receipt to your clothing, not unlike a medieval supplicant robing himself in a swatch of a saint's garment or appending a votary prayer to his own rude habit.

While I waited for the next tour to start, I studied memorials to some of the country's distinguished servants. The immediately striking ones rose directly in front of me at the Abbey's west door, threatening to snuff out the daylight. These marbles were so vast, and there were so many of them, that it was like being in the yard of an impressively spendthrift and in-demand monumental mason. There were what looked like outsize fireplaces celebrating the lives and deeds of William Pitt and the Captains Bayre, Blair and Manners ('mortally wounded in naval engagements.') Major-General Sir John Malcolm of Burnfoot, Dumfriesshire, who rested a mighty hand on his hip, had been a nineteenth-century forerunner of James Bond. The major-general's chiselled citation read that he had been 'employed confidentially in those important wars and negotiations which established British supremacy in India . . . Disinterested, liberal and hospitable, warm in his affections and frank in his manners.' The banner encomium swelled to its fulsome and premature crescendo. 'His memory is cherished by grateful millions, his fame lives in the history of nations.'

Such was the Abbey's adulatory statuary. But the mole-like

student of London noted that many great names were literally beneath his feet. There was the somehow bucking intelligence that Baron Minto of Minto had been laid to rest under the well-trodden stones. And the marble floor of a side chapel capped a rising column of late luminaries from the Middle Ages. They included four abbots who had lived in the fifteenth century, an ambassador to France, a treasurer to Edward IV. Elsewhere, and rather later, Ben Jonson achieved the distinction of being the only person to be interred at the Abbey *standing up*. He couldn't afford the price of a plot six feet by two feet, so bought a two-feet-by-two-feet one instead, and went to his reward like a tent peg.

On the hour, the verger who was guiding our tour presented himself. His name was David. He had wavy hair, spectacles and a cassock, and a way of clipping his participles and other similar-sounding usages. 'I'll be tellin' you about the history of the Abbey as we make our way around the buildin',' he said. Our party learnt that the Romans had built a temple to Apollo on the marshlands of what was Thorney Island, later Westminster. It had been so damp in these parts that the monks would report clouds of condensation gathering under the nave. After the temple to Apollo came a Benedictine order, founded by St Dunstan, Bishop of London, in the tenth century. But the credit for turning Westminster into a pre-eminent religious site belonged to Edward. By the time he became king in 1042, the capital of England was in Winchester. But he relocated the seat of power to the abandoned Roman city of London. It was Edward's dream to replace St Dunstan's monastery with a much greater building, and so work began, with a deadline of Holy Innocent's Day 1065. That was when Edward planned to have his new abbey consecrated. Unhappily for him, he fell ill and died just a week after this date. The first ceremony ever held in Edward's palace was thus his own funeral, followed by the coronation of his successor, William the Conqueror, on the same day. Ever since, Edward's tomb has been the most adored of all the distinguished plots in the Abbey. 'We try to maintain a quieter and more prayerful atmosphere in this part of the buildin',' said David, leading the tour party up a step and through a wicket behind the high altar. It gave access to a chapel bearing the kingly name. The hallowed mezzanine smelt like an old gym. The cause of this trapped funkiness wasn't far to seek: the offcuts of carpet which covered the floor like thrashed exercise mats. They protected what was left of a mosaic, which had been reverently looted over the centuries by religious souvenir-hunters. The same people had also left their mark on Edward's treacle-coloured tomb itself. It was as scratched as a bus shelter. My fellow tourists and I sat on a row of chairs before a ruined wooden choir and contemplated the Confessor. His last resting place was about the same shape and size as the vacant plinth up the road in Trafalgar Square.

Edward was barely cool in his plot before it became the scene of a dramatic dynastic twist. On Christmas Day 1066, William the Conqueror cemented the claims of the Normans to the English throne with his coronation on Edward's grave. Soon, word spread of miraculous cures effected on other visitors, and Edward the Confessor was canonised. In 1163, his body was exhumed and placed in a shrine, which attracted a crush of penitents. 'It wasn't long before they started pilin' in,' confirmed David. 'There used to be kneelin' angels around the shrine but they disappeared.' In due course, the saintly spot worked its spell on King Henry III. He made a point of attending it on the feast days of the Confessor, to whom he was devoted. In 1245, he embarked on the task of rebuilding the Abbey in Gothic style. When the work was done, the nave was more than a hundred feet high, far higher than that of any other English church. Nothing but the best would do for Henry. Purbeck marble was used in all the pillars because it produced a glassy finish with the application of a little vinegar. After twenty-five years and

£40,000 – the equivalent of all the receipts into the English exchequer for two years – and with his Abbey only half finished, Henry ran out of money. He died a disappointed man three years later, and had himself buried in a triple-decker tomb of Purbeck marble as close as he could to his worshipped predecessor. Like Gaudí's Sagrada Familia in Barcelona, Henry's astonishing, overambitious edifice languished incomplete for decades: a full century, in Westminster's case. For even longer than that, the shrine of the Confessor exerted a strange pull on the lives of the English kings. Their affairs kept them close to the palace of Edward and Henry III, and most were buried within a few feet of their forerunner.

In the legends of Edward I that have come down to us, he is seldom mentioned by that handle, perhaps to avoid confusion with his sanctified predecessor and namesake. Instead, he's 'Edward Longshanks', who stood 6′ 2″ in his chain-mail feet when his subjects thought themselves lanky if they were five feet tall; and 'the Hammer of the Scots' for his feat of relieving the Scottish of the Stone of Scone. The biblical rock on which Jacob had slept and dreamt of angels, the stone resided for centuries in the Abbey, under the wooden seat on which the kings and queens of England were crowned. It was finally returned north of the border in 1996. The coronation chair is still there, of course, though I was stunned to see the extent to which it nearly wasn't. Extravagantly scored and gouged, it looked as if it had come from a closing-down sale at the same Ofsted-busted inner-city comp which had furnished the bar in the Court of Common Council. David the verger took us to see the chair in the Abbey's House of Kings. 'Until two hundred years ago, anyone could sit in it, and it was considered lucky to scratch it,' he said. 'Graffiti is not a modern invention.'

The Hammer of the Scots was married at the age of fifteen to Eleanor of Castile, and their loving union is memorialised in the landscape of London. Charing Cross takes its name from the

Christian totem pole in the railway station forecourt, the grieving Edward having commissioned one of these monuments to be raised on every spot where his beloved wife's body rested on its posthumous return to London from what had proved to be a fatal journey to the north. Eleanor's tomb at the Abbey is decorated with designs of scallop shells, rosettes and animals on a wrought-iron fender. Edward himself was in due course buried behind the high altar, but in a simple sepulchre, the mortician's equivalent of a chest freezer. Having struck such terror into Scottish hearts in this life, Edward could if necessary be recalled from his top-loader tomb, to be pressed into service again from beyond the grave. The mortal remains of this English El Cid could be taken out at any time, and his flesh removed by boiling so that his bones could be carried at the head of an army invading Scotland.

In their turn Edward III and then Richard II were interred at the Abbey. Richard is buried with his consort, Anne of Bohemia, beneath marble facsimiles of themselves, which are quite lifelike apart from the absent arms. David explained that these had been broken off, probably by overzealous pilgrims. In 1776, an enterprising if morbid pupil of Westminster School managed to remove the king's jawbone through a hole in the tomb. A bone said to have held the royal lower set was sheepishly returned two centuries later.

Henry V lies in the shrine chapel. A recumbent figurine of His Majesty has been stripped of its decoration over the years. Finally, in 1545, the king lost his head. A replacement noggin of polyester resin was screwed into place in 1971. Henry's queen, Catherine of Valois, was embalmed and laid in an open tomb, where she reposed for a nostril-troubling three hundred years. Samuel Pepys wrote on 23 February 1669 that he 'did see by particular favour the body of Queen Catherine of Valois; and I did kiss her mouth, reflecting upon it that I did kiss a queen, and that this was my birthday, 36 years old, that I did first kiss a queen'. It was more than a hundred years after this clammy smacker that Catherine was finally hidden from sight in the Abbey, beneath the Villiers monument in the chapel of St Nicholas.

It is at this point that Henry VIII, nemesis of Merton Abbey, enters the story, and he is on familiar unsentimental form. With a kleptomania not even the most devoted pilgrim could match, Henry helped himself to the gold- and gem-encrusted canopy which surrounded the Confessor's shrine, and had it made into coin of the realm.

Today, the medieval remains housed at the Abbey are beyond even the necrophiliac curiosity of a Pepys. They have entered and permeated the fabric of Edward the Confessor's great monument. The thought may stir your warm patriotic blood, or alternatively it may creep your still-firm flesh, but that's how it is. However, I found a way of coming face to face with the late crowned heads. My means of access was underground. As attractive to trippers as the Abbey is, some parts of it are much better-visited than others. With the tombs and memorials of so many famous people to goggle at, few tourists have the time to make a full circuit of the cloister, which used to be the hub of the medieval monastery. It was on my second or third visit to Westminster that I found the undercroft. It was off the cloister, at the foot of a short stone staircase.

In your childhood, the test that every old building has to pass is whether or not it's so creepy that you couldn't imagine spending a night alone under its roof. It's no slight on the admirable attendants of the undercroft that their cellar is well up to child-scaring stuff. It's an ante-room to the afterlife; it's a primitive cryogenic lab, containing evidence that crazed and unlawful alchemists once laboured to breathe fresh life into the husks of late royalty; it's the guardroom of a vampirical night watch of the Abbey's distinguished departed. It's all these things and – getting a grip on myself – less. The undercroft, the Abbey's museum, is the repository of an extraordinary collection of effigies.

Until the Middle Ages, it was the custom for the body of a dead monarch to be embalmed, dressed in his coronation robes and regalia, and publicly exhibited during a period of lying-in-state, as well as during the funeral procession and the service itself. But because of the length of time it could take to arrange the obsequies, it became necessary to substitute a wooden effigy for the perishable loved one. This testament to the chippy's craft was placed on top of the funeral carriage for the duration of the last journey. The practice was observed until well into the seventeenth century. But after the shock to the hereditary principle that was the Commonwealth, idolatry of the posthumous royal personage was scaled down. Instead of a full-length timber facsimile, the sovereign's coffin was decked with a crown on a cushion, a practice observed to the present day.

But this didn't put the funerary sculptors out of business entirely. Effigies continued to be commissioned, now with heads and hands made out of wax, but their new function was to stand near the place of burial. As a notice in the undercroft explained, they soon became 'not so much a symbol of royal dignity and power as an object of interest to visitors and a source of revenue to the Abbey'. This trend reached its apogee in the nineteenth century, when the effigy business was still going strong. Even though Nelson was buried at St Paul's Cathedral, with the whiff of embalming cognac still on him, the jealous powers that be at the Abbey installed a bust of him anyway, to pull in the sightseers who were patronising their ecclesiastical rival to the east.

But for the fact that he was a life-size likeness, the Edward III that I found in the undercroft might have been a ventriloquist's doll. His face was clamped in a gottle-of-geer grimace. You could make out the nicks and grooves that the carpenter had left in the royal legs. This artisan's name was Stephen Hadley. Somewhere, an ochre receipt proves that he was paid for making 'one image in the likeness of a king', the oldest one still in the undercroft's care. Hadley could afford to let his hewings be rough where the monarchical extremities were concerned, as these were to be covered by the raiment of state. The important thing was to get the dimensions right, so that when the authentic togs were brought from the Great Wardrobe, the fitting was perfect. The crudely worked wood of Edward's effigy was thinly coated with plaster. The figure was hollowed out at the back, to save the royal horses and bier-carriers from a heavier burden than necessary. The face, plaster fixed onto linen, was damaged in the Second World War. When it went in for repairs, and the nose and some of the plaster on the top of the head were replaced, the restorers noticed that the rictus-lips drooped on the left-hand side and the left cheek was flattened. These details were consistent with accounts that Edward had suffered a stroke, inducing facial paralysis and rendering the king speechless, shortly before his death. It's now believed that the face is a death-mask, which would make the effigy of Edward III the earliest surviving example of this uniquely intimate form of portraiture in Europe. When the replica was carried at Edward's funeral, the head was winningly toupeed with real hair. A small dog had been plucked to furnish a pair of eyebrows.

Catherine of Valois, with whom Pepys enjoyed a post-mortem snog, is memorialised in oak. Apart from Edward III, she is the only full-length replica royal. You might have thought the woodman would have selected a voluptuous and creamy knot for the mouth which tempted the great diarist, but instead of a generously carved rosebud, the royal laughing gear is a pursed and pinched slot. The queen's hair is no crowning glory either. It's a distaff version of the Plantagenet bob favoured by the male side of the family. But even the least chivalrous onlooker must remind himself that Catherine's effigy would have worn a full wig on important occasions, and a coronet on top of that.

Half a dozen of the royal effigies have disappeared or disintegrated since the eighteenth century, notably those of Edward Longshanks and James I, but also Henry V, the husband of

Catherine of Valois. Apart from his wife, the victor of Agincourt is survived only by his funeral achievements: the helm and saddle which hung for many years from a beam in his chantry chapel, and a shield as papery, and embossed with curious patterns, as the Turin Shroud. Like royalty itself, the effigies have known the vicissitudes of popularity. You supposed that they were a talking point of royal interments – the effigy was to the funeral what the dress was to a wedding – but they became known as 'the ragged regiment', dishevelled and gathering dust in the Abbey's Islip Chantry. In a 1786 drawing by John Carter, they lean against the walls of the chapel with all the majesty of discarded shop dummies. It wasn't until the twentieth century that the ragged regiment were restored to some sort of splendour, with a new billet in the undercroft. The undercroft had been built in about 1070, and was originally the basement of the monks' dormitory (parts of which are now the library and great hall of Westminster School). The chalky roof is supported by arches sprouting from four central piers. The monks appear to have used the undercroft as a *calefactorium* – literally, a place for keeping warm. But even in this cosy nook, there was no escaping the chill left by the Reaper as he stalked by. Republicans would cheer, and monarchists mourn anew, to see that earthly corruption has treated the mannequins little better than their fleshy templates. Two hundred wormholes had to be patched in Anne of Denmark, Charles II has sunken cheeks and a Las·Vegas tan, and Henry VII had his head blown off by Adolf Hitler. His poor decapitated stomach spilled its stuffing of hay. When it was examined by botanists, it was found to contain a dozen different species of plants.

While these former crowned heads were suffering a bad case of *lèse-majesté*, I was about to ascend to the status of a titled gentleman. A letter arrived from the Chamberlain's office confirming that the Court of Common Council had 'passed an order for your admission to the Freedom of the City of London'.

I could now be made up to the rank of Freeman. But as I read on, I was taken aback to see that my prestigious ceremony 'lasts for about fifteen minutes'. Was that really long enough to do justice to such an important investiture, I wondered. Not only that but there was no mention of a special outfit. I read the letter three or four times and there was definitely no reference to a fur-lined cape or a plumed hat, to calfskin gloves or spurs. But the would-be Freeman who wants to carry the thing off in style is soon in receipt of heartening correspondence from the Freemen of England and Wales. The Freemen of England and Wales understand. The Freemen of England and Wales know that the proud initiate wants a blazer badge and a ceremonial robe; and a robe badge, too, come to that. These and other perfectly healthy, tangible expressions of the civic spirit are described by the Freemen of England and Wales in what cynics will inevitably see as a mail-order form. I for one was grateful to know that these admirable traditionalists can supply a wall plaque for £24 and a lady's scarf for a very reasonable £6 (in navy blue, maroon or green). Alas, there was no time for the Freemen of England and Wales to supply a wardrobe commensurate with the honour which awaited me. My preferment was imminent; I barely had time to learn my lines. All I could do was the same thing I did when I was going to the Guildhall crypt all those years ago as a schoolboy. Put on a clean shirt and my least eggy tie.

The afternoon teas that we used to take in the crypt were part of a great ocean of tea and a Matterhorn of cake with which the Corporation plied its visitors, I realise now, but they had seemed like the acme of this genteel meal at the time. Then, I'd had the sensation of being in a benign dungeon. The crypt was a noted example of medieval English architecture. Its walls were the oldest part of the Guildhall, pre-dating the building above. The original Guildhall was destroyed in the Great Fire and its replacement was set ablaze in the Blitz, a moment preserved in stained glass in the crypt. The livery companies were also depicted in this gallery of luminous glazing, which I remembered from my boyhood visits. The windows were like the forerunners of advertising hoardings. In their own low-wattage way, they anticipated the famous neon of Piccadilly Circus. I particularly liked the way that comparatively modern products and services had been celebrated in the Guildhall glass. The Worshipful Company of Spectacle-Makers, for example, were represented by a row of letters like an unplayable hand in Scrabble. Their stained glass suggested an early eye-chart. Then there was the pane dedicated to the Carmen's company. It featured what appeared to be a rubbish lorry and bore the legend '25 miles'. I wondered if it wasn't actually the taxi-drivers' window, twenty-five miles being the furthest their members were prepared to take a fare, or perhaps the longed-for distance at which an ambrosial tariff kicked in.

When the Clerk of the Chamberlain's Court arrived, I was pleased to see that he at least was robed. But his black gown was more or less where the formality of the ceremony began and ended. It was conducted with the familiarity of a register-office wedding. I declaimed my Freeman's oath, swearing to 'keep this City harmless ... that I will know no Gatherings nor Conspiracies made against the Queen's Peace, but I will warn the Mayor thereof . . .' Just as in the marriage vows, the master of ceremonies deftly insinuated a word of warning into the homilies. His message was plain. In the rapture of my union with the old lady of the City, I shouldn't run away with fanciful notions about what our life together would be like. It turned out that the rights I had been looking forward to were not mine to call my own. It seems they're part myth, part anachronism, those tales of Freemen driving sheep over London Bridge and debagging City of London constables with impunity.

Most crestfall-making of all, it appeared that I couldn't even puff out my chest and act the part of a swell. The clerk gave me a pocket-sized red book bearing the crest of the Corporation of

London and entitled *Rules for the Conduct of Life*. This was presented to Freemen in memory of a code once imposed on City apprentices. Before I had turned to its bromides about letting the end that I aimed at always be good, and making it the constant business of my life that I died well, an addendum slip slid into my palm. It said, 'Owing to certain persons who have been admitted to the Freedom of the City having improperly stated that the Freedom has been conferred upon them, or otherwise implying that the Freedom has been granted by the Corporation as an honour, it is necessary to remind you that you have today been admitted to the Freedom by Redemption, and to warn you that such Freedom must in no circumstances be used for self-publicity or business purposes.' If I wanted to advertise my newly cemented connection with the City of London, my best bet was to endow a stained-glass window at the Guildhall on behalf of my profession of journalism: a blotted escutcheon, perhaps, with pint tankards rampant.

THE LOVE GAMES OF HENRY VIII
Tudor London

We hobbled through the dark bent double, with the water rushing beneath our feet. It was cold, and the brick walls and brick ceiling were wet when you brushed against them. Not damp, not clammy, but wringing, squelching wet, as wet as bog. In fairness to the brickies who had done the job, their sopping handiwork was five hundred years old. It was wearing pretty well, all things considered. Water rushed into the man-made hollow. Inadvertently lowering my foot into a hidden trough, I scooped up a trainerful of rainwater. A school of eels was twisting in the watercourse. The pipe through which we staggered had once been an enlightened feat of engineering, with few equals in all of Europe. It was also said to have been used as a secret passageway by mistresses who had hitched up their skirts and trotted to assignations in a sovereign's bedchamber. It was an extraordinary feature of one of the most popular tourist attractions in London, yet it was unvisited, unknown, over-looked. Of course, I can see that hunchbacking it through the sewers of Hampton Court is not everyone's idea of a fun day out, but I must say that I've never had a better time at a royal palace.

The culverts snake for a full two miles beneath the great red-brick retreat of kings on the banks of the Thames. Improbably enough, they represent the finest flowering of the progressive sensibility which shaped this historic building. At the same time, they are utterly earthy, in keeping with the carnal personality who stamped his mark most forcibly on the place. They were the last word in gracious living, as imported wholesale from Renaissance Europe by the founder of Hampton Court, Thomas

Wolsey. They were also the stinking waste-disposal units of Henry VIII's clamorous court, with its staff of 1,200 – more than twice as large as Wolsey's – its crapulous beanos of baked carp in wine with prunes, peacock royal and stuffed boar, and its rock-festival communal toilets, capable of accommodating more than two dozen at a single sitting.

Credit for enthusing me about the Hampton Court culverts – and for guiding me through them, too, come to that – belongs to Jonathan Foyle, who was the palace's assistant curator. Oh, but he was much more than that! Jonathan was one of the rising stars of the new vogue for historical telly. How he must have made his rivals gnash and whinny, with his double whammy of well-marshalled argument and boyish good looks! Jonathan's scholarship was a model of limpid empiricism and wide-ranging reading. Within the nurturing mullions of Hampton Court, the fruits of his labours were not so much distilled into his publications as tricklingly oak-filtered into them. On the very day of our trip through the plashy pipes, at two o'clock that morning, he had completed a long article for a learned journal in which he'd argued that Wolsey's Hampton Court had been the first English building inspired by the Renaissance, anticipating by as much as forty years a more widespread trend. This was a bold claim, given that Wolsey's pile had been all but flattened beneath the rolling make-over instituted by his sovereign once he had moved in, not to mention the many home improvements initiated by subsequent royal tenants. But it was a case that Jonathan had already made in a persuasive television documentary. I had no doubt that his article, when it was published, would similarly be solidly argued and sourced, and recline on a luxurious bedding of plump footnotes.

By the light of a torch, Jonathan looked back down the culvert at me from under the brim of his hard hat, his head-boy haircut fetchingly tousled beneath it, and, if I wasn't much mistaken, a rogue smut on those healthy outdoor cheeks. How adorable his female viewers would have found him, and how older historians would have cursed the comfortable living which meant that they couldn't follow him through the stooped and narrow passages. Jonathan was explaining that the idea of the culverts dated back to the middle of the fifteenth century, when a diplomat called Sherwood was Our Man in Rome. Sherwood had picked up a book hot off the press which articulated a back-to-basics movement among Italian architects, revisiting the structural principles of the Romans. 'The Renaissance idea was that space and light and cleanliness were all desirable in planning,' said Jonathan. 'In the 1440s, King Alfonso of Naples was saying, "Destroy the squalid town and replace it with light and air!"' Sherwood brought the tract home to England, where it ended up in the possession of Charles Fox. The book, with Fox's signature in it, can be seen among his papers to this day. The significance of this is that Fox was the patron of Thomas Wolsey. Jonathan believed that Wolsey would also have read a book published in 1510 called *De Cardinal Artu*, which was the handbook on being a cardinal, and included a chapter on suitable accommodation for such an exalted servant of God.

We resumed our crouching progress. In this portion of the palace's entrails, the bricks were coated in a dull white rendering. We were heading in the direction of the kitchens. They had once been the biggest in Europe, and one role of the culverts had been to act as a giant chute for the household rubbish. From a hole in the middle of the kitchen floor, the waste had been swept out into the Thames, sped on its way by lashings of boiling water. Although my reinforced hat more than once ricocheted off the ceiling, my impression of the culverts was not that they occupied a confined space, but on the contrary, that they were surprisingly commodious. They were almost as roomy as the twin barrels of the northern outfall sewer under Wick Lane in east London. This was all the more remarkable when you remembered how long ago the conduits had been built. There was a good reason for their generous proportions, but sadly it had nothing to do with the story that Henry had provided his courtesans with a trysting tunnel so that they could enter his quarters without being seen. This rumour, this six old wives' tale, was 'a load of cack', in Jonathan's pungently apt summary. No, the sewers were almost high enough for a man to stand in because it had once been the lot of some of the palace staff to go down into them and shovel out the muck. In Tudor times, when people were shorter than they are today, it was possible to do the job at full stretch without smashing your brains out.

Jonathan and I had some members of the current staff with us, though they weren't getting their hands dirty, or at least nothing like as dirty as their predecessors had. They had joined us for a jolly in the culverts. I'd found them earlier that morning, formed up in a horseshoe around an open manhole cover on the cobbles of Master Carpenter's Court. Overlooked by the palace's aniseed-twist chimneys, the court was our point of entry into the sewers. The staff were like a retinue of old retainers, with Jonathan, wearing black polo-neck and matching slacks, cast in the role of the young master. Since I'd last seen him, on an earlier visit to Hampton Court, he'd not only taken a starring role in the documentary about the palace but he'd also recorded an edition of the history series, *Time Team*. I wasn't sure if he was joking when he said that the BBC had invited him to front a popular archaeology strand devoted to the pointing of the past. 'I was going to be Mr Brick,' he said, with an expression which was part bemusement, part gratification, and all television catnip. 'It was going to be on for ten minutes, at two o'clock in the morning.' None of us believed him. No one believed that he had been offered anything less than a sexy slot. 'They wanted to call it something like *Mortar the Point*,' said Jonathan. Judging by the admiring looks of the palace staff, they would have been happy to see him as Mr Brick.

Below ground, the rendering which covered the culvert walls

was here and there broken up by darkly protuberant shapes. On closer inspection, these proved to be short, sawn-off downpipes installed to feed rainwater and other fluids into the system from courtyards and interior floors of the palace. Hampton Court had more modern drainage arrangements now, to cater for the needs of more than half a million visitors a year as well as the palace's own employees. But this didn't mean that the Tudor culverts were redundant. I was visiting on one of those November days when what little light there is seems to be dissolved by drizzle, and evidence that Wolsey's plumbing was still doing its bit to drain rainwater could be made out beneath our shoes – and, as I say, in them, too, from time to time.

Wolsey was Henry VIII's chaplain at the age of thirty-four and the two were firm friends until 1520, by which time Henry had already been on the throne for more than a decade. The thumbnail sketch of their relationship is that Wolsey ran the country while the king enjoyed himself. Wolsey's eventual fall from grace, over his failure to secure the Pope's blessing for His Majesty's divorce from Catherine of Aragon, wasn't until 1528. So the relationship between the two men was a substantial and enduring one, which made their subsequent breach all the more disastrous. The year of 1515 was decisive. Wolsey was made Lord Chancellor, but much more importantly for both Wolsey and Henry, he was also created a cardinal of Rome. This gave him a powerful status independent of royal patronage. Wolsey had leased the manor of Hampton Court from the Knights Hospitallers a year earlier. He was now earning staggering sums of money, the equivalent of £20 million a year at today's prices. 'Elton John is the closest I can think of; Elton John is the Wolsey of today,' said Jonathan. The cardinal soon had a private staff of five hundred or more. This put a huge burden on the palace amenities. 'Think of two or three days at Glastonbury. That's what it was going to be like at Hampton Court.' But not if Wolsey and his money had anything to do with it. For six years, he lavished his wealth on his new home, indulging an Eltonian taste for silver and rich hangings. And in the midst of this extravagance, the waterworks were not neglected. As Jonathan's TV documentary had put it, 'Wolsey spent money like water – and *on* water.' One of the considerations that had influenced Wolsey in his acquisition of Hampton Court was the possibility of drawing potable water from the springs of nearby Kingston Hill. They enjoyed a reputation for being beneficial for stones, from which the Lord Chancellor suffered. Some four hundred years after Wolsey's day, an Edwardian hostess, Mrs Hwfa Williams, thought about cashing in on the mineral water, which bubbled to the surface of her estate at Coombe Springs, not far from the palace. Unfortunately, a chemical analysis of the outflow failed to support the advice of the cardinal's physicians. Indeed, one report suggested that the water was 'unfit for culinary use' since it turned vegetables black.

In Wolsey's day, a domestic water supply was a sign of glittering social distinction. Generations of Londoners relied on the uncertain facility of communal conduits, though they could be fun on high days and holidays. To mark Edward I's return from the Holy Land, 'the Conduit in Chepe ran all day with red and white wine'. There was a Little Conduit near St Paul's Cathedral, another ran from Highbury to Cripplegate while a third was built at Upper Street. It was fed by a spring in White Conduit Street and stood until the early nineteenth century, when the Regent's Canal was constructed. Lamb's Conduit Street, very near where I worked, was named after a water pipe established by Sir William Lamb. The Standard Conduit at Cornhill became the point of reference for all milestones on roads leading to the capital, some of which are still inscribed with the words 'from the Standard in Cornhill'. John Stow wrote,

These conduits used in former times yearly to be visited, but particularly on the 18th of September 1562, the Lord Mayor

Harper, eldermen and wardens to the twelve companies, rid to the conduit's head, for to see them after the old custom. And afore dinner they hunted the hare and killed her and thence to dinner at the head of the conduit. There were good number entertained with good cheer by the Lord Chamberlain; after dinner they went to hunting the fox . . . and thence the Lord Mayor, with all his company, rode through London to his palace in Lombard Street.

When Wolsey was designing Hampton Court, it was still half a century before hydraulic technology was introduced into the distribution of water in London, with the fitting of a great water wheel to London Bridge. And it wasn't until 1613 that a man-made watercourse, Sir Hugh Myddleton's 'New River', brought spring water from far Hertfordshire through forty miles of countryside to New River Head, near the site of the Sadler's Wells Theatre in Islington.

The conduit at Hampton Court was a formidable undertaking. The water was collected from the hill in brick chutes which fed mini-reservoirs known as conduit houses. From there, it was carried underground in lead pipes for more than three miles. The pipes were sunk to a depth of about six feet, to keep them clear of farmers and frost. After making a slight dogleg to avoid the already substantial development of Kingston-on-Thames, the conduit negotiated the Hogsmill River, a tributary of the Thames, before crossing the Thames itself south of Kingston Bridge. Finally, it arrived in the palace grounds, probably in the area where the water gardens, known as the Long Water, were later created. In keeping with the classical inspiration of the conduit, it was designed from a pattern introduced by the Romans. Each section of pipe was made from a narrow sheet of cast lead. The hot metal was poured into a trough, and quickly struck off level with the sides of this mould. The lead was bent into a tube and burnt, or soldered, into shape. Each pipe was twenty-five feet long, the maximum length of the casting trough, and weighed as much as twenty pounds per foot. In 1951, a display of pipe-laying was staged at Hampton Court during a pageant, and organisers found that it took at least six men to carry a standard twenty-five-foot length. Historians believe that the Tudors solved the problem of negotiating the Thames by soldering up the pipe and lowering it from a floating bridge made out of boats.

On dry land, running repairs were effected thanks to small brick buildings on the route of the conduit which were known as 'tamkins'. The word was a variant of 'tompion', meaning a plug used to close the muzzle of a gun. The tamkins were access points where Wolsey's water engineers could isolate sections of the pipeline which were in need of attention. Records survive of this maintenance work. An entry for May–June 1529 states, 'Plommers as well serching the condwyths as scowering the edds of the same and including the pipes where they were faulty.'

Incredibly, the conduit which Wolsey had ordered in 1515 wasn't finally decommissioned until the first year of the twentieth century. One of the natural springs had already been taken out of the supply chain by then, after suspicions that the water was contaminated. This was greatly to the chagrin of local land-owners, who had grown accustomed to being remunerated for allowing Hampton Court's pipes to cross their estates. Royal venison had been enjoyed in lieu of ground rent by the Duke of Cambridge, who owned all the land in the eastern section of the conduit, including the ground on which three conduit houses stood. Enraged at the loss to his game larder, the duke threatened to divert the water for his own use. At first this was treated as a piece of noble high spirits by the water commissioners, but when a messenger arrived to demand the keys of the conduit houses, they realised that the duke meant business. After lengthy negotiations, he bought the conduit houses and the pipes which crossed his property.

So much for the damp stuff coming into Hampton Court. As

for what went out again, Wolsey's requirements had included en-suites for Henry and his family in the royal apartments, which stood on the site later occupied by the Georgian rooms of the palace. During the fat years of the 1520s, Wolsey had entertained lavishly. When a French delegation came to stay in 1527, the cardinal's gentleman usher reported, 'There was also 14 score beds provided and furnished with all manner of furniture to them belonging, too long particularly here to rehearse.' The cardinal installed forty garderobes or lavatories for the guest lodgings erected in Base Court, not far from Master Carpenter's Court, where we had entered the culverts. In Base Court, the location of the garderobes was delineated by red bricks set into the courtyard, an archaeological representation of the original premises. Visitors who wander among the thousand rooms of the palace can see a garderobe for themselves. It had been the smallest room of the Tudor palace, but everything was relative: the garderobe occupied a substantial bell-shaped hollow. Its centrepiece was a velvet-trimmed thunderbox, which looked like a posh laundry basket.

To this day, the culverts shipped water down to the Thames, by means of a gully sunk in the concrete floor (this surface having been added at a comparatively recent date in the palace's history). Jonathan Foyle's underground party found a blackish spoor gathered in drifts on this concrete bed: mud, crumbled mortar, miscellaneous debris. 'That's a sycamore,' said Jonathan, shining his torch on a blackened helicopter seed. 'Perhaps there's some birdshit down here.' Where there was birdshit, there had to be birdlife. The wildlife of the culverts was remarkably abundant. Not only were there eels in the water but Jonathan spotted a mosquito among the dew drops of condensation which clung to the ceiling. These insects make surprisingly frequent appearances under London. Former Underground man Christopher Ross describes mosquitoes at King's Cross station and recalls using a colleague's naked arm as bait to trap them. With an empty plastic water bottle for a specimen jar, Ross showed his catch to a friend who was an entomologist. 'Where on earth did you get this?' said his friend. 'This species is entirely unknown in England.' Presumably the mosquito had arrived at Heathrow aboard a jet liner before completing its journey to King's Cross through the tunnels of the Piccadilly Line.

A much larger creature than a mosquito was about to make its presence felt in the Hampton Court culverts. Wild and woolly, it couldn't have been more incongruous, in the context of a riverside sewer in the twentieth century. On the other hand, it couldn't have been a better symbol of the England of Wolsey and Henry. Out of the gloom, the ceiling came down abruptly to meet our hard hats and Jonathan, ducking even lower than he had been already, exclaimed, 'We're underneath Boris!' Boris was a stuffed boar. He was the very thing for the Tudor groaning board. But Boris was only for show. He had been donated to Hampton Court by the Dutch royal family and formed part of a Tudor tableau in the kitchens which were directly over our heads. Because of his weight, Boris stood on a reinforced plinth. The base of the plinth was sunk into the floor, reducing the headroom in the culvert directly beneath him. Together with wax game, with fish and fowl which were the ornament of the mortician's art, Boris lent an air of roistering verisimilitude to the palace scullery. There was a bit of a scandal about Boris, it transpired. The director of Hampton Court palace who was in post at the time of the gift from the crowned heads of the Netherlands had immediately put the boar on show. He was reprimanded for overlooking import controls which should have seen Boris banged up in the quarantine slammer for six months.

On our haunches, we went as far as we could go. The culvert before us tapered into the middle distance, coming to an end beneath another part of the kitchens. 'It's quite steep, isn't it?' observed one of the old retainers. Jonathan studied the brickwork of the dwindling passage. 'It looks as though it may have been cut back. Do you see the layer here?' He was pointing near the bottom of this narrow duct. 'That could be from a medieval building.'

When the humbled Wolsey was forced to relinquish his place in the country to the king, Hampton Court witnessed a second whirlwind of building. In ten years, Henry blew £62,000 on the palace: £18 million in today's money. Every one of his six wives came to stay; naturally, each had to have her own brand-new set of rooms. The king also rebuilt his private chambers at least half a dozen times. By 1540, when Hampton Court was finished to Henrician satisfaction, it boasted a magnificent chapel, tennis courts, bowling alleys and pleasure gardens. Nor were fleshier pursuits neglected. Hunting parties had the run of 1,100 acres and banquets were thrown in the Great Hall. In one year, the court got through more than 1,240 oxen, 8,200 sheep, 2,330 deer, 760 calves, 1,870 pigs and 53 boar, all of them skinned and spitted and served in the kitchens above us. On a feast day, each course of a meal was made up of several different dishes in one, but even when things were quiet, the more important courtiers could expect four or five courses in the canteen hot lunch. In August 1546, Henry and his guest, the French ambassador, sat down to dinner *for six days*, attended by 1,500 close courtiers.

Jonathan led our crookbacked crocodile back the way we had come, and towards the river. Presently, the rendering ran out, and the sides of the culvert against your palm felt like clods of peat. A roaring cataract was bubbling into the passage, squirting water to about shin-height. This was presumably a direct feed from a storm drain above. It was in negotiating this babbling obstacle that I filled my training shoe with rainwater. We began to encounter small culverts radiating away from the main trunk which we were navigating. They were narrow, like the tapered one immediately beneath the kitchens, but they were also raised by perhaps a foot or so off the ground, so that water and waste would flow out of them but not wash back up again (except when the culverts were inundated by a flood tide in the Thames). One offshoot led underneath the palace pastry kitchen. Another had served a barracks which was put up in the time of William and Mary. Jonathan didn't have a lot of time for their alterations to Hampton Court. If he was to be believed, they had turned Henry's pleasure gardens into allotments.

There was a big idea behind William and Mary's barracks at the palace and it went like this: the troops would face the passing scene, so that they would act as a deterrent to intruders and insurrectionists alike. Unfortunately, the sight of these soldiers in their uniforms drew so many women of dubious repute to the palace that William was forced to turn the barracks back to front, so that the guards were now behind walls, which doused the ardour of their admirers but also undid the reason for billeting them in the barracks in the first place.

An intervention from the Hampton Court netherworld was said to be responsible for King William's death. Towards the end of his life, His Majesty suffered from dropsy. Despite this, and against his doctors' orders, he insisted on keeping up his great love of riding to hounds. He swore that this did more to relieve the pain and swelling in his limbs than all the bags of roses and lavender which he had been prescribed. During what proved to be his last ride, the king's horse had just gone into a gallop when it suddenly fell to its knees. William was thrown and broke his collarbone. He told anxious courtiers that the accident 'was a strange thing, as it happened on level ground . . . but a mole heaved it up and left a hole there in which the horse's foot stuck'. William died of pneumonia three weeks later.

Pale light lining the emerging end of the culvert announced that we were nearing the outflow into the Thames. In the van of our group, Jonathan and one of the retainers cried that they could see a fish at their feet, where the water overbrimmed the gully in the concrete. I was envious of the pair of them; they were blocking my view of the fish. I finally edged past them into the elbow of the culvert, where it went off at an angle of not quite forty-five degrees to meet the river, and caught a silvery glimpse of the tiddler. Directly ahead of us, through a metal pallisade to which weeds clung, was another gate, a watergate, light streaming through it from the riverbank.

Being in the culverts, peeking into the low-roofed side tunnels, reminded me of hiding out as a child in the treehouse-cum-camp which my brother and I built at the bottom of our garden. Our set-up had been entirely earthbound, though I suppose it qualified as a treehouse by virtue of standing at the foot of a fir. In our jerry-built hideaway, nothing was nailed or screwed or bolted. Balance, Newtonian carpentry: that was all that held it together (and often didn't). It should have felt a little frightening in there; Dad was sufficiently frightened to build us a proper treehouse. It should have felt a little claustrophobic. But paradoxically, the treehouse on the ground was too small to induce claustrophobia. I felt the same way about the culverts of Hampton Court. Under the palace, there was the same dark, wet, comfortable sensation that I had known in the igloo of wooden off-cuts at the bottom of the garden.

Henry VIII was almost as promiscuous with his residences as he was with his wives. In the address books of the sovereign's friends and relations, the pages under 'H' must have been full of crossings-out, the parchment clotted with best writing indigo. When the king was eyeing Wolsey's Hampton Court with envy, he already had substantial residences at Greenwich, Eltham and Richmond. By the end of his life, there were no fewer than sixty places that Henry could call home.

At the beginning of his reign, he followed royal precedent and based himself at Westminster Palace. When the residential quarters, the Privy Palace, burnt down, he moved into Wolsey's Lambeth Palace for a spell; this was before he snatched Hampton

Court from the luckless prelate. The king also had associations
with the Tower of London. He was the last ruler to live there,
installing timber-framed lodgings when Anne Boleyn became his
queen. Moreover, as I had discovered in the ruins of Merton
Abbey, one of the boons to Henry of dissolving the monasteries
was that it furnished the bricks and mortar, or the beautifully
worked stone, rather, for Nonsuch Park, where the king set Anne
up in a cosy palace made for two.

But there was another, even more striking, place where Henry
laid his crown. Like Nonsuch, it has not survived. Its disappear-
ance is considered to be such a cause of regret that the missing
royal dwelling has been called England's most important lost
secular building. In other words, leaving aside one or two
forgotten places of worship like Merton Abbey, it's the greatest
vanished wonder this country has ever seen. It is, or was,
Whitehall Palace. This Tudor development served to consolidate
the area of Whitehall as the seat of government. Even though the
palace was razed by flames in 1698, after a careless servant left
clothes drying too close to a fire, the site has remained the locus
of power in Britain to this day.

The point about Whitehall Palace being lost deserves to be
made doubly: it's lost from sight and lost from memory. The
tourist who includes Whitehall on his itinerary comes to see
where the prime minister lives, and to have his photograph taken
with a trooper in a busby from the Household Cavalry. As far as
he's concerned, the monarch's London home is at the end of the
Mall. He would be agog to learn that he was standing on the
ruins of the granddaddy of royal abodes, the largest palace in
Europe in the seventeenth century, covering no less than twenty-
three acres. And yet with a little prompting, and the connivance
of a sympathetic civil service turnkey, he could yet catch a
glimpse of this extraordinary pile. For though Whitehall Palace
is indeed lost, it hasn't quite gone. Moreover, as if its historic
connection with power had been indelibly imprinted into its

bricks and mortar, what's left of it is now linked via a secret doorway to the very heart of modern government, No. 10 Downing Street.

The most accessible relics of Whitehall are Queen Mary's Steps, which can be seen in the grounds of the Ministry of Defence building on the Embankment. In one of the last additions to the palace, the queen built a terrace against Henry's great river wall in 1691. It was originally seventy feet wide and 280 feet long when the fire of 1698 did its damage. In the smouldering aftermath, courtiers helped themselves to chunks of the terrace for their gardens. What remained of it was buried when Bazalgette built the Victoria Embankment, named after his monarch, and reclaimed three hundred yards of river. The Queen Mary Steps were rediscovered in 1939 and left out in the open. On the top step are the supports of a portico which once fronted a passageway. This enabled the queen to disembark from the royal barge and go to her apartments without getting the royal feet wet.

One surviving building with a link to the Tudor palace is the Banqueting House, adjacent to the MOD building. In its undercroft are tiles which are thought to have come from the floor of Henry VIII's bathroom. Under the undercroft's arched ceiling, the monarch distributed Maundy Money to the poor in Holy Week, a royal engagement which wasn't varied until the late nineteenth century. You can also see a drawing by Inigo Jones of a stage set which was erected in the Banqueting House in 1623. These splendid dining chambers had only just been rebuilt, and to mark the occasion, James I went there to see a performance of Ben Jonson's masque *Time Vindicated to Himself and his Honours*. The new Banqueting House, made of Portland stone, was intended to be the first fruit of ambitious plans by Jones and John Webb for the renaissance of Whitehall Palace under King James, but no more of it was ever completed. In 1649, Charles I walked through the Banqueting House on his way to the scaffold. Its elegant windows were still boarded up, a legacy of its occupation by the army.

The role of the Banqueting House as a place of entertainments survives to this day. When I went, I was serenaded by a troupe of minstrels who were essaying the songbook of Merrie England. 'When I-ha-hi was in the Low Countries . . .!' sang a man in gaiters, accompanying himself on what may well have been a lyre. He was joined by a man playing the sackbut and by a woman who was wardrobed as a comely wench. During a spirited rendering of a traditional air, 'Lump's Pudding', she sang, 'Such a pudding you never did see / He gave me a lump which did so agree.' This was the cue for her to put her hands beneath her pinny and to push it out as if she was nine months gone. For a rendition of the ballad of Sir Eglemon, which was about a courtly knight, one of the men rode around the hall on a pantomime horse made for one, doing all the legwork himself under the horse's skirts, his prosthetic armoured legs flapping uselessly against the flanks of his steed.

But the most fascinating remains of Whitehall Palace lie below ground, and can only be viewed by special arrangement. One of the rare occasions when they are visible to outsiders is on London Open House weekend, a popular event which sees some of the capital's most intriguing places all too briefly exposed to public gaze. One of the buildings which is sometimes included in the free-for-all is the Cabinet Office, the former Treasury building, a monument to paper-shuffling which stands at 70 Whitehall. On these prosaic-seeming premises are wonderful fragments of Henry's forgotten court, all the more remarkable for being preserved in the Sir Humphreyish surroundings of in-trays and blotters. More than any other building in London, the Cabinet Office proves the old saw about the deceptiveness of appearances.

On Open House weekend, it took two hours to go from the back of the queue on Whitehall to the lobby of number 70, where the walking tours departed. These were led not by London's established blue-badge guides but by security guards who worked for the bureaucrats themselves. The man leading my party was head of security at the Cabinet Office. He mustered us in reception. He had a fanned deck of postcards in his hand, like a game-show host. A lift opened silently, and indeed, emptily. 'That's the resident ghost,' said the head of security, with a wink.

In the interval between the medieval age and Tudor times, the royal court had migrated the short distance from Westminster to Whitehall. Ever since the Crown settled in the marshy ground by the river, its presence had attracted courtiers and suppliers, flatterers and fools. In the 1240s, the Archbishop of York, Walter de Grey, set up home between royal Westminster and the river. Within fifty years, the episcopal seat, substantially upgraded, had become York Place, and was a frequent home from home for Edward I. Incumbents of the see of York continued to make improvements in the fourteenth and fifteenth centuries. It's thought that the house doubled in size between 1465 and 1476 during the archbishopric of George Neville, eventually becoming as big as Lambeth Palace across the Thames.

Wolsey was the last archbishop to occupy York Place. On his watch it became so large that it dwarfed anything that Henry VIII could call his own. Here again was evidence of the priest's reckless extravagance. If Hampton Court was going to be Wolsey's country seat, York Place was to be his base in town. His priority, according to Simon Thurley's *The Lost Palace of Whitehall*, was 'to make York Place fit for the celebrations which accompanied the receipt of his cardinal's hat'. Accordingly, Wolsey built himself a new outer great chamber, remodelled his privy chamber with a fashionable bay window, and improved the chapel. Only the proximity of other freeholdings frustrated Wolsey's ambitious schemes, and not even these stumbling blocks detained him long. He secured a lease on land to the north of York Place, the then-rustic Scotland Yard, and snapped up the rights to a brace of estates to the south. Now York Place was ready for Wolsey's pièce de résistance, the long gallery, which graced the riverfront. The Venetian ambassador remarked that there were 'windows on each side, looking on gardens and river . . . the ceiling being marvellously wrought in stone with gold and the wainscot of carved wood representing a thousand beautiful figures'. By 1529, York Place, the heart of the future Whitehall Palace, had few rivals in all of Europe as a gracious town house. Every day during the legal term, its master processed with all the trappings and fixtures of a demi-monarch down King Street (which later became the road we know as Whitehall, the A3212) to sit in the Star Chamber, returning home each evening attended by the same pomp.

Even before Wolsey's fall, his monarch was already planning to turn York Place into a palace fit for a king. The idea was for a residence in two halves, divided by King Street but linked by a gatehouse. Old York Place, on the river side, would be retained for lodgings, while the precincts to the west of the road would be developed for diversions and sports. In due course, the monarch became so attached to Whitehall Palace that he passed his last day on earth in its royal bedchamber. Later, the palace also witnessed the death throes of Oliver Cromwell.

The Cabinet Office is the massif now looming over Henry's gaming grounds. By following corridors of institutional marigold and duck-egg blue through the lower ground floor of 70 Whitehall, you come across the astonishing sight of a high brick tower, of Tudor origin and pristinely pointed, trapped within its superstructure. This turret thrusts out a broad chest from the departmental wall. Its distant crown is blackened, by smoke or age. This was Henry's indoor tennis court. It was built more than fifty feet high – reaching to sixty-five feet at each corner – and eighty-eight feet long. The brick tower that I gazed upon was one of the corners, in fact, though the top twenty feet or so of it were missing. Despite its monumental size, the court made me think of something on a more intimate scale. It was as if a rare and exotic living thing had been pressed into the amber of a pen-pusher's paperweight, or suspended in the liquid blizzard of his desktop snow scene. The bricks were smaller than their modern, mass-fired equivalents, and arranged in the classic Tudor formation: a row of bricks laid side-on capped by a row laid end-on. (Today, these changes are rung within each row.) The bricks were the colour of dried blood, dusted here and there with mortar. 'In Henry's day, the pointing would have been covered in whitewash,' said the head of security at the Cabinet Office. What we were looking at was the remains of a decorative band of flint and chalk, which had once given the tower a striking chequerboard effect.

The tennis court is the largest surviving edifice of the original Tudor palace. In Henry's time, it was known as the Great Close, or covered, Tennis Play. It was where the king and his courtiers played sets of 'real', or royal, tennis for cash. Henry had taken to the game young, encouraged by his father. Henry VII was a keen patron of racquet sports and built courts at six of his palaces, including Windsor Castle. The Venetian ambassador, who seems to have done nothing else but look on admiringly at the domestic life of the Tudor court for the entire duration of his posting to London, reported of Henry VIII's game that 'it was the prettiest thing in the world to see him play; his fair skin glowing through a shirt of finest texture'. When Henry wasn't in his whites, he was wearing a black velvet tennis coat, which he had had specially made. After he turned the royal ankle over during a game in 1527, his cobbler produced a black slipper to match. Henry took his fun seriously and issued strict instructions to his court that on no account should anyone indulge in 'grudging, rumbling or talking of the King's pastime'.

He followed his father in constructing tennis courts, including four at Whitehall. The Great Close is one of a pair: its twin used to stand in the open air. There were also two Little Close Tennis

Courts. By modern standards, the Great Close was an absurdly grand setting for a game of tennis. But in Tudor times, the rules called for low-roofed galleries inside the court known as pentices, and players were allowed to thwack the ball off the walls and even the ceiling, as if they were in a modern squash court. On London Open House day, we looked in awe at the beautiful original windows. Set some fifteen feet above the playing surface, they made sport possible by admitting natural light to the court, which in the sixteenth century was painted black. I wondered whether kingly smashes had ever rattled the leaded panes in their putty.

Courtiers had followed matches from a viewing gallery, Cockpit Passage, so named because of its associations with another great pursuit of Tudor Whitehall, cock-fighting. Cockpit Passage can still be trod, though not in the original wood. The floor has been replaced but the brick walls are original. The bricks were once concealed behind fine tapestries. From Cockpit Passage, spectators could follow the action not only in the all-weather Great Close Tennis Play, but also on the grass courts nearby. Though you would never guess from the front door of the Cabinet Office on Whitehall that Henry's tennis courts lay behind it, there is evidence of them at the rear of the building in Treasury Green, the gardens of the former exchequer. Not only can you see remnants of the brick walls which once surrounded Henry's lawn-tennis courts. You can also make out the north wall of one of the Little Close Tennis Courts, a smaller brother to the much bigger arena. Creepers wind up the brick face of the Little Close. A large arched window once let daylight in on the tennis; below it are windows for the spectators.

The viewing windows were almost as important as the courts themselves because Henry VIII's courtiers liked to bet on the outcome of the game as they watched their favourites play. 'There was a lot of money wagered on tennis matches in those days,' said the security chief. 'Henry VIII was a very successful gambler.' Huge sums changed hands, and the nobles who liked a flutter included the Duke of Buckingham, the Duke of Suffolk and Lord Rochford, Anne Boleyn's brother. Blue-blooded sets of tennis were enjoyed at Whitehall until as late as Charles II's reign. Samuel Pepys jotted that the monarch once sweated off four pounds on the courts. I should very much have enjoyed a set or two myself in the old palace of Whitehall, but regrettably its magnificent courts ceased to resound to the thunk of tennis balls in the seventeenth century. James I converted the two little courts for his daughter Elizabeth in 1604. In 1663, the Great Close became a self-contained house for James, Duke of Monmouth, the illegitimate son of Charles II. Part of his former kitchens survives, though the noble pantry remains tantalisingly out of bounds to the subterranean tourist.

Nor was this the end of the service given by Henry's old tennis courts. After great swathes of the palace were consumed in the fire of 1698, the hardy courts found a new role as the King's Council Chamber and Treasury. They fulfilled this function for thirty years until the predecessors of Sir Humphrey warned Treasury grandees that the old tennis courts were 'in so very ruinous & dangerous a condition that we don't think it safe for your lordships to continue in (them)'. An architect called William Kent was retained to design a new Treasury. His plans were approved in 1733. Like Inigo Jones a century earlier, Kent had ambitious schemes for rebuilding a great range of royal buildings at Whitehall, including a new parliament house. But in the event, 70 Whitehall was the extent of Kent's reconstruction, and even this was only half the size of the Treasury that the architect had envisaged, though this didn't stop the work coming in at well over twice the original estimate of £8,000.

Although our tour was led by the head of security at the Cabinet Office, he was only one of the escorts. There were also two uniformed guards, a man and a woman. To the male of the pair, the presence of civilians in the building appeared to be an unaccustomed and unwelcome break from routine. From time to time, as he shepherded the stragglers, he would mutter 'Come on!' under his breath in a peremptory tone. You wondered whether this was a reflex, whether he was even aware that he was saying it.

Our tour of William Kent's Treasury included the room which was, by tradition, grace-and-favoured to the leader of the House of Lords. As we tested its springy pile, my eye was caught by panelling with a handle on it. 'What's behind that door?'

'I don't know,' said the guard. 'A drinks cabinet?'

'That's a pity. I thought it might be a secret passage or something.'

'Come on,' snapped the guard, in a spasm of bossiness.

We filed into Conference Room A, which had seen a lot of action under its old name, the Treasury Boardroom. Until the reign of George III, it was where the keepers of the coffers had gathered to carve them up with the king. A mottled wooden table with a dull patina was boxed in by two dozen walnut chairs. The table dated from 1800. Its top was decorated with a shamrock, a rose and a thistle, to commemorate the union with Ireland of the same year. 'This beautiful table was assembled here and we don't believe it's ever been out of this room,' said the head of security. 'It was the original MFI flat-pack.' Over William Kent's mantelpiece was a bust of Spencer Perceval, the only prime minister to have been assassinated. He was murdered at the Houses of Parliament in 1812 by a man called John Bellingham who blamed the government for his bankruptcy.

Even under its present name, Conference Room A had seen quite a bit of action. It overlooked the garden of No. 10, and had felt the full force of the rocket that landed on the lawn when the IRA fired three mortars at Downing Street, in another attempt to kill a prime minister. 'There was a meeting of fourteen people going on in this room and when we came up, we didn't know what to expect,' said the head of security. 'The explosion blew in every window in the room. By the radiators, you were ankle-deep in broken glass.' Fortunately, floor-length net curtains had stopped the fragments from travelling any further across the room. The curtains had shot or fishing weights sewn into their hems, to stop them from flapping out in a blast. I looked out of the window onto the prime-ministerial greensward and saw that a little blue trampoline had been set up to amuse the youngest of the PM's children, Leo Blair.

A stout couple were standing next to me. 'If walls could talk!' said the woman.

'Oh God, yes!' said her tubby hubby.

'OK, thank you very much,' said the uniformed security man, in move-along-now tones.

As the tour neared its climax, we burrowed below 70 Whitehall once more and went back in time again, from the Georgian Treasury of William Kent to the Whitehall Palace of the Tudors. We found ourselves in a thoroughfare like Cockpit Passage. Like the gallery once thronged by tennis spectators, Tudor Corridor, as this one was called, had once been a busy and VIP-choked rendezvous. Royal tennis players and their partners had tripped this way en route to the courts. The thick wooden door into the Great Close had come through the past five hundred years or so in good repair. 'In Henry's day, this was a dark passage,' said our guide. Tudor Corridor was pretty gloomy even now. We trod its darkling flagstones. Although lanterns the size of lobster pots hung from a whitewashed ceiling, they weren't lit. The head of security pointed out metal pickets which were set into doorways and recesses at shin-height. 'They were the original anti-mugging devices,' he said. Without them, footpads and cutpurses would have treated the alcoves as inglenook thieves' dens, where they could lurk in comfort before springing out at their unsuspecting victims. In the eighteenth century, another thoroughfare was installed in the middle of the former palace: the west end of Tudor Passage joined the new Treasury Passage at right angles. Treasury Passage was built to

link Downing Street to the Horseguards parade grounds. Though
it's still marked on the A–Z, this artery is considered far too close
to the heart of government to be open to outsiders.

In a hall below the Cabinet Office, my tour culminated in the
unscheduled extra of a brief grapple with the bad-tempered
guard. The hall was at one end of Cockpit Passage: it was the end
which had been nearest to the action in the days of the gaming
birds. The blood-drenched rink where their bouts took place lay
a short distance away, under the gravel where the Horseguards
now go through their paces for the tourists. The hall's
antecedents were reflected in its hangings. There were splendid
daubs of fighting cocks such as Old Trodgon, who won £200 for
his owner, a handsome purse in 1787 money. When this corner
of Whitehall wasn't filled with sporting men, it had been the
haunt of robbers and their fences, who patronised a coffee shop
on the premises.

All of this history I took in with blameless self-control, not
giving the uniformed security man the slightest pretext for laying
a finger on me. To be fair to him, though, I can hardly say the
same of my attempt to spy on 10 Downing Street. But put
yourself in my place. Our guide had just announced that the door
at the far end of the hall led directly into the official residence of
the prime minister. Who among us has a soul so dull that he
wouldn't press his eye to the keyhole? In the moment or two it
took me to reach the portal and connect with the aperture, I had
a premonition of a shirtsleeved PM hunkered around a 3-D war-
planner mainframe, his advisers taking alternate pulls on
cigarettes and beakers of coffee.

A scene like this wasn't as far fetched as it sounds. The Cabinet
Office was as bland as a filing cabinet, with a bluff façade on
Whitehall and a title that brought only manilla envelopes to
mind, but it was one of the most important bastions of the state.
Through the bulletproof doors in front of me was Cobra, the
suitably menacing acronym of the Cabinet Office briefing room.

This office, which was occupied in times of national crisis, was in use at the time of the Kosovo conflict, and it's beyond doubt that meetings were convened there during the second Gulf War of 2003. Cobra was the impregnable home of a part-time Cabinet committee which had been set up thirty years earlier to address IRA activity during the Heath government. At times of major civil emergencies and disasters, the Civil Contingency Unit could convene the heads of the Army, Navy, Royal Air Force, the security services and the SAS for urgent meetings in Cobra. From this deepest cellar of the Cabinet Office, the endgame of the Iranian embassy siege was plotted by the Home Secretary of the day and the security forces. Documents in the public domain show that Cobra was used in 1994 for a major training exercise to respond to a terrorist nuclear attack. It was also in the room in front of me that ministers, civil servants, military types and spooks met to discuss how to offset the feared repercussions of the Millennium Bug.

On London Open House day, I made out a bank of unattended workstations through the lock, the miscellaneous white goods of office life, before I felt a uniformed arm on mine. In the security man's grip, I went quietly. I rejoined the tour as it left Whitehall the lost royal residence, in favour of Whitehall the A3212. If I was trembling a little as I went, it wasn't because of my reverse at the hands of the guard but because the old stack of Henry's palace continued to reverberate to the throb of power five hundred years on, despite the fact that it was now swaddled inside the Cabinet Office. This was no more than a camouflage, I now saw, nothing other than an ingenious piece of stone-cladding on the part of the foxy mandarinate.

HIGH TREASON
The Gunpowder Plot

The most famous event that ever took place under London is an ambiguous one since, strictly speaking, it never actually happened. It has to be chalked up as a *non*-event. And yet four hundred years later, it's still such a popular fixture of our calendar that we mark it with uncharacteristic abandon. For weeks before and after the red-letter day itself, the London air is rent with the sounds of depth-charges and rapidly shredding Velcro. This fusillade of fireworks commemorates the foiled attempt by Guy Fawkes and others to blow up the Houses of Parliament. For this reason, and also because the Palace of Westminster vies with no more than one or two other institutions for the title of the best-recognised landmark in London, I wanted to include the cellars where Fawkes almost lit his seditious touchpaper on my subterranean tour of the city. What gunpowder, treason and plot failed to achieve in the early seventeenth century was partially accomplished a little more than two hundred years later, in a substantial fire of 1834. The familiar palace on the riverbank, as rebuilt by Charles Barry in the 1860s, and the one where Fawkes's cronies stashed their thirty-six barrels of explosives aren't quite one and the same. But still I hoped to tread where those insurrectionists had tiptoed, to indulge the fancy, which flares from time to time in even the most law-abiding breast, that I could drop the plunger on a chamber full of unsuspecting MPs.

Political commentators like to say that Westminster is a village, and indeed it corresponds in many respects to a thriving hamlet. On a busy day, there can be three thousand people at the palace.

Its outbuildings, and *under*buildings, are equipped to service their needs. The palace has its own power supply. There are boiler houses and car parks and storerooms below ground. There's a secret passage known as a 'crawlway' leading under the historic legal cockpit of the Court of Star Chamber. There are tradesmen serving the maintenance needs of the palace whose skills are as arcane as those of a medieval blacksmith, and whose marketplace is even more parochial. There's a shooting range where MPs, those Aunt Sallys, can work off a little aggression by getting their own back on constituent-shaped targets. There's a crypt dating back to the days of Edward the Confessor, the oldest incarnation of parliament in London. But most of all, Westminster has its own breathtakingly ripe sewage contingencies. It would satisfy the most lip-curling critic of our legislature that its very foundations are chock-a-block with sanitary ductwork. As we've seen, sensitive souls all but abandoned the place during the Great Stink of London in the nineteenth century, blaming the offensive atmosphere on the Thames. But my experience of exploring the bowels of Parliament – and for once the scatological term is the inescapable *mot juste* – makes me wonder whether MPs shouldn't have looked closer to home for the source of the smell. Of course, they don't tend to pay much attention to what goes on beneath the Commons floorboards. But anyone who has been introduced to Parliament top and bottom will tell you that, just as the most distinctive sound of the place is rhubarb, its signature smell is cabbage.

My arrangements for touring the palace entailed presenting myself at what appeared to be a side door to the House of Lords. The attendants on the door beguiled a quiet morning by exchanging camp banter with one another. 'Are you like this when you've been drinking?' one of them was asking his colleague.

'That's for me to know and you to find out!' teased the second man.

I asked if there was a Gents that I could use. Amazingly, in view of my later discovery about the palace, it wasn't well off for privies. 'There isn't one around here,' said the second attendant feelingly. 'When it rains, we have to cross our legs.'

I was waiting to be met by a member of the palace maintenance staff. The attendants at the entrance were talking about their plans for the following week, a traditional holiday period. 'I'm hoping to have it off!' said one, to shrieks from his colleagues.

A short time later in a back office, beneath a mildly bawdy calendar which had been supplied with the compliments of a water-treatment company, a man called Mike, the House of Lords maintenance manager, was filling me in on the curious subterranean architecture of the mother of all parliaments. After the blaze of the nineteenth century, Barry not only fireproofed the new roof with cladding made of cast iron, but he also rested the entire edifice on a bed of concrete. Mike said, 'It's full of drains, Victorian culverts, down here. There's one known as the medals corridor. There's a canteen at one end, and the other used to pop up underneath Speaker's Court. You used to be able to walk along it for a hundred yards. But it's been cut up, turned into changing rooms. The place is full of Victorian voids which we now make use of.' Mike's Victorian voids had been whittled away, little by little, to accommodate new equipment and machinery, to make way for progress. In the past half-dozen years or so, he said, the kitchens had been upgraded and the installation of new plant had reduced the adjacent storage space. Other voids were simply inaccessible, out of reach as well as out of sight. One of them was beneath the famous terrace of the Houses of Parliament, one of the most sought-after watering holes in London, where MPs entertained their guests over drinks on summer evenings. 'The terrace as you see it now is a new one. They had to raise it because of the tide levels of the Thames. The old one's still there, though, it's directly below it. There's a space of two to three feet. No one's fallen through yet!'

Men like Mike were the servants of the palace, and perhaps to some extent of the people who were returned there, by electoral mandate and patronage alike. Below stairs wasn't just a literal description of Mike's station: the phrase still seemed to be redolent of its Edwardian connotations. Few Members of Parliament or peers took an active interest in what went on beneath the debating chambers, Mike told me, but a handful were frequent visitors. 'Tony Benn, now he was always down here. He was forever putting up plaques. There was one for a suffragette who hid herself in St Stephen's Chapel on census day. The idea was that she could put down her place of residence as the Palace of Westminster.' Sure enough, on the back of the door of the cleaner's cupboard in the chapel, which is formally known as St Mary's Undercroft, Emily Davidson is memorialised. She hid in the little room on the night of the 1911 census. Because she could legitimately give her address as 'House of Commons', she claimed that this substantiated her claim to the same political rights as men. Two years after her ingenious protest, Wilding perished beneath the hoofs of racehorses during her famous demonstration at the Epsom Derby.

Mike and I had been joined by one of his colleagues. The newcomer was in time to hear Mike say warmly of Mr Benn, 'He wasn't a politician, he was a parliamentarian.'

Discussing the workplace in front of a scribbling visitor seemed to tempt Mike's colleague to mischievous indiscretion. 'This place is basically a gentlemen's club invaded by a lot of women.'

'Equal Opportunities!' protested Mike with an embarrassed smile. 'You can't say that.'

'All right, *inhabited*, then.'

'In today's society, they've got equal status.'

'More than equal,' said Mike's colleague, looking at me slyly.

Another of Mike's oppos, Gurmet Kalsi, showed me around the palace. We went outside and across a courtyard, Star Chamber Court. Gurmet pointed out a circular design set into the concrete of the yard. 'It's a turntable,' he said. This revolving plate had been fitted to allow delivery vehicles, including Post Office vans, to frequent the yard, which, I now saw, was otherwise cursed with impossibly tight turning circles. Thanks to the turntable, posties could pull into the yard, park on the plate and make their deliveries. Their vehicles could be swung around without the gearshift being engaged, and the drivers were free to carry on with their rounds. The one proviso, as Gurmet explained, was that the delivery people had to hit their marks exactly. Otherwise the turntable was of absolutely no use.

We inspected one of the less well advertised perks of a legislator's life, the free underground car park in the middle of central London. At the entrance to the MPs' pound were metal gates on a block-and-tackle arrangement. I assumed that these were a safety measure, perhaps introduced after the Tory spokesman on Northern Ireland, Airey Neave MP, was fatally wounded by a republican car bomb as he was driving up the car-park ramp. The subterranean facilities of the palace are especially welcome to some politicians because of their security advantages. Northern Ireland ministers and former premiers prefer to enter using an underground walkway from Portcullis House, the new home of MPs on the north bank of the Thames. Leaving the tree-lined covered piazza of this mock-Tudor billet, the more wary of our leaders descend into an underground walkway, which is lined in spanking new white tiles finished to appear old, and in genuinely old, original marble features, columns capped with gurning dragons and griffins.

Sure enough, the gates at the entrance to the members' car park had been fitted against a hazard, but this turned out to be the immemorial one of the River Thames. The car park went down four storeys below the surface and MPs were in danger of having their workplace inundated at high tide. As Big Ben was tolling the hour for midday, Gurmet and I were descending a metal staircase to look at the pumps which prevented MPs from getting their shoes wet when they collected their wheels. Our steps rang off the iron rungs. The boilers which fired the pumps were gunmetal grey and smelled of oil.

'How old are the pumps?' I asked Gurmet.

'I would say these pumps are fifty to sixty years old,' he replied thoughtfully. Mingling with the nosegay of lubricant in the boiler housing was a smell of damp, and there was a show of old pressure gauges. It was like being in the engine room of an old freighter.

Parliament was a contrary place, where, until very recently, MPs made indolently late starts and endured punishingly late finishes. It was unrepresentative, antiquated, inefficient, or so it was often claimed. In mitigation of these criticisms, the institution had evolved rather than emerged fully formed from a blueprint. This higgledy-piggledy development seemed to have been petrified in its very bricks and mortar. You might have thought that an underground tour would entail an even progress from one subterranean spot to another, but it was a much more snakes-and-ladders affair than that. From the bilges in the hold beneath the MPs' car park, Gurmet and I shot up a staircase into the fresh air of New Palace Yard, to find ourselves beneath a colonnade where an ant-column of parliamentary workers was coming and going. I sympathised with a parliamentary correspondent who could be heard saying into his mobile phone, 'I can't quite see what the story is, to be honest with you.' There were shorthand-typists lugging their stenographer's keyboards, on their way to take dictation or transcribe debates for the pages of Hansard, and policemen were studying a sunken camera which took photographs of car sills. This might have been a modern-dress re-enactment of a momentous scene from English history, the sort of thing you expect in a Shakespearean production across the river at the National Theatre. The officers were on the lookout for bombers, like their seventeenth-century predecessors who had apprehended Guy Fawkes. They were going through their drill a short distance from where that historic collar had been made.

Hardly had I caught my breath than Gurmet and I were plunging once more into the interior of the palace. We saw oil tanks and a 'chiller room', which kept computing equipment cool. We popped our heads around the door of a water-softening plant, which treated the water used in the palace heating system to prevent the pipes from furring up. We were exploring the passages beneath Westminster Hall. The hall had been built in 1097 as an extension of Edward the Confessor's original palace. This new wing was the idea of William Rufus, the son of William the Conqueror, although he was less than ecstatic with the results, dismissing the hall as a 'mere bedchamber' compared to what he'd had in mind. Perhaps this was because the most striking feature of the draughty hall was not installed until later: the staggering hammerbeam roof, made of oak and designed by a man called Hugh Herland.

Despite the reservations of William Rufus, the hall was the meeting place of the King's Council, and it was there that the Model Parliament was summoned by Edward I. After Edward's death, the Lords and the Commons began to hold separate conclaves. They would all meet in the presence of the monarch in a room called the Painted Chamber, which was linked by a passage to the king's bedchamber. The Lord Chamberlain would formally announce to the assembled parliamentarians the reason for summoning them. The peers would then retire to the White Chamber. The commoners had to mess where they could, sometimes prevailing on the monks across the road at Westminster Abbey to borrow their chapter house or refectory.

The first settled home of MPs emerged as a result of the power struggle between Henry VIII and the Vatican. St Stephen's Chapel had been founded by Edward the Confessor, rebuilt by Edward I and finished in 1347 in the reign of Edward II. It was a tall building on two floors, with high turrets at each corner and large stained-glass windows. While the monarch worshipped in the chapel proper, the court made their observances in the crypt below. But at the Reformation, the chapel was secularised, in common with all other private places of worship, under the Chantries Act of 1547, and within a few years, St Stephen's had become the recognised meeting place of the Commons. The members sat in the choir stalls which lined the north and south walls. The Mace, the symbol of the Speaker's authority, was placed on a table where the lectern had once been. An ante-chapel, behind a reredos or choir-screen, was ideal as a lobby for MPs registering their votes as Ayes, the Noes staying put. The Speaker's chair was installed where the altar had been. The custom of MPs bowing to the chair probably derives from genuflection to the altar. From the mid-sixteenth century until its destruction by fire in 1834, St Stephen's was, to all intents and purposes, the House of Commons.

Once Henry VIII had given the clergy their marching orders from the precincts of Westminster, this desirable office space in the heart of London was soon snatched up by figures representing temporal power. Members and officials of both parliamentary houses started to occupy the many vacant chambers. In 1605, one of the cellars below was hired out to Guy Fawkes and his co-plotters – and indeed, co-religionists. Fawkes's fellow Roman Catholics, including Robert Catesby, Thomas Winwith, Thomas Percy, Francis Tresham and John Wright, came in with him on the plot to remove James I, his queen and his heir, and Parliament, for that matter. They wanted to 'blow the Scots back to Scotland' and hoped that Roman Catholics would be able to take over the country in the confusion that followed this coup, so winning the religious freedom that they were being denied. The conspirators had hired a house on the site of Old Palace Yard, now the peers' car park, and stored the high explosive there before smuggling the barrels into the warrren of passageways and souterrains under Parliament. But Tresham warned his brother-in-law, Lord Monteagle, not to attend the House on 5 November. Monteagle alerted the authorities and the plot was undone. Fawkes was caught red-handed beneath the palace and taken to the Tower, where he gave up the names of his collaborators under torture. He suffered so badly at the hands of his inquisitors that Fawkes could hardly climb the steps to his own scaffold. He was hung, drawn and quartered in Old Palace Yard. Four of his collaborators, including Catesby and Percy, were apparently killed while resisting arrest. The others were hauled through the streets, executed and their heads impaled on spikes. To this day, the vaults of the Palace of Westminster are ceremonially searched by the Yeomen of the Guard before the state opening of Parliament.

In 2003, scientists from the University of Wales worked out that Fawkes and his men would have levelled large parts of central London if they'd got away with it. They'd had enough gunpowder to flatten the Houses of Parliament twenty-five times over. Thanks to the boys and girls of the Centre for Explosion Studies in Aberystwyth, we now know that everything within a radius of more than a hundred feet of the kegs would have been reduced to smouldering rubble, including Westminster Hall, the Abbey and a number of surrounding streets. The blast would have blown down walls and lifted roofs as far as three hundred feet away – that is to say, well into Whitehall – and Londoners would have been ducking flying glass and collapsing ceilings for up to five hundred yards in all directions. The boffins carried out the research for the 398th anniversary of the failed coup attempt. They're more accustomed to measuring the wallop packed by TNT than the less powerful gunpowder favoured by the plotters, but as Dr Geraint Thomas told *The Times*, 'Guy Fawkes was an expert in explosives and so knew what he was doing. If he had the gunpowder confined in barrels and well packed in, it could have been almost as powerful as the equivalent TNT explosion.' At all events, the bang would have been quite big enough to have the desired effect. It would have lifted the wooden ceiling of the cellars, carrying it up to the second floor where parliament sat. As the timbers fell back down to earth, they would have become lethal projectiles. Anybody not killed by blast or flame would have been struck by the falling debris and knocked into the burning ruins of the palace, choking on enough carbon dioxide to kill a healthy man in minutes.

In the very spot where Fawkes had once been rumbled, Gurmet and I were pressing on with our tour. We were visiting the above-advertised bowels of the palace. I was about to discover that this was a truer label for where we were going than I supposed. We were in the north basement, walking half-stooped through warm corridors towards the unmistakable smell of sewage. We tripped down a narrow flight of steps, Gurmet threw open a metal wicket leading to the humming source of this odour and said with commendable directness, 'All the shit from all over Parliament comes into here.'

I took in a handsomely tiled room with a funnelled roof. Confronting me were great, gleaming drums of waste. 'Usually we come early in the morning,' said Gurmet. 'At that time of day, it's less . . .' He faltered.

'Whiffy?'

Gurmet chuckled.

I pinched my nostrils. An unhappy suspicion descended on me. I said, 'When is the smell at its worst? When's peak time?'

Gurmet didn't even look at his watch. 'This is peak time,' he said.

He tapped a large spherical vat which had a glass inspection panel set high up in it. It was a bathyscaphe of poo. He said, 'At one stage, we used to go in to scrape it. Now it's all done by chemicals.' I didn't need to ask him what difference this had made to the working day: one look at Gurmet's face was clarification enough. An indicator board was fixed to the tiled wall. By rights, it ought to have been entirely baffling to the layman, so arcane were its calibrations: 'Metropolitan sewer gravity level: 3 feet', it said. And yet the more I read on – 'stereo pump start: 4 feet'; 'alarm bell: 5 feet' – the more its strange poetry suggested its meaning. If I was right to read the indicator as some kind of cloacal continuum, and I sensed that I was, then heaven help Gurmet and his team when the level in the tank reached six feet. This was the cue for something called the 'storm charger'.

In case you have ever asked yourself how MPs' cesspits are drained, the principle operates more or less like this. Electronic probes in the waste-collection vessels monitor the terrible meniscus. As this reaches a predetermined height, the probes go 'tilt', as it were, and trigger shockwaves of pressurised air from machines which are known without sentiment as sewage ejectors. The updraft that they produce snatches up the waste and deposits it into the palace's Victorian drains. Though this all sounds rather nifty, the sewage ejectors are in fact bogglingly low-tech and incredibly old. They date back to 1868, to Barry's refit, and they're half-timbered. They're compact, and finished in a shade of green which is a compromise between the decorous and something much more grimly hard-headed. The ejectors reside behind a big gate and within a recess which is decorated wholly unsuitably in red and gilt, as if it were one of the robing rooms found several storeys higher up in the building. The space where the sewage ejectors are kept is known to palace janitors as 'the torpedo room'. Gurmet and I gave the reeking plant the once-over, once being enough for me.

Though evidently not for Gurmet. 'They work. They work,' he purred, running a fond hand over the grain of an ejector's panelling like a classic car enthusiast admiring a shooting brake. 'They take half an hour to warm up but when they do, they work. It's wonderful when the machines are working and I've seen them working many times. *Thump! Thump! Thump!*' Gurmet mimicked the ejectors in operation.

I wasn't sure that I shared his confidence in the elderly

machinery. I could imagine irresistible pressure building up in the vats and this overwhelming the sewage ejectors, splintering their elegant panels. I pictured Gurmet's torpedo room living up to its name and shipping foul water as if it was in the bows of a scuttled U-boat. MPs in their distant chamber would hear muffled booms and fear that what Guy Fawkes and co. had schemed was at last coming to pass.

We left behind the sewage ejectors, and their paradoxically elegant quarters, but the smell of them followed me around for the rest of my visit to Parliament. Like Proust's dunked madeleine, they carried such a sensory payload that I may well be able to revisit their primal redolence for as long as I live. I couldn't shake their odorousness as Gurmet and I poked about at the foot of the Victorian tower, the splendid stack at the other end of the palace from Big Ben. The tower was a vertical repository for documents, an elaborately landscaped filing cabinet thirteen storeys tall. *Eau d'ejector* was the fragrance that wafted in with me to the electricity plant known as South Sub-station, past a wooden hutch where a stoker was reading his tabloid by a wanly glowing sodium bulb. The same perfume was saying all sorts of things about me, few of them complimentary, in both the equatorial Royal Gallery Power Plant, where I could feel the tip of my nose turning hot, and in the milder climes of the Summer Boiler Room, where a breeze ruffled my lucky hair.

Side by side in a short stretch of corridor were all the underground stalls where the craftsmen of the palace plied their trades, the clockmaker's workshop and the glazier's hidey-hole, the carpet-fitter's and the stationer and the locksmith. From a toolshed came the cauterised, singed smell of a Tube platform in August. Derek was firing up his brazing iron. Derek was the handyman at the palace of Westminster – strictly speaking, he was *one* of the handymen, but he had been there for twenty-seven years, and he wore a sweatshirt with the parliamentary motif of a portcullis on it, so some kind of distinction clearly attached to him. Derek could knock up a banister rail; he could turn you something nice out of a lump of lignum vitae – 'the hardest wood known to man' – he could make you an inkwell. 'But I have to make my own tools,' he said, moving around on the vinyl duckboarding of his toolshed with easy steps. 'There are no shops for the things I need. The technology I use is a hundred years out of date. I'm working like they did back in the 1800s.'

I suppose Derek's acommodation was really a workshop rather than a toolshed but it had the fittings and fixtures of a toolshed. There was a dartboard, and what hotels like to call 'tea-making facilities'. There was also a fishtank stocked with tropical varieties.

Derek said, 'I caught them off Westminster pier.'

'I've heard of global warming but that's ridiculous.'

Derek looked at me. 'No,' he admitted. 'I go to a pet shop in Victoria.'

I asked him about the smoking poker of his brazing iron. 'Brazing's like soldering only it's hotter, and you use an alloy of brass,' he explained. With a rueful look, he acknowledged the vapours coming off the brazing tool. 'I hope you don't mind the smell. Down here we can't get rid of the fumes properly.'

No, I didn't mind the smell. What smell? I only had nostrils for the sewage plant, even after Gurmet and I had scrambled up from deep beneath the palace once more, into the Chapel of St Mary Undercroft. It was one of the most ornate places of worship in London (ruthlessly restored in Pevsner's withering judgement). The organ looked like a rosette-winning schloss in an Austrian best-kept village contest. Recumbent Templars took their rest beneath the chapel's flying buttresses. The vaulted roof was perhaps the first 'lierne' vault in England, I learnt, a lierne being one of the ornamental, non-structural ribs which formed star-like patterns between the serious weight-bearing struts of the roof. St Mary Undercroft is a favourite spot for the weddings of MPs. They can also have their children christened in Charles

Barry's baptistry. The font, made of alabaster and marble and capped with an ornamental brass cover, is by his son, E. M. Barry. 'Here we are,' said Gurmet, standing by the font. 'Holy water, or you can say, tap water.'

It was all very well for him to bring an unbeliever's scepticism to the mysteries of the sacraments, but I had a bone to pick with him. 'I can even smell that smell in here!' I told him reproachfully.

'Yes,' Gurmet said. 'One of the sewage outflows is right outside the chapel.'

LIFTING PEOPLE
The Plague

Exploring subterranean London is an instruction in the darker side of the capital, in more ways than one. To learn about the city's other side, the underside, is to become acquainted with the things London would prefer to keep hidden: the flaws beneath the surface, the secrets under the floorboards. Another way of putting this is that you find out where the bodies are buried. This familiar usage is particularly apt in the case of my home town, which has at least as many corpses per square mile – *in* the Square Mile, come to that – as any other city you can name.

Of all the capital's deathly secrets, the one that provokes the most uneasy looks and nervous laughs, not to mention involuntary scratching, is the plague. The fascination may be put simply: so near, yet so far – thank God! We Londoners can stand directly on top of plague pits, we can stroll right through their landscaped precincts, and indulge in the tantalising vicariousness of thinking that we're almost within touching distance of this grisly history and yet are safe from its scourge. Bunhill Fields, its very name a corruption of 'bonehill', contains more bodies than there are living souls in a city the size of Southampton. 'Many who were infected and near their end ran wrapped in blankets or rags and threw themselves in and expired there, before any earth could be thrown upon them,' wrote Daniel Defoe of Bunhill Fields, where he himself was later interred. We like to tell each other tall tales about plague pits. Do you know why there isn't an Underground station at Muswell Hill? They started to dig a tunnel there and hit a plague pit! Have you noticed that you practically have to crouch as you negotiate the men's department in the basement of Harvey Nichol's? They couldn't sink it any deeper into the Knightsbridge subsoil or fashion victims would have found themselves mingling with plague victims. What lends these apocryphal stories their undoubted frisson is that the virus buried beneath us is indefatigable. It lies dormant but it never goes away, it never gives up. It has such a venerable span that the half-life of even the most unremitting radioactive element is a mayfly's term in comparison. Somewhere beneath Londoners' feet, the virus endures, and if disturbed, it could once again be extremely disobliging. But barring that unlikely outcome, the plague pits, like the plague itself, can safely be consigned to the past as surely as their unspeakable contents have been committed to reassuringly deep holes in the ground.

Or so I thought. I little imagined, when I began travelling around hidden London, that I would find myself scrambling over a plague pit, that I would be in close – indeed, confined – quarters with those who had succumbed to this blackest of deaths. It began in all innocence, with a phone call to the press office at the Corporation of London. Surely the Corporation would know some interesting subterranean things to see; now that I was a Freeman of the City, we were practically family.

At first, it seemed as though I had drawn a blank. Underground curios were in short supply at the Corporation, it appeared. But the obliging Rory Taylor of the press office asked me to give him a moment. 'Are you interested in an exhumation?' he said at last. It was at an old Wren church in the City, he said, St Andrew's, Holborn. 'Does that sound like your cup of tea?' Rory gave me a name, someone to ring.

'We're clearing out the crypt,' said Ian Grey, the clerk of St Andrew's, when I reached him by phone. As far as I could make out from this helpful and friendly man, it was something to do with the Second World War. The church had been damaged in

the Blitz, as so many of them had been. As in the case of the
Guildhall Art Gallery, it struck me as odd that the work was only
beginning now, more than half a century after peace had broken
out. Moreover, when Ian had used the expression 'clearing out
the crypt', of course he didn't literally mean—

'All told, there are up to a thousand bodies,' he said. 'They've
all got to go. They date back to the fourteenth century, which is
why there's, ah, a slight concern.'

Only a slight concern? That was all right, then. Curiously,
though, the longer Ian went on, and the more he qualified the
hazards of the crypt with soothing diminutives, the more it
sounded like a death trap. 'There's a small risk that fleshy bits
have been left on the bodies,' he said. 'There's a very small chance
of a communicable disease . . .'

The chance wasn't so small, it seemed, that you could just
drop by the crypt to have a look at what was going on. Ian told
me that if I was interested in the exhumation, I'd have to see a
doctor first. 'To make sure that you've been inoculated against
smallpox,' he added. And it wasn't sufficient to consult my own
GP. I would have to be seen at the site, by a government medic,
a Home Office pathologist who had been assigned to the project.
'It'll have to be on one of the days when she's here,' said Ian, his
voice fainter down the phone: he was checking a diary or day-
planner, to see when the pathologist would be able to vet me and
pronounce me fit to enter the plague pit of Holborn. This was a
matter of going by the rule book, I told myself, a nannying
proviso of an arcane health and safety law. That was how you
had to look at it. Otherwise, you'd have to think about the fact
that Home Office pathologists were the people who tended to get
called in after horrific deaths had made blood-spattered
headlines. You'd have to entertain the thought that the pox
doctor was on hand against the small but real possibility of the
killer bug getting loose again.

In *Oliver Twist*, Dickens's young hero walks past Holborn

Circus with Bill Sikes, glances up at St Andrew's Church clock
and notices that it is 'hard upon seven'. I had been past St
Andrew's many times. It was the largest of Wren's parish
churches. It was on Holborn Viaduct, at the easterly end of
Holborn Circus. I thought of it as marking the true boundary of
the City. The church used to face the old *Daily Mirror* building,
where I once did a handful of reporting shifts on the short-lived
London Daily News (the newspaper offices have since been
replaced by a supermarket's HQ). When I covered trials at
the Old Bailey for *Channel 4 News*, I would walk the mile or
two from the office to the court through the office refits and
make-overs that were always going on in that part of town,
cool, woody air wafting from entombed spaces, the damp,
underground air escaping, and my route would invariably take
me past St Andrew's. Unlike Oliver Twist, I didn't look for the
clock but for the figures of a male and female in seventeenth-
century dress who appeared on the west front tower. They might
have been the characters in a Stuart weathervane. In fact, they
represented the pupils of a charity school and had been
requisitioned from the façade of the former Parochial School in
nearby Hatton Garden. I had even been inside the church once
or twice and admired the gallery and the chequerboard tiles and
the stained glass in memory of John Thavie, a medieval
Londoner whose bequest to St Andrew's was, incredibly, still
holding the place together some seven hundred years later. It
wasn't that Thavie had been outstandingly rich. He had enjoyed
as many aliases as a master criminal, being variously aka Tavey,
Thavey, Thavie and Tavy, but his line was linen-armoury. He
made the padded tunics which were worn beneath the protective
iron, and had to be strong enough to keep out stray swords.
When Thavie died in 1348, he left land and property to St
Andrew's. The income from this was to pay for 'one fit chaplain'
to pray for Thavie's soul and that of his lady wife, Alice.
Charitably, the armour-maker extended the benison of these

verses to the souls of 'all the faithful departed this life'. Not even this marked the legacy as unusual. John Thavie would have been just another name on a list of forgotten benefactors if it had not been for the last clause in his will. Crucially, he had bequeathed 'all that tenement wherein I inhabit', plus his three shops, to sustain the *fabric* of the church, '*ad fabricationem ecclesiae*'. This clause couldn't be interpreted by Edward VI's grasping bailiffs as money 'for superstitious purposes' – their favourite pretext for getting their hands on the pelf of the godly – so they had no choice but to let the bequest stand. Fittingly, Thavie himself has entered the bricks and mortar of St Andrew's. He has been lying in the crypt since the fourteenth century, though not even his generosity would prevent him from joining the exodus in the twenty-first.

Thavie's open-handedness, and his lawyer's canny way with a contract, guaranteed a future for the church, which had had a tentative if tenacious foothold in Holborn since the days of Alfred the Great. In AD 951, a charter of Westminster Abbey mentions a wooden building dedicated to 'Sancte Andreas', probably a rudimentary wayside chapel where travellers and pilgrims prayed for protection on their journey or gave thanks for a safe return home.

On a morning when the Home Office pathologist and I could both attend St Andrew's, I presented myself at the church which the linen-armourer had bankrolled with such happy prescience. It was a suitably bone-cold day in the middle of December. I told myself that a low temperature ought to keep the smell of the bodies down; a strange thing to take comfort in, given the other hazards of the crypt, and not a particularly intelligent one – some of those cadavers had been in the ground for centuries; one winter's day, with temperatures marginally below the seasonal norm, wasn't going to put a crimp in the putrefaction process. But it was the stench that I had most qualms about, even more than the plague itself. If I thought about it, I could still smell the

gag-making odour of a semi-detached house that a schoolfriend
and I had cleared for pocket money one long-ago summer, after
its senile owner had been removed to a home, the orderlies
having guided her through the chicane of half-empty milk bottles
that she had been in the habit of stacking on every surface. And
though my pal and I had joked about it at the time, no one had
actually died in that house.

On the quiet side of St Andrew's, away from Holborn Viaduct
and out of the guileless gaze of the seventeenth-century orphan
pupils, blue tarpaulins the size of ship's canvases screened a
scaffolding frame. The sheets were to keep out the elements and
to conceal what was going on beneath the church from office
workers, whose buildings otherwise had unobstructed views into
the church grounds.

Ian Grey's office also looked out onto the tarpaulins. In
person, Ian was a gentle, portly man who reminded me a little of
the British actor David Troughton. He made coffee and told me
that he, too, was waiting for the all-clear from the doctor before
entering the crypt. 'Obviously, when the remains are still in the
coffin, there's no problem.' Ian was stirring hot water onto the
granules. 'But if there are spores, well, that's different. Especially
now, after September 11, anthrax, and what have you.' I began
to appreciate a hitherto unsuspected resonance to the word
'spores'.

They'd been putting off clearing out the crypt at St Andrew's
for sixty years, said Ian. The church had suffered a direct hit
from the Luftwaffe on the night of 16 April 1941, in the week
when 100,000 incendiary bombs fell on central London.
Although the tower and walls had somehow remained upright,
the interior was completely destroyed. An anonymous
eyewitness, writing in 1950, said, 'I can well remember watching
the blazing ruins, while the firemen looked on helplessly, with
only a trickle of water dripping from their hoses.' Tons of rubble
finished up in the crypt. It naturally collected there after the

bombing, though some of it had also been shoved there, out of harm's way, as the ecclesiastical dust was settling. Though the church was rebuilt, and reconsecrated in October 1961, nothing was done about the debris. For the most part, said Ian, the coffins had simply been covered up by the muck and stone, but some caskets had been ruptured, and the bodies they held had been 'exposed and desecrated'. He handed me a press release which he had prepared: 'There is recent evidence that the large volume of debris is causing structural damage to the church,' it read. 'The rubble is soaking up moisture and transmitting it to the walls particularly at the north-west and east ends of the building which are continually damp.'

There had been attempts to remedy the problem in the past, but they had come unstuck because of the costs involved. But the Guild Church Council had attracted the necessary funds this time, said Ian. The plan was to convert the crypt into a restaurant, chapel and meeting rooms. In time, the space might also stage theatrical productions. But first it had been necessary to persuade the Diocese of London to look favourably on the extraordinary petition from St Andrew's to raise a thousand dead.

Ian and I were joined by a man called Danny, the site manager. He led us to the scaffolding. Beside this framework were Portakabins stacked on top of each other, for the use of the men and women who were working in the crypt. We climbed the stairs and found a blonde woman in one of the prefab cabins, frying breakfast. On the wall were the following: a photo of the footballer Jaap Stam (one of the workers looked like him, evidently); a diagram of coffins from a variety of perspectives and elevations (it reminded me of one of those old, two-dimensional charts of a slave galley, demonstrating how the human cargo was shoehorned into the hold); a photograph of a zinc coffin which had already been recovered from the crypt; and a sheet of paper with the heading 'Sweep', a column of first names underneath this on the left-hand side of the paper, and a table of four-figure numbers on the right. This represented a lottery organised by the workers, a wager on the total number of remains that they would eventually remove from the crypt. The figures in the right-hand column of the sweepstake climbed to 2,300. This was more than twice as many as Ian Grey's estimate of a thousand-strong exhumation tally, which I had thought extravagant.

Pat Toop came into the Portakabin for a mug of tea. He was a big, craggy man in white paper overalls; craggy teeth, too. The firm which had been contracted to carry out the exhumation was named after Toop, a staunch Catholic from south London who was its boss and patriarch. It was a family business. The blonde who was now setting sausages down in sizzling fat was Toop's daughter-in-law. Toop was a wonderfully mournful name, borrowed from a lost draft of *Oliver Twist* and perfectly suited to the family business. As their trade was described to me by Toop himself, it involved 'lifting people', a euphemism which was as much for the benefit of the decent and conscientious Mr Toop, I felt, as it was for any of his more squeamish clients. Toop lit a cigarette. Veins threaded his craggy nose. He was sixty-eight. His firm had taken on the St Andrew's job themselves, Toop told me, they weren't working as subcontractors of a bigger concern such as Necropolis. I liked the sound of Necropolis, though not in the same way that I liked the sound of Toop. The toney, Greco-Roman syllables lent the concern of Necropolis a touch of class, while at the same time putting a little distance between the board of directors and the way they made their money. The name also reminded me of the 2002 novel *The Necropolis Railway* by Andrew Martin, which was based on the true story of a black-clad Victorian train which ferried coffins from storage under the arches at Waterloo station to a vast cemetery at Woking in Surrey; a kind of InterCity for stiffs. Funeral parties accompanied the dear departed on their final journeys, which left as often as a dozen times a day. The

Brookwood Necropolis Railway embarked mourners according to their social class and their religion, and these niceties were also observed in the range of accommodation provided for the dead. The company incorporated a skull and crossbones into the livery of its trains. Brookwood is still the biggest cemetery in the country but the London platforms of the railway were bombed in 1941 and never rebuilt. There was a ghostly echo of the service in 1979, when a funeral train drew out of Waterloo carrying the body of Lord Mountbatten, but all that's left of the Brookwood Necropolis Railway is the 1902 booking office on Westminster Bridge Road. It's since been taken over by a firm of shipbrokers but you can still make out the original tiles, the cornices worked in the shape of flowers, and the gas mantles over the door.

In the Toops' Portakabin, the fare on offer was not limited to the hearty breakfast which Pat's daughter-in-law was preparing. There was also a plate of mince pies, knobbily home-made and dusted with caster sugar. They were the delicious handiwork of the Home Office pathologist, who was referred to by the workers as 'the Doc'. The Doc was on site, but for the moment there was no sign of her. 'Lovely old girl but a bit strict,' Toop confided. 'She doesn't shout at you when she's unhappy about something, but you get the message all the same.'

When the Doc finally turned up at the Portakabin, she proved to be as advertised. In her spectacles and tweed skirt, she might have been the inspirational if slightly dotty science mistress of a girls' boarding school. She appraised me over her half-moons with a disinterested expression. 'Let's have a look at your arm,' she instructed. As I mentioned, it was a cold day, but the Portakabin was warm, warm with frying. I took off my anorak and my mushroom rollneck. My entire subfusc wardrobe had been picked out in the knowledge that it could end up attracting charnel-house grime, or, in the event of a particularly gory episode, my vomit. The Doc turned my bare arm over for a time.

It seemed that she was able to detect the puncture mark, the botched skin graft of a scar, which confirmed that I'd been inoculated against smallpox. I was now approved by the Home Office to enter a plague pit. It was Ian Grey's turn. Was it my imagination or was Ian slightly disappointed when the Doc passed him fit for the crypt? I put my clothes back on and went outside. One of Toop's men handed me a paper boilersuit and a hard hat. There was no getting out of it now.

Under the tarpaulins, a toxic or nuclear incident appeared to be in progress, albeit one which was being handled with textbook calm by the scrubbed and gloved figures in front of me. The activity centred on the stone flank of St Andrew's. A low arch was set in the wall, leading to the crypt. The arch appeared to be blocked up with red-brown earth, as if it had been choked by a mudslide, with only the top of this opening clear. There was an impression of light beyond it and of work going on. Hooped tinfoil tubes snaked into the crypt, supplying fresh air. Dominating the scene, however, was a conveyor belt. It was winding out of the mouth of the arch, churning soil and brick from the crypt to the surface. A ginger-haired lad in a hard hat bearing the legend 'Boy George' was sifting the contents of the belt.

'What are you looking for?' I asked him.

'Bones,' said Boy George. 'Coffin handles. Stuff like that.' I thought of the unsuspecting City workers with their bagged breakfasts, passing within a few yards of us. Items which aroused Boy George's curiosity were identified, as far as possible, and marked up. This was as meticulous as it was macabre, but it was something else as well: frankly, wasn't this tagging and wrapping a little unnecessary? After all, nobody had been interred in the crypt for at least a hundred years. Who was going to mind a fragment of bone going astray? Who would step forward to claim a used coffin handle? I was being shown around by Mark Toop, the old man's son, and I asked him about the need for such thoroughness. He nodded towards the crypt. 'They've all got descendants,' he said. 'You'd expect it, too, if it was your own family.'

He asked me, 'Are you ready to go in?'

Yes, I said. Yes, I was ready. I took a deep breath and followed Mark. We eased ourselves past the conveyor belt, half slid on the bank of mud, and by the time we had straightened up again, we were inside the crypt. Electric lights had been rigged up. I saw that we were surrounded by a series of arched brick burial chambers, each the size of a generous domestic garage, leading off a central defile. The two compartments to either side of us had been cleared of topsoil. Elsewhere, further into the crypt, the spoil gathered in drifts to waist-height. In the half-light, men were to be seen loading clods of earth onto the conveyor belt as if they were colliers, sending bony shards and rusted trimmings up to Boy George. Lead shavings like strips of ash bark were stacked near the mouth of the crypt. They belonged to lead caskets which had fallen to pieces.

I realised that I had been holding my breath all this while. Now I had to let it out, I had to risk a lungful of crypt air, to say nothing of a noseful. Like a fastidious diner sampling a questionable vintage, I tested the air on my palate and it was – well, it was OK, it wasn't too bad. It had the chalky smell of disturbed earth, of air collected in a cool, damp place.

Next to the spot where Mark and I were standing, a crouching man in a boiler suit was addressing his trowel to something poking out of the mud. The man was an archaeologist from the Museum of London and the object of his interest, I now saw, was a lump of perished wood. I recognised it as wood because it was a woody colour, the colour of a strong cup of tea. It wouldn't be that colour, couldn't be, if it was something else altogether, something else that you might find in a crypt, if it was—

'Bone,' said the man from the Museum of London, looking up at me. He was surely mistaken, though, because as he removed more earth from around the so-called bone, he exposed what was clearly a substantial tea-coloured root vegetable or tuber, a swede, perhaps, or—

'A skull,' he said. He touched its smooth pate as tenderly as if it was still connected to a living soul. The archaeologist must have noticed my expression because he went on, 'That's just the effect of the natural dye from the elm wood. They go that colour when the coffins rot.'

Could the skull have belonged to one of the famous personages interred at St Andrew's? Because of its location near the heart of the City, the church had long been associated with the great and the good, in death as in life. The dramatis personae of its story compared favourably to that of any other parish church in England. No less a figure than Henry VIII had taken the role of godfather at the St Andrew's font, at the baptism of the future Earl of Southampton in 1545. Many celebrated clerics had practised at the church, including John Hackett who defied Cromwell's troops in 1624 when they were dispatched to stop him using the outlawed Book of Common Prayer. The soldiers entered the church and cocked a flintlock to Hackett's temple. Coolly, he told them, 'I'm doing my duty. Now do yours.' At the sight of this courageous exhibition of conscience, the Puritan infantry backed down, and Hackett survived to become Bishop of Lichfield. Much later, the engineer Mark Brunel was married at St Andrew's, as was the essayist William Hazlitt, with Charles Lamb as his best man and Mary Lamb as bridesmaid. In 1827, a surgeon called William Marsden came across a young woman dying in St Andrew's churchyard. Marsden was unable to find a bed for her at any of the local hospitals. After her death, he set up a surgery in a room in nearby Greville Street to treat parishioners free of charge, and later founded the Royal Free Hospital in Gray's Inn Road (it has since moved to its present home in Hampstead).

As well as the church's medieval benefactor, Thavie, the

distinguished dead of the parish include Thomas Chatterton, the precocious poet who poisoned himself at the age of seventeen in a garret in Brooke Street. Sir Edward Coke, who was Elizabeth I's Attorney General, and who later prosecuted the gunpowder plotters, lay in the crypt, as did the renowned organist Daniel Purcell, brother of the composer, and Dr Henry Sacheverell, a former rector of St Andrew's. Sacheverell achieved notoriety in the eighteenth century when he was tried and convicted by Parliament for preaching a seditious sermon at St Paul's. It was impossible to hold a full roll-call of the dead: complete records dated from no earlier than 1831.

Mark Toop and I pressed deeper into the crypt. I was now clambering up dunes and hillocks of spoil, trying not to think too much about my next handhold, in case a hand was what it turned out to be. In the chambers which had yet to be cleared, it was apparent that more than mud awaited the Toops and their team. Fantastically buckled lead caskets were protruding from the earth like an installation by Salvador Dalí in one of his less playful moods. These sensational effects had been achieved by the vibrations of an air raid five decades earlier, by the impact of tons of rubble rattling down into the crypt, by time, by water. But to look at the caskets, you would have thought that they had been superheated until the lead was malleable, and then twisted into their profane shapes. They reminded me of the vanished fashion for blowtorching classic Coca-Cola bottles until their elegant necks were stretched into glowing icicles.

Mark told me that the Toops and their men had come across many oyster shells in the spoor. In London's gastropubs, the bivalve was the latest discovery, or rediscovery. But it had been a jaggedly prototype fast food in the days when gravediggers were lugging it to work in their snap tins. Londoners' dependency on this workaday delicacy is recorded in street names in the east of the city – Oystergate Walk, Oyster Row – and it was the poor man's dinner as late as Dickens's day. 'Poverty and oysters always seem to go together,' opines Sam Weller in *The Pickwick Papers.*

Mark pointed out the rusted links of chains which were protruding from the soil. Some of them were attached to the blood-red bricks. The chains had been used to restrain coffins: not necessarily to protect them from grave-robbers, though this was certainly a concern, but more likely to ensure that the occupants didn't lose their privileged position, as close as possible to the high altar (albeit some feet beneath it).

'But that doesn't make you more holy.' This was the unillusioned voice of Pat Toop; as befits a man in his line, he called a spade a spade. The old man had caught us up. 'It's what you do in life that counts,' he went on. All around us was proof of the levelling effect of the Reaper. Someone must once have parted with quite a sum for the handsome cartouche on the wall before us, which bore the initials GW and the date 1699. But it was an armorial in death's ante-room, to be admired by sextons and grave-robbers, and catch the eye of crypt-clearers as they took a breather three centuries later.

Despite Pat Toop's terrible solemnity, which amounted almost to a code of practice, he was absorbed by his work. He was intrigued by brick partitions which his men had come across. These pieces of pointing weren't part of the superstructure. Perhaps the deceased dignitaries of the parish were walled up behind them. The Toops thought that a brick bunker directly beneath the altar probably housed the best known of them. They would perhaps include the outspoken Dr Sacheverell, who had left instructions that this was where he preferred to repose when his time came, which it did in 1724.

The Toops showed me a casket which looked as though it had been accessed with a can-opener. This was evidence of a long-ago grave-robbing, they said. 'They would have gone straight for the arms,' said Mark. 'Get the rings, the jewellery.'

'Wasting their time,' countered his father. 'That was their

inheritance in those days, jewellery.' Pat Toop turned to me. 'I'll
bet your grandmother's still got *her* mother's ring.' His point was
that even well-to-do Londoners had eschewed the vanity of going
to meet their maker in all their finery, shrewdly endowing it to
their relatives instead.

Grave-robbing was no mere blasphemous anachronism, it
seemed. A more sophisticated villainy was practised to this day
in the lifting business. It seemed it was as driven by cost, by the
bottom line, as any other. There was some tension here, some
history. Both Pat Toop and his son expressed their dim view of
the way that some of their rivals got things done. Toop Senior
pointed out a child's coffin – a heartbreaking shoebox – and said
of an unspecified competitor, 'They'd take the lead off that to sell
it.'

With or without their trinkets and baubles, our silent
companions in the crypt were the excellent cadavers of St
Andrew's, to borrow the resonant Sicilian coinage. 'Their less
eminent friends and neighbours', as Ian Grey had put it in his
press release, had been buried in a churchyard to the north of St
Andrew's. But this boneyard had been dug up by the Victorians,
along with the late poor of the parish, in order to make way for
the Holborn Viaduct, and the bodies had been reinterred out at
Ilford where the City of London maintained a cemetery. The
viaduct was constructed in the 1860s to bridge the valley of the
Fleet, and to link Holborn with Newgate Street. The face of
Holborn was thereby transformed: Holborn Circus hadn't
existed before the work began, and neither had St Andrew
Street or Charterhouse Street. In fact, until the middle of the
nineteenth century, the tower of St Andrew's Church had
commanded all it surveyed, from atop a promontory known
locally as 'Heavy Hill'. This was such a strenuous climb that
horses were said to drop dead from exertion outside the church.
On nearby Snow Hill, part of the same range of bluffs
approaching the City, young toughs were in the reprehensible

habit of putting old ladies into beer barrels and rolling them down the slope.

It was little wonder that parishioners who occupied paupers' graves had been uprooted so summarily. To the Victorians, Holborn and especially Farringdon were synonymous with squalor, an association which may have had its psychological roots in the tarnished reputation of the Fleet, the filthiness which Jane the walking guide had explored with such relish in her tour of the buried river. Dickens disparaged Saffron Hill, in the river valley, as 'the Venice of drains'. In *Oliver Twist*, this floating city was home to the thieves' kitchen run by Fagin. Swift had written witheringly that 'turnip tops came tumbling down the flood'. (Could this reference have been in the mind of another great London balladeer, the late Ian Dury, when he left instructions for his last, posthumous album to bear the self-deprecating title *Ten More Turnips From the Tip*?) Farringdon's dubious reputation went back to the turn of the seventeenth century, when Fleet Prison on Farringdon Street was at the height of its notoriety. John Donne was incarcerated there after being found guilty of marrying a minor. Just after the Great Fire, Farringdon filled up with refugees from the charred and smoking remains of a London neighbourhood known as Alsatia, a notorious no-go area located in present-day Blackfriars.

Of course, there had been nothing unique about the dirtiness of the Fleet. All of London's waterways were fouled. At the time the viaduct was being built, Bazalgette's work had not begun and at least thirty sewers were still discharging directly into the Thames. Of the eight companies selling water to Londoners, only two failed to draw their supplies in similarly unmediated fashion from the stinking river. Not even members of the royal household were immune from waterborne disease.

Now Holborn and Farringdon were really quite respectable, and inhabitants went about their business untroubled by the fear of cholera. Nor did they have the slightest suspicion that there was a risk of plague spores getting loose in the neighbourhood. The proverbial visiting Martian might have raised an eyebrow or three at this sunny complacency. After all, London had had the plague, on and off, for a lot longer than it had been free of it: roughly speaking, a millennium or so of documented history compared to less than four hundred years. And pub folklore saw to it that even the most scientifically illiterate citizen understood that the deadly virus was merely dormant. Moreover, there was a good case for saying that the Black Death, a particularly virulent strain of the lurgy, was London's best-known or signature disease, the cockney canker.

The first recorded epidemic of plague struck the city in AD 664. Bede plotted its awful progress through the south-east of England. Two years later, it carried off the community of the newly founded Barking Abbey, the parent body of the church of All Hallows by the Tower where the annual ceremony of beating the bounds extends to the middle of the Thames. A more widespread pestilence took hold in 1248, coinciding with famine. As the price of imported corn rose to fifteen shillings a quarter, it was the malnourished poor who were hit hardest by the disease, though its prominent casualties also included Fulk Basset, the Bishop of London.

Black Death, or *Pasteurella pestis*, arrived here from the Continent and raged between 1347 and 1350. It had entered the capital by the end of September 1348 and was well established throughout the city by 1 November. The onset of Black Death was sudden. Victims suffered swellings, haemorrhages, high fever, agonising thirst and delirium. Death, briefly detained by the primitive remedies of the day, followed implacably. The cause of the fatal sickness was an awful mystery. It was often attributed to the supernatural, seen as a curtain-raiser to a biblical apocalypse. It wasn't until as late as 1905 that scientists established that rats acted as a vector for the fleas whose bites spread the contagion. One theory about the Black Death is that it was imported from France in fleeces after Edward III re-established the wool trade. Once the epidemic took hold, the king took the decision to prorogue Parliament, which had been due to sit in January 1349. 'A plague of deadly pestilence had broken out in the said place,' he said, 'and had daily increased in severity so that great fears were entertained for the safety of those coming there at that time.'

In the absence of the fortunate MPs, the plague reached its apogee. London burial grounds were soon full to overflowing, and new ones were hastily dug and consecrated. The biggest was in Southwark, where some two hundred corpses were interred every day. Historians estimate that the Black Death killed half the population of fourteenth-century England. If anything, the devastation of London was even worse. The transmission of the disease was encouraged by the narrow, busy and filthy streets, crowded houses and noisome sanitary conditions. The toll among Londoners has been variously put at between 50,000 and 100,000. Records of the day attest to the extent of the scourge. Wills presented to the Court of Hustings increased tenfold in the plague years and reveal that entire families perished. Eight warders of the Cutlers' Company died in 1349, and six men who had been created officers of the Hatters' Company in 1347 were all dead before three years had elapsed. The Abbot of Westminster and twenty-seven monks died and were buried in a mass grave in the cloister, not far from the undercroft where the ragged regiment of royal effigies is on parade today. With one exception, the brothers and sisters who served at the Hospital of St James died in May 1349. The survivor, the warden, succumbed himself not long after.

The Black Death exhausted itself in the early 1350s but its impact on London continued to be felt long afterwards. Because of its terrifying cost in human lives, Edward ordered measures to improve hygiene and sanitation. In 1361, he commanded the Lord Mayor and the sheriffs to exercise greater control over the slaughter of cattle within the city. His Majesty wanted to prevent 'the putrid blood running down the streets and the bowels cast into the Thames whence abominable and most filthy stench proceeds causing sickness and many other evils'.

Despite royal concern, the plague came and went among Londoners like the flu does now, albeit with a drastically less favourable prognosis. Parliament, and even the court itself, were frequently relocated as far as possible from the overcrowded streets and poor hygiene which were understood to exacerbate the epidemics. However, a doom was coming which would overshadow all previous afflictions. 'Some heard voices warning them to be gone,' wrote Defoe, 'for there would be such a plague in London that the living would not be able to bury the dead.' Sure enough, among the rat-infested alleys of north-west London, and into Whitechapel and Stepney, spread the 1665 epidemic which would later merit the sobriquet 'the Great Plague', if for no other reason than its sheer body count. In that year, there were more than ninety-seven thousand recorded burials in the London area, perhaps a fifth of the entire population and five times the usual number. In Stepney alone, they were somehow disposing of six hundred corpses a week in high summer.

If my inspection at the hands of the Home Office pathologist wasn't enough to alert me to the remote but real hazard of plague spores in St Andrew's crypt, there was also documentary evidence that parishioners had died of the disease. 'In every parish along the Fleet, the plague stayed and destroyed,' wrote a London doctor. St Andrew's, found hard by this reeking waterway, certainly qualified. In *A Journal of the Plague Year*, Defoe said of the Holborn area, 'It began to be suspected that the plague was among the people at that end of town, and that many had died of it, though they had taken care to keep it as much from the knowledge of the public as possible.' Defoe totted up the bills of mortality kept by the parish clerk at St Andrew's, and by his counterpart in a neighbouring City parish. 'The increase of the bills stood thus: the usual number of burials in a week, in the parishes of St Giles-in-the-Fields and St Andrew's, Holborn, were from twelve to seventeen or nineteen each, few more or less; but from the time that the plague first began in St Giles's parish, it was observed that the ordinary burials increased in number considerably.' As early as January 1665, there were two weeks when the tally of bills at St Andrew's was 23 and 25.

It was a while before Londoners woke up to the crisis, perhaps because they had been misinformed, as Defoe claimed. Samuel Pepys did not deem it necessary to send his wife to the airy environs of Woolwich until July, only joining her there himself a month later. The moderns would say that the diarist was in denial. He had seen houses daubed with the crude red cross signifying the plague as early as June, when he had walked up Drury Lane 'on the hottest day that I ever felt in my life'. In truth, the inferno was already raging. Defoe wrote, 'It began at St Giles's and the Westminster end of the town, and it was in its height in all that part by about the middle of July, viz., in St Giles-in-the-Fields, St Andrew's, Holborn, St Clement Danes, St Martin's-in-the-Fields, and in Westminster.'

In the summer of 1665, the toll rose to more than eight thousand a week. With layers of bodies buried only inches below the surface of the earth, the air quivered with rankness. Orders were given for the digging of plague pits, huge holes sunk in vacant patches of ground and coated with quicklime. Gravediggers, often very understandably the worse for drink, worked in shifts, day and night, but were outpaced by the daily cartloads of cadavers. The prophecies recorded by Defoe had come true: the living weren't able to bury their dead. It proved impossible to inter all the corpses within twenty-four hours of death and some lay stacked like wax figures in the streets for days at a time.

Efforts to impose quarantine broke down. It's said that overcrowding in the wards of London hospitals and pest-houses was so great that visitors had to walk *across* the beds instead of around them. By August, most of those who were accustomed to exercising authority in the city had either died or fled. 'But now, how few people I see, and those walking like people that had taken leave of the world,' wrote Pepys.

Some ten thousand citizens made a home for themselves on the Thames. Others wandered the countryside, sometimes finding themselves on the receiving end of a volley of rocks and dung hurled by villagers who feared contamination. When one sickly Londoner, far from home, crept into a farm hut in Dorchester to die, the locals dug a vast pit and swept the entire building into it, corpse and all, sooner than risk handling the body. In the metropolis, some of the men who drove the carts laden with bodies contracted the plague themselves, and died at the reins; their horses are said to have plodded on all the same, dragging their horrific burden.

In St Andrew's crypt more than four hundred years later, plague victims were entombed in gloom and mud. You couldn't think of the hundreds – *thousands* – who occupied the dunes beneath your boots without shuddering, especially when you contemplated the bane which had removed so many of them. I was grateful to be in the company of old man Toop and his son, to be in their tender if horny hands. What this meant in practice, though, was that I had the benefit of their experience and the example of their dignity rather than, say, the tension-dissipating distraction of gallows humour. To Londoners of the twenty-first century, the plague was an ungraspable monstrosity. But exposure to death of any sort, let alone ugly, premature death, was thankfully rare. The Toops, by contrast, had supped long on the horrors of the flesh. They recalled a previous job, in which they had been engaged to lift bodies from beneath the car park of Guy's Hospital near London Bridge. 'We found loads of arms and legs,' Mark told me.

'By themselves?'

'By themselves. People used to get paid to donate their limbs. The doctors would practise amputations on them and then get rid of them.'

Dan, the site manager, joined us, as our conversation continued to dwell on matters of mortality. At one time, he said, four out of five infants in London failed to survive. But apart from the child's coffin which Pat had shown me, the team had so far come across a disproportionately low number of undersize caskets. They were at a loss to account for this. At the other end of the growth charts and development indices was the putative Giant of Holborn, a man of seven foot or more whose femur had one day glimmered from the topsoil. Mark mimed where this outsize leg bone would come to against him. In this dumb show, he might have been demonstrating the crutch-brushing proportions of a fisherman's wader.

I made a terrible mistake and asked the Toops if their work had given them a different attitude to death, a more philosophical approach. Pat turned his head away and so it was left to Mark to tell me about the death earlier that year of his twin sister. 'We thought about chucking it in after that, didn't we?' he said, looking at the old man. After a moment, I heard Pat say, 'She would have wanted us to carry on.'

Later, Pat told me about a commission the firm had once had to exhume two dozen nuns from a rural convent. 'I had a priest in to bless my men every day,' he said.

'Every day? Was that really necessary?'

Toop rounded on me in the gloom. 'Would you want to lift twenty-two brides of Christ without being blessed?' he asked, unanswerably.

The Toops were active in raising money for charity. After a hard week on site, limited only by Corporation of London rules, which specified no work before eight o'clock in the morning or after five at night, the weekend would find the Toops on market stalls. They sold large toy animals in aid of good causes. Indeed,

in the church garden was an old estate car belonging to the
Toops, with its back seat full of big stuffed cats. The sight of it
made me think of the gangster film *Donnie Brasco*, in which
Cosa Nostra foot soldier Al Pacino is given a lion and keeps it in
his car, prodding morsels of steak to it through a rear window.

By the autumn of 1665, the terrible blight which had fallen on
London began to lift. In November, the weekly head count of the
dead was still appalling – nine hundred – but then it had been a
great deal worse. Those who had fled the capital began to return.
The Lord Mayor threatened a levy on the homes of the
prosperous unless they made haste and opened them up again.
The court of Charles was restored to the capital on 1 February,
1666, to a peal of bells from St James's.

We left the crypt and went out into the crisp winter morning.
In the Portakabin, Mark's wife cooked us a late breakfast: the full
English. I heard the terrible story of Mark knocking down and
killing a woman of ninety, who had stepped off a bus to buy
some eggs and walked into the path of his car without looking.
She was taken to hospital but was pronounced dead. A short
time later, she turned up at the family undertaking business. 'That
really done me in,' said Mark, looking grey.

I thought of the idea I had sometimes come across, the
consoling proposition that pain and hardship were somehow
attracted to those who had the moral equipment to deal with
them. It was like the myth that only the good die young. The
Toops' daily contact with death had not left them blasé in the
face of it. Instead, it had reinforced their faith. Under the screen
of tarpaulins at St Andrew's, an unmarked white van pulled up
in the late afternoon. The Toops and their men filled it with
discreet containers of remains. They were bringing them out at
a rate of more than a hundred a week. Every morning at seven
o'clock, the van left for Ilford, where the wealthy of the parish
were posthumously reunited with their poorer brethren. Every
morning, Mark Toop saw the van off, his hard hat sombrely

doffed. Six months into the exhumation, the thousand remains that Ian Grey had expected to emerge from beneath St Andrew's, the 2,300 chalked up as the top guess in the sweepstake, had become 3,000, and the crypt still wasn't empty yet.

SPOILS

London's Treasures

A wine cellar in the middle of London was once the cobwebby setting for cloak-and-dagger meetings held by the future emperor of France. He summoned his co-conspirators to a wine shop and, armed with a candle and a couple of decent bottles, led his allies deep into the dusty vaults. To the muffled accompaniment of horse-drawn carriages rattling on the cobbles overhead, he insisted on searching the cellars, tapping the casks and peering into empty ones, before getting down to business. At last, surrounded by cases awaiting dispatch to distinguished clients, he began to speak, dictating his messages from exile to his beloved French nation. This was not Chesterton's fictitious *Napoleon of Notting Hill* but the real-life founder of the Deuxième Empire: the Napoleon of St James's.

One of his subterranean secretaries was a man named Sherer, of *The Standard*. He found the work hard going. 'It was no light job with which I was confronted,' Sherer wrote.

> Besides appeals to the French army and people, there was over a score of proclamations for distribution in the chief towns of France. The proclamations were devised to suit the tastes and feelings of the inhabitants of the different cities. During the whole time Napoleon never once left my side. Suspecting all, trusting none, even at this period in his career, he evidently thought that were he to turn his back, I should pocket one of his copies.

Napoleon's anxious draughtsmanship indirectly benefited London, repaying the city's hospitality to him. When he finally presented the Prefect of Paris, Baron Haussmann, with plans for redesigning the French capital, the main thoroughfares were highlighted in primary colours, in red, yellow and green, according to their importance. This unheard-of finishing touch was taken up by later planners and designers, most notably the Mondrian of the Tube, Harry Beck.

It wasn't all business when Napoleon had one of his clandestine get-togethers. Following in his footsteps, modern-day visitors to the wine shop, Berry Brothers & Rudd, can still see the outsize set of scales on which, for light relief, Napoleon had his companions weighed. He spent two years in London, from 1838 to 1840. This was at the time of the Chartist riots, when the movement for universal suffrage which had begun in provincial England culminated in disorder and panic in the capital. Louis Napoleon was sworn in as a special constable and paced a beat in the West End, in the company of the cook from the Athenaeum. 'In the same unit was my great-great-great-great-great-grandfather, George Berry,' Simon Berry told me. 'The pair of them became firm friends. When the heat became a little too much, Napoleon hid in the cellars.' Simon gestured towards the bottle-lined vaults. 'I'm sure there must have been worse places to lie low.'

I had turned up late and scruffy for my meeting with Simon, scion of the vinous dynasty which has given its name to the business. By contrast, Simon was a character part in a Richard Curtis screenplay, with his chalk-stripe, his creaseless skin and a sandy fringe powdered grey. He wasn't the least put out by my untidiness. When I promised – untruthfully, as it turned out – to be more presentable if invited back to one of the firm's celebrated tastings, he waved away such rot. 'Oh, don't worry about that.' He wasn't offended by my lateness, though he did warn that he would have to be away by – I didn't catch the hour, in

Simon's attractively diffident groping for his watch-face. Around us, well-spoken young men traversed a rolling wooden floor. It was like the deck of a tea-clipper. There were bottles and barrels, and a sit-up-and-beg clerk's desk. It was all a far cry from Victoria Wine.

'Great old place,' I said.

'Rather fun, isn't it?' agreed Simon. He steered us into a far room with a view onto a yard. 'The smallest courtyard open to the public in London,' he said. 'Goes back to William and Mary.' Simon and I stood framed by the window. Beyond the courtyard was a building faced in white brick, and beyond that, the yellow elbow of a crane. Wider still and wider, this was a part of town which was in no hurry to catch up with modernity. Perhaps only P. G. Wodehouse could have done justice to the inter-bellum streets of St James's. You felt that the members of the Drones Club might at any moment windmill onto the pavement in a sandstorm of breadcrumbs. Creaking toffs still levered themselves from their clubs, and tradesmen continued to offer the personal touch. In this quarter, you half believed, Bertie Wooster drew breath. His shoes came from Lobbs bootmakers, his toiletries from a fogeyish purveyor of emollients (though in reality, of course, it was wealthy foreigners who did a lot of the spending).

Simon told me that the office we were in had once been a dining room, though it seemed on the small side for that function. Now it was a consulting room, a sommelier's surgery. There was a piece of cloth on a rod behind the glass in the door: it could be pulled across to ensure discretion. There were sketches, Edwardian caricatures, on the walls, and books had been laid down like bottles. Simon started to fill me in on the history of the cellars. 'Oh, it's cold in here,' he said suddenly, as if reproaching himself for a lack of manners. I was glad of the cool; I told Simon I was fine. (I thought that he had left the ancient bar-fire off, in deference to me, but by the time we returned to the room, hours later, one bar had begun feebly glowing.)

Berry Brothers have been trading from 3 St James's Street for three centuries. They're the oldest wine and spirit merchants in Britain, perhaps the world. As well as Simon Berry himself, half a dozen members of the family continue to oversee the operation, the seventh and eighth generations of the tribe to do so. As early as 1760, the firm was meeting the bibulous needs of George III. It supplies the royal family to this day, holding warrants from the Queen and the Prince of Wales.

Simon and I descended old flags to the cellars. Spirit flasks lined the staircase, one of them cast to resemble Asquith. 'In the old days, wine was always cheaper than the bottle it came in,' said Simon. 'Glass was very rare. Grandfather began the collection. I think he bought a job lot of stoneware.' I liked Simon. He was unstuffy, open, apparently happy enough to have me. I decided that Berrys' were peculiarly media-friendly when, down in the cellars, we got wind of an imminent party from BSkyB. But this wasn't a film crew, recording light relief from the 'war against terrorism'. It seemed that Sky executives quite often booked the wine merchants' dining room to do their brainstorming. I told Simon that I ought to bug the room, to eavesdrop on their Napoleonic plotting.

When Ford Madox Ford described the 'ragout of tid-bits so appealing and so innumerable' that made London what it was, he singled out 'miles of port-wine cellars'. He might have been talking about Berry Brothers, and probably was. The cellars were a fruity grotto of arched stone and brick, surmounted by splintered beams. Some of the wood below ground had originally formed part of the superstructure of a tennis court, an outhouse of St James's Palace. It was the brainchild of that tennis-mad monarch, Henry VIII, who was evidently not content with the four courts he had commissioned less than a mile away at Whitehall. Dating from the late seventeenth century and enlarged in the 1730s, Berry Brothers' vaults stretch from St James's Street along Pall Mall to Crown Passage: it's thought that the cellars were once linked by a door to the royal palace, a secret passage alas long since sealed up. The basement occupies a total of eight thousand square feet, as much as three of Henry's tennis courts. It's claimed to be the largest working wine cellar in London. It's split-level: in the lower basement are a dining room and lecture theatre, which Simon guided me around. There were water biscuits on a sideboard in the dining room, and thick iron hinges screwed to the long table, which falsely conveyed an impression of great age in this groaning board. In the adjacent lecture theatre were stainless-steel sinks which doubled as spittoons. The theatre was to be subsumed into the dining room when the latter was expanded. In turn, an unused chalky vault would be made habitable as a new lecture theatre ('the wine school').

In the upper basement, some of the 150,000 bottles on the premises could be seen stacked in pyramids of a dozen or so. These formations bore an authentic patina of unsmudged dirt. Berry Brothers' oldest wine was a comparatively impudent vintage, dating from no earlier than 1811, but there was sack going back to 1642. The firm's earliest list, from 1898, enterprisingly included four wines from Australia, following a well publicised tour by Robert Louis Stevenson of the vineyards of that country.

Located as far away as possible from the fumes and faint rumble of St James's, a smart young man called Michael was bent over a laptop and a sheaf of computer printouts in a blue-checked shirt. Despite his youth, it was clear at once that here was an adept of the wine trade, a magus of the methuselah. Michael and his laptop – and the firm's finest wines – were preserved in the humid conditions of the cellar, these discreetly maintained by a state-of-the-art extractor fan from France. I told Michael that I'd like to see the firm's most expensive bottle and he duly looked out a '28 Petrus from the musty recesses. It was worth £8,000, he said. I remembered a fuss over a dinner party of City traders who had toasted a deal in Petrus. Hadn't it cost them £8,000 at the restaurant, I wondered aloud?

One look at the barely suppressed incredulity on the faces of Simon and Michael and I knew that, once again, the puckish presence of a late British humorist was dogging my progress through St James's. Now I had become a buffoon from a Bateman cartoon: the man who thought dealers would run up a bar bill of four figures when enjoying a blow-out! Gently, the others corrected me. Lunch had set the party back a cool £44,000. 'Washed down with a couple of Kronenbourgs,' added Michael in a sorrowing voice. (Perhaps because of Michael's age, in other surroundings I might have reckoned him to be a man who is partial to a Kronenbourg, as, come to that, am I.)

'Of course, in a restaurant, they'd mark up the wine to at least twice what we charge,' said Simon. In fact, the six dealers had paid a top whack of £12,300 a bottle during lunch, which had been taken at the Petrus restaurant, then under the intimidating skillet of volatile celebrity chef Gordon Ramsay. The diners plumped for an agreeable '47. In the course of the same meal, in July 2001, they had also got through another two bottles of Petrus, at £11,600 and £9,400 respectively; a dirt-cheap '82 Montrachet at £1,400; and a £9,200 dessert wine. The six worked for Barclays Bank, which had just announced a round of redundancies. Officially, the bank took the view that staff dining was a private matter, but a source confided to the *Evening Standard* that bosses were 'apoplectic' about the publicity surrounding the dealers' beanfeast, and the six in turn paid with their jobs. One of them, Dayananda Kumar, told the newspaper that he was setting off to the North Pole. 'The whole situation is particularly funny because I'm a teetotaller,' he said bravely. Kumar had nevertheless chipped in £9,000 towards the bill.

One way and another, my trip through Berry Brothers' cellars was a reminder of the terrible potency of the grape. One of the lines of which Simon was fondest was a frisky Hungarian tipple first produced in the nineteenth century. The booze of choice of emperors and tsars, Tokay was made underground in the little town of Mad. It was swigged in tiny quantities, said Simon. 'The juice just comes off the grapes by itself.' In fact, Tokay was just so damn juicy that left to its own fructifying devices, it would simply tear through the cork: the wine had to be stored upright. Berrys had tipped a glass or two of the Mad firewater down the wine writer Hugh Johnson when he had last come to lunch in the dining room. But otherwise the Hungarian hooch was kept behind a sliding steel wicket in Berrys' holy of holies, with the wines that the firm was not prepared to sell.

'You won't sell them, Simon? Are you serious? So you keep them here just to drive your customers mad?'

He smiled. 'We offer them to our guests at tastings, and we auction them for charity. As a matter of fact, we auctioned a rather good bottle when we turned three hundred.'

Berry Brothers can trace its origins back to the restoration of the monarchy. It set up in premises which were considered highly desirable among tradesmen and courtiers by dint of their handiness for St James's Palace, which Henry VIII had fashioned out of the unpromising material of a medieval leper colony. In 1698, the Widow Bourne established her grocery, or 'Italian warehouse', opposite the palace, facing the royal tennis court. The weighing scales in the shop are a relic of the origins of the business as a general goods store. At first, the firm measured out bags of coffee, tea, spices and snuff for its customers. But by 1765, it had become fashionable to place your own personage on Berry Brothers' apparatus. This was in the days before you could reckon the pounds in the privacy of your own bathroom. Napoleon III included, the substantial figures who tipped the scales at 3 St James's Street amount to a veritable Who's Phew! of historical avoirdupois. To the gambler Charles James Fox, who plied his trade in the clubs of St James's, Berry Brothers was what a weighing room is to a professional jockey. The family's scales also took the strain of Pitt the Younger in 1783, shortly before he became Britain's youngest prime minister at the age of twenty-five; the seven sons of George III; Queen Victoria's 'wicked uncles', including the Prince Regent, later George IV; Robert Peel; Lord Byron; and Beau Brummel. The celebrated dandy had himself weighed no fewer than forty times, including once in 1822, six years after he had supposedly quit England for France in order to outrun his creditors.

A decade or so after Napoleon and his friends were making plans in the cellars, Berry Bros had the builders in to shore them up. This was for Wellington's funeral in 1852, when the vintners feared a cave-in as the Iron Duke's cortège drew heavily by. In the last century, orders made by Berry Brothers customers went to the bottom of the Atlantic with the *Titanic*. In the Second World War, 3 St James's was hit by an incendiary bomb, but a lot of the stock had already been evacuated by then. The firm once maintained nine cellars in London, but by the mid-sixties, the company had moved the bulk of its wine to Basingstoke. In their long history, Berry Brothers had seen many changes in drinking tastes. Simon himself was partial to elderly, flat champagne. 'It's a bit like dry sherry,' he admitted, 'but it's got an amazing depth of flavour.' He went on, 'What's the least fashionable wine you can think of?'

'A Blue Nun or something, I suppose.'

'Exactly.' Simon fetched out an unidentified bottle from Berrys' private stock. 'A 1921 Liebfraumilch,' he said, cradling it tenderly. 'It's actually very decent, and collectable.'

Simon and Michael told me about buyers from the Far East, of whom there were a growing number. 'They are insistent about presentation,' said Simon. 'If you showed them a bottle like this,' he went on, weighing the impressively aged but correspondingly grubby Liebfraumilch in his palm, 'they'd say, "Can't you take it away and clean it up?"' He made a slightly pained face, impersonating the fastidious wine novice. Simon himself was on the right side in this. 'It's only fermented grape juice,' he said.

It seemed that oriental sluicers were also emphatic about seeing labels on their wine, no matter that this was a comparatively new feature of the trade. Michael proved the point by digging out a port of great antiquity, and costliness, in an unmarked bottle. 'Some of the so-called labels you see are just faxes in reality,' he said. 'They've just been faxed over from the dealer to the customer, to keep him happy.'

A bottle of wine priced at £10,000 was sold at one of Berrys' outlets at Heathrow airport within twelve hours of its going on sale. Some at St James's had doubted the wisdom of putting such an expensive bottle on display. But it was snatched up by a Hong Kong Chinese, who carried it onto his flight. Simon was intrigued, and made some enquiries among friends in Hong Kong. They told him that they had heard of Simon's extravagant customer.

'Simon, don't you worry,' one chum told him. 'How long was this man in your shop?'

'It couldn't have been more than ten minutes.'

'Well, in that ten minutes, he would have *made* £10,000.'

Simon said, 'Some people have a problem finding ways to get rid of their money.' He eventually met the customer, who told him how much he had enjoyed the bottle of wine. ('That was a relief. I thought he was going to say that he hated it. Or that he'd dropped it.') The man had called friends who were also wine enthusiasts and they had opened it and 'seen it off'. This was what should happen, said Simon, the wine being drunk by people who enjoyed it, not put on a shelf to be looked at.

The Berrys had a sense for what would go down well with their customers. You could call it a nose. It had served the business well ever since Old Mother Bourne had allowed the aristocracy to loll about on her snuff scales as if they were hammocks. In addition to outlets at airports, Berry Brothers threw open their basement to meetings and presentations 'with up-to-date audio-visual equipment'. Berrys' handsomely printed price list included pen portraits of selected growers. Under the entry for a 1998 Rioja was a photograph of a scowling, bespectacled young man in a beard, and the following blurb: 'The philosophy of the estate is very traditional, with Juan Carlos Lopez de Lacalle adamant about producing hand-crafted wines.' Ludwig Hiedler, the viniculturist of a competitively priced Austrian dry white, bore the distinguishing mark of what looked like a recent duelling scar.

The range of services offered by Berry Brothers even included a cellar plan. 'Funded by standing order from as little as £75 a month', customers could acquire the habit of laying down wines. Sadly, the storage space in question wasn't the mature chambers beneath St James's – 'generally clients opt to have wine stored in our own temperature-controlled cellars in Basingstoke' – but at least wine-lovers could come to the place where the firm's story began, to take classes in wine, or to sample different vintages.

Berry Brothers' tastings were trendy. Kate Moss had been spotted at one, and they had been written up in the glossy pages of *Vanity Fair* ('wine buffs can clink glasses at Berry Brothers and Rudd's Wine School'). They were fashionable in the way that shooting briefly was, after Madonna and her English husband Guy Ritchie were said to have taken it up. Tastings had that indefinable tweedy quality that money can't buy – until it does. For the newly rich, the attraction was perhaps that the events were attended by antique-seeming ritual even more venerable than some of the vintages under consideration.

At my first tasting, I was immediately presented with a quandary of etiquette. Not to put too fine a point on it, it came down to this: 'Do you spit or do you swallow?' You might have thought that the title of the event made such a question unnecessary. It was a port *tasting*, after all; nothing there about port swigging, or port necking. But how wrong you would be. Although some fanciers of fortified wines were hawking into steel pails and scribbling notes with pencils, as if in some hellish emetic experiment, others were not.

'I start off spitting, but as the night wears on, I swallow,' allowed Mark, an investment manager built like a ninepin. He ruminated on the words in the same way that he savoured his drink, practically chewing a mouthful. You couldn't begrudge him leaving the tasting with more port inside him than when he went in, since he was paying £80 for the privilege. For this, his palate had the run of a score of the finest vintages bottled on the slopes of Oporto. Not to mention the chance of sluicing them amid the mellow brick of Berry Brothers' basement.

To the accompaniment of the silky, ship's-screw noise of air conditioning, tipplers circulated among damask-draped tables, accepting the equivalent of an optic or so of the ruby-coloured stuff from the Berry staff. The punters glugged and spat – or swallowed, at their discretion – before jotting down their thoughts on the ports. The illusion that these smartly dressed men and women were fastidiously keeping dance-cards reinforced an impression that the evening belonged to a bygone age.

I overheard one vintage being praised for its jam. Another was 'the Saab of ports': as good value and reliable as the Swedish tourer. Yet a third had an undertow of linctus, I felt, but it was a welcome change for me from the Ladas and Trabants of house wines. Seeking out Mark, the roly-poly investment manager, for further pointers, I found him holding his glass up to the light and squinting at it like a mechanic working on an axle. I made a note that he wasn't agitating it, as you might a balloon of cognac. (Here was a useful lesson: no storm in a port.) He said, 'I'm checking whether it has a watery edge. Do you see?'

The more port you drank – I mean, tasted – and the warmer the basement became, with the circulation of glowing aficionados, the more the chemical element of the drink seemed to separate in the glass, to stand up and be counted independently of the bouquet of fruit. In addition, I noticed that an attractively rosy bloom had begun to steal across one or two faces. An old boy who worked for one of Berry Brothers' suppliers came over to enquire whether I had ever been to the region of Portugal from where the eponymous grog hailed. I told him that I couldn't remember.

'One of the most unspoilt parts of Europe,' he said mistily.

'Perhaps you're not paying your workers enough,' I heard myself say.

He looked at me. 'Could be!' he said genially.

Naturally, there was an opportunity to go home with alcohol at the end of the night, though this was nothing so redolent of the high-street offie as reeling into St James's with a case of plonk in the crook of your arm: arrangements were made to have the port collected at a later date, or delivered. In the reception of 3 St James's, where the wooden floor seemed even more corrugated than before, I was fighting my way into my coat when a City boy told me that it had been one of the best tastings he had attended. 'I generally find I'm fifteen years younger than everyone else at these things. It's usually a case of, "Right, line up, we're all going to try this one now!" But this was very informal.' We stepped into St James's. 'Someone got me a ticket to this as a present. Thought it would be a good way of taking my appreciation of wine forward,' said the young man. We took a long draught of cool night air.

'So you're a bit of a port expert, then?' I asked him.

'Me? You're joking! It's just a brilliant way of getting mullered at the end of a meal.'

Like my friend from the City, I wouldn't normally have thought of a port-tasting as my cup of tea. But I enjoyed my time at Berry Brothers. Perhaps it was the sumptuously lived-in cellars; perhaps it was the sense of being surrounded by history bottled and stoppered; perhaps it was all that strong wine I had put away. You had to hand it to Simon Berry and his team. As British as they were, they managed to carry off that elusive style that can only be put into words in the language of a wine-making country: *savoir faire*. Although they appeared to be marooned on the wrong side of progress, together with all the huntsmen and headmasters of public schools and everyone else who was an apologist for the anachronistic ways of Olde England, Berry Brothers & Rudd deflected the criticisms that even the most committed class warrior was likely to offer. Their wares could be seen as the essence of extravagance, it's true, as a veritable distillation of privilege, but Berrys seemed to say of them that they were only a little drop of what you fancy. They left it to their clients to decide how far they wanted to throw themselves into the drawing-room farce of wine appreciation.

Cellars, basements, lower ground floors: because they're out of sight and out of the way, they're among our most trusted and treasured places. In London, venerable bottles of sack are only one commodity of an infinite variety stored below ground. I went to look at grottoes groaning with great riches. They were buried bazaars of jewels and costly metals. They were storehouses in which people had secreted their most valuable belongings; in some cases, the possessions dearest to them in all the world. Compared to Berry Brothers and the rubicund sluicing that went on there, though, these were lonely spots, where the nearness of wealth, you felt, would never wholly assuage a fear that it would all somehow drain away into the London soil, that all the furtiveness and fortifications would never be quite enough.

Silver vaults under Chancery Lane, by an irony as black as tarnished plate, resembled nothing so much as a horde of Nazi loot. 'An Aladdin's cave,' a posh saleswoman, tall and tweedy, corrected me when I tried the analogy on her. But I wasn't so sure. In sunken, impregnable corridors, dealers in precious metal were operating out of rooms like strongboxes, and going by the names over the doors, it seemed that a number of the traders were Jewish. In the aftermath of the al-Qaeda attacks, you had the thought that the dealers were bunkered with their goods as a hedge against the present unpleasantness. But the tweedy saleswoman, for one, was not susceptible to such terrors. She wanted to tell me about the collecting bug, how customers developed a passion for certain articles and then pursued it. A woman, one of her clients, had a thing for mustard containers made out of silver. Having collected more silver boats than she would ever have enough tangy Dijon to fill, the client had moved on to snaffling up every silver grapefruit dish she came across. I picked up and turned over something called a quaich, which sounded as though it belonged in a Harry Potter story but was actually a drinking vessel of Highland origin. As if to confirm what I'd just heard about determined silver-fanciers, a couple could be observed going from dealer to dealer along the off-cream corridor, asking for a 'heart-shaped frame'. She was in good shape for a woman in her late forties, or even early fifties, with long dark hair which was grey where it brushed her face. At every corner of the maze or labyrinth of shops, which were thoughtfully signposted in four languages, including French, German and Arabic, I heard the pair telling the dealers of their desire for a frame in the shape of a heart.

In their cavernous retreat, the traders kept a low profile. That was the way everyone liked it. But the vaults were an open secret among serious players on the silver circuit, heavy metallers from the UK and overseas. By *sotto voce* reputation, the vaults were *the* place to go to buy and sell silver. Under one reinforced roof, they were a covered market of stalls and stands trafficking in the finest hallmarked products. They were the natural successor to Silver Street in EC2. All the silversmiths used to live in that part of town in the sixteenth century, according to John Stow's survey. The street had marked one corner of the old Roman fort. At the beginning of the seventeenth century, Shakespeare took lodgings in the area, over the shop of a man called Christopher

Mountjoy, a French Huguenot refugee who made lustrous headdresses for ladies of the court. But Silver Street itself vanished when London Wall was widened.

In its modern successor below ground, there were silver bottle-stoppers and cufflinks made of silver. There was a silver letter-rack in the shape of a swan. There was a George I marrow scoop, made in London in 1717, and a George III cheese scoop from 1804, with an ivory handle which was stained or discoloured to a greenish hue. What I took for a silver pillbox was in fact a container for bandages. The lid was worked with the motto 'We heal all wounds save those of love'. There were hideous, outsize bluebottles, in silver and gold, and a table-setting consisting of a cow with a large fly in the middle of her back. On closer inspection, the insect proved to be the handle of a detachable lid – perhaps admitting access to a horseradish spoon.

Thanks to the low ceilings and narrow passages of the vaults, all intended to thwart the larcenist's drill, the Chancery Lane shopping experience was a little like going below decks on a cruise liner. The dealers' rooms were like cabins. Some were even fitted with porthole-shaped windows and a manufacturer's crest in the style of an anchor. Finding yourself temporarily alone in a corridor, you felt like Charles Ryder when he was on board ship during a storm in *Brideshead Revisited* and all the other passengers had retired to their cabins with seasickness.

In a salesroom barely big enough to swing a ship's cat, a man was reading the obituaries page of *The Times*. 'How long have you been here?' I asked him.

'Too long. Twenty-two years. But it's all right, I surface every night,' he assured me. He had his spectacles on a lanyard and wore a yellow, patterned tie over a blue shirt which was showing signs of foxing. He had regular customers, he said, some of them dealers like himself. He worked in the vaults three days a week; the rest of his week was spent travelling, bargain-hunting, buying. Despite having made a little joke about surfacing after dark, the dealer reacted jerkily, like a marionette, when I asked him to name the oddest thing he'd ever handled. He appeared to be at a loss for an answer so I mentioned the first thing I could think of, which was the bandage box I'd just seen.

'They used to make everything in silver,' said the dealer, with the air of a man regaining familiar ground. 'Too many things. You'd need a football pitch for all of them. And you'd have to keep them clean. And they wear out.' After two decades of buying and selling, there was a sense in which the dealer was a little shop-soiled himself. Another man went past his tiny room carrying a pair of wooden boxes. The dealer shouted out in a teasing voice, 'Going abroad?' I wondered whether this was a joke, if 'going abroad' was a fond euphemism among the silver fraternity for doing a bunk, a flit, for escaping the taxman or creditors or the wife.

I thought about the dreary stuff-ness of the vaults. My dealer who talked about football pitches of silverware had surrounded himself with stuff: costly, shiny, pointless stuff. And then there was the stuff-fixation of the couple who were looking for a heart-shaped frame. This is what the end of the world might be like if you were a silver obsessive or a dealer, or if you were moderately, not fabulously, rich. There, under the ground, in the rinsed air – but for how long would it stay sweet? – clinging to your stuff for dear life.

In a batsqueak echo of Dante's *Divine Comedy*, I discovered that the further I went below ground in search of material riches, the more unhappiness I encountered. While the clients and friends of Berry Brothers cheerily swigged drink in their brick basement, there was an atmosphere of melancholy and futility in the silver vaults. It was as though the salesmen and their patrons had walled themselves in with their precious metal, only to find that it wasn't the bulwark against insecurity that they were looking for. And by the time I reached an underground chamber where people stashed their most prized things, I was face to face with real tragedy, though, in keeping with the 'discretion' on which this place prided itself, it was at first well hidden.

Geoffrey Knowles admitted me to his interview room like the ex-copper he was. 'Go in now! Go in now!' he commanded, depressing a switch which sprang a lock. He was a big man, with a coordinating tie and breast-hankie combo. Inside the interview room was a mean little chair and a counter. Some trick of the strip lighting made me think for a moment that I was looking into a two-way mirror. Perhaps I was bracing myself for Knowles to set a tape recorder running with the words 'Geoffrey Knowles entered the room at 14.15 . . .' On the wall of the interview room was a watercolour of Westminster Bridge, perhaps painted by a Victorian hand, but otherwise the cubicle was exactly the sort of inhospitable space in which you might expect to be quizzed by the DHS or Customs or indeed the Met. In fact, I was in the safety-deposit vaults of which Knowles was the manager.

While I was waiting for him to appear on the other side of the counter, I heard a woman talking to him outside the door. She was complaining about an invoice which she had received. She had a posh accent which didn't quite sustain. 'I shouldn't be here, doing all this,' she said. 'You should have checked your rentals,' she told Knowles.

I heard him say, 'We'll reimburse you by cheque.'

'Where will the cheque go?'

'Oh yes, of course. You've changed your address, haven't you?'

'I live abroad. I'm coming back on the twenty-second.'

Finally, Knowles came into the interview room. He sat down and looked at me. He had blue eyes and he was wearing a Poppy Day flower in his lapel. Before becoming an ex-policeman, Knowles had been an ex-soldier. He asked me about the bag I was carrying: had it been searched? He looked unhappy when I told him that the caretaker types at street level had failed to satisfy themselves about the contents of my rucksack. I saw at once that Knowles was the withholding type. This made sense.

How much had he sweated out of rattled villains and, in another life, the foot soldiers of the IRA, by forcing them to talk before he'd ever say a word?

We were sitting at the centre of the safety-deposit company's principal asset, a massive concrete tank buried twenty feet below ground. It had been built to a specification of immense strength and thickness. It was equipped with the latest security aids and surveillance measures, said Knowles. 'We're on a par with the Bank of England and the Tower of London.' All this was to protect several thousand metal boxes: reinforced pigeonholes, drop boxes. Once you were accepted as a client, said Knowles, you came and went as you pleased. 'You give your name, your box number, your password, and you get your key.'

The safety-deposit vaults were part of the same shrewd excavation beneath Chancery Lane that also housed the silver market. Those below-decks salesrooms were separated from Knowles and me by a few feet of earth and reinforced concrete. The safety-deposit business was the longer established of the two, and had been going since 1885. There was a picture of it in the *Illustrated London News*, said Knowles. In those days, the vaults had boasted marble floors and walk-in safes. They were patronised by the landed gentry and the titled people of London. 'The butler of the house would put the silver in here overnight for safe keeping and come and get it in the morning.' At the beginning of the twentieth century, there was a large influx of Jews into London following pogroms in Eastern Europe. 'They went into the rag trade in the East End, but around here, near Hatton Garden, they were jewellers. They used the safety deposit to put their jewels in at night.' Hitler's bombs failed to dent the vaults, but damage from fire, and from all the water used to put out the fire, led to a refurbishment. And out of this came the silver vaults, in 1953.

This much I cribbed from Knowles, but our conversation was by no means one-way. After all, the cubicle we were sharing wasn't called the interview room because it was where Knowles was accustomed to unburdening himself to journalists. Broadly speaking, it was where *he* did the interviewing. He taxed me on my background, my methods and motives. After satisfying himself about me, he agreed to lead me into the vault. We left the interview room and stepped through a portal like the bomb-bay hatch of a Trident submarine.

Knowles was explaining what the procedure would be if I was one of his clients. 'You would come and see this custodian here,' he said, indicating with a motion of his arm a middle-aged woman who was blinking at us in the half-light of a booth. She might have been manning a kiosk which dispenses change in an amusement arcade. 'She checks your name and ID against a ledger,' Knowles went on. I smiled at the woman, whom Knowles referred to only as 'the custodian', and she smiled back. 'If you're who you say you are, she hands you your key,' said Knowles.

There was a free-standing display of boxes of different sizes. They were like a nest of boxes, or perhaps a range of unwieldy luggage. Rentals started at £141 per annum, including VAT. This bought you a box measuring four-and-a-half inches high by five-and-a-half inches wide and eighteen inches deep. At the top of the scale was a box with the dimensions of fifteen inches by twenty inches by twenty-four inches – two foot deep – for which you'd pay the Devil's own money: £666 precisely.

As Knowles led the way, the vault opened up before us. The atmosphere was uninviting. You might almost say stealthy, or even ashamed. No fountain splashed. The only noise was the hum of an air duct fitted in the concrete wall. There were no muzak loops, no soft furnishings, no ziggurats of complimentary Ferrero Rocher. Knowles and I might have been in the locker room of a police station. This was no glittering hoard. It was all very well men burying their treasures in the wormy deep, but as graveside homilies remind us, in time everything is reclaimed by the earth whence it came. In May 2003, the safety-deposit rooms of top people's bankers C. Hoare and Co., which were located a short distance from Chancery Lane in Fleet Street and had held the valuables of Samuel Pepys, Lord Byron and Jane Austen, were found to be infested with mould.

I saw that Knowles's safety-deposit boxes could be compared to a vast crossword, 3-D and interactive. I noticed several black squares. 'That's where the boxes have been drilled,' said Knowles. The client might have mislaid his key, he said, in which case he would have been charged £120 to have the box opened with a Black & Decker. Alternatively, the client might have cancelled his account, or died, or detectives might have demanded a look inside.

'Who are your clients?'

'They're from across the board. Some of them just want to keep their mortgage deeds or their share certificates in a safe place. Or they're putting their jewellery in the safe to keep the insurance premiums down. We get market traders, car dealers, very rich people—'

'—and fences, stashing moody gear?'

'Obviously, we don't condone anything illegal but our clients have complete confidentiality,' said Knowles. 'Unless the police turn up with a warrant.'

'Has anyone ever tried to break in down here?'

'No. Frankly, it's much easier to rob a bank.' The producers of *Sexy Beast*, a cult British caper movie, had approached Knowles about shooting their memorable safe-blowing scene on his premises. But, as he had told them, professional protocol forbade it. Knowles had referred the film-makers to other facilities in London. I thought of the vaults of the old Midland Bank building at Poultry, where the producers of the James Bond films had set scenes from *Goldfinger*. Knowles drew the line well short of upsetting his clients by attracting that kind of publicity.

But this didn't mean that he kept all of his inside gen to himself. 'Please believe me, please believe me, please believe me:

we've got *everything* in here,' said Knowles, unrecognisably expansive from the narrow-eyed ex-policeman in the interview room of half an hour or so earlier. It seemed that pearl-handled revolvers, those pretty arbiters of affairs of the heart, had found their way into boxes beneath Chancery Lane over the years, even though the rules expressly forbade firearms and explosives as well as noxious substances and drugs. 'There was once a gentleman, from South America, I believe, who deposited a Samsonite suitcase with us,' Knowles recalled. 'Well, some time later he disappeared. Vanished off the face of the earth. When we finally opened the case, it was full of gems.'

Gems! Had Geoffrey really said 'gems'? He had! This was probably a workaday usage in his line of business, given all the eyeglasses and miniature weighing-scales around the corner in Hatton Garden. But with the exception of the word's own immediate circle in the jewellery world, it was never spoken, and was not previously thought to exist outside the nonsense language of journalism, a fate that 'gems' shared with words including 'dossier' and 'probe'.

Now Knowles had said 'gems'. It was like a taboo being broken. 'What happened to the gems?' I asked him, for the pleasure of saying the word as much as anything.

'They were auctioned eventually. Of course, we took out our costs, as we were entitled to do.' Not all of Knowles's competitors had got off so lightly with the criminal fraternity. In the summer of 2003, a confidence trickster walked away with at least £1.5 million from vaults just round the corner from Knowles's premises in a heist which the newspapers immediately compared to the film *The Thomas Crown Affair*. The tall, dapper thief, thought to be in his fifties, had rented four strongboxes at Hatton Garden Safety Deposit eight months earlier in the name of Philip Goldberg. One Saturday morning, dressed in a smart black suit and a homburg, he took a holdall with him into the vault and stuffed it with cash and jewellery. It was two days before the robbery was even detected, when another customer found his safety-deposit box had been glued shut. 'Goldberg' had often taken diamonds to show to jewellers in the Garden. 'He established himself in the community, becoming known, visiting people regularly, so that he'd never look out of the ordinary,' said a police spokesman. *The Guardian* reported that his audacious crime won him a reputation as a figure of mystery in the jewellery quarter, 'a man known to one's acquaintances, rather than to oneself, and someone whose nerve and evident talent was thought deserving of some kind of grudging respect'.

Reflecting on the curious patrons of safety-deposit vaults perhaps encouraged Knowles to reappraise his description of his customers. At any rate, what he now said was, 'If I take a hundred per cent of my client base, I would say that thirty per cent are normal. The other seventy per cent are oddities.' This was a strikingly high proportion, and an extraordinary thing for Knowles to say. The 70 per cent presumably included the High Court judge who had fondly stashed a cache of what Knowles described as 'Evelyn Waugh-ish' letters, chronicling his lordship's weekends in Brighton with a lady of pleasure.

Other secrets of the vault were rather less uproarious. Knowles told me about a late client, a woman, who fell pregnant in the thirties. Perhaps she was unmarried; perhaps the baby wasn't her husband's. 'She went to France to have the baby and she gave it away,' said Knowles. In her safety-deposit box she kept letters and photographs of the child, and a pair of baby shoes. There was also what Knowles called the 'macabre' story of the woman who came to the vaults once a year, always on the same day in June. She would take her safety-deposit box into one of the private cubicles provided, and after an hour or so, return it. This went on for year after year until the woman grew old. One summer, it wasn't the woman who came to the vaults in June but a nurse, the matron of the home to which the old woman had been admitted. The matron went away with the contents of the box, returning them to Chancery Lane the following day. This became the new pattern with the tenancy of this particular box until finally word came from the nursing home that the woman had died and the box wouldn't be needed any longer. Only when it was being emptied by the old woman's executors was its secret finally revealed. It contained nothing but a plait of jet-black hair. The woman had been incarcerated in a Nazi prison camp with her daughter. The Nazis had cut the girl's hair off before killing her; the mother had saved it, smuggled it away somehow in her clothes. Every June, she came to look at it, on what would have been the girl's birthday.

You might imagine that the private cubicles would be like hotel rooms, or at least the interiors of expensive cars. I put my head around the door of one and it couldn't have been more utilitarian. If there had been a window in it, it would have been a peep-show booth or a prison-visit hutch. How wretched that old woman must have felt, stroking her daughter's hair in such a place.

There was only one bona fide visitor to the vaults that afternoon, a stooped type in thick lenses. He wanted the help of one of Knowles's staff, a custodian like the woman in the booth, except that this man's role was as a warder, a turnkey. No youngster, the screw of the safety-deposit vaults rose effortfully from a desk where he'd been looking at a brochure of property on the sybaritic sod of Jersey. He couldn't have been rich himself, I thought, not unless he'd been dipping into the till, so I could only assume that he had caught the habits of the wealthy. He accompanied the visitor to one of Geoffrey Knowles's bigger boxes. As the client opened it, I saw that it held a coarse hempen bag with a word stencilled on it. Disappointingly, the word wasn't 'SWAG', but it was almost as good. It was 'GEMS'.

The rule that the customer's peace of mind dwindled in direct proportion to the density of the concrete surrounding his goods also worked in reverse, I discovered. The tattiest and least secure of subterranean storehouses was a joy to browse, with its extraordinary lines of coffins, artificial hips, stuffed parrots and monkey suits. This was an auction house selling off unclaimed spoils of crime, and it traded out of the rundown brick arches of the former Bishopsgate goodsyard in the east of the City. On a typical day, a crowd of about thirty punters, some in tracksuits, others blue rinses, cast their eyes over goodies including hooky computers, mobile phones, jewellery, and bicycles. It was booty recovered from police raids on burglars and shoplifters. The profits went to community anti-crime initiatives. Spencer Davies, who rapped the gavel on some four hundred lots a month, said, 'You name it, we've sold it. We've sold a rickshaw, a set of ten parachutes and even a hot-air balloon complete with basket. I'm not surprised by anything any more.'

I went to Bishopsgate at the suggestion of John Hawks of Merton Abbey Mills. On his mobile, John had arranged for me to meet a man named Nigel, who was in charge of the old goodsyard. Both John and Nigel worked for Eric Reynolds, the entrepreneur credited with rejuvenating Camden market, the land around Regent's Canal and Dead Dog Basin, before moving on to other neglected corners of London. He'd had his work cut out at Bishopsgate, which had been disused for more than a century and been badly damaged by fire. Eric and others had given the Piranesian labyrinth a new lease of life but now it faced its biggest threat. London Underground wanted to tear it down to make way for a £600 million extension to the East London Line. Permission had been granted as long ago as 1997 but a legal battle had since ensued.

Ironically, it was railway bosses who'd put up the arches in the first place. In 1834, the Eastern Counties Railway company proposed building a passenger line from London to Norwich and Yarmouth, and work began three years later. By 1840, the

London end of the line occupied a handsome Italianate building on Shoreditch High Street. It was the fifth of the great railway termini to appear in the capital. But the station was badly located. Moreover, it was 'confined, somewhat dingy, and ran slow and uncomfortable services' according to a contemporary account. By 1864, the railway had merged with the Great Eastern. A decade later, with the opening of nearby Liverpool Street station, Shoreditch ceased to be a passenger terminus. It became a freight station, at one time the biggest in London, occupying the space of twenty football pitches. But latterly its role as a whirligig of goods was confined to knocking down ill-gotten gains.

Under the arches were plaques, intensely eaten away by the elements, which memorialised the railway and its founders. 'They just shut the doors and walked away,' said Nigel. 'The goodsyard nearly burnt down in 1961. It's been grotty for forty years: drunks, drugs, prostitutes and unbelievable fly-tipping. This place is filthy now, but compared to what it was, it's an operating theatre.' Nigel strode through an unreconstructed corner of the catacombs, 'confined and somewhat dingy' even on an unseasonably bright January day, with his head down. He was ex-military – the Royal Greenjackets – and had ex-military hair. It was wavy like the late Alan Clark's. Nigel had been a helicopter pilot, he said, 'but I wasn't terribly good at it.'

'Why was that?'

'I lacked confidence.' It wasn't until he was on Civvy Street that he learned to make the most of his army training, he said.

With money from Europe as well as some of his own, Nigel's friend Eric had made the goodsyard habitable for small businesses who had been priced out of nearby Spitalfields. There were the inevitable gym and car park in the arches, but other tenants included Christie's, who had a repository there, and a company called Future Fibres, who manufactured cables for yachts competing in the America's Cup. The long brick arches were ideal for paying the cables out, testing the five-ton breaking strain of the company's revolutionary product, zylon.

Nigel was a little vague about the occupancy of the arches. 'There are thirty-nine of them and we've let them all,' he said. 'No, that's not true. All bar sixteen. About half of them. We *could* have let the whole lot twice, four times, over, but the council wouldn't let us.' With the people who worked in the old goodsyard, Nigel played the good-egg company commander. These were officer-and-other-ranks conversations, but Nigel was friendly and genuinely interested. In Future Fibres, I heard him saying to a young rope technician, 'I think you'd be good SAS material: quiet, placid – no, that's the wrong word, not *placid*.' To my surprise, the young man looked flattered.

Nigel revealed that the breakthrough in his career came after he had left the Greenjackets and secured a perhaps unlikely position with Lucy Clayton, the world-renowned finishing school for young ladies. 'The army background means you can go straight to the heart of things and say, "Right, stop buggering about. What are we trying to do here?"' At the college, Nigel found himself surrounded by women who were 'billowy' – he made expansive gestures with his arms, as if he was shooing cattle. This performance was so antediluvian that I expected some qualifier or signal from Nigel to show that he was kidding, that he knew he was being old school about the women of the college, but it never came.

Nigel had been a success at Lucy Clayton – another expansive gesture, as if he was demonstrating some wonderful ropeway to the stars, possibly made of zylon. He got rid of all the curtsying, the deportment, 'the girly stuff. They teach them all that at public school now anyway.' Nigel had insisted on introducing hard-headed business techniques to the gels. 'They're intelligent, they've all got A-levels. They want to know how to be organised, to run a career.' Out had gone the legendary technique for access and egress to even the most cramped cars without revealing a flash of knickers. 'Oh, yes, gone,' confirmed Nigel, 'I sold the car, in fact.'

The centrepiece of Bishopsgate was the Braithwaite viaduct, which sounds as though it ought to have been straddling a gorge on the Settle-to-Carlisle railway. It was one of the oldest constructions of its kind in the world and English Heritage had listed it. They had retained engineers who passed the viaduct fit to take the strain of the East London Line, but the arches below remained vulnerable to London Underground's wrecking ball. Tube bosses weren't the only ones who wanted to see the back of Bishopsgate. Ken Livingstone, the Mayor of London, Railtrack, and the Corporation of London were all united in wanting change. There were plans for a major development, including up to four million square feet of office space and at least one tower which would stand twenty storeys high.

However, the Prince of Wales, who couldn't see a threatened brick building without throwing himself in front of it, had urged the preservation of the goodsyard, saying it would be a 'desperate tragedy' if it was razed. 'Within its subterranean depths, now hidden from public view, there are some of the very finest brick arches to be found anywhere in the world,' he wrote in the *Standard*. 'Perhaps I am not alone in feeling that we owe some sort of responsibility to the hundreds of Victorian craftsmen and builders who worked to construct this most remarkable of buildings.' In his latest cause, Prince Charles found himself up against his old adversary, the architect Richard Rogers. Lord Rogers of Riverside was chair of the Mayor's architecture and urbanism unit, which had already drawn up a shortlist of architects to plot the reconstruction of Bishopsgate.

If the prince was the figurehead in the fight to save the goodsyard, the prime mover was a pensioner from south-west London, 65-year-old Keith Hammerton, who had been beaten up for his pains. He took London Underground to the High Court, arguing that its planning permission to level Bishopsgate had lapsed. In October 2002, a month before the hearing, Mr Hammerton was assaulted by men who he believed were trying to frighten him into abandoning his action. He also received threatening telephone calls. The Underground condemned the assault and there's no suggestion that it had any connection with Mr Hammerton's attackers.

Mr Justice Ouseley found in Mr Hammerton's favour, on the technical point that the Underground had breached the terms of the planning permission by failing to provide an exchange of land on an alternative site. The judge went on to praise Mr Hammerton's courage. 'His assailants made it clear that they were trying to deter him from continuing with these proceedings. The police should treat this as a very serious matter.' The pensioner himself was not in court – he was still recovering from his injuries – but he welcomed the decision. 'This means that London Underground cannot wriggle out of its legal responsibilities,' he said. But the ruling was only a stay of execution. It didn't remove the threat of demolition. Bishopsgate was one of the ancient portals to London, established when the Romans built their city within the stones. In his memoirs, V. S. Pritchett, born in 1900, recalled the railways he took when he was an apprentice: 'the trains come in and go out over those miles of rolling brick arches that run across London like a massive Roman wall'. But the people who had reinvented the goodsyard were resigned to the fact that they would be leaving sooner or later and the brick walls would come tumbling down.

GOING OUT WITH A BANG

Victorian London

On the far wall of the darkened chapel, ghostly images of an officer in the Royal Navy and of a much shorter matelot eerily materialised. The senior man appeared to be cradling the shrunken sailor in his arms. 'Arthur Prince and Jim,' a man's voice intoned. A two-bar fire was blazing in the chapel though it was a close May night. The smaller of the two flickering figures had the body of a small man but there was something distractingly odd about him, something stiff and prosthetic. 'Prince died in 1948,' the voice went on. 'He lies in a simple plot in Hampstead. He was buried with Jim. Yes, he was buried with his doll. You must never, ever, call it a dummy, by the way, ladies and gentlemen. Vents get very uptight. It's a *doll*.'

The Dissenters' chapel at Kensal Green cemetery was built in the nineteenth century to cater to any foreseeable lying-in-rest requirement. It was based on the Temple of Ilissus in Athens, with other features borrowed from the Monument of Thrasyllus, also in the Greek capital. After years of vandalism and even partial demolition, it was restored by English Heritage and others in the late 1990s. In its long and colourful history, it can seldom have witnessed an engagement like tonight's. It had been booked for a talk and slide show by Terry Lomas from the British Music Hall Society, whose subject was the graves of variety artistes. His projector rested on a wooden bier.

Arthur Prince and Jim, his doll, his imaginary friend, once had an act called 'Naval Excursions', said Lomas. 'He was the first vent to drink a glass of water while the doll was talking.' Lomas could be dimly made out in the glow cast by the projector. He was a broad, dark man with spectacles and a moustache. There was the sound of the projector shuffling its pack, its deck of the kings and queens of music hall. Then the image of a woman appeared on the wall and Lomas said, 'Lottie Collins, the "Tara-ra-Boom-de-ay" lady.' Shuffle, went the projector. 'Harry Champion: now he performed "A Little Bit of Cucumber" and "I'm Hen-er-ee the Eighth I Am".' Lomas accompanied his slides in song, though there had been no mention of this extra in his billing for the night. As he sang, he swivelled about the fixed point of his hips like a skittle wobbling on its base.

'Now this is Herbert Campbell,' said Lomas, as what looked like a retouched daguerreotype swam into focus. Campbell was the doyenne of pantomime dames. He is buried at Stoke Newington. He was the partner of the legendary London turn Dan Leno. On the chapel wall, Campbell was succeeded by Leno, a man with a smile and bomb-gone-off hair. You had expected that Lomas's selection of studies would dwell on the big-name board-treaders of yesteryear. Less probably, he had also included a good number of photographs, most of them by his own hand, recording the last resting places of these heroes. One of them was up on the wall now. It was of a lump of stone peeking between leaves and wild flowers. The trouble was, so were all the others. Like the entertainers they commemorated, these indistinguishable memorials had in many cases fallen into neglect, although the Music Hall Society had embarked on a programme of restoration.

Lomas was playing to a fullish house, which was sharply divided along unlikely lines. One half of his audience were twinkly pensioners who dimly recalled variety. The other 50 per cent, much younger, affected the blanched maquillage and widow's weeds of the fashion-resistant strain of youth culture known as goths. When I first arrived at the chapel – north along Ladbroke Grove to the bridge over the Grand Union Canal; then through a gate in a wall and down a metal staircase into the cemetery precincts – I ran into a woman wearing a frock coat and a shirt and tie. With her cigarette, she looked like an undertaker on a break, or a cabaret artiste from 1930s' Germany. Sitting directly in front of me in the chapel was a woman in her twenties who was almost nunlike in her blackness. Her raven tresses fell down the back of her boned and fitted dress (intensely charcoal) which coordinated perfectly with her boots (profoundly penumbran). There was little obvious overlap between the two blocs of Lomas's demographic, between the showpeople and the morbid types, the death fanciers, the *no-show* people. The goths didn't join in when the old-timers called out the names of music-hall stars at random, inviting their guest to say where the late crowd-pleasers were interred, as if he himself was a bill-topper at the Alhambras and Empires and Roxys: Lomas the Memorial Man.

You couldn't get much more uncompromisingly subterranean than the grave – the grave of a music hall legend or anyone else, for that matter – I reflected in the partially sunken Dissenters' chapel at Kensal Green, which was nothing but a splendid anteroom to the hereafter, frankly, especially given that its wooden floor was all that separated you from dank catacombs below, catacombs that I would be tremulously exploring by and by. I'd noticed on the way in that a gloomy staircase leading down from the chapel had been ominously curtained off. It was like wandering onto the set of a cheesy British horror film, called something like *The Slide Show of Doom*.

These were the sort of thoughts you might have been entitled to have as the evening began. But taking stock of the alternately wrinkled and whey-painted faces around me, I had a different vision of underground London, one made up of submerged, *unimagined*, interest groups and ginger organisations. This was another sort of hidden city, a community which somehow embraced not only old-time song and dance fans but also pall-bearer groupies.

We heard that Marie Lloyd was born in Hoxton in 1870 and went on to become the biggest crowd-puller the halls had known. When she died, 100,000 people lined the streets to watch her funeral procession. '"Oh, Mr Porter",' said Lomas, embarking on an inventory of her smashes in somehow actuarial tones, '"When I Take My Morning Promenade"; "One of the Ruins that Cromwell Knocked About a Bit".' Lloyd had married a racing tipster. She divorced and married a coster king. Her third match was a jockey, a Derby winner, who was twenty years her junior. But this last union was particularly ill starred. Not to put too fine a point on it, she was one of the ruins that hubby knocked about a bit. Or as Lomas had it, 'She went in fear of her life.' The occasional archaic usage such as this only complemented Lomas's performance. Another feature of it was his knack of extending the last syllable of every other line he sang, often by use of the suffix '-er', so that the man's name 'Jim', for example, which had apparently been resorted to by the librettists out of all proportion to its incidence in everyday life, was rendered by Lomas as 'Jim-er'.

'I'm a broken-hearted milkman,' sang Lomas. 'In grief I'm arrayed-er.'

We had arrived at a picture of the 'Yorkshire comedian', Tom Foy. Tom Foy with his donkey, in fact. That was the act: Foy and the donkey. This provoked a titter from a row of chairs somewhere over my shoulder. 'Late laugh?' said Lomas. 'Glad you came, madam!' Foy was buried at Brompton: cue virtually generic shot of headstone bordered by greenery. Lomas recounted the extraordinary story of the death of Lafayette, a contemporary and colleague of the great Houdini. Lafayette was killed in a house fire. It was only after he had been buried that another body was discovered in the house. This second corpse was that of the real Lafayette. He had employed a double for the act, it seemed, and the authorities had interred this unfortunate man, Lafayette's all-too-dead ringer, by mistake. But this wasn't the end of the complications surrounding his passing. Lafayette had left instructions that he wished to make his final journey accompanied by his much-loved dog. But he was Jewish, and the rabbis wouldn't hear of his last request, so the obsequies were performed by a Presbyterian instead. The dog was embalmed and Lafayette's ashes placed in an urn between the beast's paws.

When the lights went up and Lomas invited questions, there was only one thought on my mind. Considering the story we had just been listening to, and linking this to the earlier account of Arthur Prince and his doll Jim, I wanted to know if Tom Foy had been laid to rest with the donkey.

'I don't think so,' said Lomas, who gracefully managed a laugh. I had a sense that one or two of the goths, by contrast, were glowering at my naive sunniness from behind their eyeliner.

Outside the chapel, it was still light but the streets were empty. A wind had got up, freshening the muggy evening. The only other person who was heading my way was the woman in her twenties who had been sitting in front of me in the chapel, wearing black. Now that I saw her ensemble in full, it was even more strikingly monochrome. Over her dress she wore a black coat and in her hand was a furled black umbrella. My route took me in the same direction as the woman for half a mile or so. We walked in silence through the deserted and windy streets, the woman steadily outstripping me, even on the high heels of her black boots. She was a businesslike witch, I decided, stomping off to her cauldron to attend to a backlog of spells.

It would be hard to imagine a more instructive case study of nineteenth-century London than the making of the General Cemetery of All Souls at Kensal Green, as it was formally known. If its own history were to be celebrated in a lurid monument of the kind which litters its grounds, the stonemasons could do worse than a marmoreal triptych showing an outstretched arm (reach exceeding grasp), a woman suffering an attack of the vapours, and the affronted nostrils of a gentleman. The original Victorian values of enterprise, appalled fascination with the human body, and snobbery had underpinned the founding of the necropolis. By the 1820s, there was growing unease at overcrowded graveyards which were situated in the middle of cities. It was becoming increasingly difficult for mourners to look the other way when each interment had the effect of propelling a decomposing inmate to the consecrated surface on the end of a sexton's shovel. Handkerchiefs soused in lavender could restore the gagging bereaved, but Londoners were worried about more serious and widespread health risks. The few Victorians who didn't blame cholera on miasmas rising from the Thames linked it to unwholesome airs in oversubscribed graveyards. In May 1830, Andrew Spottiswoode, MP for Colchester, presented a petition to the Commons urging that metropolitan burial grounds be removed to locations where they would be 'less prejudicial to the health of the inhabitants'.

Although Kensal Green was then an airy spot in the countryside, located a fairish drive by horse-drawn carriage from the centre of the Victorian metropolis, it wasn't at the top of everyone's list as a resting place. An architect called Francis Goodwin favoured Primrose Hill for his 'Grand National Cemetery', with buildings in the Greek Revival style. He pictured it containing 'facsimiles of some of the most celebrated remains of Greek and Roman architecture'. By contrast, John Loudon, a landscape gardener and writer, proposed a chain of cemeteries, equidistant from each other and from the centre of London. They would boast every type of hardy tree and shrub, in order to serve as botanic gardens as well as burial places. But the most ambitious, not to say outlandish, vision belonged to Thomas Willson, the man behind the 'Pyramid Cemetery for the Metropolis'. As its name suggests, this was a borrowing from the Nile delta. But instead of accommodating a solitary late pharaoh plus entourage, Willson's grand design envisaged bunk-space for no fewer than 'five millions of individuals' in a huge multi-storey tomb. The base of this structure would occupy eighteen acres, so providing a thousand acres of burial chamber. In plans published in 1831, Willson anticipated that his pyramid would cost about £2.5 million to build and would contain freehold vaults retailing at between £100 and £500 each. Any space left over would be let to parishes which had run out of room in their churchyards. Willson claimed that his solution to overcrowding among London's dead was 'compact, ornamental and hygienic'. He estimated that his scheme would net profits in excess of £10 million, and 'go far towards completing the glory of London'.

But the great and the good who served as trustees of the new General Cemetery Company elected instead to purchase thirty-two hectares of land at Kensal Green, and encouraged architects to submit drafts. An outbreak of Asiatic cholera in 1831 came along at the right time to galvanise MPs into passing a bill for 'establishing a General Cemetery for the Interment of the Dead in the Neighbourhood of the Metropolis'. When it became law, the act stipulated that the main chapel at Kensal Green was to be reserved for the use of Anglicans. Objections to the idea of a purpose-built burial site had been led by the clergy, who were accustomed to making a tidy living out of the dead. A further condition of the legislation, intended to make up the burial fees lost by London parishes, was compensation of up to five shillings a head.

When it was finally built, Kensal Green recalled the formality of late-Georgian town planning in the West End. In other words, it was 'the Victorian Valhalla for the Quality . . . the cemetery provided a development that deliberately echoed the parts of London occupied by aristocratic society, and offered those who chose to bury or be buried there plots in perpetuity that represented not only real estate, but had connotations of class, respectability, gentility, and positions in pecking order'. The words of the admirable Professor James Stevens Curl in *The*

Victorian Celebration of Death of 2000. (On the back cover of his book, which may very well become the standard work in its field, the Professor dispenses with the customary author photograph in favour of a picture of a marble bust of himself. The blurb, in which he may or may not have had a hand, unimprovably hails his book as 'an outpouring of the great black cornucopia of Victorian agony and the terrific paraphernalia of the Last Act . . . an agreeable companion to the non-eternal bedside'.)

The very active Friends of the cemetery put on tours every other weekend, with a visit to the catacombs of Kensal Green included on one Sunday a month. On the June sabbath when I signed up, I shared a stroll to the Anglican chapel under a canopy of trees with a middle-aged couple. He was the shorter of the pair, and his eyes were watering. It was one of those changeable days of early summer, cool enough for a jacket if you were on the towpath of the Grand Union Canal, but the worst day of the year so far for hay-fever sufferers, this not helped by the fact that the cemetery was like a meadow, a meadow with outcrops of stone and marble in it. I mentioned the book I was writing and the man said that he used to work in Brook Street and a river had run through the basement of the store. He admired the funerary architecture all around us and provoked his wife into scolding him when he wondered aloud about taking some of it home to scatter across the lawn. I asked him if he'd like to be buried at Kensal Green when the time came. There were several places around the country that he'd considered, he said. 'Perhaps I'll leave a bone in each.' The woman thought that Freddie Mercury was buried at Kensal Green even though 'the authorities' had opposed the singer's interment, fearing that the place would be overrun by his fans. I learnt later from a man called Henry, one of the Friends and a guide for the day, that Mercury had indeed been cremated at the cemetery but his ashes had been returned to his native Zanzibar. 'I think the cemetery company asked a lot of money for a plot,' said Henry. Kensal Green was still run by a private company, the successor to the Victorian General Cemetery Company. 'I think they thought they were on to a good thing.'

The chapel was dusty and smelled of damp. There was modern stained glass in lurid shades, replacing a window which had been sucked out by a Second World War bomb. Perhaps it was only the fact that sunlight was suffusing this chapel, that it was pierced by daylight, but there was more of an apple-cheeked look to the tour party than the chalky assembly which had listened to Terry Lomas.

Henry the guide, a lanky, enthusiastic man, told us about the architect of the chapel, John Griffiths. Griffiths had based his drafts on a hall at the Bank of England, which had been designed by his mentor, Sir John Soane. Henry asked us not to take photographs in the catacombs. 'The people who are buried here never foresaw that it would one day become a visitor attraction.' Then he said, 'Don't wander off or you might not come up again for a very long time.'

But it was hard to concentrate on Henry for looking at the mesmerising centrepiece of the chapel. This was the catafalque, a great hydraulic contraption for lowering coffins to the catacombs below. It was a mortician's trapdoor, a moving floor, a nifty gadget which was none the worse for being a little creaky-looking, like the motorised sofas and revolving daubs of Tracey Island, which removed the altruistic puppets from the view of their loved ones whenever *Thunderbirds* were go. The catafalque could spin a coffin through 180 degrees, said Henry, who saw plainly enough where our gaze was tending. A marvel of the 1830s, the elevating, revolving bier had been restored by the Friends. Henry said, 'It's the only working catafalque in the country. It's a marvellous sight.' I thought of how mourners at a crematorium dreaded seeing the coffin conveyored into the ovens. 'It's a wonderful thing, if you get the chance to see it in operation,' said Henry.

Demand for the tour was so great that we couldn't all enter the catacombs at once. Those of us who drew the short straw were treated to a warm-up circuit of the cemetery's highlights above ground. For the first eighteen months or so after Kensal Green opened, there were very few takers. But then William IV died, and the Duke of Sussex, attending his funeral at Windsor in 1837, vowed that he would never allow himself to follow the king into 'that stinking hole'. More prosaically, the duke knew that his second morganatic wife, whom he had married illegally, could not be buried in the royal chapel. If the couple were to stay together beyond the grave, then the grave would have to be dug somewhere other than Windsor. Accordingly, the duke became the first royal patron of the new cemetery. The bigamous royal and his wife lie beneath a massive Cornish-granite ledger surrounded by unfluted Doric bollards. The duke started a fashion for plantings at Kensal Green which soon caught on among the well-to-do.

Around us, the grass stood waist-high. An Asian woman filled a vase at a standpipe. She retreated down an aisle between graves, where the undergrowth had been trodden flat. A black woman in a polka-dot sweater noisily filled a polythene carrier bag at the same pipe. We admired the tombstone of the great Blondin, while Henry told the story of how the tightrope-walker had once cooked an omelette high above Niagara Falls. A couple of middle-aged men – balding, in shades – walked past carrying their shopping. The largest plot in the cemetery belonged to the fifth Duke of Portland, the hero of *The Underground Man*, who devoted his life and wealth to tunnelling beneath his Nottinghamshire pile. The duke went so far as to hollow out a vast underground ballroom, though no one ever trod its burnished marble. Except when he was excavating, the reclusive William John Cavendish-Bentinck-Scott seldom left his rooms, going to extravagant lengths to see that his physical needs were met without exposing himself to company. One such wheeze, the 'perpetual chicken', ensured that a fowl was forever roasting on a spit, so that whenever the Duke was hungry, the bird could be dispatched at speed on a miniature underground railway from the kitchens to his door. In Mick Jackson's novel, his lordship becomes so engrossed in his subterranean activities that eventually it's impossible for him to tell where he ends and his tunnels begin. 'When I woke I was all in a lather, having dreamed how a tiny carriage had got inside me and how its progress through my personal tunnels was making my stomach ache. I was, if I remember rightly, the man in the carriage as well as the man whose innards I journeyed through.'

The high summer of Kensal Green's fashionability arrived with the death of Portland's brother peer, the Duke of Cambridge, who was committed with full pomp at the turn of the last century to the grandest of the cemetery's mansions dolorous. The duke occupied a mausoleum, after King Mausolus, who insisted that he reposed *above* ground. Despite Cambridge's best-laid plans, not to mention his substantial outlay, his burial chamber, set as it was in this thoroughfare of mourners and gawpers, was a reminder that death was democratic, or at least demotic. Be they ever so mighty in life, the dead were in no position to decide who could look upon their last resting place.

Behind us, the black woman with the bag full of water was tending a grave in the long grass. When she knelt down, she vanished from sight. Some of the people on the tour were moved to discuss their own ends. One man said, 'I like the idea of being left on the Tube, just going round and round.'

'On the Circle Line?' asked his girlfriend.

The General Cemetery Company had entertained the notion of installing a water gate at Kensal Green, to provide access for funeral barges bearing their sad burdens along the canal from Harrow and Little Venice. Henry showed us an artist's impression from the period. It was a vision of a lowering London everglades, the proposed water gates draped with willows, which were empathetically weeping. The plan, by Henry Kendall, was not proceeded with. It seemed a pity that waterborne departures had been ruled out. The canal, which dawdled past the cemetery less than a hundred yards from where we were standing, was a pleasingly incongruous feature of the environment, its pipe-sucking bargees chugging imperviously through what was otherwise ambiguous territory, to say the least, a place with a reputation for fecklessness and drug-selling. Had things turned out differently, the west London cemetery might have staged funerals to compare with the full-blown send-offs popularised in the East End, with black-plumed horses pulling mournful longboats swagged with crêpe.

At last, it was the turn of our party to enter the catacombs. We descended a staircase beside the Anglican chapel. A draught of cold air goosed the flesh. The stairs led into an arched chamber, which stood perhaps twice as high as a man. There were damp flagstones underfoot. A man called Kevin introduced himself, saying that he would be our guide to Kensal Green below ground. He was in his late thirties or early forties and wore a pair of gold-framed spectacles and a ginger beard. 'How many of you come from London? I come from Milton Keynes. Somebody has to,' said Kevin, reworking an old Bill Bryson joke about Des Moines with the air of a man who is breaking the ice. Was it my imagination or were all the guides at Kensal Green a bit on the thin side, a little pale and – yes – ever so slightly cadaverous?

The catacombs were lit by lamps set in the brick ceiling, (100-watt bulbs, said Kevin), and by daylight, which could be made out at the end of passages radiating away from us into the middle distance. There had once been skylights, too, but these had been shattered in the same air raids which had removed the stained glass from the Anglican chapel.

Kensal Green was fortunate to have 'the largest working catacombs in England', said Kevin. He made them sound like steam engines or shire horses. Altogether, there were three different sets of catacombs, each one identified by the chapel it served. The galleries attached to the Anglican chapel, chapel A, were the largest. The Dissenters' chapel should by rights have been referred to as chapel C, said Kevin, but it was feared that the C might be misunderstood to be short for consecrated, so instead it was chapel Z. This sounded like the title of a TV show from the sixties which was so avant-garde that it had never been broadcast, although on second thoughts, chapel Z had a nice ring about it for a place of eternal rest.

In the great catacombs where we were standing beneath the Anglican chapel, there were more than two hundred vaults, with space for four thousand bodies. Kevin showed us a set of plans in which the vaults were revealed as the cells of a terrible gulag, or the chalets in a holiday camp run by cowboys. Or like the bedrooms in a vast hotel. A hotel of the dead: this was what the catacombs were, of course; competitively priced accommodation for those, unlike the Duke of Cambridge, who weren't quite flush enough to run to one of the de luxe suites on the surface.

We followed Kevin towards the patch of daylight at the end of a corridor. There was a mulch underfoot: was it of leaves? The mulch, the silt of decay, made the floor slippery. In this respect and possibly in others, following Kevin along the corridor reminded me of walking through Bazalgette's sewers, trying to keep my balance. Grime stippled the damp walls in strange patterns. Here and there, undersea algae bloomed. Kevin stopped beneath the shaft of sunlight, which was admitted by a grille, and waited until everyone had caught him up. At his back, caskets lined an arched vault. 'The dead are on the shelf,' said Kevin, with a theatrical sweep of his arm. Some of the caskets were wearing better than others. Several were warped and buckled. In some cases, the boxes were behind iron wickets which were secured by padlocks. One lay beyond a rusty iron lattice, which had been twisted out of true by corrosion. Others were screened by glass. Yet others could only be viewed by means of spyholes which penetrated their concrete carapaces. The caskets had faded metal plates on them which identified their occupants; or had done, rather, until time had wiped the slate clean. Kevin explained that the keys to the locked metal wickets were in the care of the next of kin. That was the idea, at any rate. In the case of the caskets mouldering behind rust-spotted defences, it was assumed that the keys had been mislaid, or that the familial line had died out, or that the next of kin had simply ceased to care. Frankly, this wasn't a surprise. What was a surprise was the idea that people might still come and mourn here, might even have their own names down for the eternal shelving. But what had Kevin said? These were the 'the largest working catacombs in England'.

High overhead, beside the light-admitting grille, hung stalactites like knitting needles. The only other things I could recall seeing which looked remotely like them were the long fingers of plastic I once found in my oven after I had neglected to remove all the wrapping from a pizza.

Not all of the old caskets were impregnably protected. You could reach over and touch some of them. I tapped a lead one and a wooden one. 'People are worried about grave-robbing,' said Kevin, looking at me with a mixture of concern and irritation, like a teacher at a zoo who spots a pupil trying a set of bars for size. 'The bodies have already been embalmed,' Kevin went on, 'so they're of no interest to latter-day Burke and Hares.'

In confiding tones, he continued that mourning jewellery probably 'fell off' before the bodies arrived at Kensal Green, i.e. the mourning jewellery found its way into the morning trousers of the undertakers. I had begun to notice a confusion or at least an inconsistency in Kevin's use of tenses. He talked about jewel theft as if it was in the past, but not so grave-robbing, for example. Was this part of a more general, and revealing, confusion on his part as to whether the inmates of the catacombs were still with us or not? 'Sir William Clay,' he said, 'has bought himself a prime site.' Was he really referring to a yet-to-be interred toff who had been shopping wisely?

Kevin went on, 'You're down here for ever, so you'd better prepare yourself. You go to the plumber and he puts you in a lead case.' The case in turn was slipped inside the more familiar wooden coffin, and this was finished with handles of brass or another metal, and then covered with velvet. In time, the velvet turned into a brown powder, like sawdust.

In the second half of the nineteenth century, it had cost £199 to buy a space in the catacombs: a shelf, I think Kevin meant, rather than a whole vault. The shelves at eye-level, being the most prominent, the most eye-catching, had commanded steeper fees. I thought, *£199!* The Victorians had marketed the repository as shrewdly as shopkeepers, knocking a pound off to keep their prices on the right side of discouraging round numbers.

Kevin pointed out the caskets of Eliza Abud, who died in 1860, and her husband, Richard, who perished thirteen years later. Their iron modesty grilles were furry, bearded, with rust. The technical term for this process was delaminating. 'It's the same thing that's happening to the *Titanic*,' said Kevin. As for the caskets themselves, they had crumbled. It was as if Miss Havisham had not only held on to her untouched wedding breakfast but also a brace of his 'n' hers pine boxes in which she had thriftily invested, in the same misplaced confidence of a lifelong union. Though the caskets were set well back in their shelves, you could still make out the extent of their disrepair. You were able to do this thanks to a huge torch which Kevin wielded. I had an image of him allowing it to be used – only under his strict supervision – at the municipal fireworks display on Guy Fawkes Night in Milton Keynes.

'Caskets can weigh up to half a ton,' he said. 'They go in feet first, because the feet are lighter than the head, and because people like to come and talk to their loved ones and the head is naturally the thing to aim for.'

Like all guides who are accomplished in their fields, Kevin had his own particular riffs and moves, his tics and tricks. 'Black underwear started in Victorian times. I think I'll change the subject there,' he said, as coquettishly as Marie Lloyd. With a deft movement of his torch, he picked out a line of caskets in varying stages of decay. 'Going, going, gone,' he said. He made a point of marshalling us in front of a murky vault. 'If you look up there' – he threw a light switch – 'they're children up there.' We groaned, as he knew that we would.

In vault number 82 were coffins on rails. 'I think they look like railway lines. Have a look at these coffins. Strange thing to do on a Sunday afternoon,' said Kevin, a little defensively. 'Have a look under them. Aren't they good?' The idea behind raising the coffins an inch or so off the shelf on a set of tramlines was to make the boxes less susceptible to moisture, which accumulated on the flat surface. Kevin pointed out that the underside of a coffin was never finished, but deliberately left unsmooth. This was done with the pallbearers in mind. 'A highly polished box balanced on your shoulder doesn't bear thinking about.'

Looking at me now with that schoolmaster stare of his – me and my unquiet notebook – Kevin said, 'Don't write this but – we're not supposed to mention this, so please don't write it down.' From time to time, Kevin continued, watching our faces as resentfully as a relief biology teacher about to say the word 'penis' and knowing the imbecile sniggering it will provoke, from time to time the coffins exploded. There were gasps and giggles. Kevin went on quickly that the blasts were caused by a build-up of waste gases in the caskets. *Exploding coffins!* We were all thinking the same thing. What noise would it make? What would it look like? Was one about to go off? Favouring each of us in turn with his minatory expression, Kevin said that old-fashioned clay pipes were used to forestall detonations. Injuncted against taking notes, but needlessly fearful that I might forget what my disbelieving ears had just been hearing, I jotted down a samizdat – but upper-case – 'CLAY PIPES!' when Kevin's back was turned. For some reason, I thought of the late author and countryman Laurie Lee enjoying a well-filled clay over a flagon of cider. 'Down here, we really only make use of the pipe stems,' said Kevin. These were thin enough but also sufficiently hardy and discreet to be slotted into apertures in the caskets. Tin plates were slid aside like peepholes, and the clay pipes were put into the narrow punctures behind them. The decomposition gases were burnt off. I imagined Kensal Green flaring at night like an oilfield. Is it a wicked thing to say that I should quite like to see an exploding coffin; indeed, wouldn't mind taking my leave that way myself, going out not with a whimper but a teak-splintering bang? Yes, set me up in one of those matchstick-makers when my time comes.

We moved on to the lube shop or exhaust while-you-wait or axle bay which actually housed the moving parts of the catafalque. We were peeking behind the metaphorical bombazine. This was where the levers were pulled to jolt the great Frankenstein's gurney above us. This apogee of the mortician's art ran on water pressure. It employed the same technology as the bicycle pump: eight mighty pumps, in this case, drawing water from a reservoir which was housed somewhere beneath our feet. When a coffin was about to be disappeared into the catacombs, it was imperative that the water pressure in the catafalque was high. Below the chapel, well away from the reddened eyes of loved ones, the undertaking industry's equivalent of tattooed stokers would be opening valves and dodging geysers of steam to make sure that the catafalque was taking the strain.

What happened next, to be fair to Kevin, was his attempt to put these hydraulics in the context of the funeral rites. But what we got in practice was an almost blasphemously perfunctory show-and-tell. '"For as much as Almighty God—" anyway,' said Kevin, with a sweep of his hand. '"We commit his body—"

whatever.' He seemed to be trying to suggest that he was comfortable with modern, atheistic sensibilities, though I suspected that his heart wasn't in it. He was trying to show that he was in touch. In reality, he was a traditionalist. He would say things like 'If you're lucky enough to get into Brompton Catacombs . . .' He'd catch himself getting a little sentimental in front of us about old-time funerals with all the trimmings. 'Lovely sight, six Belgian horses.' He called the dead by their first names.

Kevin said, 'The First World War finished this place off' – he blew his nose heavily into a handkerchief – 'and, if you'll excuse the pun, it died a death.' His argument was that the morbid fetish of the Victorians could not survive the surfeit of death in Flanders. Now the catacombs were the haunt mainly of the Friends of the cemetery, and their guests. Kevin's group weren't the only ones still poking about down there that afternoon. A beam of torchlight emerging from an avenue of vaults announced another party of visitors, led by a man dressed as a roadie in a black T-shirt, a baseball cap and a ponytail. 'All right, Kev,' said the roadie. 'Shall we do my trick?'

'No, John,' said Kevin.

'No?'

'I'll talk to you about it later,' said Kevin firmly. John and his torch disappeared into the darkness: he was a locomotive towing a train of people. (I learnt later from an Irishman who had been in John's party and was breathing hard in the cemetery grounds for some time afterwards that John liked to lead a full-on tour. He had shown his group a cracked coffin. Perhaps it was one of the coffins that had exploded. John had informed the group that the decomposing human body becomes a tar-like substance. 'It looked exactly like Marmite on the floor,' said the Irishman. 'It looked as though it was still wet. It turned my stomach.')

To us, Kevin said, 'I'll explain something to you in a minute. Something I'm not happy with. Bit of politics.' But Kevin was visibly distracted, and it was only a few moments before he returned to the subject of his encounter with John. 'John wanted to turn all the lights off and I said no. Health and safety. Don't want anyone tripping over and injuring themselves.'

It seemed there was more to John's prank than turning all the lights off. Kevin led us through the catacombs, to show us exactly what John had had in mind. 'Smallest coffin,' said Kevin. 'Having the lights off, as a special effect for someone.' Kevin was upset. He was speaking in broken sentences, but it was clear enough that he was talking about John. John had wanted to extinguish the lights, and in the darkness shine his torch on the smallest coffin. 'Brings us back to basics, this place does,' said Kevin in a different voice. 'Really does.' I found myself on Kevin's side, even though I remembered him throwing a switch in a vault a short time earlier and announcing, 'There's children up there.' The smallest coffin, clearly made for a baby, was a pathetic little knot of wood.

Perhaps it was just as well that we were approaching the end of the tour. We saw the last resting place of the Earl of Clare. His casket was finished in velvet, with coronets set over the handles. Kevin referred to something called a viscera chest.

I said, 'What's a viscera chest?'

'Well, if he was a chicken, it would be a plastic bag.' Yes, the noble giblets had been popped into the eternal equivalent of an overnight bag, and on the same principle: that the earl would have all his important bits and pieces with him, should they be needed.

Standing beside a tumbledown vault, which had collapsed twenty years earlier, trapping a workman and breaking his leg – 'The owners decided it was an omen and left it,' said Kevin – the guide and I had a private word.

'What's your interest in all this, Kevin?'

'Oh, I'm in the business,' said Kevin.

'You're an undertaker?'

'No, I work for Volkswagen.' If only I had thought of a way to explore this nonplussing non sequitur – there was no imaginable link between the catacombs and the teutonic car-maker. Had I misunderstood Kevin? Did he perhaps imagine that leading tours in itself qualified him for a black armband? As I say, there was no opportunity to pursue any of this because Kevin was saying, 'I hope that was interesting to you. Sorry about the exploding coffins but I'm not supposed to mention that.'

No, Kevin, no. *I'm* sorry.

EUSTON, WE HAVE A PROBLEM

London Underground

Discovering subterranean London meant exploring it, penetrating it. In turn, it was penetrating me, I realised, it was filling my thoughts. I always had my head in a book that I thought might tell me something about this hidden city. I plumbed for it in newspaper libraries and on the Internet. I went to talks, I went on walks. My first intimation of the subterranean metropolis had come as I travelled on the Underground and I found myself spending more and more time in this labyrinth. One day I looked up from the book I was reading and found that I was sitting on the Tube. Not standing by the doors, not gasping at the open window like a hooked fish, but serenely commuting. Perhaps I had unwittingly performed successful aversion therapy on myself. Flaubert wrote, 'It is only by gazing down at the black pit at our feet that we remain calm.' At all events, I was quite at home in the greatest buried thoroughfare in the world.

The Underground occupies more than 630 square miles. A poster of Piccadilly Underground station, shown in cross-section, was like a biopsy of one of London's vital organs. This was the hidden London that all Londoners encountered. Outposts of the network which were exotic to me, places like Totteridge & Whetstone, Cyprus and Theydon Bois – exotic in the same way as, say, the brothel that madam Sylvia Payne once ran behind the net curtains of Streatham – these were as familiar to some commuters as their own front doors. That wasn't to say that they thought of them anything like as tenderly. In fact, most Londoners saw the Tube as a necessary evil, a punishment to be endured twice daily. They believed that the system as a whole was dirty and overcrowded, neglected by indifferent authorities and, with the advent of the public–private partnership, left to the mercy of businessmen who were chiefly interested in number one. In this, they were of the same mind as the generation who had watched the Underground burrow its way beneath the capital in the first place. From the beginning, it had been a device for removing traffic from the streets and into often disagreeable conditions below ground, while entrepreneurs watched from their comfortable offices, hoping, often in vain, for a return on their investment.

Interpreting London the way the archaeologists do, by reading her history backwards, we find the Tube embedded in the Victorian substrata of the city. By the middle of the nineteenth century, horse-drawn vehicles and omnibuses were no match for the transport needs of the capital, now a city of more than two million people. The crush was exacerbated by the crowds pouring out of the new railway termini. London Bridge was the first to open, in 1836, and within twenty years, it was disgorging more than ten million passengers a year. In all, the exodus from the other great stations of the Victorian age – Waterloo, Victoria, Paddington, Euston, King's Cross, Shoreditch (later Liverpool Street) and Fenchurch Street – amounted to sixteen million people, getting on for eight times London's indigenous population. A lack of transport links within the city was not only a nuisance. To the entrepreneurs of steam, it was also an opportunity going begging. When the Great Western Railway deposited City gents at Brunel's terminus at Paddington in the morning, a long haul through central London to their desks still awaited them. Men such as Charles Pearson, an advocate of garden suburbs for the poor, and of underground mains to supply Londoners with their gas, proposed a subterranean railway for the heart of the metropolis. A financier called William Malins dreamt up a scheme to connect Paddington, Euston and King's Cross with a railway running under the Marylebone and

Euston Roads. Eminent Victorians including Robert Stephenson and Isambard Kingdom Brunel backed the idea, though there were also voices ranged against such godlessness. At an open-air meeting in Smithfield, a preacher called Dr Cuming warned, 'The forthcoming end of the world would be hastened by the construction of underground railways burrowing into the infernal regions and thereby disturbing the devil.'

Nonetheless, Malins's plan became the Metropolitan Railway, the first of London's underground lines. From Paddington, where the façade of sooty tiles of the original Metropolitan station now looks upon the Paddington Hilton, a rejuvenated Great Western Hotel, the route ran for four miles to Farringdon. In 1858, the aspiring railway company paid the Corporation of London £179,157 to purchase the Fleet valley. The river, which I had traced with Jane and the other walkers from its source on Hampstead Heath, which had been the midwife to so much development in London over the centuries, was rendering the city another service. Not that it suffered the irruption of digging lightly. The engineers were confronted by major problems in diverting not only the Fleet but also other lost London waterways, including the Westbourne and the Tyburn. In November 1860, a water main burst in Farringdon Street, flooding the dig. In April 1862, the Fleet roared in on the works. Arnold Bennett wrote that 'the terrific scaffolding of beams was flung like firewood into the air and fell with awful crashes. The populace screamed at the thought of workmen entombed and massacred. A silence! The whole bottom of the excavation moved in one mass. The crown of the arch of the mighty Fleet sewer had broken.'

The railway was built using the cut-and-cover method. This involved ploughing up roads to create trenches in which the line was laid. The walls of the tunnel took the strain of the sagging topsoil and the line was roofed over before the road surface was restored. The prospectors of the underground railroad rubbed their hands together. To them, the great advantage of cut-and-cover was that it involved minimum disruption to the houses lining the roads, so they didn't have to pay a fortune in compensation to home-owners. This was only true as far as the middle classes were concerned, however. Rev. William Denton, the rector of St Bartholomew, Cripplegate, claimed that the construction of a half-mile stretch of the Metropolitan had seen the levelling of nine hundred dwellings, home to ten thousand of his poorer parishioners. The establishment greeted the works with scepticism. *The Times* said it was 'an insult to common sense to suppose that people would ever prefer to be driven amid palpable darkness through the foul sub-soil of London'.

This was part of a wider association between soil and commercial interests, between muck and brass, in the Victorian mind. In *Our Mutual Friend*, it's never entirely clear how inheriting some dust heaps makes Mr Boffin rich – the heaps are metaphorically as well as literally muddy – but students of Dickens's novel have concluded that the mounds held sewage and other stinking refuse. Since it was first conceived, the Underground has been associated with the foul, with the rank and the odoriferous. This is about our visceral fears of being away from the surface of the planet, the place we think of as our natural and exclusive environment. But it's also about a similarly ingrained recoiling from the uses to which the ground beneath our feet has been put: it's a burial chamber, it's a cesspit. Taught by our parents never to put clods of earth anywhere near our mouths, we shrink from the soil. The Tube authorities have always had to work at persuading London that their network is sanitary and pleasant. Brunel had to satisfy MPs that the Metropolitan had sufficient ventilation to mitigate the effects of steam-driven trains running through its tunnels. He explained that lengths of the railway were left open to the sky – at Farringdon, for example. In addition, the directors of the Metropolitan claimed that their engines would 'consume their own smoke and condense their own steam'. The theory was that the exhaust gases would be trapped in tanks behind the engines to be released safely when the trains emerged from tunnels into overground sections of the railway. This led to the erection of a brace of the most extraordinary architectural curiosities in London. From the front, 22 and 23 Leinster Gardens, W2, are pukka stucco buildings. They stand on an avenue of hotels which are not quite as grand as their Bayswater address would perhaps lead visitors to expect. But they are false. They are *trompe l'œil* devices, stage flats. Their depthless façades and lightless windows, never glazed, were designed to shield polite society from a stretch of railway which was otherwise open to the elements and used as a place where engines could vent their fumes. Underground trains still emerge into daylight from under Leinster Gardens, though they no longer let off steam there.

Despite such decorous arrangements, the milieu of the railway proved to be less than airy. The London correspondents of foreign newspapers astounded their readers with accounts of carriages which were smoky both inside and out. While travellers sucked on their pipes, the tunnels around them filled with coal gases. A passenger on the Metropolitan in 1879 complained that he almost suffocated and had to be helped out of the train and up onto the street. As he recalled, he was taken to a nearby chemist's. 'Without a moment's hesitation, he said, "Oh, I see, Metropolitan Railway," and at once poured out a wineglass full of what I conclude he designated Metropolitan Mixture. I was induced to ask him whether he often had such cases, to which he rejoined, "Why bless you sir, we often have twenty cases a day."'

The Metropolitan dismissed this scaremongering. Colonel John Bell, the general manager, assured MPs that the railway's fumes were actually health-giving, and that Great Portland Street station was 'used as a sanatorium for men who had been afflicted with asthma and bronchial complaints'. His own recovery from decades of tonsilitis Bell attributed to the boon of the 'acid gas' which accumulated in the tunnels. Other reports from the Underground claimed that its environs were efficacious in relieving anorexia. Poisonous or not, the atmosphere on the Underground, once experienced, made a powerful impression. A traveller with experience of Africa compared the smell of the tunnels to the breath of a crocodile. Ford Madox Ford wrote in *The Soul of London*, 'I have known a man, dying a long way from London, sigh queerly for the gush of smoke that, on a platform of the Underground, one may see escaping in great woolly clots.' No doubt every city has its signature stink. In Venice, it's the canals; in present-day Amsterdam, the heady fug of decriminalised pot, and so on. In London, the peasouper famous from a dozen Sherlock Holmes stories disappeared from the streets only to reappear underneath them.

The airs of the subterranean railway were not improved until the introduction of electrification led to the phasing out of steam trains. (They survived as vehicles for transporting night-time maintenance crews. The last one ran in June 1967.) But the fragrancy or otherwise of the network remained a noisome issue. Old bill matter for the Central Line has Father Neptune, in a crown and a skirt of weeds, up to his hips in the sea, blowing through the Tube as if it was a giant conch. 'The most enjoyable form of travelling in London,' claimed the copy. 'Every trip invigorates you. Father Neptune blows 80 million cubic feet of Ozone through the Tube daily.' Ozoning plants were built at Edgware Road, Goodge Street and Charing Cross. Another marketing strategy, intended to convey how pleasantly cool a subterranean journey could be, represented the Central Line as a prize-winning cucumber.

Today's commuter would smile wryly at that, provided he had been sufficiently sedated first. Although 'strap-hanging' is the best-known gerund that metropolitan travel has given us, the vocabulary of every Tube passenger in possession of an olfactory sense also includes 'nostril-pinching', or a variant of it. Armpits, insteps, ox-felling halitosis – this is the nosegay of the Underground. It lacks air conditioning, unlike the transit systems of other great conurbations, and the earth of the city can still be noxious. In the Paris Metro, trains at one time sprayed perfume as they entered stations. In the spring of 2001, London Underground itself trialled perfume on the Tube. An apothecary of pongs was retained from a French scent house and tasked to create a bouquet for the Tube. The result was Madeleine, a pot-pourri of rose, jasmine and fruit, which was applied to the surface of platforms and released by passing feet. It was tried at Euston, Piccadilly and the flagship halt of St James's Park, which is situated beneath London Underground's art deco HQ. Even when Madeleine was right under the noses of commuters, many said that they couldn't discern it above the familiar stew of the Tube. Of those who expressed a preference, most felt it was cloying and overpowering. It didn't catch on.

As for the foul subsoil of the pioneering Metropolitan Railway, it had a curious afterlife. The general manager of the railway received a telegram from the manager of White's Club in St James's not long after the line had opened. The club official sought an answer to a puzzle which had been the subject of large bets among members: what had the railway done with all the earth which had been removed to make way for the trains? The clubbable gamblers were advised to visit Chelsea. The spoil from the site had been dumped just off the Fulham Road, at a place called Stamford Bridge. In 1905, when Chelsea Football Club was founded, the terracing was built upon the spoor of the Metropolitan Line.

The success of the railway led to a scramble to build more lines, a kind of steam rush, with no fewer than 250 schemes in the year after the Metropolitan's inaugural run. Some had more going for them than others. The more fanciful ideas included draining the Regent's Canal and laying tracks in it; opening a railway powered by windmills; and establishing another, circular route, entirely covered in glass. More realistic plans for an 'Inner Circle' system led to the creation of the District and Circle Lines, built using the same cut-and-cover method. The idea was that the District would run south of the Metropolitan and parallel to it. At either end, the District would curve northwards, the Metropolitan southwards, and the two would link to form the Circle Line. The risk of tunnelling in central London, with its hazards of potentially ruinous compensation, was mitigated by laying track in the new Victoria Embankment, handily provided by Bazalgette. To let smoke and steam escape from the locomotives, he installed ventilation shafts in Victoria Embankment Gardens, which can be found to this day, disguised as plinths. Work began on the District Line in 1865. For a year, two thousand labourers, two hundred horses and 58 engines hacked their way underground. The clay they extracted was fired into bricks at two huge kilns at Earl's Court.

Sir Edward Watkin, the chairman of the Metropolitan, embarked on grandiose plans for an empire of rail. Not only did he push his own line out as far as Harrow, Amersham and Chesham, creating the 'Metroland' which was later celebrated by John Betjeman, but he also entertained notions of making London the hub of a railway linking Manchester and Paris. Watkin was an early advocate of a Channel tunnel. A shameless booster of his own businesses, he set out to build a soaring tower, fifteen feet taller than Gustave Eiffel's Parisian landmark, to attract tourists to the Metropolitan at Wembley. The Watkin tower wasn't a great success and was never completed. The site eventually became Wembley stadium, the second London football ground associated with the Metropolitan Line.

Although the earliest routes are considered part of today's Underground network, they lie only a few feet beneath the surface of the streets. For significant stretches, the trains run in the open air. These are not the magma-scrapers that brought London's Tube international renown. The technology which made the deeper lines possible was developed by Mark Brunel as he and his son Isambard built the Thames Tunnel, the first under a river anywhere in the world, which is itself now a splendidly arched, bone-white tunnel between Wapping and Rotherhithe on the East London Line. Brunel patented a tunnelling shield in 1818. The principle was that the shield pressed against the face which was under excavation. At any one moment, only a small section of the shield was drawn back to permit digging, while the rest of it served to buttress the seam. Brunel's shield consisted of twelve massive cast-iron frames. Each of them was more than twenty-one feet high and three feet wide, and divided into three compartments in which a miner could work. After the Thames Tunnel opened in 1843, the new shield technology was adapted to build the first genuinely underground railway. The contractor, James Greathead, excavated the line between King William Street in the Square Mile and Stockwell. Greathead's achievement is commemorated in a statue outside the present-day Bank station and by a piece of a Greathead Shield, as his device became known, which can be seen by commuters using 'the Drain', the Waterloo and City Line.

In its first two weeks, the King William Street to Stockwell railway, the forerunner of today's Northern Line, carried 165,000 passengers. Small electric locomotives dragged the three-car trains, and hydraulic lifts ameliorated the inconvenience to passengers of descending more than forty feet through the earth to the platforms. The carriages were dubbed 'padded cells' because they were upholstered from floor to ceiling: no windows had been fitted, on the grounds that there was nothing to look at. The service was thought to be quick and clean. This was the high water mark of the route's popularity, before it developed a reputation for tattiness and sloth as 'the Misery Line'.

King William Street was to become the first of those fascinating London fixtures – part ghost train, part secret passageway – the disused, or 'dead', Tube stations. It was opened by the Prince of Wales, the future Edward VII, on 4 November 1890. It was originally conceived as the City terminus of a cable-traction operation, the City of London and Southwark Subway, rather than of a prototype electric railway, the City and South London Railway, as it later became. This showed in its specifications. Moreover, the approach to the station was awkward because the line snaked beneath narrow streets. The tunnels crossed each other, so that the 'keep left' rule which usually obtains on railways became a 'keep right' rule (this is still a feature of the line between Moorgate and London Bridge). In places, the northbound tunnel was even stacked on top of the southbound one. The City & South London Railway was extended northwards to Moorgate and Bank. The board wanted to flatten Hawksmoor's church of St Mary Woolnoth and even got parliamentary consent to do so. But an outcry saved the building. Instead, the railway underpinned the church's foundations and quarried a booking hall out of the crypt. The directors decided to bypass King William Street and the station closed in February 1900. A farmer applied to grow mushrooms in the tunnel but he was refused. In 1914, following a tip-off to police at the outbreak of the First World War, the station was searched for enemy agents who were said to be equipped with a cache of explosives. Officers found nothing to substantiate this rumour, which recalled the legend of Guy Fawkes, as well as more primeval anxieties about threats from beneath the earth. The police boarded the tunnels up just in case. Outside, the entrance to the former station was incorporated into an office building at 46 King William Street. In 1930, the Underground Group, as the line's then owners were known, decided to dispose of this property, and invited the press to see King William Street for the last time. Reporters found that the entrances to the pedestrian tunnels were marked by those reassuring, vanished symbols of Victorian England: pointing hands, protruding from double-folded linen cuffs. On tattered posters, property auctions were advertised in the same eye-catching font used to bark up trade for freak shows. The derelict wooden signal box, like a lifeguard's lookout post, was still standing on the platform. As for the southern end of the first tube railway, the original platform at Stockwell was in use until 1923. It was replaced after the line was extended as far as Clapham Common, but you can still see where it stood if you squint through the windows of a passing train.

The phantom, chimerical architecture of the Tube was part of the occult city that I was attempting to document. At London Bridge, with station manager Ian McCrory as my guide, this major interchange was revealed as a honeycomb of tunnels and passages, both in service and in delicious desuetude. For instance, directly above the Northern Line tunnel we found ... the Northern Line tunnel. An abandoned stretch of the railway was bricked up on top of its successor. The old tunnel was like an elongated Nissen hut. The floor was striped, indicating where the sleepers had once been. Lights were mounted on the walls and there was a white door at the far end of the truncated tunnel. It had been decommissioned after managers decided that it wouldn't stand up to all the traffic that would be passing through the station.

Elsewhere in the warren – at a bridge connecting the Northern and Jubilee lines – Ian opened a door which admitted us to a dripping chamber, where a dirty metal staircase rose steeply away. This chamber afforded access to another disused part of the station, the old City and South London line. A curving tunnel bent away out of sight. To enter it was to climb the gently ascending wall of an industrial chimney thickly lined with dust. You placed your feet on slabs which protruded from the inner face of this stack. Something in the dust made it glitter.

Ian and I shinned up the slabs to emerge into another sawn-off tunnel. This one had been used as an air-raid shelter during the Second World War. There was a graffito of an only slightly less cobwebby vintage: 'Millwall' accompanied by a date from 1988. There was also the plaintive slogan 'Waiting for the Northern Line'. Ian said that the directors of pop videos sought this location out. It was also used by the fire brigade when they held exercises for tackling smoke in confined quarters. The firemen were brought to the disused tunnels below London Bridge at night, and exposed to fumes including CO_2 and burning oil. Ian said, 'I was on a platform of the Jubilee Line during one of these exercises and you couldn't see your hand in front of your face.' The station was fitted with fans at either end of the concourse: they soon dispersed the smoke. 'The fans also make passengers feel more comfortable. Since we got them, we've had fewer people keeling over,' said Ian with satisfaction. There was plenty to contend with, as things were. Up to 63,000 people went through London Bridge station on a busy day. Some of them were unruly, even violent. Five members of staff had struggled with one man: three of them had sat on him before his rage abated. In another incident, three youths set fire to a woman's hair. One regular at London Bridge used to repair to the platforms to take his toilet. 'Used to bring his own loo paper and everything.' Ian once rounded a corner to come face to face with a six-foot-tall Dalmatian which was standing patiently on the platform with the other commuters. Another discovery of his concerned a passenger who had shed his outfit rather than donned an unusual one. He found a full set of clothes laid out neatly on the station concourse: top, trousers, shoes, underwear. There was no sign of the Reginald Perrin figure who fitted this ensemble.

The drunk and the delinquent and the plain dirty ought to know that every operative nook of London Bridge falls within the all-seeing eyes of Ian and his team, or rather of their CCTV cameras. The mischievous youngster who sets off an alarm on a platform would be amazed to know that everyone in the control room is looking at him within seconds. The cameras are programmed to focus immediately on any point in the station where the alarm has been raised. Alarms from two or more points at the same time have to be followed by an evacuation, even if it's just a drinker who's pressed one red button, gone round a corner and done the same thing again. With heroic restraint, the staff make only the most sparing use of their terrible power. For example, the teenager who tosses his empty jeroboam of milkshake onto a platform may have his conscience pricked, and his cheeks reddened, by an almost simultaneous Tannoy injunction against dropping rubbish. The litterbug might not be identified as such, but he'll know who the announcer was talking about and so will everyone else near him. The best message I heard at London Bridge was made by the admirable Mr Wong, a staffer of Chinese descent. Somehow sensing from his distant eyrie in front of a bank of CCTV screens that there was tension on a fast-filling platform, Mr Wong cooed into his mic, 'When the wind blows, that means the train is coming.'

In the stretch of old tunnel where Ian and I were, you could make out marks on the walls where the wartime bunks had been rigged up. Ian said that a colleague of his had spent his time in and out of the shelters of London Bridge as a boy and had gone on to clock up thirty years' service or more on the Underground.

'Do you ever hear of people living in the Tube today?'

'Only the staff,' said Ian. 'My wife says I spend more time here than at home.'

London Bridge was one of seventy-nine Underground stations which became makeshift but effective shelters during the air raids of the Second World War. Londoners also took refuge in the disused King William Street tunnel, which held 100,000 people alone, and the Piccadilly branch line between Holborn and Aldwych, which was now frequented only by Barry, the manager of the ghost station, in his personal train. At the outbreak of war, the authorities were wary about people fleeing the bombs for the

Tube, on the grounds that they might never come back up again. Those who allowed their fears to get the better of them were seen as inadequate, as 'Tube Cuthberts'. The *Railway Gazette* was relieved to find that few of the 'offenders' letting the side down were native Londoners. 'We are happy to record that a vast majority of offenders are members of alien races, or at least alien extraction.' London Transport put up notices expressly forbidding the practice of using stations as shelters. The rules were that only fare-paying passengers were admitted during raids. But Londoners weren't stupid. In their thousands, they simply purchased the cheapest ticket available and headed for the platforms. The spectacle of so many people cheek by jowl in the gloom awed Henry Moore, who produced a sketchbook of drawings based on what he'd seen.

> One evening after dinner in a restaurant with some friends we returned home by Underground taking the Northern Line to Belsize Park. As a rule I went into town by car and I hadn't been by Tube for ages. For the first time that evening I saw people lying on the platforms at all the stations we stopped at . . . I had never seen so many reclining figures and even the train tunnels seemed to be like the holes in my sculpture. And amid the grim tension, I noticed groups of strangers formed together in intimate groups and children asleep within feet of the passing trains.

After this experience, Moore frequented the Tube during air raids, particularly Liverpool Street. A new Central Line tunnel had been built at the station before the bombing began and London Transport, growing less hard-hearted the longer the Blitz wore on, tarmacked it over to accommodate more people. At night, rows of sleeping families occupied the entire length of the tunnel. The artist made notes to himself on the back of an envelope instead of sketching the shelterers where they lay. 'It would have been like drawing in the hold of a slave ship,' he said.

Sanitary conditions were appalling. Many preferred to stay in their homes and brave the Luftwaffe rather than endure the foul-smelling platforms. For the rest, there were compensations to the troglodyte life in the amenities that station regulars set up for themselves. There were canteens, lending libraries, first-aid posts. There were even puppet shows for the children and theatrical productions. The Tube stations nevertheless became breeding grounds for dissent. At Swiss Cottage, the shelterers produced their own newsletter. After a child died of meningitis at the station, *The Swiss Cottager* railed against the authorities for 'indifference amounting almost to callousness, neglect, soulless contempt for elementary human decencies ... red tape, authoritarianism and officialdom'.

If this was the lot of ordinary Londoners, some found more agreeable billets. The rich resorted to a shelter beneath the Savoy Hotel and the subterranean Turkish baths at the Dorchester. In his diary, Cecil Beaton recorded the revels at the latter. 'There the noise outside is drowned by wine, music and company, and what a mixed brew we are! Cabinet ministers and their self-consciously respectable wives; hatchet-jawed iron grey brigadiers; calf-like airmen off duty; tarts on duty; actresses (also); déclassé society people, cheap musicians and motor car agents. It could not be more ugly and vile.' This carousing led to ill feeling among the less well favoured. On 15 September 1940, Phil Piratin, a Communist MP, led a hundred East Enders into the Savoy shelter. The staff could not lawfully bar them. The visitors left after the all-clear, not forgetting to tip the waiters.

The Tube saved countless lives but it was far from bombproof. Twenty people were killed at Marble Arch station during a raid on 17 September 1940. A bomb smashed a water main at Balham, where six hundred people were sheltering. The road over the station collapsed, filling the tunnel with tons of earth and water. The bodies of sixty-eight people were dug out of the quagmire. In 1941, a bomb dropped into the crypt at St Mary

Woolnoth, the booking hall built by the City and South London Railway. By terrible and improbable misfortune, it bounced down the escalator of Bank station and exploded on the platform, killing 117 people. Londoners were not deterred by these reverses. A few days after the fatal Marble Arch blast, for instance, no fewer than 117,000 people were sleeping in the Underground. Nonetheless, plans were hatched for shelters which were even deeper than Tube stations, and hence more secure. The idea was to build ten of these deep-level shelters a hundred feet down, directly underneath existing Tube stops. Two would be under the Central Line and eight beneath the Northern Line. But a proposed bunker at the Oval was undone by the waters of the buried River Effra, while another at St Paul's was ruled out because of fears that the cathedral would be undermined. The eight remaining shelters were commissioned and were ready by 1942. They were at Chancery Lane, Clapham South, Clapham Common, Clapham North, Stockwell, Goodge Street, Camden Town and Belsize Park, and the Northern Line shelters are given away to this day by the distinctive Martello Tower entrances which can be found nearby. The shelters each comprised a pair of parallel tunnels, 1,200 feet long, divided into upper and lower floors and equipped with iron bunks. There were also sickbays, wardens' posts and enough ventilation equipment to bring air to these subterranean hideouts. Because the shelters were lower than Bazalgette's sewers, engineers contrived to get rid of waste by using compressed air. This propelled the effluvia up to the level of the mains, in much the same way as the sewage ejectors tenderly curated by Gurmet Kalsi at the Houses of Parliament.

Chancery Lane and Clapham Common were designated as emergency command posts in anticipation of the bombardment of London by V1 and V2 rockets. Military planners feared that these unfamiliar weapons might carry atomic payloads. Stockwell was used as a hostel for American troops and Goodge

Street became the secure headquarters of General Eisenhower. Hard-pressed civilians could take cover in the other redoubts, which were designed to house as many as eight thousand people each.

The entrance to the Clapham North shelter is at the rear of a car park behind a pair of locked gates on Bedford Road, SW4. A sign on the old brick chimney of an air shaft in the car park reminds the visitor that it is the property of the defunct 'Ministry of Public Buildings & Works'. A nondescript doorway opens onto the entrance hall of the shelter. It's really a foyer, with a counter on one side. Perhaps this was a check-in position, where a marshal tallied the numbers entering the bunker as the air-raid sirens sounded. On the wall is a Ministry of Works plan. The shelter's secure housing begins at the far-off foot of a broad concrete staircase. Lining the staircase are decrepit boxes, like something a fruiterer might once have stacked apples in.

The endless tunnels, secured by rivets, are like the bulkheads of a vast freighter. Wartime planners hoped that the tunnels would be knocked through in peacetime to create a new high-speed Tube line. This was never done, though the deep-level shelters are wistfully cited by those who speculate about secret tunnels spanning the entire underground metropolis. In their time, the shelters have been put to many other uses. In 1948, 236 Jamaican immigrants who landed in Britain on the *Empire Windrush* had their culture shock compounded by beginning life as Londoners in the Clapham South shelter. This dugout inadvertently made a major contribution to the multicultural life of the capital. Because the nearest labour exchange was in Brixton, many of the *Windrush* arrivals settled there and it became the spiritual home of black London. The Camden Town shelter has provided a backdrop for episodes of *Doctor Who* and *Blake's 7*. Eisenhower's old bunker at Goodge Street was used by troops en route to action in the Suez crisis in 1956 and now stores Channel 4's back catalogue of programmes. Other shelters have similarly been converted into data banks and archives. Deep underground at Clapham North, an untidy workbench stands abandoned behind a polythene screen, tools and dirty mugs and dockets left exactly as they were when the workmen exited, perhaps on the very day indicated by a yellowing tabloid: 24 May 1986.

There was plenty of hidden Underground to see, provided you knew where to look, who to talk to. Another of my guides was a man named Billy McKeown. If you happen to be tucked up in bed as you read this, spare a thought for Billy. He's deep below London now, about as deep as you can get, in fact, and all by himself in the blackness. He's down there every night for hours at a stretch, in one of the furthermost reaches of the capital. His workplace is transiently and unthinkingly occupied by millions of Londoners during the working day – though not transiently and unthinkingly enough for most of them – but deserted in the small hours. It's imagined in its nocturnal condition, if at all, in the same way that the fortunate householder, or reader, snugly abed, contemplates wild weather outside his double-glazed window, hugging himself at the sound of the rain on his impermeable roof. Billy was a good guide to the lost Underground. But I had to find him first – he was lost in it.

Billy's job is to walk the line: the Northern Line, in fact. In addition to doing one of the two things the average passenger of the London Underground would prefer not to attempt – being alone in the system after dark – he does the other one as well, and steps nervelessly onto the track. Billy is no fool, and besides, he's been doing his job for a long time now. The only reason he goes anywhere near the live rail is because he knows that the power is switched off during the hours he works. This is the period between one o'clock in the morning and about five a.m., between the last Tube taking home the drunks and the workaholics, and the City trader earlybird specials. It's the time when the Underground replenishes itself. In the four or five hours when the current is turned off, the Underground system, a giant octopus uncoiled on a seabed, goes through its intimate routines of preening and taking its rest. It's the interlude when advertisements are scraped off their hoardings like old wallpaper and their replacements are pasted in place. Litter which has been overlooked during operating hours is collected; the same goes for escalator repairs. Platforms are swept and tunnels are purged. The night shift is also when London Underground maintains its antique and groaning infrastructure. Chipped and distressed concrete sleepers are effortfully levered from the bottom of inverts and swapped for fresh slabs. At a distance of up to several miles from the nearest track crew, Billy McKeown makes his solitary rounds. He's a patrolman, pacing out the deserted tunnels with his lamp and his walkie-talkie and his large box-spanner. Although Billy's most important job is to keep a lookout for any flaws in the line, any kinks or cracks, and then report them, he also checks the bolts which hold the rails onto the sleepers: he tests their grip. With his great monkey wrench, he can screw any loose bolts to a better-than-finger-tightness.

I was looking forward to meeting Billy. Through the incongruous medium of the country and western lyric, Billy's occupation of patrolman – lineman, to Americans – has been mythologised as a romantic one, the calling of a self-reliant loner. 'Because you're mine, I walk the line,' sang Johnny Cash, as if love kept him on the straight and narrow, or conversely, as if footslogging the rugged and inhospitable margin was the penance he served for love gone bad. Although I wasn't quite ready to imagine Billy McKeown of the Northern Line as the Marlboro Man, I was keen to meet someone who seemed to be so well adapted to London's last frontier, the subterranean city. Billy was only a conversation away by walkie-talkie, but he was lost to the eye in the maze of dark tunnels.

In the middle of the night, Billy's boss, Mick Murphy, was leading the way through a deserted London Bridge station. Mick was in charge of maintenance work on the railway. He had been working on the Tube for years. He walked to the end of the Northern Line platform, where it met the tunnel, and stepped off the edge. Even though I knew that the power was off, the hop onto the track was a leap of faith, going against everything that had been drummed into me in all the years I had used the Tube. I placed the reinforced sole of a complimentary LU welly on the rail – and didn't fry.

We were going north to Bank station, a journey which would take us under the Thames. Just as I had on my earliest, childhood visits to London, I allowed myself to be swallowed up by a Tube tunnel. Somewhere up ahead, Mick's gang were at work. We couldn't see them yet, but vibrations travelling through the rails would have given them away to a Red Indian scout. Billy McKeown was supposed to be on his way to the tunnel too, though no one had seen him since the start of the evening and Mick hadn't been able to raise him on his walkie-talkie. Mick was in touch with the Northern Line control room, at Coburg Street behind Euston station, in an attempt to solve the problem of the missing patrolman, but the night managers hadn't heard from Billy either.

In the tunnel, Mick and I discussed the smirk-raising matter of the fluffers. Now a euphemism, or near-euphemism, for women who get male porn stars in the mood before the cameras turn, the fluffers used to be the name of the workers who had the unmirthful task of keeping the Tube tunnels clean. 'They were lovely big West Indian ladies, most of them,' said Mick mistily. (I was going to say 'Mick carried a torch –' meaning that his flashlight enabled me to glimpse the faraway look in his eye; on second thoughts, perhaps I stumbled upon the apposite phrase at the first time of asking.) 'Do you know the main thing the fluffers had to get rid of?' he asked. 'Human hair.' With so many people circulating through the Tube network every day, moving and bumping up against each other, there was hair loss of alopecian proportions, as well as a massive sloughing off of skin. The Underground was a wind tunnel of psoriasis. Unfortunately, the fluffers didn't work underground any longer. They had been replaced by a machine which trawled the Tube for flakes of epidermis and tufts of hair, like a giant prototype of a device you might see advertised on a shopping channel, a grooming aid which was claimed to banish the distress and embarrassment of dandruff for ever.

The other unlikely detritus in the tunnels was wallets. I was baffled – why would wallets turn up on the track in significant numbers? – until Mick explained that it was a by-product of the mugging and pickpocketing that went on in the Tube. Thieves snaffled purses and pocketbooks, filleting them and dropping what was left through the windows at the end of the carriages. The place where I preferred to stand for ventilation's sake was integral to the craft of the Tube criminal.

We approached the middle of the tunnel. Directly above us was the merest margin of London clay, and above that, the Thames itself, insistently pressing. Mick pointed out dense metal panels folded against the sides of the tunnel, upon which nature, that reckless graffiti artist, had left its sprawling tag, even so far from what was fresh and bountiful – what was *natural* – as the middle of a Northern Line Tube tunnel. The mineral of the panels had fused with a vegetable, even perhaps an animal, element. The metal was matted with moss, shiny with the tunnel's own secretions. The panels were floodgates. In the unlikely event of a riverine incursion, they were meant to stop the water from inundating the Northern Line. London's rivers were a constant challenge to London Underground: with its pipes and pumps, it was the second-biggest shifter of water in London after Thames Water. It wasn't too fanciful to see the Tube train drivers as the pilots of skiffs. Like the canny, live-on-their-nerves skippers of the dragontail boats of Bangkok, they nosed and clipped their way through the piers and pontoons of the Underground. The trains were junks, sampans, rude and unimaginably antique, plying the city's reeking, soupy-warm channels and backwaters.

At the height of the IRA's threat to the British mainland, Mick told me, the Underground had posted a man on the floodgates every night, just to make sure that there wasn't a bomb anywhere near them. This recalled the police search of King William Street station in 1914. In the seventies and eighties, the IRA was considered the chief threat to the network. In March 1976, a republican called Vincent Kelly was carrying a bomb on a District Line train at West Ham when his device started giving off smoke. Kelly panicked and threw the bomb onto the floor of the carriage. It injured nine passengers, including himself. He fled from the train but was chased by the driver, Stephen Julius. Kelly shot Julius dead, injured a Post Office engineer with a second round, and put a bullet in himself. But there was no recorded incident of the paramilitaries hiking through the Tube tunnels, looking for a place to leave their explosives. As Mick and I contemplated the gates under the Thames, the recollection of doing IRA-watch made him almost as sentimental as the thought of the vanished fluffers: what a glorious skive it had been, to be the man who kept lookout from the floodgates for the Provos!

The most recent scare was the threat of an anthrax attack on the Tube. A London Underground official was asked if there was an emergency procedure for such eventualities. 'Well, put it this way: we've had plans about what to do in a chemical attack and it's along those lines,' he said. 'But we've also had to get the cleaners to switch to a new powder when they're clearing up sick, to stop passengers coming along afterwards and panicking. The old stuff was white, you see.' In 2002, the chief constable of the British Transport Police complained that the government had been parsimonious with security measures against possible attacks on the Underground, compared to resources for incidents above ground. In any crisis, the first clue to commuters that anything untoward was going on would be a message over the public address system for 'Inspector Sands'. This fictitious employee was always summoned in the event of an emergency in an Underground station.

Down in the dark tunnel leading to Bank station, Mick and I were approaching the gangers, or at least we were nearing the source of muffled clanging and echoing voices. We were taking a bend. It's one of the unanticipated features of walking the line that Tube tunnels don't follow an unvarying route over flat planes. On the contrary, they swerve and dip. The physics of a Tube train moving around a bend meant that there was greater wear and tear at such a point. Mick said, 'What you're basically trying to do is to get a square metal box around a corner.' To skew the physics in favour of LU, and indeed the travelling public, trackside sumps known as greasers were to be found on corners, dispensing lubricant onto the rail at the trigger of a passing train. A battery of floodlights on tripods came into view and below them, a knot of men in orange boiler suits were backlit in attitudes of toil. This was the track gang, Mick's boys. As we drew nearer, it was possible to make out the men's faces. They were as black as colliers.

The men were maintaining sleepers, and small wonder. I was astonished to learn that some of these groynes dated back to the 1920s, and even now were not considered to have reached the end of their useful lives. Before the gang could get at the sleepers, however, they had to move the track out of the way first. This entailed undoing the bolts that held the rails in place, in brackets known as chairs. The next task was to jack the rails up. With this done, the men could at last get their hands on the sleepers themselves. As I was learning, the backbone of the railway wasn't lightly transplanted. If there was any prospect that there was life left in a sleeper, it would be taken out, turned the other way round – so that the onside of the sleeper, so to speak, was now the offside – and then put back. This might be a worthwhile exercise on a bend, for example, where the sleepers were ground down at one end but had a few hundred miles of wear left in them at the other. Sleepers which were of no value even to the miserly maintenance men were broken up with electric drills and removed in pieces.

The gang was led by a charge hand named Scott. He was built like a rugby forward, an impression in no way qualified by the front tooth he was missing. Scott told me that it was only in the past few years that maintenance teams had been supplied with electricity in the tunnels at night. Once the juice had been turned off in the control rooms overground, the gangs had worked by Tilly lamps fuelled by paraffin, or by the lights on their hard hats. 'We had to use picks to smash the sleepers, and sometimes a hammer and chisel,' he said. It was a gruelling job even now, and a man in the night gang might earn no more than £24,000. How safe was it? Scott pointed out that the men were equipped with hard hats. He said, 'We're supposed to wear them, of course, but why? They only make you sweat. If something falls on your head down here, a hat ain't going to save you.' It was sobering to think of the graft, and risk, involved in swinging a pick in a confined space when the practice had been to do this in near-darkness. It was a hard life underground, I suggested to Scott.

'In ways you don't always think of,' he said. 'One of the biggest problems is relationships. I've seen a lot of them break up. You've got to have a good woman behind you.' In the heat and grime of a Tube tunnel in the middle of the night, this sounded nothing but noble.

As we came out of the tunnel into Bank station, I checked my watch. It was 3.05 a.m. The Northern Line platform was quiet; there was no sign of anyone. More to the point, there was no sign of patrolman Billy McKeown. Where could he be? Soon, we would be setting off on our return journey, to complete the trip back to London Bridge before the railway woke up for another day. I didn't like to think that we would fail to run into Billy, after all.

Perhaps Mick's many years on the Underground had given him a sixth sense about a man like Billy. He suggested that we carry on as planned. If we started for London Bridge, we might spot him coming towards us. Sure enough, hardly had we clambered down onto the track again, and squinted into the tunnel before us, than a light winked like a glow-worm in the gloaming, and into sight came a figure with a mighty spanner over its shoulder. Was it the implement he was carrying – in the half-light, it might have passed for a club, or even a sword – that lent Billy's entrance a heroic aspect? He might have been a pioneering railwayman, a Casey Jones.

Blinking in the comparative noonday of Bank station, Billy was fazed to be met by a welcoming committee. He had started his shift by getting onto the line at Kennington as soon after midnight as it was safe to do so, he told us, and it was his intention to reach Old Street before sun-up – or, more pertinently, before the power came back on again. 'I should be there by about 4.15, I hope,' he said in his Ulster twang. The route he had set himself was a little over four kilometres long. Unlike Mick and I, who had walked up the northern tunnel and would be promiscuously returning by the southern passage, Billy was monogamously husbanding the two thoroughfares one after the other, with his northbound trek tonight followed by a southerly sojourn the next night. 'It's a one-man job patrolling, so you can take more detail in,' he said. 'You might make wrong decisions but you won't make bad ones.'

Billy was a solitary type, an uncompromising ploughman of his own furrow. This cussed quality was not helped by Billy's strangely mimsy Presbyterian tones. When he said 'Actually', it came out as 'Ectually', in the accents of Miss Jean Brodie. But he was a terrific bloke, a man who was sure of himself without feeling the need to impose this certainty on others. He was fifty-five, he said, and his bearing suggested a hinterland not confined to the miles he had conquered of otherwise little-trodden track.

That was a point: I asked him, 'If someone brought you down here blindfold and took the mask off, would you know exactly where you were in the tunnel?'

'I could probably give you the km-mark,' he said. In other words, he'd know to the nearest kilometre. I was briefly crestfallen. This wasn't the uncanny precision I'd hoped for from the man who took his daily constitutional in the Underground. But I rallied when I considered how difficult it must be for even the most seasoned tunneller to tell one stretch from the next. The deceptively homogeneous defile gave up clues to Billy of which the stumbling stranger was oblivious.

Billy came from a God-fearing background but had at one time, by his own admission, been overfond of the bottle. London Underground had been very understanding while he sorted himself out, he said. These days, he was stone-cold sober. He wasn't a fanciful man. So, although the hour and the place were congenial to supernatural cogitations, I expected only the shortest of shrifts from the Ulsterman when I asked him who or what might occupy the tunnels at night; other than himself, of course. I was duly surprised by his reply. He said, 'I didn't necessarily see a ghost but there was a very strange experience once.'

It was about ten years ago, said Billy. He was walking the Jubilee Line in those days. It was 2.30 in the morning and he was patrolling between Baker Street and St John's Wood. He had clocked on some hours earlier and was ready for a breather. 'I was sitting on what used to be called the "anti-noise",' he said, referring to a baffle set into the hollow of the tunnel. It was at a stretch of the railway which was quite well lit. 'I was just sitting there, having a drink of Coke, and suddenly I felt this wee draught. You know how warm it can get down in these tunnels? Well, it was very surprising to go cold all over like that.' Billy had been staring directly ahead of him, his gaze fixed on the line. There was a dusty, powdery ballast between the rails, he said. 'As

I was looking, I saw footprints appearing in the ballast. It was going right past me, whatever it was. I was frozen.' As Billy watched, the ballast continued to be disturbed in the same way, with what appeared to be footprints heading deeper into the tunnel, as if an invisible figure was walking away from him. 'After it got about ten metres away from me, it stopped,' said Billy. 'The worst part of it was that I had to go in the same direction.' He decided to move as quickly as he could. 'I felt incredibly cold, like I was in a freezer. But after I got past those first ten metres, I started to feel OK again.'

Risking ridicule, Billy described what had happened to his fellow patrolman, a man named Wilson, as the pair of them were changing at the end of the shift. 'I thought Wilson was going to laugh at me. But not a bit of it. He said that at one time, a long time ago, there was a patrolman killed on that stretch of the railway. He was knocked down by a runaway train.' Billy smiled apologetically. 'They say the driver got out at Finchley Road to go to the loo and never put the brakes on.'

As well as its ghost stations, the Tube is known for its ghosts. In the abandoned stop of Aldwych, Barry the station manager is sometimes in the mood to show visitors a spiral staircase which ascends into murk. He says, 'I always imagine a headless ghost on these stairs, perhaps pursuing a damsel in distress.' In its prime, Aldwych served the theatres of the Strand, and even today, its showbusiness connections are not confined to the film crews who are accommodated by Barry. 'Supposedly an old theatre was demolished to make way for the railway,' he says. 'The leading lady didn't like it, so she haunts the old station.' She had yet to reveal herself to the phlegmatic Barry. At Covent Garden station, a member of staff put in for a transfer in the fifties after seeing a tall, slim ghost in a grey suit and glasses. Perhaps the most exotic shade in the Underground inhabits British Museum, a lost halt on the Central Line. The station opened in 1900 but within half a dozen years there was competition a short distance away from Holborn station on the Piccadilly Line. Eventually, Holborn was expanded and Central Line trains no longer called at British Museum, though its tiled walls can still be seen from trains heading west out of Holborn. Before it closed in 1933, there were reports that the station was frequented by the ghost of an ancient Egyptian, a mummy who had fled from the nearby repository, and newspapers offered rewards to anyone prepared to spend the night on the platform. This legend is echoed in the sarcophagus motif on the walls of the present Holborn platforms.

Now that I had finally found Billy McKeown, he was able to lead me around another part of the ghostly Underground. It was the old Angel station. Angel was still very much in business, and boasted the deepest escalators in Europe, but part of the station had been closed during refurbishment in the 1990s. The redundant booking hall was now used as a billet by Mick's men, by Scott and Billy and the others. It was where they showered and changed after a shift, where they kept their kit. The dead station was at the western end of City Road, where it met a confluence of five roads at Angel. In the old ticket hall, a portion of the original green tiling lustrously survived, as well as a poster from a long-forgotten marketing campaign, encouraging trips to the bosky extremities of the Tube network. The booking hall was further evidence that abandoned parts of London's past lingered on overlooked into the present.

Billy led the way to a chamber which had once housed the winding gear for the passenger lifts. In the middle of the concrete floor, directly over the disused lift shafts, was a hole. On second thoughts, it was more of a gap, or even a chasm. 'It's quite a long way down,' said Billy, peering into the abyss. He wasn't kidding. If I hadn't been up all night, I might have been worrying about the integrity of the floor.

Billy and I set off to explore the depths of the dead station. We opened a door to find ourselves at the top of a spiral staircase, in the dark. The stairwell was lined with metal panels, which brought to mind provisional, military building: the staircase was like a pontoon bridge turned on its side. Like the floodgates in the Northern Line tunnels, the panels displayed signs of water damage, blotches of corrosion. As we wound deeper into the clay beneath N1, Billy drew my attention to a brace of lamps glowing feebly in the stairwell.

'What does that mean, Billy?'

'It means no one's been down here in a while. They need replacing.'

We could make out another source of light from what was presumably the bottom of the staircase. We advanced towards it, and it slowly resolved itself into a porthole which looked onto a brightly lit and well maintained platform. This was evidently where Northern Line trains stopped at the redeveloped Angel station. There by the porthole, at the foot of the stairs, Billy and I had arrived at an intersection of subterranean passages, to compare with the Catherine wheel of roads radiating from the Angel junction up on the street. These were the workings of the lost Tube station. We discovered the pit of a lift shaft. We found a pair of low brick arches, like an undercroft. Billy thought that this had once been a cable tunnel, carrying telephone lines. But he was baffled by the well of yet another shaft. He thought that this couldn't have been a second lift, because there was a narrow stainless-steel staircase ascending beside it. 'Maybe it's a fire escape,' he mused.

Through the dusty mesh of a locked wicket, Billy's torch picked out the tattered remains of a poster for long-lost 'Intercity' trains, and beyond it, a tunnel leading away into deep darkness. 'That's a dead tunnel,' said Billy, exploring through the grille with his beam. The tunnel appeared to serve as a ramp. Billy said that it ran for about a hundred yards before connecting to the main Northern Line tunnel.

Did my pulse quicken on these subterranean recces just because I was enjoying myself, I wondered, or did anxiety have something to do with it, too? I thought about how much the natural adrenalin reaction you felt at finding yourself below ground – down where you were only supposed to go when you were buried – was exaggerated by the difficulty of orienting yourself in this strange environment, deprived of the clues and pointers familiar from the surface: horizon, depth of field, daylight?

Where were Billy and I going, come to think of it? There was the door giving access to the Northern Line platform, of course, but Billy was regarding it warily. 'It might be alarmed,' he said. We weren't supposed to be down in the dead station. Gingerly, Billy tried the handle. It gave, and no sirens sounded. I was holding the torch and Billy told me under his breath that he didn't want me flashing it down the platform. 'They might see us on the CCTV,' he said. It was not yet five o'clock and the station wasn't open. On the other hand, the platforms had been swept, in preparation for the morning rush hour, and the juice was back on. Billy and I looked at each other. Once we stepped through the door, it would close behind us and we wouldn't be able to get back through it, to open it from the platform side. Another pressing consideration was whether Europe's deepest escalators would be working. It was a long way up if it was a climb. As I looked at Billy, I saw him make his mind up. 'If we go quickly, they might not notice us on the cameras,' he said, snuffing the torch and stepping smartly through the door. A distant-waterfall rumble told us that the escalators were already operating. In the smart, modern booking hall of the new improved Angel station, Billy exchanged nods with a ticket collector, already at his post. We weren't in any hot water. It was only Billy's Presbyterian conscience which had troubled him. I thought about the dead station and how tempting passengers would find the unremarkable door at the end of the platform if they remotely suspected what lay behind it, if they only knew that they could step through the portal and back into the Angel's past. Old Tube stations, or bits of old stations, had become as resonant as boarded-up priest holes.

Of course, several of them were now more than a century old. The great boom in Underground excavation had been at the turn of the twentieth century. The Bakerloo Line was introduced in 1906, followed by the Piccadilly in December of the same year. The so-called 'Last Link' was a route from Charing Cross to Hampstead, a spur of today's Northern Line. There was strong resistance to the idea of Tube lines under Hampstead Heath, to man-made conduits mimicking the immemorial flow of the Fleet. In 1900, *The Times* said, 'The Heath has been hitherto considered sacred ground . . . A great tube laid under the heath will, of course, act as a drain and it is quite likely that the grass and gorse and trees on the heath will suffer from lack of moisture.' Nonetheless, consent was given for the new stretch of line. It was opened by Lloyd George on 22 June 1907, when 140,000 Londoners enjoyed a complimentary inaugural ride. The line had the deepest tunnels in London. Just north of Hampstead station, the trains ran 250 feet below the surface. A new station was built, North End, between Jack Straw's Castle and Manor House Hospital. But the strength of local opinion forced the Northern Line to scrap it before a single commuter had darkened its tiles. North End, also known as Bull and Bush after a nearby pub and a treasured cockney anthem, remains the only dead station which was never fully alive in the first place. Passengers travelling between Hampstead and Golders Green on the Northern Line can catch sight of its remains.

The work under Hampstead Heath was backed by an American financier, Charles Yerkes, to the tune of £100,000, enough to put a hole in even the deepest pockets at the beginning of the twentieth century. Yerkes could be called a visionary of the London Underground, although what he chiefly had before his eyes were dollar signs. His pithy business philosophy was 'Buy up old junk, fix it up a little and unload it upon other fellows.'

Yerkes had interests in the District, Bakerloo and Piccadilly lines, and built a huge power station at Lots Road, Chelsea, to keep his railways supplied with electricity. He was only one of a group of self-interested financiers whose connections and apparent wealth won them an entrée to the establishment, but whose methods did not always withstand close scrutiny. Whitaker Wright, though an Englishman, had made his pile from mining in America. A millionaire at thirty-one, he returned to his native land to take a stake in the Bakerloo Line. But his holding company ran into difficulties, and Wright's illicit attempts to fix its share price proved insufficient to bail it out. It was declared insolvent and Wright did a runner. He was finally tracked down to New York and brought back to London to face the music. In 1904, he was convicted of swindling investors out of £5 million and sentenced to seven years in prison. He left court swearing his innocence and his intention to appeal. A few moments later, however, Wright was dead. He had swallowed a cyanide capsule which he had been concealing in the courtroom. Police also found a loaded revolver on him. Wright was buried in the grounds of his Surrey mansion, surrounded by his landscaped gardens, private theatre, observatory, lakes and an underwater billiard table encased in glass.

Death by one's own hand has been a grim feature of the Underground, the locale most often resorted to by Londoners desperate for an escape, the cockney Beachy Head. In his memoir of working at King's Cross station, Christopher Ross says that there were an average of two suicide attempts a week in the Underground. Ross recalls being shown the section of track where a young man had leapt to his death a few hours earlier.

I thought I could see a trace of blood, but it was only a KitKat wrapper, discarded on the scattered sand. Something drew me to return to this spot again and again throughout the morning, as if trying to surprise an elusive clue as to why someone might choose to die in this sad place.

Next day, chatting to a Bakerloo driver I mention the incident. He tells me he knows the driver concerned; he has been given compassionate leave. 'Lucky bastard!' he says, assuming we are all the same, that we all want to be paid without having to work. 'Wish it had been me!' But I didn't believe him.

Tube workers have their own slang – a derailed train is 'on the floor', for instance – and refer to a suicide as a 'jumper' or a 'one-under'. They've become squeamish about filling the rest of us in on what has happened. A few years ago, announcements about 'a passenger under a train' were not uncommon but now all you hear is a call for Inspector Sands or an opaque mention of 'an incident'. News of a suicide, or even an intimation of one, can hardly fail to provoke a shudder, though I remember feeling disbelief on finding that I couldn't catch a Tube into central London, after reporting from the scene of the Clapham disaster in 1987, because one poor friendless soul had chosen that day of all days to end his own life.

Of course, the Underground has had its own terrible accidents, too. After Moorgate in the seventies, there was the King's Cross fire of 1987. Attending the public inquiry as a reporter, I heard that a match discarded on a wooden elevator had sparked the inferno in which thirty-one people died. It seems incredible in retrospect but smoking was still allowed in the Underground until the blaze. The right of passengers to light up had been enshrined by the Victorians, libertarians and smokers to a man. In 1868, the philosopher and MP John Stuart Mill had been instrumental in getting railway smoking cars established in law. The inquiry found that the King's Cross fire was the proverbial accident waiting to happen. Since 1956, there had been forty-six escalator fires, most of them attributed to careless smokers. In 1981, one person died after rubbish caught light at Goodge Street station, and this led to a ban on smoking in trains and on platforms. But gasping passengers were still apt to light up on the escalators. At King's Cross, all it took was for the smouldering match to drop onto the dry and oil-soaked rubbish which had accumulated beneath the escalator and within minutes the booking hall was full of choking fumes. The inquiry led to the end of smoking in the Tube. Wooden escalators were replaced and sprinklers installed.

Throughout its history, the Underground has been the scene of violent death. In May 1957, Countess Teresa Lubienska, the descendant of a Polish landowning family, was fatally stabbed at Gloucester Road station. A survivor of the Ravensbrück concentration camp, she had settled in Kensington and was a leading member of the exiled Polish community. Her killer was never found. In 1959, detectives arrested a criminal called Gunther Podola while he was blackmailing a housewife from a phone booth at South Kensington station. Podola shot Detective Sergeant Raymond Purdy dead. He was found guilty and executed in November 1959, the last person to be hanged for killing a police officer. Baroness Orczy, who claimed to have come up with the idea of her most famous work, *The Scarlet Pimpernel*, while buying a ticket at Tower Hill station, set a fictional murder on the Metropolitan Line. In *The Mysterious Death on the Underground Railway*, a young woman is found murdered at Aldgate station and the lack of other passengers in her carriage helps the killer to avoid capture. More recently, in *The Director's Cut*, novelist Nicholas Royle has a psychopathic film-maker living in a dead station and murdering passengers on the Tube.

The Underground remains the scene of often dramatic crime. In the spring of 2003, a man died after running in front of a District Line train at Plaistow to avoid detectives who wanted to question him over suspected drugs offences. And a man who assaulted a security guard escaped police by fleeing into the tunnels between Notting Hill Gate and High Street Kensington. Power to the District and Circle lines was turned off but a frantic search of the tunnels failed to find the fugitive. A police spokesman said, 'He's lucky to be alive, he must have resurfaced where the line goes overground.'

To soothe the nerves after such dramatic events, patrons of the Tube and clocking-off railwaymen were once able to enjoy a drink in the Underground. During the First World War, when opening hours were limited elsewhere, there were more than thirty licensed buffets on the network. Two bars were actually on the platforms themselves. Pat-Mac's Drinking Den, on the eastbound Metropolitan Line platform of Liverpool Street station, was open for business until 1978. It became a café called the Piece of Cake. The other bar, The Hole in the Wall, was on the westbound platform at Sloane Square. In Evelyn Waugh's *Vile Bodies*, the Sloane Square buffet is briefly *the* place to be seen after newspaper diarist Adam Symes pens a mischievous paragraph claiming that it is 'the haunt of the most modern artistic coterie (Mr Benfleet hurried there on his first free evening, but saw no one but Mrs Hoop and Lord Vanburgh and a plebeian toper with a celluloid collar)'. Last orders at Sloane Square were not called until 1985, when it became an underground version of a corner shop. 'The concept of the Tube station bar excited me,' wrote Iris Murdoch. 'In fact the whole Underground region moved me, I felt as if it were in some sense my natural home. These two bars were not just a cosy after-the-office treat, they were the source of a dark excitement, places of profound communication with London, with the sources of life.' Mansion House used to have a bar near the platforms, and at Baker Street, Sherlock Holmes could drop into the Moriarty, a licensed buffet named after his great adversary which was close to the Metropolitan Line platforms. The bar was hymned by Betjeman in 'The Metropolitan Railway Baker Street Station Buffet'.

Now the Tube was dry, so workers leaving after a thirsty-making night shift sometimes found their way to Smithfield meat market. I had promised Mick Murphy of the Northern Line maintenance team a pint at one of the pubs that opened in the early hours for the meat porters. Mick hadn't been for a drink in the market in ages, he said, and was looking forward to a nightcap – or was it a liquid breakfast? It was 5.30 in the morning. The market was filling with refrigerated lorries and men in white coats. Many of the porters had bulked out their outfits with fleeces and hats, against the February cold. We'd been putting our faith in a boozer on a particular side street off the market. Apparently, this was where the night maintenance crews would go after they finished work. Mick said that the landlord used to let them in as early as five o'clock, if they tapped on the window 'and he knew you'. But this morning the pub was dark. We completed another circuit of the market in Mick's car. I counted two closed pubs, then three. Mick decided that the porters would know where to go. 'We'll ask these,' he said, winding down his window beside a knot of blood-boltered bummarees. 'Is there an early house?' he said.

We were directed to the Cock Tavern on Poultry Avenue, within the very halls where the carcasses were bought and sold. This was at the heart of the market, not to mention its lights, tripes and offal. As we parked, within sight of St Bart's Hospital, the dawn was being serenaded by birdsong. It was turning six o'clock but the Cock looked closed. Suddenly a man appeared on the doorstep, opening up, clearing the way to a staircase which led down to his subterranean establishment. We ducked through an arch to find a restaurant, with curtained-off banquettes, and beyond that, the bar proper. Great blown-up black-and-white stills of the market and of its VIP visitors hung on the walls, beside large wooden blazons of the names of the old family firms. Breakfast television was on in a corner and a bloke with blond hair, wearing his white coat and hat indoors, was pumping coins into a fruit machine. I got the first round in. The landlord, a bloke in glasses heading towards corpulence, told me that he was open from six in the morning until four in the afternoon. The coming hour was his busiest, he said. On cue, the bar was suddenly peopled by porters ordering full English breakfasts, served by a woman with whom they had a spot of banter. The Cock also attracted doctors and nurses from Bart's and off-duty police from the City of London nick on Snow Hill. A restaurant reviewer from one of the newspapers reported, 'At one stage, I have *The Bill* to my left, *Casualty* to my right, and an episode of *EastEnders* directly ahead.' Mick and I also came across a handful of white-collar types. One man was blond, Germanic-looking, in a good shirt and tie. He was swigging mugs of tea with a couple of men in white coats. Was he the client from Munich, perhaps, who'd had no idea of what he was letting himself in for?

The market's prime location made it ripe for gentrification: Iain Sinclair, the master psychogeographer, appeared to think that last orders might soon be called at the Cock, 'that fan-cooled dungeon beneath Smithfield meat market' as he described it. (Admittedly, this was going by what he said in a short story, which wasn't entirely scientific, but then who was he to complain about that?)

'It's a privilege to be here, at all, don't you think?' the young woman, Katie Harwood, asked. 'Before it disappears.' Give her credit, she could put away a decent plate of meat, two kinds of sausage, a couple of kidneys, liver black as treacle, nestling on a bed of refried potato, a bright wink of egg. She passed on the stout.

In the filling underground bar, Mick and I didn't read the runes in the same way as Sinclair, we didn't suspect that time was running out for the Cock. But just in case he was on to something, we didn't pass on the stout.

POST RESTANTE

London's Lost Railway

If the dead stations of the Underground exert a fascination, how much more so an entire subterranean railway running the breadth of central London, decommissioned and shut down but still in perfect working order beneath the streets of the city? This deserted line is all the more intriguing for being pint-sized, a scale model, a *miniature* railway. If you stumbled upon this faerie railroad and gazed in astonishment at its secret silos, a child's idea of the lair of a criminal mastermind, you'd be obliged to conclude that the Wizard of Oz and Austin Powers had gone into partnership in a privatised Tube franchise.

This unlikely transport link is one attraction of buried London capable of evoking wonder in the beholder. It's so spellbinding that it's hard to believe that the rationale behind it was self-consciously earnest, that it was intended to serve a vital national interest, its charms or lack of them being in the end quite incidental. The men who championed the railway thought of themselves as sober-sided men of affairs and viewed their project as a matter of strategic importance. In recent years, the accountants have successfully argued that what they created was every bit as romantic and fanciful as it looks, that it wasn't commercially viable, though there's a school of thought that a more imaginative approach could yet realise economic benefits from the railway. As I say, this landmark of nether London beguiles in spades. But even so, it's not something that you'd be well advised to come across in anything less than top form. To be taken unawares by it would be like stumbling into a hall of mirrors where everything appeared to be smaller than life. So it was far from ideal that I had just disembarked from a long-haul flight on the day that I finally clapped red eyes on the Post Office's underground railway, otherwise known as the Mail Rail.

In its final few months before mothballing, I had a last chance to see it in operation beneath the biggest Post Office depot in the capital, Mount Pleasant. Mount Pleasant was where I had paused on my walk along the route of the buried Fleet and learned from Jane the guide that the locale had been named ironically, after a high-smelling rubbish dump. Later, Mount Pleasant was the site of Clerkenwell gaol, but now the Post Office occupied six acres of it. 'Royal Mail welcomes you to Mount Pleasant,' read the formal card, the stiffie, that I was carrying. It was like an invitation to a Buckingham Palace garden party. 'The tour will include – The Journey of a Letter from the time it arrives at the Sorting Office and how it is processed. We will also show you the latest in mechanised sorting and finally how the mail is despatched. You will also visit Mail Rail, we are the only Post Office in the world with our own underground rail system.'

The idea of moving letters and parcels beneath London was as old as the penny post itself. An underground connection between London's busiest sorting offices was thought to be a quicker way of shifting the mail than through the clogged streets overhead. The theory went that if posties didn't have to contend with charabanc jams and nose-to-tail horses and carriages, their record of swift and reliable deliveries would be enhanced. But in view of the Mail Rail's eventual demise, it's important to note that it would never have been built, or persevered with, except for political considerations. From the beginning, Post Office bosses expressed doubts about its cost advantages, but those in high places attached strategic value to getting the mail through in the days before everyone had a telephone and e-mail. In June 1855, Rowland Hill, the secretary to the Post Office and progenitor of the everywhere-for-1d scheme, urged the Postmaster General to install an underground tube for conveying mail from the General Post Office at St Martin's-le-Grand to Little Queen Street and Holborn. The idea was that a narrow, fifteen-inch-diameter pipe would run beneath the line of the streets. It would operate pneumatically, in the style of a system for carrying messages which had been successfully trialled at the Stock Exchange three years earlier by a man called Josiah Latimer Clark. If the postal tube was a hit, it could be extended to serve the entirety of the capital, or even the rest of England, or so its boosters fondly assumed.

At the same time, an engineer called Thomas Webster Rammell was also hatching plans for pneumatic railways. He and Latimer Clark eventually set up the Pneumatic Despatch Company together in June 1849. After trials in Birmingham, they laid a demonstration line 452 yards long at Battersea, on the spot where the famous power station stands today. Air pressure propelled little trucks through the two-foot-diameter tubes from one end, while a vacuum created by a steam-driven fan at the other sucked the carts in the same direction. They reached speeds of forty miles per hour. Although they were meant to carry freight, the *Illustrated London News* reported that 'two gentlemen occupied the carriages during the first trip. They lay on their backs, on mattresses, with horsecloths for coverings, and appeared to be perfectly satisfied with their journey.'

The success of the trials led the Pneumatic Despatch Co. to build a similar line which ran from the parcels office at Euston underneath Eversholt Street as far as the Post Office's north-western district office six hundred yards away. It was opened in February 1863, one month after the Metropolitan Railway. The journey took just over a minute for a rail truck a little over eight feet long. A larger pipeline, completed in January 1865, was constructed from Euston railway station and ran beneath Drummond Street, Hampstead Road, Tottenham Court Road and High Holborn to a station at 245 Holborn. On its inaugural run, some guests braved the wagons, although they later complained to newspapermen that 'the sensation at starting, and still more so upon arriving . . . was not agreeable'. A large steam engine was required to drive the wagons, which were just over ten feet long and fitted snugly within a U-shaped tunnel. At their destination, the wagons were met by a cushion of air, which served to arrest their onward rush towards the buffers.

Despite their technical merits, the pneumatic railways suffered financial problems. A banking collapse in 1866 interrupted the progress of the next phase of the letters pipeline, which had been due to be extended to the General Post Office at St Martin's-le-Grand. Rammell had the same trouble, despite scoring a popular hit with a pneumatic passenger railway in Crystal Palace Park, where a carriage full of whooping South Londoners was sucked and blown along a six-hundred-foot tunnel. On the strength of this, MPs were persuaded to approve the laying of a pneumatic railway from Great Scotland Yard beneath the Thames to Waterloo, but work was stalled by money problems.

In 1868, the Pneumatic Despatch Co. finally got their hands on fresh funds. They extended the postal pipeline from Holborn, beneath the new Holborn Viaduct, to the General Post Office. It now stretched a total of 4,738 yards, all the way back to Euston. In a development which was to be repeated in the history of the Mail Rail, Post Office nabobs weren't convinced by the new tube, and only agreed to operate a limited service through it. When they found that it suffered problems with air pressure leakage, and that in any case it was only four minutes quicker than a horse-drawn van, they declined to have anything further to do with it and refused to send mail through the tube. By late 1874, the line had been written off. In the 1960s, some of the original railway cars were discovered by workmen who were building the Euston Road underpass. One was put on show at the Museum of London. Stretches of the old pneumatic railway serve today as telephone and electrical ducts underneath Tottenham Court Road. The railway's legacy also included the

Mail Rail, which it directly inspired. In 1913, Parliament approved proposals for a Post Office railway and tunnelling began the following year. After delays caused by the First World War and the General Strike, the trains finally began rolling in December 1927, just in time for the Christmas rush. Within a year, a quarter of mail vans had vanished from the streets of London.

The journey that I made in order to visit Mount Pleasant, travelling across London from west to east on the Central Line, more or less mimicked the trip that the Post Office railway had laid on below ground for the lucky letters of London. From the post office at Paddington, they sped under Edgware Road before the Mail Rail made its first stop at the western parcel office on Bird Street, behind Selfridge's. The next call was at Rathbone Place, north of Oxford Street, where the Post Office had its western district post office. The single nine-foot-diameter tunnel wormed under the site where Centre Point stands today to arrive at the western central district post office at High Holborn. From there, the tracks ran under Bloomsbury to Mount Pleasant. Heading east of the sorting office, the railway buried its way under the old Roman fortifications at London Wall to call on Post Office headquarters at King Edward's Buildings, near St Paul's Cathedral. It also made a stop under Liverpool Street station before terminating at the eastern district post office on Whitechapel Road. Its full length was six and a half miles. Of the seven original stops, only Paddington, Rathbone Place, Mount Pleasant and Whitechapel were still operating in 2003, and these too were facing decommissioning, the fate which awaited the entire route in a matter of weeks.

I'd passed Mount Pleasant many times, and seen the posties lounging outside, on fag break. I admired the way that they adapted their fatigues with the élan of rappers. Some of them went to the barber's where I got my hair cut. One or two of them came in for change to put into fruit machines. Tony the barber

would exchange their five- and ten-pound notes for coins from
his till. Later, the transaction would happen in reverse, Tony
obligingly converting the posties' jingling winnings into folding
currency. Tony himself preferred the football and the horses, but
he was happy to accommodate a fellow betting man if at all
possible.

At one of the depot's many portals, I showed my invitation
card and was directed to a – or perhaps, *the* – 'reception room'.
It had the hermetic quality of the soundproof booth that marital
partners took it in turns to occupy on the long-running television
quiz show *Mr and Mrs*. It contained a grey three-piece suite and
monochrome photographs of Mount Pleasant taken in the
twenties and thirties. Presently, a Sikh man in a turban and Royal
Mail tank top, Mr Harjit Bhurji, arrived to show me around. Mr
Bhurji was courteous, but hard to make out perfectly. Jangling
with jet lag, I didn't by any means catch everything he said. What
made matters worse was that I was following him through the
busy office, through the susurrus and clicking of sorting
machines, the most animated of them shuffling at hysterical high
speed, as if they were automated croupiers in a vast casino. Had
the machines somehow hypnotised the posties, I wondered,
programming them to tilt at the tumblers of fruit machines
during their lunch hour?

There were machines that sorted letters according to depth. If
a letter was more than six millimetres deep, it became a parcel.
There were machines that sorted them by size, there were others
that read postcodes with their electronic eyes. One piece of kit,
operated by a person using what looked like a primitive
typewriter – as clunkily die-cast as the Enigma code-breaking
machine of the Second World War, as deceptively short of keys as
a court stenographer's desktop – converted a postcode into
microfilm. Tiny dots of what appeared to be blue polythene were
gummed to the envelopes, in another boon to sorting. Yet
another gadget told first- and second-class stamps apart. Mr

Bhurji explained that the first-class had a tiny cellophane highlight or bar, which the machine looked for in the same way that a shop assistant might scrutinise banknotes for a watermark.

For the items of post which had been successfully screened and assigned by the machines, there were mailbags suspended from the hoops of metal frames like rubbish sacks inside wheelie bins. The frames had resonant names: Ashgahat, Turkmenistan, Roseau in the Windward Islands. Other letters were intended for NASDAQ, Czarniken, the *Methodist Recorder*. As for air mail travelling in the opposite direction, bound for addresses in the United Kingdom, 96 per cent of it passed through Mount Pleasant. The depot had its own Customs and Excise outpost, where the staff had authority to open any suspicious items. They looked for drugs, obscene publications, anything with terrorist connections, policing the post just as the successors of Geoffrey Chaucer in Lower Thames Street patrolled the river.

A transfixing part of my visit to Mount Pleasant was the call we paid on the corner given over to something called the Blind Transaction Duty. This was the cloak-and-dagger section of the Post Office. It was the job of the people employed in this cranny to work out where to send post which had been poorly, bafflingly – practically *non-* – addressed. The undisputed expert here was Bruno Valentino, as irreplaceable in his own way as the typing-pool grannies who cosset 'M' in John Le Carré's spy novels. Indeed, he made me think of the seamstresses who were retained by the intelligence services before the war to unpick diplomatic mail undetected.

It's my recollection that this deft man introduced himself as '*Miss* Bruno Valentino'. Was this a trick of my jet lag? The din of the sorting machines? Or some terrible in-house joke, of the sort it was all too easy to imagine in a place like the Mount Pleasant post office? Like all big institutions, it had its own language. A notice referred to 'ghosters', who turned out to be postmen and women doing overtime. They could also be said to be working on the 'tap': the boss tapped them on the shoulder when he wanted to know if they'd put in a few extra hours.

Bruno was wearing a standard-issue Post Office light-blue shirt. His eyes were vivid with enthusiasm behind their glasses. Bruno kept an encyclopedia by his desk but his knowledge of the world's remote spots had been learnt – and, importantly, imagined – from the years he had spent poring over envelopes, working on what he called 'scriptures': the different spellings that people of the same country favoured for their capital city, how such and such a tribe represented a town in their peculiar argot. 'The people twenty miles away would write it an utterly different way, they wouldn't know what you were talking about,' he said.

Half-Italian, fluent in French – the international postal language – Bruno also spoke Spanish and German, and had a self-taught working knowledge of many other tongues. He had devised his own guide to Cyrillic phonetics. Before he had been given the job, he had had to sit an exam, in front of a panel. The questions he must have been asked by this daunting horseshoe in postal blue! 'What is the capital of Uzbekistan?' 'What is unusual about the letter "R" in the Cyrillic alphabet?' Bruno had been doing this kind of work, on and off, he said, for fifteen years.

The words tumbled out of him. 'I have the knowledge, I have the confidence behind me.' He addressed these remarks not to anyone within earshot, it seemed, but to the pigeonholes of letters in front of him, as if daring them to defy him, as if this refrain, heard more than once, was what Bruno told the shaving mirror before girding himself for a shift at Mount Pleasant, notwithstanding his pass at the interview board and his fifteen years' experience.

Did Bruno have his favourite countries? He simpered to be asked, luxuriated in the thought of his favourites. 'Well, we've got a soft spot for Malta, haven't we?' he said, enlisting the, I thought, reluctant support of his Asian colleague at the next desk, a man who was cast in the role of Bruno's junior. 'Yes,'

Bruno went on, 'there's the good, the bad and the ugly.' People in Israel who wanted to post letters to parts of the Arab world were loath to put stamps on their letters, *Israeli* stamps, he said, because this was a sure way of having them set on fire. Bruno told me of hapless correspondents, unschooled in English, who erroneously put down gobbledegook like 'This is not a circular' in lieu of an address, or confidently penned their own addresses where the letter's intended destination should have been displayed, and vice versa.

As I said, I was used to seeing knots of workers hanging about outside Mount Pleasant, but I wasn't prepared for the air of bookish, monkish solemnity inside – I suppose I'm thinking of those religious orders who used to sequester themselves in order to copy out the gospels in copperplate. It's true that there was some banter; yes, there was obscene graffiti covering a notice in a lift (so-and-so was a so-and-so). But in the silence of the great room, where a master computer, a big brain, mutely petitioned the humans for help, showing them 'grabs' of envelopes with their baffling, flawed postcodes and entreating them with the frank question 'What does this mean?' on its screen, I felt that I might have been witnessing the final, long-hoped-for emergence of a new order, or religion, in which men worked harmoniously with superintelligent machines. The sheer number of employees at Mount Pleasant – could Mr Bhurji really have said four thousand? – and their bluish fatigues, not to mention their myriad colours and polyglot tongues, suggested an idealised version of the UN.

Despite the hubbub of the sorting room, there was one phrase of Mr Bhurji's that I couldn't miss, that he really had off pat. It was 'Cheers, mate'. This was his 'Open Sesame': delivered with the right intonation – that is to say, with no intonation at all, but in the most perfunctory, you might even say cheerless, fashion – it opened all doors to us, including, I would presently discover, that of the coach depot, the cavernous and strictly speaking out-of-bounds shunting yard of the mini-railway itself. But first we had to descend two floors beneath Mount Pleasant. Mr Bhurji led me to the lifts. He tugged the lattice-doors closed behind us and pushed the button to go down.

Although the First World War had halted work on the railway, that wasn't the same thing as saying that it was abandoned during this period. On the contrary, finding a safe storage space underneath their feet, wartime officialdom in London was quick to make use of the half-completed Mail Rail. Canvases from the Tate and National Portrait Gallery collections, and documents from the Public Records Office, were stashed in the tunnel beneath the King Edward Building. The Elgin Marbles were among treasures from the British Museum which went into safe keeping under New Oxford Street. The stretch of railway at Paddington became the temporary home of valuables from the King's Pictures and the Wallace Collection. When peace broke out, the treasures were removed and construction finally resumed. The two-foot-gauge track was laid, and shafts were sunk in sorting offices so that mailbags could helter-skelter down steep chutes to the platforms below. From here, the bags were loaded on trolleys which were wheeled onto the trains. Deposited in this way in one part of the system, the mail was taken off the train elsewhere, and hauled up to another sorting office by conveyor belt. The Mail Rail was fully automatic. The driverless trains ran on electricity, their speed governed by the current which flowed through a central rail. As in the Underground, the stations were slightly raised, so that trains lost speed as they approached a platform, and picked it up swiftly as they exited.

Mr Bhurji and I were seventy feet below ground when the lift doors sighed ajar and we stepped out into what indeed appeared to be a shrunken but to-scale version of a Tube station. For ventilation, propeller fans revolved in the concave ceiling. The station was brightly lit but deserted. In front of us, a red display board showed the icon of a puffing loco and indicated that a train was temporarily at rest at a spot identified as E14. This was presumably a station, and going by the prefix of an 'E', it was in the east: Whitechapel, presumably. The utilitarian nomenclature wasn't fooling anyone, however. It couldn't disguise the sentimental origins of the Mail Rail. It was a patriotic sentiment, by no means ignoble, but sentimental all the same, an emotional attachment to making sure that Her Majesty's post got through. The puffing steam icon of the Mount Pleasant signage, the lusty LED, was just as misleading, but it inadvertently told you rather more about the psychology of the system. Because no matter where 'E14' was, no matter in which part of the railway the train had been secreting itself, when it finally emerged from a tunnel to our left, it was dinky, a *toy* train, purring alongside Mr Bhurji and me to stand no taller than waist-high. Nor was the train pulling a conga line of carriages. The entire thing measured just twenty-eight feet from bumper to bumper. Where you would have expected to find the locomotive was a boxy little generator. Behind it were four barrel-shaped containers, each the size of a village-fête tombola. Michael Frampton, who was an engineer on the Mail Rail for thirty-seven years, said, 'It's been such fun to work on, like a big boy's plaything.'

Indeed. The Mail Rail was a train set. On such a conveyance might Ken Dodd's Diddymen have embarked for the face of the chip-butty mines of Knotty Ash. Straining to grant the thing a little more sinew, a little more menace, I suppose it could conceivably have conveyed one of James Bond's adversaries to his compound, provided that he'd ducked whenever the train went into a tunnel. The railway seemed made to measure for Mini-Me, the half-sized sidekick of Dr Evil in the ersatz-Bond franchise of the Austin Powers films. The Mail Rail did in fact have a cinematic pedigree. If you saw the Bruce Willis thriller *Hudson Hawk*, you might recall a sequence in which our hero runs down a railway platform beneath the Vatican, the Holy Father apparently having his own subterranean rapid-transit scheme. The Mail Rail at Mount Pleasant stood in for the papal station.

To give the twinky railway its due, the trains could pull half a ton of letters and parcels at a very respectable forty miles an hour, a performance that any gridlocked London haulier would envy. It was the only conceivable way of moving a mailbag from one side of London to the other inside half an hour. Unfortunately, the imperative to do this was no longer what it was. From handling twelve million letters a day at its peak in the fifties, the Post Office railway was shifting only a third as many by the time it closed in May 2003. Royal Mail claimed that keeping it open was costing four times as much as hiring lorries to replace it. It was claimed that mothballing Mail Rail would save £5 million a year. This was part of a broader policy by Royal Mail to withdraw from rail altogether. In the days of the travelling post offices, the mail vans in which post was sorted as sleepers clattered through the night to the four corners of the country, an undertaking celebrated by Auden in *The Night Mail*, it made sense to have a fast, secure link from the capital's big depots to major terminals such as Paddington and Liverpool Street. But the mobile post offices had the black spot on them, too. It was only a week or so after the subterranean railway was suspended that Royal Mail announced it was no longer entrusting its deliveries to trains. In future, all post would be moved by road, a decision which was hard to credit in commercial terms, let alone environmental ones.

As for the Mail Rail, it had a putative asking price of £15 million. Post Office executives were hoping that businesses would recognise the benefits of a first-class delivery system that was rapid, self-contained and exempt from the Mayor of London's congestion charge. One idea was to turn it into a conveyor belt for moving fine wines below ground, ideally with a station at St James's for Berry Brothers & Rudd. Another suggestion was that it could transport jewels and other valuables, perhaps linking all the strongrooms of London, including the Chancery Lane safety-deposit vaults. But since its tracks ran directly beneath the big department stores of Oxford Street, realistic hopes centred on retailers there.

In Mount Pleasant station, the prospective buyer would be getting a repair workshop and turn-around tunnels, all arranged in tight curves to maximise space. The network also included twin 'blind' tunnels, which ran for a short distance under Cubitt Street and along the Fleet valley before coming to an abrupt halt. The blind tunnels were to have been extensions of the railway, a north-west loop taking in King's Cross, as the Post Office schemed to develop its own titchy Circle Line. The plan was not proceeded with, but later realised in a different form, in a system of Post Office tunnels beneath central London.

On the condemned platform, Mr Bhurji allowed himself a rare moment of romance. He was talking about the passenger coaches of the Post Office railway. 'They're supposed to be quite posh,' he said dreamily. Mr Bhurji himself had never seen them.

'They sound good. Can I go in one?'

'No. They're never used these days,' he said. But he took me to the coach depot. 'Normally it's out of bounds, but at four o'clock on a Friday afternoon . . .'

The depot was housed in a deep bunker, within concrete emplacements, and was entered through great plastic flaps, like an abattoir or a cold store. The experience reminded me of the old Fleet Street, of looking over the sunken newspaper presses. The depot was a shunting yard for the thirty-four trains that ran on the Mail Rail. Of the half-dozen in the yard that evening, the most cheerful was the inspection train, with its yellow mesh cages and plumply upholstered vinyl banquettes.

Closure meant the loss of seventy-six jobs. Most employees took voluntary redundancy or retrained for other work. Dave Dyer, who had put in thirty years' service at Mount Pleasant, was still pondering whether to stay with Royal Mail when I met him, so he declined to confirm my suspicions that workers went joy-riding on the inspection train, and betrothed men awoke from stag-night revels to find themselves lashed naked to locos, Jiffy bags rattling onto their unprotected rear ends. However, Dave said, 'One thing we did do was have Father Christmas down here. One of the lads would put all the gear on – beard, robes and everything – and then all the kids would come and see him and get a present.'

The underground train set naturally appealed to youngsters, and the station at Mount Pleasant was indeed a grotto. However, as well intended as the seasonal gift-giving had undoubtedly been, the children would have been awed and even a little fearful, I felt. It was just as I'd guessed. I said that the Mail Rail reminded me of *The Wizard of Oz* and the posties' offspring could have been forgiven for thinking that Mount Pleasant station was what really lay at the end of the Yellow Brick Road.

Of course, there was one major wrinkle. In the film, the thing about the magic kingdom was that a diminutive sorcerer was behind all the bigger-than-life special effects. But the same pay-off was never likely to await the visitor to an already dwarfish project like the Mail Rail. On the contrary, the thrills and spills all had to work the other way round: because everything was so small, anything of normal size appeared outlandish. On the day of my visit, the duty controller of the Mail Rail was busy in a signal box on the platform. I should estimate that this blameless soul stood no more than 5′ 10″ in his stockinged feet. But because of my jet lag, and a Lilliputian sense of disorientation brought on by my surroundings, he struck me as a veritable Gulliver. Goodness knows what the tots made of him. They must have quaked at the sight of the Monster of Mount Pleasant, I thought, as I watched him pressing a dooda suspended from the ceiling which set off another tiny train. He might have been firing up the conveyor belt in a sushi restaurant.

BUNKER MENTALITY

Cold War London

'I hate being late,' said Bob. He wasn't talking about himself. He was talking about me. It was supposed to be an eight o'clock start, from outside Redbridge Tube station in north-east London. It was now ten past. A hangover, I'm afraid. I couldn't risk blaming the Underground because Keith, who was giving us a lift, was a train driver on the Northern Line. He was in a position to verify my story, or otherwise. I didn't think I'd done badly – it was Saturday morning, after all, and I'd had to travel across town – but I sensed an atmosphere as I climbed into the back of the car. An atmosphere and also a climate. Keith's Rover was one of the hottest models I have ever been in. It was a February morning but the sun was out. Why was the heating on full blast? Perhaps this was why the Tube was always so hot: the drivers felt the slightest draught. Keith's car wasn't small but the three of us were all quite big. In the front, Bob's coat pressed close to Keith's coat. We turned onto Eastern Avenue and there was an explosion from the driver's seat, a stentorian sneeze from Keith. I felt wretched. I only had myself to blame for feeling sick in a Rover, I thought, for being ignored by my new friends.

I decided to make a fresh start of things. I asked Bob what he did for a living. He looked a little old to be going out to a job every day, but I didn't want to give further offence by suggesting this. 'I gave up working,' Bob confirmed. 'It's a mug's game.' At this early stage, I had a hunch that I'd get more out of Bob than Keith. But that was all Bob had to say for the time being. I sunk back into my seat. No, I didn't feel Bob and Keith were pleased to see me. I don't imagine they'll be pleased to hear from me again now, either. They're members of Subterranea Britannica.

Now I like Subterranea Britannica, I'm a member myself and proud to be one. The society runs an informative website and I always look forward to receiving the newsletter of their research study group. I don't think you'll take much convincing when I say that the heart lifts at the sight of a new *Siren* on the doormat. And it would be wrong to think that my fellow underground explorers were anoraks. Well, all right; it would be wrong to think that they didn't think it, too. They can be winningly self-deprecating about their pastime. If it hadn't been for them and their infectious interest in the subterranean state, I might never have met an extraordinary man who is a highly favoured habitué of it, a man described in the following pages but who might have stepped out of an espionage thriller, the sort of man who makes a journalist reconsider his scepticism about conspiracy theories as the most callow naivety.

So why, after these glowing words in their praise, do I fear that my mates Bob and Keith, and other members of Subterranea Britannica, won't be pleased to catch up again? It's because – and I'm sorry to have to say this, fellas – they're completists, they're hair-splitters. In their view, no one ever gets anything entirely right about what's underground, not even each other.

There may be a defensive tone to the above passage. As I write, I admit to premonitory touchiness, phantom bristling, at the thought of the curt and dismissive reception my book can expect, if any, from my pals in the SubBrits. Of course, the hobbyist lives in a hermetic world. No one understands his football team, his train numbers, his chloroformed and pegged butterflies, quite like he does. So I'll get this out of the way now and save us all some time later: you're right, Bob. Keith, you've got me there. That schoolboy blunder on p. 38; the elementary howler in chapter 4: don't waste your stamps, save your green ink. I'm bang to rights.

Dear reader, please overlook these chippy animadversions. If I hadn't realised before that I was mixing with serious accuratists and monomaths, I certainly knew it when I was riding in the back of Keith's Rover. Keith, Bob and I were going on an expedition to a Cold War radar block. There's nothing the members of Subterranea Britannica like better than a nice run out to a reinforced country pile. They were probably the only people in Britain who understood a man called Colin Woods when he chose to spend Christmas in a nuclear bunker. In a televised auction for the ultimate get-away-from-it-all break, Woods' £300 surpassed other bids. The bleak nuclear midwinter found him tucking into a Yuletide spread of cold baked beans, cold Spam and a glass of water a hundred feet below ground in Kelvedon Hatch, Essex, a former government shelter against atomic and biological attack. The financial services worker said that he was glad to get away from the bickering which traditionally accompanies the festive season.

Companions from past outings, Keith and Bob were chatty enough with one another. It seemed that Keith had not long returned from a trip to the Isle of Wight, where, he said, the trains were made up of cashiered rolling stock from London Underground. Trippers disembarking from the Portsmouth ferry found a Tube train waiting for them at the end of the pier. Keith went in for funny voices, pitched in the register of some of Peter Sellers's *Goon Show* characters. I decided that he was probably in his forties. His good hank of dark hair showed no signs of greying. He wore specs with a yellow tint, and an expression of pasha-like complacency behind them. I gathered that Bob had been a policeman, doing duty on various manors in south London. Before that, he had spent twelve years in the navy, including a golden spell in Singapore. By experience and disposition, Bob was an old salt. He had finally weighed anchor in Croydon. It was particularly shaming that Bob had arrived at Redbridge punctually, because he'd had to travel from south of the river.

At the time of our field trip, English Heritage had announced that it was thinking of listing Cold War architecture. Inspectors were visiting what survived of the A-bomb building boom, including weapons silos and military bases as well as fallout accommodation. The Department of Culture, Media and Sport would be deciding which addresses were preserved for the nation. Could the publication of *Pevsner's Shelters*, and afternoon tea in the west bunker, be far behind? Conservationists were coming round to the challengingly minimalist lines of the concrete radar post, but in this, as in much else, they were way behind Bob. He knew more about the early warning system of the 1950s than any man of his age who didn't have a degree from Cambridge and a flat overlooking the Kremlin. 'I'm just nosy,' he explained. 'You can't study these things in isolation, you need the complete picture.' Bob had a plastic wallet of notes and maps on his lap. He was full of observations and stories for Keith. As we headed north, the older man pointed out every passing water tower, CCTV turret and radio mast. It was like I-spy for spies.

Despite the earlier tut-tutting over my lateness, it seemed that we had some time in hand before our rendezvous at the radar station with other members of Subterranea Britannica. My unspoken preference was for breakfast but Bob and Keith took the opportunity to have a look at Wittering aerodrome instead. We passed a sign to a – or perhaps *the* – Minimal Disease Pig Unit. Keith parked by a bin of turnips. We saw the unstirring runway of the aerodrome and its deserted-looking control tower through the wire of the perimeter fence. 'There are such interesting places around airfields,' said Bob happily.

'Yes, they're very interesting,' agreed Keith.

A man was exercising a pair of large dogs behind the fence. 'Dog training,' said Bob.

'Patrolling,' said Keith.

'He might just be walking his dogs,' I said, to silence.

We visited a hamlet called Barnack. Keith pointed out a bus

stop. In a funny voice, the tones of a man who had neglected to wear his false teeth, he said, 'The bush comes oncesh a week!' We parked. Rising purposefully from his seat, Keith said, 'I want to take a picture of a rural police station.'

'That'll put the heebie-geebies up them,' said Bob.

In Market Deeping, I asked Bob why he was taking a photograph of RAF houses. 'Remember what I was telling you. It's about building a complete picture.' Keith and Bob were quite harmless. Bob's wallet of documents was like sealed orders for a mission which was taking place years after the top brass had called the whole show off.

In order to get a word in from the back seat, and also to take advantage of having two clued-up members of Subterranea Britannica with me, I mentioned some of the places that I'd been investigating. But I made the mistake of bringing up the secret government tunnels beneath Whitehall. At first blush, it was an easy error to fall into. Government buildings excite a particular frisson among subterranean snoopers – because of their very inaccessibility, as much as anything, I suspect – but the *secret* government tunnels amount to a Shangri-La. We all dream of the hidden eau-de-Nil door which yields unexpectedly to the touch, of surprising the prime minister and the chiefs of defence staff as they move missile-shaped Monopoly pieces across a lightbox. It was said that John Major's Cabinet had taken refuge in the tunnels when the IRA had mortar-bombed Downing Street and blown in the windows of Conference Room A over Henry VIII's tennis courts. It was rumoured that the passages were extensive enough to include an underground escape route from Buckingham Palace, close to the Ranelagh sewer. There were stories that this corridor led to a secret platform of the Piccadilly Line, a last resort for the royals in the Blitz or the Cold War, enabling them to catch a plane from Heathrow if all else failed. Other myths suggested that the way out was via the Victoria Line, which also ran beneath Buck House, and thence to Victoria

Station and the boat train to Canada. In 1998, the Queen and
Tony Blair reportedly donned protective suits and gas masks and
took cover in a bunker underneath Downing Street as part of an
exercise which simulated a biological attack on central London.

I wasn't to know it, but partly because everybody had had the
same fantasy about discovering the tunnels, and partly because
of the sheer hopelessness of this project, it tended to be treated
as kids' stuff, a foolish distraction, by serious subterraneans. All
unknowing in Keith's Rover, I described a recce I'd made to the
Gents' loo at the ICA on the Mall. From this unlikely location,
you can eavesdrop on the concealed corridors of the
Establishment, or so I'd heard. In the cubicle furthest from the
door, you can peep through a louvred window into a tiny
hallway – by standing on the loo seat, if necessary. On the other
side of this hallway, an external door opens onto the Duke of
York Steps, although it doesn't look as though it's been opened
in years. From your teetering vantage point, you can see that a
piece of wood has been nailed across the back of the keyhole, to
prevent anyone drilling through, a ruse that any London flat-
dweller might recognise. A short flight of concrete steps leads
down from the external door to an internal one, a shabby,
neglected-looking wooden panel. Through a mesh-lined window,
you can make out what appears to be a fire extinguisher in blue
livery, perhaps suited for chemical blazes. Is this a point of entry
to the Whitehall warren? I noticed a rubber doorstop in the well
of the stairs. Was this wedged in on special occasions, when men
with a lot of scrambled egg on their hats needed to keep an
urgent rendezvous in the hardened basement of No. 10? You
strain your ears in vain for the sounds of footsteps, voices. To
your surprise, you find that you're listening out for the
anachronistic clack of typewriters. But all you can hear is the
hum of air conditioning. Is it from the Gents, or from the secret
passages?

Out on the Duke of York Steps, the external door is finished

in dark wood. There's a doorknob that might have come from a
metroland semi, and – yes! – there's even a bell-push. But for the
metal wire criss-crossing its frosted panes, and a yellow sign
saying 'WARNING This door is alarmed', it might be the offices
of an old-fashioned firm of solicitors. On the day of my visit, the
usual knot of tourists at the bottom of the steps was being
invigilated by a pair of motorcycle policemen. I took a chance
and pressed the doorbell. There was no sound, except for the
same purring of air conditioning.

All this – or, to be honest, some of this – I was allowed to
recount to Bob and Keith as we motored hotly north. They
weren't impressed. 'The ICA leads to the tunnels?' Bob turned
halfway around in his seat. 'Where did you hear that?' If I
wanted to know about the secret tunnels, he said, they were
accessed from the first street you came to as you walked down
Whitehall south of Trafalgar Square, a cul-de-sac so
unremarkable that most people passed it without a second
glance. On Bob's recommendation, I subsequently checked this
street out. It was called Craig's Court, a road which had been
around since the early 1700s without making much of a mark on
the popular history of London. If Bob was right, then this low
profile was hardly surprising. But was he right? Was Craig's
Court a portal to tunnels known only to ministers and civil
servants with top-level clearance? Put it this way: behind a set of
forbidding doors was a British Telecom office, and in the
unpeopled lobby was a sign indicating not which conferences and
training sessions were in progress, but the current gradation of
perceived security threat. When the first secret government
passage of modern times was excavated in 1939, from Trafalgar
Square down Whitehall to the Cenotaph, a shaft eight feet in
diameter linked the northern end of the tunnel with the then
Whitehall Post Office telephone exchange in Craig's Court.

At last Keith, Bob and I arrived at a rutted farm track in the
raw Lincolnshire countryside. Our fellow SubBrits had already

begun to gather. A couple of them were in potholer's boiler suits and hard hats. There was also a good show of fleeces and facial hair. The farmer and his family lived beside the track in a brick bungalow which had once been an RAF guardhouse. At the back of an ad hoc breaker's yard, screened by a wood of mature trees, was the large concrete bunker of the old radar post. It was built in 1942 but had been substantially refitted in the fifties when Britain's early warning system was upgraded. For a time, the radar station had been in the front line of the Cold War. As many as eighty men and women had lived in it, monitoring the movements of aircraft in the skies over the east coast and beyond. In March 1958 the post was reassigned to a 'care and maintenance role', according to the Ministry of Defence, and in the sixties it was sold to the farmer. He'd been using it as somewhere to stash his rubbish ever since. The bunker was full of every kind of junk: old JCB parts, broken bikes, piles of tiles, road signs, miscellaneous tubes and linings and flanges. Presently all this was joined by the wrapper of Bob's BLT sandwich from Tesco's. Bob was talking animatedly to one of the potholers. I struggled to follow the minutiae of Bob's conversation. Then I realised that to follow it was to miss the point of it. Bob and the potholer were both talking more than they were listening. In the old radar post, each man was sending out his data stream, his call sign, but neither was paying much attention to the pings identifying incoming traffic. 'Do you know about . . .?' Bob would begin. But the potholer would transmit across him, 'I knew there would be a mezzanine. I found exactly what I expected to find.' Facts, if that's what they were, were flourished like winning hands of cards.

A stocky, mustachioed man cut in. 'What did you expect to find?' he asked the potholer. Was he winding him up, I wondered. I saw that he wasn't. 'Nothing I *didn't* expect to find,' repeated the potholer firmly.

The mezzanine that he'd found was entered through a

trapdoor. I dropped through it and found myself on a false floor, a liminal storey which had been secretly interposed between the ground floor and the basement. It was a chalky tunnel, not quite high enough to stand up in. It was lined with a row of glass bowls: the bunker's original lampshades. The other surviving features of the radar post, the *Dr Strangelove* outhouse, included the serving hatches in the galley, the cubicles in the Ladies, and a brace of steel blastproof doors. Nor was it quite deserted. As the SubBrit website reported, the farmer's children had claimed to have seen a large cat, a puma, prowling the ruins; 'it's been identified from paw prints and droppings'.

In the basement of the radar post, Nick Catford, the membership secretary, was taking photographs. He set up his tripod and shooed everyone out of the shot. To compensate for the minimal light, his camera was prepped for exposures which lasted minutes at a time. The stocky man was looking around at the pigeon-limed concrete. He said, 'I find it wonderfully ironic that we gave up the Cold War not for ideological reasons but because we couldn't afford to go on with it.'

Outside, the air was brittle with hail. We walked across a field to see an R7 bunker. It was much smaller than an R6, almost entirely below ground, and full of rainwater.

'Do you want to see a picture of a Type 7?' Bob asked the stocky man over the noise of the wind.

'That's the best chat-up line I've heard all day,' he said.

One of the potholers showed me a text message he'd received on his mobile phone. 'Don't become an anorak,' it read. 'Watch for people in anoraks. You might become one.' He said to me, 'I thought you'd like to see that.'

'Who's it from?' I said, wondering if the potholer had a girlfriend.

'Someone I know,' was all he would say.

It would be hours before the most ardent fanciers of Cold War arcana in the group had finished tooth-combing the chaotic R6.

Down in the darkness, fussing over his camera and its glacial exposures, Nick Catford would be the last to leave. But it was cold, and it would be getting dark in a few hours. The expedition began to break up. Everyone was going their separate ways. There was no talk of finding a pub, no suggestion of taking a glass to keep the chill out. Bob and Keith were happy to be getting under way again. For them, the formal business of the day was an excuse for the real fun of side trips, rambles, digressions.

Keith's Rover nosed back down the track. Bob said, 'You'll have to excuse me, I'm afraid I must take in some victuals,' and out of his knapsack came a triple-decker sandwich. 'Did you bring any food?' he asked me.

'No. I'm fine,' I said. This evidently relieved Bob of any obligation to offer me anything.

'The thing about Nick is, he's totally selfish,' said Bob, munching strenuously. 'Lovely bloke, but he never considers anyone other than himself.' On an earlier foray to a different bunker, a location to which access had been hard won, members were setting up to take their photographs when Nick had shouldered his way to the front.

Bob's butty was making me hungry. I was gagging for a cup of coffee. When a McDonald's appeared on the East Anglian horizon, I suggested a pit stop. Bob and Keith had been a bit sniffy about McDonald's because Nick never ate anywhere else, according to them. On one trip, they'd visited the chain seven times in one day, said Bob. 'Breakfast, elevenses, lunch, tea, supper . . .' By contrast, another of their fellow members, a man who had a penchant for the finer things in life, was known to them as 'Quails' eggs and pink gin'.

The reference to this high-living friend led to a discussion about the attitudes and outlook of the SubBrits. 'Nobody brings politics into it,' said Bob as we trayed our Value Meals to an MDF bench. 'By nature, everyone's conservative with a small "c". And most of them with a large "C", too.'

'What are you on about?' said Keith. 'I'm not a Conservative. I've always hated the Conservatives. Hate the loony left, too.' I had offered to buy lunch, but I wondered if I'd done the right thing. Had I offended Keith? Had my money transformed his quarter-pounder and cola into quail's eggs and pink gin?

Later, calling in at Sutton Hoo, a stately pile and former military billet, we found ourselves shut out by a pair of gates and I suggested ringing the bell. Instead, assuming a toff's voice, Keith cried, 'Working-class person on the premises!'

We embarked on a revealing conversation, with Bob saying that he found a kind of retrospective reassurance in knowing that officials had been providing for us during the Cold War. 'They had XX tonnes of powdered egg,' he said, naming a figure so unthinkable that I immediately uncommitted it to memory. 'And XX tonnes of bacon. So we'd have been all right for—'

'—breakfast?'

'Bacon and eggs,' laughed Bob.

'The point is, you've got to have someone to organise the survivors, haven't you?' said Keith with chilling quiescence.

With Redbridge almost in sight again, Keith pulled into a filling station. As he jockeyed the pump, Bob and I watched him in silence from the car. It had been a long day. Without turning to look at me, Bob said, 'You probably won't be coming again, will you?' It was heartbreaking – did I hear the faintest note of wistfulness in his voice? – the hoped-for but shattering moment of lucidity at the nursing home bedside.

As it turned out, I was at another Subterranea Britannica function a few months later, though there was no sign of either Bob or Keith. They were outdoorsmen and this was very much a classroom-based event. It was a conference at the Royal School of Mines in London. The school's proud crest, featuring an axe rampant, was mounted on the staircase. Members were signing in. 'Do you have badges?' one man was asking the register monitor.

'No, I'm not doing badges any more,' he said.

'Oh. I like badges.'

The star speaker was the author and journalist Duncan Campbell, a man who occupied an extraordinary place in the hearts of SubBrits because of his investigations into the secret state below ground. Priestly and aloof, left-wing and gay, he was adored by the fellow-travellers of Keith and Bob, the men in sweaters who were hard-to-please and conservative, if not necessarily Conservative. After lunch, the speaker who was on before Campbell, his warm-up man, boosted and flattered him from the dais. But Campbell was oblivious to these bouquets, munching a pear and scrolling through spectral images on his state-of-the-art laptop.

When he finally took the platform for his presentation, a speech enhanced by visual images cued by mouse, Campbell began by telling his listeners what they wanted to hear. They weren't wasting their time and energy on ruins renounced by history, he said. On the contrary, their pet subject was swoon-makingly fashionable. If the fall of the Berlin Wall had tended to put the mockers on the study of secret fortifications, then September 11 had put it right back on everyone's agenda. 'What we thought of as our special interest was becoming history. But is now becoming very relevant again.' Campbell introduced his speech as 'Above ground and underground'. It was also familiar ground, or at least some of it was, and none the worse for that, as far as the SubBrits were concerned. 'Twelve miles of deep-level tunnels were built in London, mostly after World War Two,' Campbell said, and his listeners settled back on their benches with satisfaction, an audience who were reassured that the headliner was going to perform his much-loved old repertoire, after all.

Campbell had made his name among this fraternity with an account of penetrating secret government tunnels. In his case, the SubBrits were more than happy to waive their unwritten rule about giving short shrift to fanciful talk of this kind. In Campbell's case, it wasn't fanciful. He'd been there, done it, and had the photographs to prove it. In 1980, the Christmas number of the *New Statesman* carried his account of pulling off the coup that every SubBrit secretly dreamed of. He described lifting a manhole cover on a traffic island near the Bishopsgate goodsyard, between Bethnal Green Road and Sclater Street, E1, and descending into a tunnel carrying Post Office cables. He found a door which opened onto a shaft a hundred feet deep. Campbell claimed that he entered an underground labyrinth stretching from the East End to Maida Vale; from Euston station in north London to Waterloo in the south (the intrepid reporter had taken a collapsible bicycle with him, to help him get around). Originally a secure wartime link for telephone communications, this warren was enlarged in the 1950s and 1960s so that favoured officials could use it and, if necessary, take cover. The network was designed to protect the machinery of government from the A-bomb. Campbell had been fortunate to find that the tunnels were deserted after five o'clock in the evening, because that's when the patrolmen all went home. At a distance of more than twenty years, this was the clinchingly corroborative detail somehow, the fact that the guards had all knocked off at teatime.

Campbell's was perhaps the only first-hand report of the tunnels in the public domain. In his account of pedalling down a tunnel codenamed 'L', he described arriving at an 'interchange' directly underneath the former Post Office headquarters on King Edward Street. Tunnels shot off in all directions. Two rose to join the Central Line. Another pair made a circuit beneath St Paul's Cathedral. At Holborn, there was an underground complex with six shafts below the Post Office's telephone exchange. The Kingsway exchange had been earmarked as a vital project by Cold War planners, who had created it out of the abandoned deep-level shelter which was built beneath Chancery Lane Tube station during the Second World War. The new subterranean construction was fitted with five thousand trunk lines. It was served by its own artesian well and stocked with six months' supply of food. Peter Lurie, Campbell's eminent predecessor as a mole, claims that Kingsway was entered through an inconspicuous door on High Holborn. 'Its size – to walk round it takes at least an hour and a half – its cleanliness, order and quietness are an impressive testimony to the government's determination to protect itself,' wrote Lurie in *Beneath the City Streets*. 'If the government can hide this from us, it is plain that they can hide anything.'

In subterranean Whitehall, the true seat of power, the Post Office tunnels radiated away to Fleet Street, to Leicester Square and the Post Office Tower, even under the Thames to Waterloo. A hundred feet beneath the statue of George IV in Trafalgar Square, one of the tunnels joined the Q-tunnel. This passageway, which shared an initial with the gadget-fancying quartermaster in the James Bond stories, was the inner sanctum of the state-in-hiding, the holy of holies to the SubBrits. From the Q-tunnel, narrower passages, eight feet in diameter, radiated to the great departments of state. There was one to No. 10 Downing Street, another to the Treasury, another to the Cabinet Office, to the rooms I had peeked into where Cobra meetings were convened. The tunnels were connected to a Ministry of Defence underground operations centre which was equipped with the nuclear button.

I felt vindicated that Campbell didn't rubbish the ICA connection. According to him, 'a ventilator fan, linked to the Admiralty's bit of the Whitehall bunkers, has been tucked into the fabric of the ICA – beside the Gents, to be precise. The fan may be heard and observed by taking a discreet footing on the ICA's sanitaryware.' So it was a secret Admiralty fan I'd heard! (In case you're tempted to take a peek yourself, I should warn you that a white piece of board was put up over the louvred window in 2003, perhaps to deter snoopers.)

The tunnels were the spine of the subterranean set-up. They linked four underground fortresses known as Citadels, which were built in 1941. One was the King Edward Street telephone exchange; another was the ivy-clad Admiralty blockhouse at the eastern end of the Mall, described by Churchill as 'the vast monstrosity which weighs on Horse Guards Parade'. This gave members of the services access to the tunnels. A third bunker was in Curzon Street, Mayfair, in the ground floor of a former Department of Education and Science building. The remaining Citadel was established on the site of old gasometers in Marsham Street. When government offices were going up there, the Citadel was installed in the foundations. For many years, the Marsham Street buildings were home to the Department of the Environment and some of the vast space below ground was bagged by civil servants for their cricket nets and model railway. The buildings were finally torn down in the summer of 2003. From an observation position kindly provided by the contractors, students of the underground state were able to watch the great concrete blocks of the Citadel being broken into rubble.

The SubBrits in the schoolroom loved to hear it all over again: how a tunnel terminated beneath the Whitehall Banqueting Hall, that harmless old lady who lived on the meanest street in the government barrio; how the reporters who used the press centre in the basement of the QEII building little guessed that they were standing right on top of a 1950s' bunker. Campbell was a good turn. He sent the SubBrit crowd home happy. They never tired of hearing about his subterranean bike ride in Whitehall, his tour de Petty France. But as he had astutely foreseen in his original write-up, it had been a once-only escapade. He anticipated that the tunnels would become much harder to enter as a result of his exposé. Faced with the provocation of Campbell's article, the spooks had not been idle. I'd been in touch with the journalist some time before his lecture, posing one of those questions which have to be asked even though the answer couldn't possibly be in doubt: was there any chance that the tunnels were still accessible? No, he replied, he didn't believe there was. I went to the spot where Campbell had embarked on his adventure. I couldn't find a manhole that wasn't tightly sealed; one appeared to have been overlaid with a block of dauntingly dense sculpture, in case it had occurred to anyone to try jemmying it up.

For twenty years, one part of the government's underground compound has been open to public gaze: the Cabinet War Rooms opposite St James's Park, the glorified air-raid shelter from where Winston Churchill plotted the fight back against Hitler during the Blitz. The War Rooms were part of a massive stalactite of an office block that took shape underneath the junction of Horse Guards Road, Storey's Gate and Great George Street. In the 1930s, the ground floor of the present Treasury building was filled with concrete to a depth of seventeen feet, turning it into a protective carapace for the edifice below.

Since 1984, the War Rooms have been on the tourist trail, though you might not think so if you came upon them unsuspectingly. They are gained from a nondescript entrance set into the side of Clive Steps on King Charles Street. In a hint to the original purpose of this unremarkable nook, an outer wall is wainscoted with sandbags; although, spoiled and spent as they are, what they actually look like is used teabags. The impression is not that this place came through a Blitzkrieg but that it came through a burst pipe. Was an effect being strived for here? Perhaps the officials who decommissioned the War Rooms, and converted them into an attraction on Civvy Street, felt that it would detract from their USP to make them vulgarly obvious to passing trade.

As you enter the lagged portal, however, the thinking becomes clearer. In Churchill's old Cabinet Room itself, a waxworks Marine is putting out papers as if prior to a meeting. There are blotters and pencils and a glue pot, and what look like pliers, for punching holes in documents. A map of the world, flushed with imperial pride, overlooks a wooden seat with a lattice back, once occupied by Winnie himself. You can see all this because curators have cut away one of the external walls of the Cabinet Room. It gives the impression of a ship's wardroom, thanks to its air vent and boilerplate and thick girders, though the latter were installed for no more fanciful reason than that they might hold the ceiling up if the building above took a direct hit and collapsed. In a foreword to the visitor's handbook, Robert Crawford of the Imperial War Museum, which oversees the place, writes that the room is just as it was when Churchill and co. left it. 'Its occupants are long since departed, the dense pall of cigar smoke no longer hangs in the air,' writes Crawford. 'But, as we walk the corridor, passing the Prime Minister's suite of offices on our right, the walls still seem to echo to Churchill's footfall and we walk back over fifty years in time.' The dull finish of the marigold paint; the coat-pegs like treble clefs; the little wooden postbox with its sign saying 'Stamps are on sale in the mess. Cleared at 08.30-11.30-16.00-17.15': these are all said to be authentic.

After the aerial bombardments of the First World War, military planners began to consider arrangements for the evacuation of the prime minister, his Cabinet and the upper echelons of the defence staff in the event of a war over London. Several solutions were evaluated in the thirties, including the conversion of basement offices, and the tunnelling of deep shelters in central London and in the capital's north-west suburbs. A major concern was that the people shouldn't suspect that their leaders were deserting them. As a stop-gap solution, a dead Tube station was brought back to life. The last Piccadilly Line train had called at Down Street in 1932. It was too close to its sister stations of Green Park and Hyde Park Corner to be viable, but it was turned into emergency accommodation. Air raids would sometimes find the War Cabinet standing on the disused platforms, discussing official business and waiting for the all-clear. Churchill was seen

walking through Green Park, apparently on his way from
Whitehall to the Down Street shelter, and a rusty metal bathtub
in its recesses is said to have been reserved for his use. Later,
Down Street became the secure headquarters of the railway
authorities. If you travel between Green Park and Hyde Park
Corner today, you may be able to make out the pale tiles of the
dead station. At street level, its terracotta façade, designed by
Leslie Green, is instantly recognisable. A newsagent's is now
where the booking hall used to be.

Down Street was never seen as a permanent answer to the
problem of safeguarding the Cabinet. A 'Central War Room' was
the favoured option. The War Rooms as they appear today were
installed in what used to be the basement chambers of the Office
of Works building. It was the strongest structure of any in
Whitehall, and handy both for Parliament and Downing Street.
The War Rooms, otherwise 'the Hole in the Ground', became
fully operational on 27 August 1939, a week before Germany
invaded Poland and Britain declared war. Under Churchill, 115
War Cabinets were convened in the bunker, or about one in ten
of all such meetings. The clocks in the Cabinet Room have been
set at 16.58, and the tables prepared as if in readiness for the
prime minister's arrival, so that visitors can imagine that they're
about to witness the grim-faced powwow which began at five
o'clock on the evening of 15 October 1940, the day after a
German bomb badly damaged No. 10 and convinced its tenant
to relocate his meetings underground.

A light above the doorway of the room used to warn the
occupants when an air raid was in progress. In the corridor
outside, a small bell performed the same function. Otherwise, the
minions who toiled in the complex relied on the pithy dispatches
of weatherman George Rance to keep them abreast of the
situation. The man from the Ministry of Works, Rance was
responsible for operating a crude wooden weather gauge which
displayed a brief summary of meteorological conditions, along

the lines of 'Fine and Warm'. Rance's colleagues knew that when the gauge showed 'Windy', however, it was really his way of telling them that there was a flap on.

The War Rooms had once been home to a large – and noisy – population. As well as being a workplace, they were a makeshift living space, too. Even deeper below today's Treasury building than the Cabinet Room, a full floor lower, in fact, was the 'dock', a sub-basement running the full length and breadth of the building. This is where Churchill's butler laid his head. The dock was also a cramped home-from-home for typists and clerks. The doors to the dormitories were no more than four feet high and gave onto cells with concrete floors and bare brick walls. Though chemical toilets had been installed, those who slept in the sub-basement described a long and embarrassing trek up two flights to follow the call of nature. They were invariably followed by one of the overzealous Marines who guarded the Cabinet Room. Many workers preferred to go home and risk air raids and blackouts rather than squeeze into the Cabinet office dungeons for the night.

Betty Green was personal secretary to General Hastings Ismay, Churchill's representative on the Chiefs of Staff committee. She wrote, 'I used to spend every other night sleeping in the office . . . sometimes I was there for about three nights running, because I just couldn't get home, so in some ways I was fortunate that even in this revolting place called the dock one could get a good night's sleep, because you didn't hear the bombs raining down, which is just as well, because we'd all have been buried alive in the Cabinet War Rooms.'

Another part of the bunker had once reverberated to the clattering keys and pinging carriage-returns of the prime minister's typists. It was this celestial pool that I had strained to hear from across St James's Park, in the Gents of the ICA. It turns out that the most secret arm of the British war machine was dedicated to the covert production of memos. Room 60A, the typing pool, was a paper mill, a clanging shop floor of document manufacture. Accurate minutes and reports had to be typed up, with two carbon copies, and made available for circulation within a matter of hours, regardless of the time of day or night. It chimed happily with the homely mythology of the Blitz that the signature noise of the Cabinet War Rooms was not the droning of doodlebugs but the thud of typewriters.

A transatlantic hotline, linking the bunker to the White House, had been installed in a former broom cupboard. A repro PM could be seen on the phone in this cubicle, an inch of waxworks ash depending from his stogie. In 1943, Bell Telephone of the United States developed a scrambler, codenamed Sigsaly. It was ahead of its time in using electronics. So far ahead, in fact, that its circuits were the size of tree roots. This was a real-life version of the old joke about the impossibly elegant technological boon which is dependent on batteries the size of suitcases. Sigsaly, or 'X-ray' as it was known in London, relied on an intermediate scrambler apparatus five feet high which the prime minister had to squeeze past before he could place a call. But encrypting a single conversation also demanded more than thirty relay racks, which stood seven feet tall and weighed a total of eighty tons; a power supply capable of producing thirty kilowatts; and a room large and cool enough to prevent the whole lot from blowing up. There simply wasn't enough space at the War Rooms. The basement of Selfridge's was the nearest location capable of accommodating X-ray's elephantine entrails. Churchill's partially enciphered telephone conversation was transmitted by cable from the bunker to the department store, where it was fully scrambled and beamed by radio to Washington. Only Churchill himself was allowed to use the link to the president. The door to the transatlantic telephone room originally came from a lavatory, and it's said that this helped to keep the secret of the hotline safe even from Churchill's fellow denizens of the bunker. They naturally assumed that he had bagged the only tolerable loo in the compound for himself.

At the time I was going round the War Rooms, the serving British Cabinet had been placed on a 'war footing' by Mr Blair for a forthcoming general election. As I write, Blair now has a War Cabinet of his own. Britain is at war 'against terrorism'. Even if the successors of Churchill's Cabinet don't meet below ground at present, the option will certainly be available to them. To protect ministers and others from hijackers crashing planes in central London, from the release of chemical or biological weapons, from a cloudburst of anthrax, officials will have been dusting down the corridors and bunkers beneath Whitehall in case they're needed again. Such are the state's arrangements for its own preservation. 'You've got to have someone to organise the survivors, haven't you?' as Keith of Subterranea Britannica had put it. It occurred to me as I neared the end of my tour of the War Rooms that the surreptitiousness which surrounded the government's contingencies continued to permeate these old corridors long after the stale cigar fumes had dissipated. It was this sensation that had struck you at the sandbagged threshold. It wasn't that officials had decided to keep the place low-key for reasons of authenticity, or at least it wasn't only that. It was more that a distrust of outsiders, of *civilians*, has been absorbed into the marigold matt.

On 16 August 1945, the day after VJ Day, the officers in the War Rooms finally tidied their desks, turned the lights out after six years, and left the place in utter secrecy, as it had been throughout the war and would remain until the 1980s. This touched on the real attraction of the subterranean. Nothing is more hidden, more secret, than what's below ground. The sense of a lair, the thought that you could pass directly overhead without suspecting a thing, is integral.

The image of Churchill in his bunker is by now well established: the sinew-stiffening broadcasts in the Hannibal Lecter-style siren suit; yes, even the footfall and the pall of tobacco smoke. What's much less well known is that a second, back-up shelter was created in London for the PM, in the event that the Germans not only levelled No. 10 but threatened the Cabinet War Rooms as well. Unlike them, Churchill's other bunker was designed to be completely bombproof. Known by the codename 'Paddock', this retreat was well away from the centre of the city. In *Subterranean City*, Antony Clayton does his best to make the location sound impressive. 'It was intended to form a last bastion of defence in the event of a German invasion . . . and from its position built into the northern heights commanded a panoramic view above ground over the rest of London.' In fact, the shelter was sunk in the unglamorous environs of Dollis Hill, though of course the very lack of airs and graces of this address made it highly suitable. The hideaway is nowadays accessed by a door that isn't there. Its secret, unnumbered entrance is between 115 and 117 Brook Road, a brace of modern maisonettes. It's like the chimerical railway platform at St Pancras station where Harry Potter boards the train for wizard school.

Unlike the War Rooms near St James's Park, the dugout at Dollis Hill is not normally open to the public. The site had belonged to the Post Office before the war, and in peacetime had reverted to them and to their successors, British Telecom. Now it was open to outsiders just once a year. I was lucky enough to go into Paddock on one of its rare openings. A handwritten sign on a concrete outbuilding in Brook Road welcomed visitors to 'Churchill's Bunker', and waiting to greet arrivals were my old friends, Subterranea Britannica. Some of my fellow members had volunteered for the job of showing the curious over the site. It was immediately clear that this was indeed a task for them. Paddock had fallen into disrepair. The bunker had been quarried out forty feet beneath an old GPO research station, where the boffins had helped to devise the Ultra code-breaking system. In wartime, camouflage netting had concealed steel-reinforced concrete three and a half feet thick. Below this was a deep chamber covered by two layers of concrete six feet thick, which were separated by loose sand to absorb the shocks of heavy bombing. Unlike the Cabinet War Rooms, Paddock had not been given a lick of paint in years. There was no brochure or pre-recorded tour. There was no functioning lighting, except for a temporary arrangement that the SubBrits had contrived. Walls and floors ran wet. Up on Dollis Hill, nature had been doing its immemorial thing of returning dust to dust. In one sunken chamber, a beautiful snowy fur, the most exotic fungus I had seen below ground, grew luxuriantly from the ceiling. Nearby was the old map room, the domain of Churchill's military planners. The Nazis never even came close to penetrating this sanctuary, but the boards on which the generals had unfurled their charts had been put to rout by rot.

'When we had a look here last year, it was eighteen inches deep in water,' said a SubBrit I recognised as a potholer from the trip to the R6 radar station.

His mate chortled happily. 'It's like *Star Wars* where they're trapped in a trash compactor.'

I very nearly knew what he meant. There was something fantastic about the place. Paddock had been so shrouded in subterfuge that not even the King had been let in on its exact whereabouts, so it would have come as a complete surprise to him if the royal household had ever been removed to Dollis Hill. In his memoirs, Churchill was deliberately vague about the bunker, writing that it was 'near Hampstead'. He described it as 'a citadel for the war cabinet . . . with offices and bedrooms and wire and fortified telephone communication . . . On September 29 [1940] I prescribed a dress rehearsal so that everybody should know what to do if it got too hot. I think it important that Paddock should be broken in.' Accordingly, the Cabinet met 'far from the light of day' on 3 October. 'Each minister was requested to inspect and satisfy himself about his sleeping and working arrangements.' This necessary but disagreeable business having been dispatched, the Cabinet enjoyed a 'vivacious luncheon' to fortify them for the return to Westminster.

'It's quite possible that Churchill actually carried out that Cabinet meeting in this room,' said one of the SubBrits. There were gravy splashes of mould up the walls. 'The notes at the time say it was held in "a long narrow room" just like this one.' On the old, curved steel shapes of ventilators, droplets of water had been cultured into jewels by immobility. There was a galley with a pair of sinks and the remains of kitchen cupboards. Original light fittings survived. An old telephone exchange near one of the entrances looked like a wine rack. A small room where a bed and some furniture were uncovered, marked with the number 13, is thought to have been set aside as Churchill's bedroom.

After sixty years, Paddock had at last been opened up to daylight, or at least torchglow. Incredibly, it might have remained hidden to this day, but for a decision to build over the top of it. A housing association won permission to put up three dozen new homes in Brook Road. The association was astonished when the Ministry of Defence made contact, requesting access to the site before a pile was driven. Contractors for the MOD removed maps, files and pieces of equipment from the bunker. Once the housing association, Network, realised what they were sitting on, they felt that they should give the public at least one opportunity a year to see the bunker. Spokeswoman Maria Michael said, 'People just can't believe it when they see this huge complex beneath them that they didn't even know was there.'

The guide from Subterranea Britannica was inhaling contentedly. 'There's still that engine-room smell,' he said in the engine room. Gauges measuring amperes and volts were like the rusted round facemasks of deep-sea divers. There had been no central heating at Paddock, said the guide, because once you were deep enough in the ground, there was a more or less constant temperature in the upper fifties Fahrenheit.

Paddock had once contained a broadcasting studio. A plan

was hatched for the actor David Niven to impersonate Churchill at the mic if the situation became so tight that the old boy was forced to flee the country with the royal family. In reality, although Clement Attlee did at some stage chair a meeting at Dollis Hill with the Australian prime minister, Churchill's inspection of 3 October 1940 proved to be his one and only visit. Not even his good lunch had tempted him to return. The SubBrit guide said that the PM had never cared for the place: he detected a slight in Churchill's comment about it being 'far from the light of day'.

Other evidence points towards Churchill's low opinion of Paddock. Downing Street was behind a decision to purchase a pair of flats in Neville's Close, near Brook Road. When Churchill's secretary, John Colville, wrote about accompanying his boss on a recce to 'the flats where we should live', it's thought that he was referring to Neville's Close. A local historian called Jack Valentine believes that Churchill agreed to hang his tin hat at the flats, as a gesture towards removing himself from the heavily bombed centre of town, but refused to endure the confines of the bunker itself. In Paddock, the installation of flushing lavatories had been overlooked, notes Valentine, and on his one visit, the PM was constrained to use a fire bucket as an ashtray for his cigars. These were not aspects of life underground which were calculated to win the PM over.

Exiting the bunker by the narrow staircase of the emergency exit, you ascended into the down-draught of cool currents, harbingers of the pleasant airs of Dollis Hill. Squirming through the tight chicanery of the climb, the guide from Subterranea Britannica spared a thought for his wartime forerunners. 'They obviously weren't as well fed as me,' he said.

I've already indicated that the glittering prize of underground exploring in London, the great white that obsesses every hunter as he voyages through the sewers and submerged rivers, is the secret government labyrinth. It's not that mole-men are subversive by nature, let alone any kind of threat to national security. On the contrary, if Subterranea Britannica are anything to go by, our rulers couldn't wish for a more responsible and law-abiding crowd. But the seekers after sunless places are driven by a strange mixture of curiosity and one-upmanship. On the face of it, at least, nothing could be quite so satisfying as to claim a trip to the heart of the hidden state, to bag a corner of unseen Whitehall. But not since Campbell climbed from his manhole cover in 1980, folded his bicycle and wrote up his trip, has such a feat been convincingly claimed. Of course, it's a reasonable assumption that the underground state is in pretty constant occupancy. But the people who enter it don't write about it, just as those who write about it don't enter it, in a state of affairs no less stymieing for being symmetrical.

Reader, I've cracked my poor skull on the bulkheads of this great underground monolith. I've made approaches both official and irregular, I've faxed and phoned and e-mailed, and I've taken every chance to test inviting door handles and jink past the guards. I even managed to get a stride or two inside the Admiralty citadel, the ivy-clad blockhouse at the eastern end of the Mall, the entrance to the Q-tunnels for the military. They had the removal men in, and I followed a couple of chaps in overalls as they lugged a table over the threshold. But the pair of naval ratings I ran into had not heard of the open day that I claimed to be attending.

Formal requests have been politely nixed. No, you cannot come into the Ministry of Defence to have a look at the remains of Henry VIII's wine cellar, because a substantial refit is in progress. 'Your project was given the utmost consideration,' said a Buckingham Palace spokeswoman after I'd enquired about touring the cellars. 'Although your ideas are certainly intriguing, I am afraid that we are unable to offer you any assistance.' The applications that weren't turned down went serially unanswered.

After an old school friend in British Telecom failed to come up trumps on the tricky matter of access, I approached a senior BT tunnel man several times without ever hearing from him one way or the other. With another *grand fromage* on the London tunnel scene, a pleasant and well-meaning man, I went through a monthly pantomime in which he assessed the security situation before reaching the invariable conclusion that it was too risky for him to let me in.

It was in the course of these frustrating exercises that I encountered a man who, I suspect, knows what's under Whitehall as well as anyone else alive. I enter a caveat because he was almost too good to be true, the sort of man whose stories mark him out as either a privileged insider or an inspired charlatan. I'm a poor member of Subterranea Britannica, God knows, but the best of us are amateurs, dabblers, compared to him. Always assuming, of course, that he can be trusted to be who he says he is. On balance, I think he can. Our meeting was arranged by a highly reputable go-between who certainly knows his subterranean stuff. The sit-down was fixed for a part of the underground Q complex. It was in a borrowed office beneath Whitehall, inaccessible to most of us but one of my interlocutor's easier ports of call. Beneath a substantial girder, papers sprawled across an untidy desk. On the wall was a clock that wouldn't have looked out of place in a railway waiting room of the pre-Beeching era.

What to call my contact? A pseudonym is the least that he'd insist on; an enigmatic initial, on the other hand, would be absurd. I think I'll refer to him as the architect, since that was his stated occupation. I nearly said it was his cover. No doubt he practised his profession to the highest standards, but in his case, this had the fortuitous effect of enabling him to pass unchallenged in circles outside the experience of his fellow draughtsmen. The architect told me that he once had a pass to Mecca. A patent infidel from the top of his close-cropped head to the soles of his lily-white feet, he had been able to come and go as he pleased at the holy of holies, on the personal say-so of the King of Saudi Arabia.

The go-between left us after half an hour, but the architect and I sat on for two hours, discussing the overdraft of the late Queen Mother – £5 million, he thought, run up on the horses – and the prestigious London civil engineering project which was then in trouble – undone, so the architect claimed, by the vainglory of the designer. 'He skimped on a layer of rubber so he could spend the money on a bit of the thing that the public would see,' said the architect with disgust.

He had a pass that I, for one, coveted as much as his ticket to Mecca: it gave him entry to all Ministry of Defence establishments in Whitehall.

'Exactly how high up the food chain are you?' I asked him.

'Pretty high up,' he said, as if it was the first time he'd given the matter a thought.

'So how much is there down here? How many tunnels are there?'

'I'd say there are about twenty-five miles of tunnels.'

'Twenty-five miles! That's a hell of a lot. It's possible to go from one government department to another, then.'

The architect smiled at me.

'I mean, to go from one to another without going out onto the street.'

'That's what I thought you meant. Oh yes, there are several ways of doing that.' His features were a little doughy, befitting someone who spent a lot of his working life away from daylight. His looks also went with a kind of unpindownable quality about him. Though he was entirely affable, he hadn't the slightest intention of admitting me to his secret lair, of piloting me through the eau-de-Nil door.

I said, 'Look, I'm not a terrorist. I'd let you see what I'd written before I published it.' Leaving out a few identifying features and technical references struck me as a fair trade for having a look at the buried state.

'That's fine,' said the architect cordially. 'But you see, even if you didn't publish certain details about what's down there, you'd still *know* them. Do you follow me?'

In other words, I might be tempted to spill the beans in the pub to my mates. The conversation took a detour into the topic of design in Japan. The architect wondered whether the remarkable window frames he had seen in that country owed anything to origami. It was impossible to say, afterwards, whether this had been a sleight of hand on his part, a deliberate attempt to change the subject, to move us on as silkily as possible from his implied lack of confidence in my discretion, from the rebuff he had administered to my hopes. As he went on to describe his interest in military history, the architect could almost have been a member of Subterranea Britannica, albeit one with access that the rest of us could only dream of. He told me about a friend of his, an old boy who had once served in the SAS. 'He was involved in the assassination of Mussolini.'

'But I thought the Italians strung him up from a lamp post.'

'Exactly.' In another time and place, the tale would have seemed preposterous. The last refuge of the impostor – and often the first – is a claimed kinship with the SAS. Perhaps it was all an act. In the same genial vein as before, the architect explained how it was possible to incinerate a room with a light-bulb bomb, a tip he'd picked up from his SAS crony. 'You pierce the metal bit of the bulb and dunk it in a beaker of petrol,' the architect was saying. 'You plug the hole with chewing gum . . .'

Though I was still smarting at the suggestion that I couldn't keep a secret, I realised that the architect had been right not to trust me. I could already imagine myself telling friends how you made a firebomb out of a standard lamp. There really were two types of people: those who enter the government labyrinth and don't write about it, and those who write about it but don't enter it. I got no inkling from the architect of whether he had a family or not, so I asked him if was necessary for him to keep his friends in the dark about what he did. He said, 'I might tell them I was working on an MOD building but I wouldn't mention anything about tunnels.'

The architect was agreeable – the tritest observation from me was met with 'Absolutely!' – but also entirely slippery. He talked about a marksman who had been recruited in the forties in an abortive operation to shoot Hitler. The project was codenamed Foxley. 'The man's wife found out years later and she was absolutely stunned. She said, "We used to go pheasant-shooting and he never hit a thing."'

I said, 'Is there a touch of Foxley about you?'

'Oh yes,' said the architect.

POOL OF LONDON
The Essential City

In the new are traces of the old. One of the most striking pieces of engineering in the modern city, the Thames Barrier, recalls the first London Bridge. Its signature conch shells are a visual echo of the turreted 'starlings', or pontoons, of the prototype span across the river, familiar to us from the earliest canvases of the city and reproduced in the twenty-first century in Tod Hanson's deadpan drawing-board piece *The Pool of London*.

The barrier was a reminder to cockney landlubbers that their home was built on water, with all the vulnerability that that implies. In Roman times, the river oozing through Westminster was three times the width it is today and was effectively non-tidal. But as the city developed, reclaiming land from the Thames and squeezing it into a narrower course, the danger of inundation grew. In 1236, water poured into the Palace of Westminster and 'men did row with wherries in the midst of the Hall', according to one account. On 7 December 1663, Samuel Pepys told his journal that 'there was last night the greatest tide that ever was remembered in England to have been in this River all Whitehall having been drowned'. The problem has recurred within the last century. Torrential waters claimed the lives of fourteen people in 1928. In 1953, a flood tide swept over the river walls at Canvey Island just before midnight. Within half an hour, the bridge to the mainland was impassable. The first that most islanders knew of the danger was when the river burst into their homes, many of which were bungalows, no match for the flood water. Some survived by smashing holes in their ceilings and clambering to safety on their roofs in their nightclothes. But fifty-eight people were killed on Canvey Island that night, out of a total of three hundred who lost their lives in the Thames estuary.

Even in clement conditions, the river waxes and wanes by a full seven metres. According to the Environment Agency, tides are getting bigger, because of factors including higher mean sea levels, the settlement of London on its bed of clay, and the tilting of the British Isles: to put it bluntly, the south-east is slowly sliding into the Channel. The effect of this is that the Thames is rising, by about sixty centimetres every hundred years. What every Environment Agency man dreads is a surge tide. This is caused by low pressure moving across the Atlantic, dragging a mass of water in the shape of a hump or inverted saucer. If the trough passes the north of Scotland, and travels as far as the relatively shallow water in the southerly reaches of the North Sea, there is cause for alarm. Suppose that there are high winds and a spring tide as the hump of water meets the bottleneck of the Straits of Dover and the mouth of the Thames estuary. You would then have the perfect conditions for a flood along most of the tidal Thames. Water would be driven into the estuary, raising the normal level of the river by as much as four metres. A tidal wave would bear down on the city from reaches resonant of threat, from Sunk Head and Black Deep, from Knock John Channel and Shivering Sands.

If a flood was to overwhelm London's defences, the effects could be catastrophic. Would those little-used floodgates I had seen in the Northern Line tunnel between London Bridge and Bank be laboriously sealed? If they and other bulwarks failed, the Underground could be crippled. Foul water could contaminate drinking supplies, and sewage bubble up from its courses to decorate our sitting rooms with doilies of dung. Amenities like gas, power and telephones could fail. It wasn't just the riverbank that was at risk. The waters would cover London City airport and the Dome. They would pour into the disused chalk mines in Greenwich Park, flood the Royal Naval Hospital and surge up

the hill to the Observatory. The shopping mall of Bluewater
would live up to its name: it was, after all, a former chalk quarry
only a mile from the Thames. At the Oval, the middle would be
distinctly unplayable and there would be a horrible hiss from
Victoria station as trains were engulfed. Flooding could extend
as far as Clapton in the north and the borders of Wimbledon in
the south. The Environment Agency has estimated that the cost
of a severe dousing could be a mind-boggling £30 billion
'without counting the cost in human suffering and potential loss
of life'. This was the cataclysmic scenario envisaged in Richard
Doyle's popular and well-researched novel of 2003, *Flood*
('London has stood for 2000 years. Until Today'). Less a pot-
boiler than a pot-filler, *Flood* imagined mountainous seas along
the east coast of Britain and a huge wave sweeping up the
Thames. The barrier is struggling to keep back the waters when,
unhelpfully, it is rammed by a cargo ship.

London's historical solution to the problem of flooding has
been to bolster river walls and embankments. After the Thames
Flood Act was passed in 1879, and again after the floods of
1928, the banks were built up. The last major improvement of
this kind was in 1971. But there was an uncomfortable suspicion
that this strategy wasn't adequate, while it also had the drawback
that, if extended indefinitely, it would obscure the river altogether
behind dreary fortifications. In 1966, the government
commissioned an investigation into the feasibility of a flood
barrier. In all, more than forty different schemes were evaluated
at six separate sites. The successful project had to satisfy four
criteria. It had to be reliable, compatible with tidal flows,
navigable by the shipping on the river, and easy on the eye. Little
by little, the competition process moved in favour of the bulwark
we know today. A man called Charles Draper had advocated the
use of rising sector gates: he got the idea from studying the
humble domestic gas valve. In the judging process, it was
recognised that Draper's gates would impose minimal hindrance

on river traffic and would be relatively easy to build. Woolwich Reach, at one of the river's narrower points, was attractive as a location: surprisingly, the barrier is little more than five hundred yards long. The other local advantage was that the barrier's foundations could be built on solid chalk. Draper's scheme emerged victorious. The necessary legislation was passed in 1972 and construction began two years later.

In the gull-loud fastness of Woolwich Reach, it's easy to imagine that the barrier stands alone as London's insurance policy against freak tides. But it's part of a larger flood-defence package. For more than twenty miles downstream, the riverbanks have been raised by two metres, and at the mouth of Barking Creek stands the great guillotine of the Barking Barrier, a hair-trigger drop-gate resting between two towers which loom sixty metres over the quayside. Well to the west, eighty kilometres of bank have been built up between Putney and Purfleet. Nevertheless, the Thames Barrier is *primus inter pares*, the front line.

As I say, it looks like a scattering of shells, like the abandoned lunch of a giant who is fond of his seafood. Or perhaps it can be compared to a line of stepping stones. On most days, there is clear water between the middle stones, to allow shipping to pass, but for now they are threaded by a chain of metal. This metal consists of Draper's concave gates. They fulfill the remit of the barrier. The shells are dazzling in their metal carapaces, but it's the gates that do the dirty work. They are hinged baffles; for most of the time, they're invisible, lying under the surface of the river. In the event of a flood, however, they appear from underwater, rolling up like visors. Their job is to prevent the swollen Thames from passing through to the densely populated parts of the capital to the west. On this sunny but breezy Sunday in September, the day of the barrier's annual test, scores of people have come down to the riverbank to watch engineers prove that the Thames's silver bracelet is practical as well as elegant. It's quite a thing to see the gates rising up from the waves, pushed by rocker beams, the tense yellow legs of the giant grasshoppers who seem to be nesting in the shells. The environmental picture is uncertain, which is why the barrier was built in the first place, of course, and it would be rash to predict how this eye-catching feat of engineering will be fulfilling its job description even a few years from now. But this morning, the reality of it may be put in a conch shell: the barrier rules the waves, it tames the Thames. Downriver of it, the briny estuary is dammed, until it laps greenly at the embankment, splashing onto the partly covered walkway which leads from one side of the beautiful obstruction to the other. If you follow the walkway, a short stretch of the Thames path, you find yourself looking in astonishment not at a mighty river but at listless shallows, a weed-choked stewpond. Fish are practically flapping on the mudbanks.

A sudden squall has the sightseers sprinting to a café, part of the Thames Barrier visitor centre on the south bank. The café stocks a pencil-sharpener modelled on the barrier: a tiny slide rolls up to reveal the blade. Doing his best to keep spirits up is a giant cat wearing a sou'wester and walking upright in red gumboots. This moggy is Inspector Down Pour, according to a label pinned to his oilskin. One of the dads is talking to the cat, wanting to know how the barrier works. He averts his eyes as the mascot briefs him. He is embarrassed to make eye contact, to acknowledge that he's having a conversation with an outsize tabby.

In mid-afternoon, the gates move to the 'underspill' position. Yielding from their implacable head-on posture to the tide, they rise a little on their hinges and the Thames starts to boil beneath them. From the riverbank, the sound of the hydraulics is a low, reassuring hum. The emerging metal is shiny with river. Fish are channelled into cones of white water and gulls wheel over the sudden waves, which race to the muddy banks and slap against the boardwalk.

To see the barrier in action, even if only in make-believe, in a not-so-dry dry run, is enough to make your day. But to see what goes on in its deepest depths, what makes it tick, is a rare privilege. The idea of looking at the barrier in this fashion, from *below*, was planted in me by a contact at Subterranea Britannica. In his itinerary of underground places, classified as to the ease or otherwise of getting into them, the Thames Barrier was in the category of maximum difficulty. Some 25,000 people went to look at it every year, and enjoyed a tour of the visitor centre. But the barrier's service tunnels were one place even my contact had not set foot. From then on, the barrier wasn't only on his list, it was on my list, too.

You could see why the Thames path wasn't automatically routed through the barrier. Given the strategic role of this construction in keeping Londoners dry, it was no surprise that access to it was restricted. It was classified as an 'economic keypoint', according to Steve East of the Environment Agency. Steve and his colleagues were responsible for running it. But when it came to keeping the barrier safe, the people they took their orders from were the security services. In the aftermath of September 11 and the start of 'the war against terror', I had become accustomed to outlining my interest in a part of the city where I lived and worked as though I was stating the purpose of my visit to an immigration official at a foreign airport. At economic keypoints, the mood was dark. Paradoxically, confirmation of this was that the colour denoting the level of threat, the official pigment of anxiety selected from a government wall chart, was lurid. I was told that I could tour the barrier, only to be updated that the green light for my visit had been replaced by a forbiddingly cheerful shade. I had to wait until the level of ambient danger had been downgraded to a cooler colour before a date was definitively set.

With his chewing gum, his aftershave, and his M&S suit, Steve was waiting for me at Woolwich Reach. He gave me a hard hat and led me across an access bridge to the nearest shell: strictly speaking, a 'pier'. Steve was going to the far side of the river, to make enquiries about a security man who had called in sick after suffering what he claimed was an injury at work. The barrier's burnished and deckled finish – the conches seemed to anticipate the Guggenheim Museum at Bilbao – gave little indication of the mass of machinery bunched within it. Each pier was really a multi-storey energy plant. Under its stainless-steel eaves were the power packs which drove the moving parts; on the next level down was one of the compressors which put the kick into the grasshopper's legs; below that was the shift-and-latch mechanism which guided the nearest gate into position; this in turn was on top of a second compressor unit. Only after you had descended past all these floors did you reach the tunnels. One way of gaining them was by lift. If you've ever looked at the barrier, you'll know that the gleaming piers are split in two; they're on the half-shell. The smaller, downriver halves of the shells housed the lift shafts.

From the foot of the lift shaft, Steve and I walked through a tunnel of thirty-five metres to a second pier. There, we climbed down to yet another level before entering the main subterranean causeway, ten times the length of the first. Before disaster strikes in *Flood*, a party of government ministers and officials is taken through the tunnels by Angus the barrier chief, a fictional version of Steve East. 'Angus leads the way through a steel door into a broad, brightly lit passage, as spacious as a tube tunnel ... Twelve metres below the river, this is one of the hidden marvels of London. The twin tunnels – there is a second lying parallel with this one – run inside the concrete sills sunk into the riverbed in which the barrier gates rest. They extend from bank to bank, a private crossing reserved solely for barrier staff, a permanent and safe means for engineers to reach the gate piers, regardless of weather, and to bring equipment in and out.'

The underwater gangway was wide enough for two people to

walk side by side. Water pipes were racked on one wall of the tunnel. On the other were electronics and a thin red cable, part of a fireproof loop. The cable was meant to break in the event of fire, triggering an alarm. Yellow dots on the floor, showing which way was south, were to guide any fireman who became disoriented by smoke during an emergency. Drains ran away beneath gratings. The tunnels were cold and well lit, the clinical light making them seem even colder. 'If you're down here when a ship's going overhead, you can hear her propeller,' said Steve. 'It's like being in a submarine.' It felt as though we were a long way from the romantic, Sydney Opera House sails admired from the riverbank. To be under the river, in the chill of these sunken corridors, was to be reminded as if through your own skin of the barrier's function. It was to keep London from drowning.

'How deep are we right now?' I asked Steve.

'Deep enough,' he said.

I thought about the great metal shutters above our heads, the rising sector gates which awaited the call to save London, to turn again. There were six of them and they rested in curved concrete recesses on the brown riverbed. In the event of a surge tide, they were moved up through ninety degrees until they were side-on to the flow. Each one was as high as a five-storey building. The clearance from one gate to the next was more than sixty metres, which is the same span available to shipping at Tower Bridge when its bascules are raised. The gates weighed the best part of four thousand tonnes each and were capable of withstanding a load almost three times as heavy. They had been positioned to within a fastidious tolerance of less than half a millimetre.

When the barrier sets its metal face against Father Thames, the rising gates are joined by four falling radial gates, the smaller barriers nearest the riverbanks. As their name suggests, these hurdles are moved in a downward direction to assume their defensive positions. The barrier can be slammed shut in five minutes, but if this was all the time that the Environment Agency had, it would be a rush job, an all-hands-on-deck scramble. After all, closing the barrier in haste could produce exactly the disastrous effect it had been designed to prevent. An ebb tide could find its path out to sea obstructed, creating a 'reflective wave' which would wash back up the Thames towards the centre of the city.

As far as possible, the agency sees to it that, even in the worst weather, closure proceeds according to a timetable as methodical as a moonshot. The countdown goes as follows. At T minus thirty-six hours, the barrier's control room on the south bank starts receiving satellite pictures and other meteorological data indicating that low pressure and bad weather are moving across the Atlantic towards the British Isles. A full twenty-four hours before shutdown, these trends are confirmed in updated weather bulletins, and at T minus twelve hours, tide gauges begin to register a surge rippling down the North Sea. The men who operate the Barking Barrier are called out and the Port of London Authority, which oversees shipping in the Thames, is put on notice. Before the barrier can safely close, thirty-seven subsidiary gates and defences downstream of Woolwich have to be confirmed shut. These include massive gates at the King George V docks, a thirty-metre barrier across the River Darent at Dartford, and the Tilbury barrier. Private concerns at particular risk of flooding, such as the Woolwich Ferry and a huge Tate & Lyle depot, also have their own defences. With nine hours to go, and tides high on the east coast, a message confirming a tidal alert is issued. Barrier closure teams and floodgate inspection staff are paged to come in. They converge on the barrier within an hour, and by T minus seven, they are at their stations, with the barrier's exclusive power supply turned on. There are three mains supplies and as many back-up generators. Six hours before the tide arrives at Woolwich Reach, the falling radial gates swing into their defensive attitudes,

followed by the main gates an hour later, with the central gates
left until last. With the countdown at T-minus four, the control
room is in a position to announce, 'The barrier is closed.'

The sealing of the barrier is performed by two technicians,
sitting at separate workstations. Each man can see two monitors.
One tells him whether the gates are open or closed and the other
registers the oil pressure in the hydraulic systems. All of the
barrier's gates can be closed from either workstation. When an
operator clicks his mouse over a gate icon, the only immediate
sign that anything has happened is an increase in oil pressure
represented on the hydraulics display.

As Steve and I approached the northern end of the tunnel, he
was telling me about the film crews who were always asking to
shoot in it. He said, '*Alas Smith and Jones* filmed here. *The Fast
Show*, *The Bill*. We've also had pop videos and fashion shoots.'
Like several of the subterranean places I had explored, the
tunnels had been built for practicality, for prosaic reasons. But
perhaps because of the way that they condensed space, the
architects responsible had inadvertently created an aesthetic
which was attractive to less practically minded people, too.

Out in the open air again, we arrived at the security hut on the
north bank. 'I've come to examine your killer door,' Steve told
the occupant of the hut. 'Did you hear about Dave Finch?' Dave
Finch had claimed to have strained his arm opening the door.
'He's off sick today. Gone to the doctor's,' said Steve. He tried the
door for himself. It seemed to work all right. But then Steve
stumbled. He lost his footing and took a pratfall on the path.
'The pathway is much worse than the door,' said the security
guard loyally, stretching out a hand.

On the northern side of the Thames, there were signs that
development was creeping up on the barrier, in the shape of
riverside condos. But for the moment, the place was popular with
wildlife. A cormorant on a rock was stretching its wings,
unfolding them like a map. 'We sometimes see the odd dolphin up

here,' said Steve. Below us, a great, long ship, covered with piping and ducting, a vessel whose business was obviously muck, was shooting the rapids of the barrier.

In the first ten years of its operational life, from 1982 to 1991, the gates were closed in anger only nine times. In its second decade, the barrier was much busier. By the summer of 2001, the total number of closures had risen to sixty-three. The Environment Agency has predicted that the barrier could be shutting thirty times a year by 2030. But even this seems to be a significant underestimate. In the winter of 2001–2, the barrier was in action more than twenty times. At the end of 2002, the rainfall of a typical London December was concentrated into just ten days and water levels in the Thames estuary rose to four feet above the norm, their highest levels in half a century. As a result, the Thames Barrier was closed an unprecedented fourteen times *in a week*. According to the *Standard*, 'Experts believe that if the barrier had not been closed, parts of the capital including Westminster, Docklands, Chiswick and Fulham, and up to 26 Tube stations, would have seen serious flooding.' In the capital's constant if overlooked struggle with her watery element, the barrier occupied the no man's land between the sea and the city. Woolwich Reach was the outer reaches, the barrier a frontier. On a wintry day, it might seem to the men and women posted at this lonely fortification that they were the heirs of the legionnaires who had kept watch over the first city from the Roman wall, itself now submerged beneath the high water mark of the modern town.

The threat of a riverine catastrophe has led London's civil defence chiefs to apply lateral thinking. If you were looking for somewhere to establish a flood-control room, where's the best place to put it? Imagine yourself in the authorities' waders. They would tell you that it was probably best to keep the nerve centre out of sight, to avoid spreading alarm and despondency. The ideal spot would be the last place anyone would think of looking for it.

In this aspect of their brief, the location scouts for the flood-control room did their job immaculately. Though thousands of people pass its entrance every day, none of them could be expected to guess that such an important strategic bunker had been squirrelled away in the depths of an old tram tunnel on Kingsway, W2. In every respect, Thames Flood Control could not have presented a greater contrast to the Thames Barrier.

As its name suggests, Kingsway was once the poshest street in London. It was opened by Edward VII in 1906. Kingsway had been planned in the late nineteenth century as a solution to congestion in Drury Lane and Chancery Lane, the ancient routes linking the Strand and Holborn. Part of a wider scheme which also involved New Oxford Street, Shaftesbury Avenue and Charing Cross Road, the 100-foot-wide Kingsway would run between the old, clotted roads and become the main north–south artery. The £5 million project also included slum clearance and the development of new homes in adjoining streets. As Kingsway was being constructed, the tram subway was being quarried beneath it. A little over half a mile long, it began under Waterloo Bridge, where it was built using the cut-and-cover method familiar from the earliest underground railways. The tunnel became a deep-level excavation under the Strand, reverting to cut-and-cover once more below Kingsway itself. A stairwell was sunk at Holborn, serving one of two subterranean stations – the other was at Aldwych – and the tunnel finally surfaced on Theobald's Road. It was the interchange between the trams of south London, which radiated away from the Embankment, and those of the north, which travelled from Theobald's Road. Trams emerging onto the Embankment were preceded by a guard waving a flag, to warn oncoming traffic. In 1931, the tunnel was enlarged to accommodate double-decker trams. It was the heart of the city's tram network for half a century. The last one ran on 5 July 1952, though the Mayor of London has said he wants to restore the tram to the city.

In the seventies, the section of tunnel between Waterloo Bridge
and Kingsway was effectively converted into a pair of wedges:
one wedge was an underpass for road traffic, with its blunt end
at the bridge and its thin end where the Aldwych meets Kingsway
in the shadow of Bush House, home to the BBC's World Service.
Underneath this wedge was its twin, the remainder of the
subway. Only the Greater London Council had found a use for
it, when they were casting about for a hush-hush location in
which to establish a civil-defence field-control room.

My journey home from work took me past the northern
entrance of the old subway, where Southampton Row meets
Theobald's Road. I didn't have a clue about what, if anything,
might be hidden in it. One summer evening I noticed through
the rush-hour traffic that the gates leading to the slipway were
open. I had never seen them unlocked before. A man was
stacking a flatbed lorry with bricks. I crossed over to this
entrance, which is effectively an island in the middle of a dual
carriageway. Beyond the man and the lorry, the mouth of the
tunnel was blackly inviting. 'I'm a bit of a tram nut,' I told the
workman. 'Mind if I look around?'

He said, 'All right. Be careful in there, though, it's dark.'

In the entrance to the tunnel were piles of paving materials,
kerbstones of different sizes and finishes. There were railings,
some of them quite old; traffic cones; a street sign for 'Star Lane
W2' (an address I've combed the A–Z for without success); and
blue signs for a cycle route through Holborn. The subway itself
was rectangular, with tiled walls. It was an impressive size,
comfortably bigger than a Tube tunnel, say. For once, the
qualifier which reflexively sprang to mind was the right one to
use: you could drive a bus through it, or rather a double-decker
tram.

The former subway was in darkness apart from columns of
light descending from ventilation grilles. Directly beneath each
grille was a mulch of leaves and litter, London's compost. I could

also make out the lights of a distant JCB. Presumably this was being operated by a colleague of the workman on the slipway. As I made my way into the tunnel, I sensed a groove or hollow underfoot. It was the furrow of an old tramline.

Because of the disorientating effects of the dark, I couldn't say for sure how far I'd gone before I came across a Portakabin, but it must have been a couple of hundred yards. There were no signs of life. Through the Portakabin's windows I made out a sign to 'Thames Flood Control', and another to 'Thames Flood Engineering Control', with arrows to the two ends of the hut. I tried the door and it opened, but I didn't go in. Not yet. I was afraid that the man on the JCB might throw me out of the subway. He didn't know that I had permission from his mate. He was heading towards me, or at least that was the impression I had from the lights of his vehicle in the darkness. I thought that I'd better introduce myself. I stood and waited in a bright spot, beneath a grille, hoping that he would see me. Sure enough, the JCB pulled up. The driver was a big man with a shock of greying hair. Over the noise of the engine, I said, 'Sorry if I startled you. The bloke on the ramp said I could have a look around. I'm a bit of a tram nut,' I repeated.

The driver's name was Mick. He said, 'You can't see very much. You can go down there if you want, but only as far as that light.' He indicated a distant shaft of light, sunk by another grille in the surface of Kingsway. 'That's where the road goes over the top of the old tram lines.' He turned the engine off. He was very amiable. I wondered if he was going to offer to show me around. Instead he handed me a large torch. 'You take this. When you get back here, I'll go out with you.' Mick said he would wait for me to come back before he knocked off for the weekend. I had been worried that he would order me to get out, but more troubling than that was the fear of becoming stuck. Would I fall and injure myself? For all my adventures under London, I was not immune to these primal anxieties, these cave concerns.

'Don't shut me in,' I joked.

'Oh, you wouldn't want to be shut in,' agreed Mick.

I took the torch and set off, preposterous in my suit and with my briefcase. I thought about putting the briefcase down but I doubted that I'd ever find it again. Thanks to Mick's help, I could make out the contents of the tunnels more distinctly. Dozens of crush barriers were stacked against the walls. There were small yellow road signs of the sort you see attached to lamp-posts detailing parking restrictions. The subway was a highway planner's den, it was the secret London museum of street furniture.

When I reached the shaft of light which Mick and I had agreed as the point where I would turn back, I saw that there was a dogleg in the tunnel. An avenue of concrete pillars stretched down this turning. I had to satisfy myself that they *were* concrete: what they looked like were timbers, wooden props. In time, I realised that the props weren't of uniform height. They were beginning to get shorter. The roof was tapering to a point. I kept expecting Mick to cry out, calling me back, or to hear his JCB thunderously approaching. This was where the wedge of the redundant subway ended and the wedge of the traffic underpass planed on top of it. It was dusty and damp in places, but otherwise it was remarkably well kept. There were even lights fitted to some of the props, though these were dark.

I thought that I'd reached the end of the subway, but there was a small doorway to my left, set three or four feet off the ground. There was a black smudge on the ground in front of it. I took a step towards the door and sank to my shin in water. By torchlight, I saw that the black smudge was an oily puddle. Poking out of it was a plank. There was nothing else for it: I rolled up the legs of my suit trousers and stepped onto the plank and went through the doorway at a crouch, my briefcase swinging from my shoulder. I found myself in a much narrower passageway, which I assumed was some kind of service link to the old subway. Though the passage was tight, I could straighten up again. The top of this tunnel was as high as the main shaft had been before it began to contract. I went up a short, narrow flight of metal steps and across another wobbly wooden board. I was following a large pipe which had been installed just off the ground. Perhaps because of the pipe, the floor was swampy, with water or oil or both. Every few paces, I met a junction in the pipe. I hopped and scrambled between these struts until at last the passageway itself came to a dead end. I couldn't see a way over the sheer concrete face that confronted me. What had kept me going through the oily route was the hope of finding a tunnel leading into the BBC World Service, but I had exhausted this possibility. The sound of traffic over my head was noticeably louder now. I was directly underneath the roundabout at the Aldwych.

As I set off to retrace my steps, I found that my thighs were aching. I was also sweating, and not only from exertion. I didn't want to be left behind when Mick and his mate, despairing of seeing their torch again, put the padlock back on the gates of the tram subway and left for the weekend. Ducking through the little door at the end of the passage, I re-entered the main tunnel with a noise like a spinnaker cleaving from its mast. Thanks to the clear subway acoustics, I was left in no doubt that I had torn the crotch of my suit trousers. It was the third suit I'd ruined in this way during my underground explorations, though none had been written off as decisively.

Shyer now, I decided I could afford to spend a few moments in the flood bunker before returning to the surface. At least if I was kicked out now, I'd already seen the tunnel. I went into the Portakabin and shone Mick's torch at the arrow pointing in the direction of 'Thames Flood Control'. I expected to find some combination of the dourly practical and the institutionally self-interested, perhaps a list of out-of-hours undertakers and bespoke wetsuits for every alderman. I certainly hadn't anticipated a room full of old Christmas illuminations. But there they were, neon robins and winking elves and light-box snowmen, stacked and dusty and forgotten but waiting in the true spirit of Christmastide for delivery at the hands of a messiah figure, in this case, the municipal handyman.

'Thames Flood Engineering Control', in the Portakabin's other room, was a bit more like it. There was a businesslike blackboard on the wall, and a whiteboard for 'breaches'. This was where flood control technicians would grimly inventory failings in the riverbanks and London's other tidal defences. But not any longer. I can't say I was surprised that the cabin had been abandoned. Though the subway tunnel undoubtedly answered the need of the civil service for concealment, it would have been a dark and dirty place to work, with no obvious amenities. But plainly the real reason that the Portakabin had been abandoned was that it was a folly to have the capital's river defences run from an underground location which was well within the flood delta; indeed, less than half a mile from the Thames itself.

One way and another, managing the waters of London is a major undertaking for those with responsibility over the subterranean city. When we citizens are not in peril of being overwhelmed by our aqueous surroundings, it seems that we're facing the opposite hardship of not having enough to drink. Like every generation before us, we still rely on the Thames for potable water. Three-quarters of what we consume every day comes from the river. But demand is predicted to increase by 13 per cent within the first decade of the new millennium. With this in mind, the most important tunnel under London is the Thames Water ring main, though it's as unregarded as the old tram route of Kingsway. Longer than the Channel Tunnel, the ring main stretches for more than sixty miles. It is London's watery orbital, an M25 of H_2O. If a map of subterranean London was ever compared with the more familiar overground chart, the ring main would be a mirror image of the blue band representing the motorway.

One of the few superficial markers of this vast loop is a cool blue column on a wooded traffic roundabout at Holland Park, tall enough to clear the treetops of this desert island. Idling at the lights, the lynx-eyed motorist may notice coils of water hula-hooping around the trunk of this column. Water under pressure is a clue to its function, for it is in fact a vast pump, a 'pump-out shaft' in the sexy argot of the hydrologist. With ten other cylinders dotted around London, most of which are less easy on the eye because they're out of the public gaze on land owned by the utility, the pump extracts water from the main and feeds it into the water pipes which supply homes and offices. Each pump is capable of drawing enough water to fill an Olympic-sized swimming pool in less than a minute. The pumps also act as the safety valves of the water main, which may be likened to a great tyre or rubber ring being held at intense pressure forty metres below ground; that is to say, twice as deep as most Tube lines.

Not even the mole-like student of London gets to go inside the ring main, for the very good reason that it is chock-full of water which customers of Thames Water expect to be able to drink. The next best thing is to be invited to a bunker not far from Kempton Park racecourse where shirtsleeved men oversee the flow. In the still of their ergonomically manned control room, you could be on the bridge of a spaceship which was quasaring through light years of deep space while most of its company hibernated. Thames Water says that only three operatives are needed for the vital work at hand. Thousands of signals coming in from the ring main through fibre-optic cables feed information to their all-seeing computer, which monitors and controls pressure and flows, and keeps tabs on indicators of water quality. If you ask nicely, the skeleton crew may let you nudge a fader or tap a keyboard to open a sluice gate or tighten a stopcock.

Here at Thames Water's high command, you see that the ring main is a ragged lasso thrown around the suburbs and dormitories to the west of the city. From Holland Park to Kew, it extends as far as Ashford Common and crosses the Thames at Walton before returning to the other bank of the river at Hampton: it's a deep, subterranean shadow of the conduit that Wolsey installed through the water meadows to supply his palace. Surbiton and Merton are points along the main in south London before it goes inner-city at Streatham and Brixton. The loop is drawn tight through Battersea, Park Lane and Regent's Park. A vast orbital tank, it is filled from five water treatment plants. Once the water has been through the plants, it simply drops in great waterfalls to the ring main below. The effect of gravity does the rest, pushing the water along for the remainder of its journey. The main supplies half of the drinking water that London needs each day: 1,300 megalitres, enough to fill the Albert Hall eight times over. Thames Water are thrilled with the main because it means that they don't have to dig the roads up so often, or so they say.

Like the layers of history which are interleaved with each other in London, the ring main is plumbed into older technology. One of the most august of the capital's waterworks, as vast as the most vaulting cathedral, would rightly inspire awe if it was exposed to public gaze. Indeed, if anyone knew of its existence at all. It is a reservoir, but not one of the blank-faced ponds of J. G. Ballard's Shepperton. The Honor Oak reservoir occupies a hollowed-out hill in south-east London. It's the biggest in Europe, capable of holding enough water to fill a small sea: sixty million gallons. It was such a place that Doris Lessing had in mind when she wrote, 'They say that if you know the man who has the task of guarding the precious waters, one may be taken through a small door and find oneself on the edge of a reach of still black water, under a low ceiling where lights gleam down. One may add to this attractively theatrical picture the faint plop of a rat swimming away from the sudden light, and a single slow-spreading ripple.'

A man called Beachcroft built Honor Oak reservoir in the late nineteenth century, behind the respectable villas of Peckham Rye. Work began in 1898 and was not completed until a decade later. Arising from its own blazing kilns, which worked day and night on site, the reservoir was formed out of no fewer than sixteen million bricks, which were made and hod-carried and mortared into place by four hundred men. Like the Stygian labyrinth of Bazalgette's sewers, Beachcroft's Honor Oak is a fantastically overdesigned monument to the brickie's craft, beautifully pointed and supported by scores, if not hundreds, of immaculate arches. There's a very sound engineering principle behind the arches, though, as I discovered when I paced out one of the four endless chambers, or cells, of the reservoir. The cell had been emptied of water, to permit maintenance work. 'With a space like this, you have to watch that as you drain it, you don't pull the roof in with the suction,' said Adrian Hartland of Thames Water, my guide. 'That's why you need good ventilation and something sturdy to hold the roof up.' We padded across the shelving seabed of the reservoir floor. It was cold and dark but it was dry. When it was full to its working capacity, the water level was three times as high as Adrian and me. Two great iron pipes which serviced the cell, the inflow and the drain, were barnacled with oxidation.

The retaining walls between the cells were no less than five feet thick. Like everything else, they were made of solid brick. Water was bubbling up into the floor of our cell. It was entering through a leaking valve, because of pressure from an adjacent tank. 'There's an eight-foot tunnel down there,' said Adrian, training his torch on the floor, 'but you wouldn't want to go in it.'

'Why wouldn't I?'

'Because there are dirty great fan blades in the middle of it. They'd cut you to ribbons.'

We hadn't passed through Doris Lessing's small door to reach the cell, but climbed down a zigzag of metal ladders like a fire escape. Here and there, one or two other ladders, no bigger than the cherry-pickers that council workers use to change the bulbs in street lights, were propped against the high arches. They were to enable Thames Water's specialists to carry out their inspection. Strings of lights had been installed for the duration. They threw dark, elastic shapes through the watery undercroft. When Adrian and I were out of their range, I could make out pinpricks of daylight in the head-craning nave. These were ventilation holes, and boreholes which had been sunk to allow the quality of the water to be tested when the cell was full.

Honor Oak: the words were redolent of the Arcadian idyll. This former hamlet, a once remote and bucolic outpost of London, was noted and named for the tree which had marked the boundary between Camberwell and Lewisham. Queen Elizabeth I is said to have rested beneath its sheltering boughs. Dick Turpin found Honor Oak a happy hunting ground, stepping out from behind the gnarled trunk with his neckerchief and his pistols. In the Napoleonic wars, the Admiralty came to Honor Oak to raise one of its early-warning beacons, the predecessors of the R6 radar stations like the one I'd rummaged around in on my day trip with the SubBrits. All in all, then, there was every reason to assume that the mound which dominates the Aquarius Golf Course was all part of the same verdant heritage. Only on closer inspection do the contours appear a little too angular to be natural; and what business does that Edwardian brick folly have, cluttering up the fairway like that? The hill is in fact man-made, the earthworks commissioned to enclose the reservoir and its vasty draught of water. The brick gazebo is a ventilation inlet, a rococo chimney.

The club members are affable types who can be imagined having a G and T in the White Horse or the Morning Star or the Heaton Arms, the unchanging post-war pubs of Muriel Spark's *The Ballad of Peckham Rye*. As a rule, players are expected to play through the 824-foot reservoir. But during the maintenance work, they sportingly walked around it. No loose tee shots pinged off the brick hazard. The contractors had the hill to themselves and were scooting across it in one-man, fun-size JCBs. They were raising the turf and laying a film of plastic sheeting beneath it. This was in order to allow rainwater to drain off the mound. Far, far below the links, Adrian and I sensed the whale music of these distant undertakings.

I said, 'There's a very unusual atmosphere down here.'

'It's quite serene,' agreed Adrian. 'When we first came here in October, the weather was terrible. It's always cold where you and I are right now, but the wind was blowing outside, it was chucking it down. You get in here and you don't know what's going on outside. The light could go for the day and you wouldn't notice.'

I imagined the reservoir when it was full, the terrible gravity of the massed water in its underground loch. And then I thought about being in the control room near Kempton Park racecourse and working the levers for Honor Oak, seeing in my mind's eye an oil-strike of water which would drench a startled four-ball to their squelching plus-fours.

In *Invisible Cities*, Italo Calvino says, 'The city does not tell its past, but contains it like the lines of a hand.' The map-book that I had carried with me throughout my odyssey, my battered and bandaged *A–Z*, was scrawled and scored with lines. They marked the places I had visited which lay beneath the streets. My *A–Z* was a kind of palimpsest of London under London. A peopled urban topography thrived out of sight, just like the one we were familiar with in the overground. 'The Underground has its streets and avenues which the pedestrians quickly recognise and follow,' says Peter Ackroyd. 'It has its short cuts, its crossroads, its particular features (no escalators at Queensway, deep lifts in Hampstead, long escalators at the Angel) and, just like the city itself, areas of bright lights and bustle are surrounded by areas of darkness and disuse. The rhythms of the city are endlessly mimicked beneath the city, as well as its patterns of activity and habitation.' This was the city under the city, and I could disappear into it whenever I wanted.

Retracing the capital to her Roman origins, I'd read the book of London backwards. From buried rivers to the Thames Barrier, I'd explored the underground metropolis, and in the end, it came down to water, to water and clay. That's what London was made of, just like the rest of us. After the air-conditioned and thermostated precincts of the surface, the foul subsoil of London was candidly elemental. Installed in it, the steel and concrete Tube had become part of it. Surreptitiously, the Thames slicked the tunnels of the Underground and decay speckled its floodgates with liver spots. The city was a living thing. 'Like the human body, London hides its organisms within it. There are arteries bearing the body's fluids, lungs enabling it to breathe, bones giving it support, muscles endowing it with strength, nerves carrying signals, and bowels disposing wastes,' say Trench and Hillman.

Dante travels to the forbidding subterranean City of Dis and is soon embroiled in a discussion about 'dead clay'. 'On every side, the vast and reeking mire surrounds this city of the woe-begot.' 'When we die, we turn back into ooze. We just leak!' as Jamie the guide had put it on our walk through the valley of the Fleet, addressing matters of mortality more jauntily. Our lives begin in darkness and end in darkness. We're returned to the earth, dead clay. An ambitious theatrical production based on Coleridge's druggy poem 'Kubla Khan' which was staged in the old train shed of the Camden Roundhouse, was like a serene near-death experience. Wearing a headset which played a recording of the verse as well as projecting suitably hallucinatory images, the theatregoer followed a 'hostess' down the dimly lit tunnels of this brick pleasure dome and reflected that this was how it might be on Judgement Day, if he was lucky.

The running of the Tube was like the cycle of life. 'Near hospitals, one always finds a florist, an undertaker and a subway station,' says Marc Auge in his book on the Parisian Metro. On this side of the Channel, Royal London Hospital was near Whitechapel, St George's near Tooting Broadway, Great Ormond Street near Russell Square. Everyone who takes the Tube connects with a folk past. Travelling on the Circle Line, G. K. Chesterton noticed that the names of St James's Park, Westminster, Charing Cross, Temple, Blackfriars 'are really the foundation stones of London'. As station succeeds station, it's like a chronology of important moments in our past: Victoria, Waterloo, Aldgate. 'The train threads its way through our history at an accelerated speed,' says Auge, 'it commutes among great people, high places, and great moments . . . taking the subway would thus mean, in a certain way, celebrating the cult of the ancestors.' For Londoners, a Tube ride was also a more intimate excavation, a return journey to our own lives. This stop was once home, that one would be forever associated with a job, yet a third was the trysting ground of a long-ago love affair. For us, the unloved stations were points of departure. 'Surely it is our own life that we confront in taking the subway.'

In Cricklewood, the miners digging the London Connection for the electricity utility had made contact underground with the other miners who were digging in the opposite direction, towards them. They had their breakthrough party in a pub across the road from the pit. They arm-wrestled each other for cash at a table by the bar. It was a surprisingly civilised affair – chicken wings and thousand island dressing and pressed polo shirts in the upstairs function suite – though there was a possibility that it would be gatecrashed by travelling folk looking for a fight, spoiling for a return match. The food had been laid on by the cook from the site. He was up at four o'clock to go to market to pick out fresh produce for the men, he told me. This seemed to be above and beyond the call of duty. Surely all he had to do was

wait until Iceland opened, then trolley all the burgers and chips
he needed to the checkout? Was he telling me that there were
vegetarians, *vegans*, down the pit? 'Do you buy rocket for them?'
I asked him.

'All right, all right. Why would they want rocket, anyway?'
returned the chef. He had a good point. How pleased did I think
I'd be to find a sprig of peppery salad waiting for me after eight
hours' digging under Cricklewood? 'As long as they keep coming
back, that's the main thing,' said the chef. 'That's as good as a
compliment to me.'

I hadn't seen Mark from Newport since he'd had a fortnight
in Benidorm, a last family holiday with his eldest son. 'It was
grand,' he said. 'I had my wallet pinched in a bar but apart from
that, we had a brilliant time.' He was driving to Liverpool first
thing in the morning with his boy, hoping for tickets to see the
Reds. A miner who hailed from Birkenhead was drinking lagers
and Red Bull. He said, 'I'll kip in my car. I'll have a fucking
headache tomorrow, but what can you do?'

In London, if not in the coalfields, there was plenty of work
for miners. The government might finally get around to
commissioning Crossrail, a long-delayed scheme linking
Paddington to Liverpool Street and Stratford. It would boost the
city's chances of hosting the Olympic Games in 2012 and provide
a fast connection between Heathrow and the City. More urgently,
it would ease the crush on the Central Line. The plan called for
a twin-bore tunnel from Paddington to Whitechapel. It would
use main-line trains, calling at enlarged stations to be built at
Bond Street, Tottenham Court Road, Farringdon and Liverpool
Street. Then there was the rail link of the Channel Tunnel,
excavating its way from Stratford and expected to reach St
Pancras in 2004. The road was up in front of the old terminus.
They were spending £300 million on converting it into a hub of
this international line. Eighteen months of subterranean
preparation were needed before tunnelling could even begin.

Sewers, water mains and utility cables were all diverted. In east London, the dig was a multinational project. They'd had the top managers over from Japan to smash a barrel of sake over the great tunnelling machines which would stealthily advance on King's Cross.

There was always talk of new runways for London, even of entire new airports, and that meant more mining. One possible solution to the holes which had undermined the A2 at Blackheath was to excavate tunnels through the heath and put the traffic down there instead. The city's population would grow by almost 10 per cent by 2021, much faster than anywhere else in the country, and one of the few ways it could grow was down.

At the breakthrough party, a tough old tunnel man called Gary – Gal – told me over several large ones that the game wasn't what it was. But it seemed to me that the miners earnt their wages – as much as £90,000 a year – the hard way. Gary told me a story about the old days, about coming out of a dig in Dartford and ordering a meal at his favourite Indian restaurant and suffering a sudden attack of the bends, an occupational hazard for men emerging from deep underground in less safety-conscious times than our own. When the ambulancemen arrived, Gary asked them to collect his food and wine. 'It was Blue Nun in those days,' he said. The ambulance took Gary to Harley Street where a specialist saw him at once. He ordered Gary into a remedial decompression chamber which had been installed in the surgery, to simulate a slow, pain-free ascent from below sea level. The doctor allowed Gary to take his meal in with him but confiscated the wine. As Gary forked his lonely madras, he watched through a porthole as the doctor and his nurse drank the lot.

SELECT BIBLIOGRAPHY

Ackroyd, Peter, *London: The Biography* (Vintage)

Adams, Anna, (ed.), *London in Poetry & Prose* (Enitharmon)

Adams, Tim (ed.), *City Secrets: London* (The Little Bookroom)

Auge, Marc, *In the Metro* (University of Minnesota Press)

Ballard, J. G., *Collected Short Stories* (Flamingo)

Ballard, J. G., *High-Rise* (Flamingo)

Baron, Alexander, *The Lowlife* (Harvill) ·

Berger, John, Gee, Maggie, et al., *Diaspora City* (Arcadia)

Calvino, Italo, *Invisible Cities* (Vintage)

Chesterton, G. K., *The Napoleon of Notting Hill* (House of Stratus)

Clayton, Antony, *Subterranean City* (Historical Publications)

Connor, J. E., *Abandoned Stations on London's Underground* (Connor & Butler)

Conrad, Joseph, *The Secret Agent* (Penguin)

Curl, James Stevens, *The Victorian Celebration of Death* (Sutton Publishing)

Dante, *The Divine Comedy* (Penguin Classics)

Defoe, Daniel, *A Journal of the Plague Year* (Penguin Classics)

Dickens, Charles, *Oliver Twist* (Penguin Classics)

Dickens, Charles, *Our Mutual Friend* (Penguin Classics)

Doyle, Richard, *Flood* (Arrow)

Duffy, Maureen, *Capital* (Harvill)

Duncan, Andrew, *Secret London* (New Holland)

Duncan, Andrew, *Walking Notorious London* (New Holland)

Dyer, Geoff, *Yoga For People Who Can't Be Bothered To Do It* (Abacus)

Dyson, Tony, *The Medieval London Waterfront* (Museum of London)

Ford, Ford Madox, *The Soul of London* (Everyman)

Gilbert, Pamela K. (ed.), *Imagined Londons* (State University of New York Press)

Glancey, Jonathan, *London, Bread and Circuses* (Verso)

Glinert, Ed, *A Literary Guide to London* (Penguin)

Graham-Leigh, John, *London's Water Wars* (Francis Boutle)

Green, Henry, *Caught* (Harvill)

Greenblatt, Stephen, *Hamlet in Purgatory* (Princeton University Press)

Halliday, Stephen, *The Great Stink of London* (Sutton Publishing)

Halliday, Stephen, *Underground to Everywhere* (Sutton Publishing)

Hardingham, Samantha, *London: A Guide to Recent Architecture* (Ellipsis)

Hill, Tobias, *Underground* (Faber & Faber)

Inwood, Stephen, *A History of London* (Papermac)

Jack, Ian (ed.), *Granta 65: London: The Lives of the City* (Granta)

Jackson, Mick, *The Underground Man* (Picador)

Kelly, Michael, *London Lines* (Mainstream Publishing)

Kersch, Gerald, *Fowlers End* (Harvill)

Laurie, Peter, *Beneath the City Streets* (Penguin)

le Vay, Benedict, *Eccentric London* (Bradt)

Lessing, Doris, *London Observed* (Flamingo)

Litt, Toby *Corpsing* (Penguin)

London, Jack, *The People of the Abyss* (Pluto Press)

Macinnes, Colin, *The Colin Macinnes Omnibus* (Allison & Busby)

Martin, Andrew, *The Necropolis Railway* (Faber & Faber)

Moorcock, Michael, *King of the City* (Scribner)

Moorcock, Michael, *London Bone* (Scribner)

Moorcock, Michael, *Mother London* (Secker & Warburg)

Moore, Tim, *Do Not Pass Go* (Yellow Jersey Press)

Nicholson, Geoff, *Bleeding London* (Indigo)

Orwell, George, *Down and Out in Paris and London* (Penguin)

Paling, Chris, *The Repentant Morning* (Jonathan Cape)

Pevsner, Nikolaus, *The Building of England: London* (Penguin)

Platt, Edward, *Leadville* (Picador)

Porter, Roy, *London, A Social History* (Penguin)

Pritchett, V. S., *A Cab at The Door* (The Hogarth Press)

Pritchett, V. S., *London Perceived* (Penguin)

Ross, Christopher, *Tunnel Visions* (Fourth Estate)

Royle, Nicholas, *The Director's Cut* (Abacus)

Self, Will, *Dorian* (Penguin)

Sharp, David, *The London Loop* (Aurum Press)

Sinclair, Iain, *Downriver* (Vintage)

Sinclair, Iain, *Lights Out for the Territory* (Granta)

Sinclair, Iain, *London Orbital* (Granta)

Sinclair, Iain, *Lud Heat and Suicide Bridge* (Granta)

Sinclair, Iain, *Rodinsky's A to Z* (Goldmark Uppingham)

Sinclair, Iain, *Sorry Meniscus* (Profile)

Sinclair, Iain, *White Chappell, Scarlet Tracings* (Granta)

Spark, Muriel, *The Ballad of Peckham Rye* (Penguin)

Stow, John, *A Survey of London* (Sutton Publishing)

Thurley, Simon, *The Lost Palace of Whitehall* (RIBA)

Time Out Book of London Short Stories Vols 1 & 2 (Penguin)

Time Out Book of London Walks (Penguin)

Trench, Richard, Hillman, Ellis, *London Under London* (John Murray)

Waugh, Evelyn, *Vile Bodies* (Penguin Classics)

Weinreb, Ben, Hibbert, Christopher (eds), *The London Encyclopaedia* (Macmillan)

Weinreb, Matthew, *London: Portrait of a City* (Phaidon)

Wilson, A. N. (ed.), *The Faber Book of London* (Faber & Faber)

Wolmar, Christian, *Down the Tube* (Aurum Press)

Wright, Patrick, *The River: The Thames in Our Time* (BBC)

INDEX

A-Z guide 15, 68, 156, 364
A2: 21, 368
A24: 110
A3212: 150
Abbey Mills 57
Abbey of Barking 88
accidents on the Underground 6–7,
    287–288
Ackroyd, Peter 87, 91, 364
Admiralty 324, 325, 336, 363
AK47 100
AK74 100
Albert Hall 361
Aldersgate 68
Aldgate 66, 68
Aldgate station 288, 366
Aldwych 91, 355, 358
Aldwych branch 267–268
Aldwych station 19–20, 281
Aldwych tram station 354
Alfonso, King of Naples 135
Alfred the Great, King 91, 181
Alias Smith and Jones 352
All Hallows Berkyngechirche 88
All Hallows by the Tower 86–88, 89,
    91–92, 94, 193
Alsatia 192
America's Cup 227–228
Amersham station 262
Amsterdam 260
Angel Islington 282

Angel station 282–285
Angle station escalators 364
Anne Boleyn, Queen 113, 146, 153
Anne of Bohemia, Queen 123, 127
anthrax 276
'anti-noise' 280
Apocalypse Now 36
aquarium 29, 75
Aquarius Golf Course 363–364
archaeologist 187
archaeology project 63–65
Ascension Day 85
Ashford Common 361
Assizes of Nuisance 47
Association of Port Health Authorities
    117
Asterix 70
Asticus 70
Athens 233
Attlee, Clement 335
Auden, W. H. 306
Auge, Marc 8, 366
Augustinians 111–112
Austen, Jane 222

babbling brooks 35
Baker Street station 280, 289
Bakerloo Line 285, 286, 287
Balham 57
Balham station 269
Ballad of Peckham Rye, The 363

Ballard, J. G. 16, 361
Bangkok 275
'banjos' 3, 24
Bank station 263, 264, 269–270, 274, 278, 344
Banqueting House 147–148, 325
Barcelona 122
Barclays Bank 208
Barking 88, 109
Barking Abbey 193
Barking Barrier 346, 351
Barking Creek 57, 346
Barking Wharf 109
Barnack 314
barracks 144
Barry, Charles 161, 162, 170, 173
Barry, E. M. 173
Base Court 141
Basingstoke 210, 212
Basset, Fulk 193
Battersea 297, 361
Battersea Park 55
Bayre, Captain 119
Bazalgette, Sir Joseph 56–58, 147, 192, 262, 270, 362
BBC World Service 355, 358
beating the bounds 86, 91–92, 94–97, 193
Beaton, Cecil 269
Beck, Harry 11–14, 17, 204
Becket, Thomas 108, 112
Bede, the Venerable 90–91, 193
Bedford Road 271
Bell Telephone 330
Bellingham, John 154
Belsize Park deep-level shelter 270
Belsize Park station 268
Ben Hur 81
Beneath the City Streets 324
Benn, Tony 164
Bennett, Alan 113
Bennett, Arnold 257
Berger, John 39
Berry Brothers & Rudd 203–215, 218, 306
Bethnal Green Road 323
Betjeman, Sir John 262, 289
Bhurji, Harjit 300–307
bibliography 369–371
Bidder, H. F. 113
Big Ben 46, 165, 171
Bilbao 349
Bill, The 352

Billingsgate Fish Market 89–90
Bird Street 299
Bishopsgate 68, 226–230, 323
Bishopsgate railway arches 114
black burnish ware 65
Black Death 193–195
Black Deep 344
Blackfriars 38–39, 68, 192
Blackfriars Bridge 32
Blackfriars Underground station 366
Blackheath 21–22, 368
Blair, Captain 119
Blair, Tony 316, 331
Blake's 7: 271
Blake, William 23
Bleak House 71
Blind Transaction Duty 301
Blondin 242
Bloomsbury 299
blue guides 95
boar 32, 142
Bond Street station 367
Bond, James 20, 119, 222, 305, 324
bones 63–64, 187–188
Book of Common Prayer 188
Boris [boar] 142
Borough 90
Boudicca, Queen 38, 67, 90
boundaries 31, 66, 85–86, 363
Bourne, the Widow 209, 211
Braithwaite viaduct 229
'breaches' 359
Brideshead Revisited 217
British Museum 304
British Museum station 281–282
British Music Hall Society 233–237
British Telecom 317, 332, 337
British Waterways 36–37
Brixton 271, 361
Broadwick Street 56
Brodie, Miss Jean 279
Brompton 236
Brompton catacombs 250
Brook Road 332, 334
Brook Street 240
Brooke Street 189
Brookwood Necropolis Railway 185
brownfield development 23
Brownjohn, Alan 39
Brummel, Beau 210
Brunel, Isambard Kingdom 256–258, 263

Brunel, Mark 188, 263
Bryson, Bill 244
Buckingham Palace 56, 315, 336
Buckingham, Duke of 153
building boom 89
Bull and Bush station 285
Bunce's Ditch 114, 115
Bunhill Fields 177
Burgess, Anthony 52
burial chambers 258
Bush House 355
Byron, Lord 210, 222

Cabinet Office 148–150, 324
Cabinet Office briefing room 156–157
Cabinet War Rooms 20, 326–332
Calvino, Italo 364
Camberwell 363
Cambridge, Duke of 140, 243, 245
Camden Lock 114
Camden Market 36, 226
Camden Roundhouse 365
Camden Town 32
Camden Town deep-level shelter 270,
    271
Camomile Street 68
Campbell, Duncan 322–326, 336
Campbell, Herbert 234
cane-sword 100
Canterbury Tales, The 86
Canvey Island 343–344
Carter, John 127
Cash, Johnny 273
Castle Baynard 109
catacombs 242, 244–252
catafalque 241, 249–250
Catesby, Robert 168–169
Catford 92
Catford, Nick 22, 319–320
Catherine of Aragon, Queen 137
Catherine of Valois, Queen 123–124,
    126, 127
cattle slaughtering 195
Caxton, William 30
Cenotaph 317
Central Line 7, 260, 268, 270, 281–282,
    299, 323, 367
'Central War Room' 328
Centre Point 299
cesspits 49–50, 170, 258
Chadwell 38
Chamberlain of London 104, 127–128

Chamberlain's Court 104, 107
Champion, Harry 234
Chancery Lane 215–225, 307, 354
Chancery Lane deep-level shelter 270,
    323
Chancery Lane station 12
Channel 4: 180, 271
Channel Tunnel 262
Channel Tunnel Rail Link 37, 367–368
Chantries Act 1547: 168
Chapel of St Nicholas 124
Charing Cross 122–123
Charing Cross Road 354
Charing Cross Underground station 260,
    285, 366
Charles I, King 147–148
Charles II, King 127, 153, 199
Charles, Prince of Wales 206, 229
charnel house 20–21
Charterhouse Square 21
Charterhouse Street 191
Chartist riots 204
Chatterton, Thomas 189
Chaucer, Geoffrey 86, 99, 301
Cheapside 90
Chelsea 86, 261
Chelsea Embankment 55, 58
Chelsea F.C. 261
Chesham station 262
Chesterton, G. K. 203, 366
Chief Commoner of the Court 117
Chiswick 57, 353
chloroform of lime 46
cholera 56, 192, 238, 289
Christ Church, Spitalfields 65
Christie's 227
Churchill, Sir Winston 107, 325–335
Circle Line 9, 243, 262, 288–289, 366
Citadels 325, 336
Citadels 336
City and South London Railway
    263–265, 270
City of London and Southwark Subway
    264
City of London boundary 31
City of London Freemen's School 77,
    104–105
City of London School for Girls 117
City Road 282
Civil Contingency Unit 157
civil defence field control room 355
Clapham Common deep-level shelter 270

Clapham Common station 265
Clapham North deep-level shelter 270–272
Clapham railway accident 287
Clapham South deep-level shelter 270, 271
Clapton 345
Clare, Earl of 251
Clark, Alan 227
Clark, Josiah Latimer 297
Classicus 68
claustrophobia 7
clay 25, 365
Clay, Sir William 246–247
Clayton, Antony 332
Clayton, Lucy 228–229
Clerk of the Chamberlain's Court 129
Clerkenwell 32, 38
Clerkenwell gaol 296
Clive Steps 326
cloaca 47
Cobra 156–157, 324
Coburg Street control room 274
cock fighting 152, 156
Cock Tavern 290–291
Cockpit Passage 152, 155, 156
Coke, Sir Edward 189
Colchester 67
Cold War 100, 313–321, 323–324
Coleridge, Samuel Taylor 365
Colliers Wood 115
Colliers Wood station 110, 115
Collins, Lottie 234
Colville, John 335
Commissioners of Sewers 48
Comptroller of Customs and Subsidies of Wools, Skins and Hides 99
condensing engines 258–259
Conference Room A 154–155, 315
congestion charge 306
Coombe Springs 138
Cornhill 73, 138
Coronation chair 122
Counter's Creek 29
Court of Common Council 115–118
Court of Common Council 105, 108, 115–118, 122, 127–128
Court of Hustings 194
Covent Garden 91
Covent Garden station 281
Craig's Court 317
Craigmore, MV 98
'crawlway' 162

Cressfield Close 35
cricket nets 325
Cricklewood 4, 22–23, 366–367
Cripplegate 68, 138, 258
Cromwell, Oliver 150, 188
Crossness 57–58
Crossrail 367
crown-jewels 20
Crown Passage 206
Croydon 313
Crystal Palace Park 298
Cubitt Street 307
Curl, James Stevens 239–240
Curzon Street 325
Customs and Excise 86, 98–100, 301
Customs House 96–100
'cut and dried' 78
cut-and-cover 257–258
Cutlers Company 194
Cyprus station 255

Daily Mirror 180
Dalston 54
Dante 44, 218
Darent, River 351
Dartford 351, 368
Davidson, Emily 164
De Cardinal Artu 135
de Grey, Walter 149
de Lacalle, Juan Carlos Lopez 212
de Worde, Wynkyn 30
Dead Dog Basin 36, 226
dead dogs 36
dead stations see disused Underground stations
Death Line 21
decompression chamber 368
Defoe, Daniel 52, 177, 195–196
Department of Culture, Media and Sport 314
Department of Education and Science 325
Department of Environment 325
Deptford 57
Description of a City Shower, A 35
Dickens, Charles 71, 179–180, 189–190, 192, 258
Die Another Day 20
Diocese of London 183
Director's Cut, The 288
Disraeli, Benjamin 46, 107
Dissenters' Chapel 233, 235, 245

dissolution of the monasteries 113
District Line 262, 276, 286, 288–289
disused Underground stations 13, 76, 189, 263–265, 281–285, 327–328
Divine Comedy 44, 218
'Doc, The' 185–186
'dock, the' 329
Docklands 353
Docklands Light Railway 40–41
Docquets for the Hospital Seal 117
Doctor Who 271
'Doctors, Diseases and Death' 95–96
Dodd, Ken 305
dog fights 51
Doggett's Race 93–94
Dollis Hill 332–335
Dome, The 344
Donne, John 192
Dorchester 64, 197
Dorchester Hotel 269
Dorian 55
Down and Out in Paris and London 87
Down Street station 327–328
Downing Street 146–147, 156, 316, 324, 328
Doyle, Richard 345
dragons 165
'Drain, the' 263
drains 19
dramatic crime on the Underground 276, 288–289
Draper, Charles 345–346
Drones Club 205
dropsy 144
Drummond Street 297
Drury Lane 196, 354
Duke of York Steps 316–317
Dunciad 35–36
Dunstan, St 120
Durham, Bishop of 92–93
Dury, Ian 192

Eagle Wharf Road 64, 66
Earl's Court 262
Earl's Sluice 29
early-warning beacons 363
East London Line 226, 229, 263
East Saxon 87
Eastern Avenue 311
Eastern Counties Railway 226–227
Edgware Road 299
Edgware Road station 260

Edward the Confessor, King 118, 120–121, 162, 167
Edward I, King 97, 122–123, 126, 138, 149, 167
Edward II, King 167
Edward III, King 123, 125–126, 194
Edward IV, King 120
Edward VI, King 181
Edward VII, King 264, 354
eels 29, 141
effigies 124–127
Effra, River 29, 114, 270
Eiffel tower 262
Eisenhower, General D D 270–271
Elephant Man's hat 15
Elgin Marbles 304
Eleanor of Castile, Queen 122–123
Elizabeth I, Queen 48, 153, 189, 363
Elizabeth II, Queen 51, 206, 316,
Elizabeth, Queen, the Queen Mother 338
Elstree aerodrome 4
Eltham 145
embalming 125
Empire Windrush 271
'energy line' 87
English Druidical Order 87
English Heritage 229, 233, 314
Enigma machine 300, 332
Environment Agency, The 345, 348, 351, 353
Epsom Derby 164
Erith Marshes 58
escalator fires 287
Euston 297–298
Euston Road 41, 256–257, 298
Euston station 256, 261, 274, 297, 323,
Evelyn, John 48–49
Evening Standard, The 11, 208, 229
Eversholt Street 297
exhumations 178–200
exploding coffins 248–249

Falcon, River 29
Farringdon 192
Farringdon Lane 38
Farringdon station 257, 258, 367
Farringdon Street 192, 257
Fast Show, The 352
Father Neptune 260
Father Thames bust 29
Fawkes, Guy 161, 166, 168–169, 189, 247, 264

Felixstowe 98
female gladiator 82
Fenchurch Street station 256
Finchley Road station 281
Finney, Albert 56
fires
  60 AD 67, 90
  1666 Great Fire 31, 49, 97, 128, 192,
  1698: 147, 153
  1715: 97
  1814: 97
  1834: 161, 168
  Customs House 97
Flask Walk 34
Flaubert, Gustave 255
fleet 33
Fleet Bridge 31–32
Fleet Lane 31
Fleet Primary School 34–35
Fleet Prison 192
Fleet Road 35
Fleet sewer 257
Fleet Street 30, 222, 307, 324
Fleet valley 32–34, 307
Fleet, River 29, 30–39, 96, 191–192,
  195, 257, 296, 365
Flood 345, 349
floodgates 275, 283, 344
floods 80, 343–345, 353
fluffers 274–275
flushers 40–47, 50–51, 55, 58–59
flushers' walk 53
Ford, Ford Maddox ix, 15, 206, 260
foul drainage 42
Four Weddings and a Funeral 33
Fox, Charles James 135, 209–210
Foy, Tom 236
Frampton, Michael 305
Freedom of the City of London 103–108,
  115–118, 127–130
Freedoms, types 107–108
Freeman of the Corporation of London
  178
Freemen of England and Wales 128
Freud, Sigmund 17
Friends of the Kensal Green Cemetery
  240–252
frightening the horses 19
Fulham 353
Fulham Road 261
Fumifugium 49
Future Fibres 227–228

garderobes 141
gas-monitoring device 53
gasometers 37–38
Gaudi 122
General Cemetery of All Souls 233–252
General Post Office 297–298
General Strike 1926: 299
Gentleman's Magazine 32
George III, King 154, 206, 210
George IV, King 210, 324
George VI, King 333
'ghosters' 301
ghosts 149, 280–282
Giant of Holborn, the 198
Gilbert, Sheriff 111
Gladiator 81
Glancey, Jonathan 16
Gloucester Road station 288
Goddess beauty salon 35
gold leaf 64
golden jubilee celebrations 51
Golders Green station 285
Goldfinger 222
Goldsmiths' Hall 51
gong-fermors 46–47, 50
Goodge Street deep-level shelter 270–271
Goodge Street station 260, 287
Goodwin, Francis 238
Goon Show 313
government tunnels 315–317, 323–326,
  335–340
Gowman, Alice 117
Gracechurch Street 72–74
Grand National Cemetery 238
Grand Union Canal 234, 240
grave-robbing 190–191, 246
graveyards 19
Gray's Inn Road 38, 188
greasers 277
Great Bear, The 11
Great Close tennis courts 151–152, 155
Great Conduit 90
Great Custom 97
Great Dover Street 82
Great Eastern Railway 227
Great Fire 1666: 31, 49, 97, 128, 192,
Great George Street 326
Great Ormond Street Hospital 366
Great Plague 52, 195
Great Portland Street station 259
Great Scotland Yard 298
Great Stink of London 46, 56, 162

Great Stink of London, The 46
Great Wen 49
Great Western Hotel 257
Great Western Railway 256
Greater London Council 29, 355
Greathead Shield 263
Greathead, James 263
Green Park 328
Green Park station 327–328
Green, Betty 329
Green, Leslie 328
Greene, Graham 59
Greenwich 145
Greenwich Observatory 345
Greenwich Park 344
griffins 165
Grimes, William 70–72, 88
Guardian, The 225
Guggenheim Museum 349
Guild Church Council 183
Guildhall 74–82, 103–108
Guildhall Art Gallery 74–82
Guildhall crypt 77, 103, 105, 128
Guildhall Yard 77, 104
Gulf War, Second 157
gunpowder 48
gunpowder plot 161, 166, 168–169, 189, 264
Guy's Hospital 197–198

Hackett, John 188
Hackney 57, 64
Hadley, Stephen 125–126
Hadrian's Wall 67
hairdresser's 72–74
Halliday, Stephen 46
Hallowe'en 21
'Hammer of the Scots' 122
hammerbeam roof 167
Hampstead 32, 57, 115, 188
Hampstead Heath 34, 257, 285
Hampstead Road 297
Hampstead station 285
Hampstead station lifts 364
Hampton 361
Hampton Court conduit 139–140
Hampton Court culverts 133–146
Hampton Court Hotel 64
Hampton Court Palace 133–140, 361
Hampton Court sewers 133–145
Hanson, Tod 18, 343
'Hardy Tree, The' 37

Hardy, Thomas 37
Harley Street 368
Harper, Lord Mayor 138–139
Harrow 243
Harrow on the Hill station 262
Harvey Nichol's 178
Hatters Company 194
Hatton Garden 180, 220, 223
Hatton Garden Safety Deposit 223–224
Haussman, Baron 204
Hawksmoor, Nicholas 65, 264
Hazlitt, William 188
Heath, Edward 157
Heathrow Airport 142, 211, 367
Heaton Arms pub 363
'Heavy Hill' 191
Henry I, King 111
Henry III, King 47, 112, 121
Henry V, King 123, 126–127
Henry VI, King 112
Henry VII, King 127, 151
Henry VIII, King 113, 124, 134–146, 143, 167, 151–153, 168, 188, 206–207, 209, 315, 336
Herland, Hugh 167
heroin 98
Heseltine, Michael 89–90
Hiedler, Ludwig 212
High Court 229–230
High Holborn 297, 299, 324
High Street Kensington station 288–289
Highbury 138
Highgate Ponds 32
Hoare and Co., C 222
Hogsmill River 139
Holborn 90, 178–200, 297–298, 323, 354
Holborn Bridge 31
Holborn Circus 179–180, 191
Holborn Hill 71
Holborn station 282
Holborn tram station 354
Holborn Viaduct 38, 180, 191, 298
'Hole in the Ground' 328
Hole in the Wall, The 289
Holland Park 360, 361
Hollar, Wenceslaus 18
Holmes, Sherlock 260, 289
Honor Oak 363
Honor Oak reservoir 361–364
honorary Freedoms 107
Horseguards Parade 156, 325

Horseguards Road 326
Hospital of St James 194
Houdini 236
Houndsditch 36
House of Kings 122
Household Cavalry 146
Houses of Parliament 161–173, 270 *and
    see* Palace of Westminster
Hoxton 236
Hubbard, Sue 18
Hume, Cardinal Basil 111
Hungerford Bridge 58
Hutchinson, Maxwell 11–12
Hyde Park Corner station 327–328
hygiene 47–59, 195

ICA 316, 317, 324, 329
Ilford 191, 199
Ilissus, Temple of 233
Illustrated London News 220, 297
Imagined Londons 14
Imperial War Museum 327
'in the room of' 117
'Inspector Down Pour' 347
'Inspector Sands' 277, 287
intercept sewers 57
interventions 89
Invisible Cities 364
IRA 154–155, 157, 165, 276, 315
Iranian embassy siege 157
Isle of Wight railways 313
Islington 139
Islip Chantry 127
Ismay, General Hastings 329

Jack Straw's Castle 285
Jackson, Mick 52, 242–243
Jamaican immigrants 271
James I, King 126, 147, 153, 168
jellyfish 29
Jenkins, David 92–93
Jerusalem 23
John, Elton 137
John, King 31, 97
Johnson, Dr 96
Jones, Inigo 147, 153
Jonson, Ben 120, 147
*Journal of Public Health and Sanitary
    Review* 45
Journal of the Plague Year, A 52,
    195
Jubilee Line 7, 9, 90, 265, 266, 280

'jugging it' 93
'jumper' 287

Kelly, Vincent 276
Kelvedon Hatch 313
Kempton Park racecourse 360, 364
Kendall, Henry 244
Kenditch, River 33
Kennington station 279
Kensal Green 57, 238–239
Kensal Green cemetery 233–252
Kensington 86, 288
Kent, Duchess of 69
Kent, William 153–154
Kentish Town 37
Kentish Town Road 35
Kew 361
Kilburn station 11
King 39
King Charles Street 326
King Edward Building 299, 304, 323
King Edward Street 323, 325
King George V docks 351
King of the City 113
King Street 150
King William Street station 263–265,
    276
King William Street tunnel 267
King's Council 167
King's Council Chamber and Treasury
    153–154
King's Cross
    Channel Tunnel rail link 37, 368
    Fleet River 32
    Post Office Railway 307
    Queen Boudicca 38
    station 256, 368
    Underground station 141–142,
        286
    Underground station fire 6, 287–288
King's Cross Road 38
King's Pictures 304
Kingston Bridge 139
Kingston Hill 138
Kingston-on-Thames 139
Kingsway 323–324, 354–355
Kingsway tram subway 354–359
Knights Hospitallers 31, 137
Knock John Channel 344
Knowledge, The 15
Kosovo 157
Kubla Khan 365

Ladbroke Grove 234
Lafayette 236–237
Lamb's Conduit Street 138
Lamb, Charles 188
Lamb, Mary 188
Lamb, Sir William 138
Lambeth Palace 145, 149
latrines 47–49
lavatory 330
Laystool Court 33
Laystool Street 33
Le Carré, John 301
Le Corbusier 8
Leadenhall Market 72–74
Lee, Laurie 249
Leicester Square 324
Leinster Gardens 259
Leno, Dan 234
leper colony 209
Lessing, Doris 9, 361, 362
Lewisham 363
Liberty's 110
licensed bars on the Underground 289
Lichfield, Bishop of 188
lierne 173
lifting business 191
light, absence of 4–5
liminality 75–76
Lincoln's Inn Fields 37
linen-armoury 180
Little Close tennis courts 151–152
Little Conduit 138
Little Queen Street 297
Little Venice 243
Liverpool Street station 227, 256, 299,
    367
Liverpool Street Underground station
    268, 289, 367
livery companies 106, 128–129
Livingstone, Ken 229, 306, 354
Lloyd George, David 285
Lloyd, Marie 236, 248
LMO number plate 94
Lobbs 205
location, location, location 114
Lombard Street 139
London
    iceberg comparison 15
    illimitable 15
    noblest builders 56
    paintings 18
    redevelopment in magpie fashion 68

sea port 29
sight unchanged for 100 years 55
sights not visited by Londoners 119
vertical city 16–18
London Archaeological Archive and
    Research Centre 63–65
London Bridge 18, 49, 67, 139, 197, 343
London Bridge station 256
London Bridge Underground station
    264–267, 273, 279, 344
London City airport 344
London Connection 4, 22–25, 366–367
London Daily News 180
London Electricity 4, 22–25
London Open House weekend 148, 152,
    157
'London over the Border' 66
London Under London 50
London Underground headquarters 261
London Underground Limited see The
    Underground
London Wall 67, 69, 71, 217, 299
London, Bishop of 193
London, Jack 66
Long Water 139
Loophole 56
Lord Mayors 77, 85, 91–92, 103, 116,
    138–139, 199
Lord's cricket ground 4
Lost Palace of Whitehall 146–157
Lost Palace of Whitehall, The 149
Lots Road power station 286
Loudon, John 238
Louis Napoleon 203–204
Lower Thames Street 96, 301
Lubienska, Countess Teresa 288
Ludgate 68
Lump's Pudding 148
Lurie, Peter 324

M25 17–18, 76, 359
Macaulay, Rose 9
Mace 168
Madame Jo-Jo's 43
Madeleine 261
Madonna 212
Megalosaurus 71
Maida Vale 323
Mail Rail 295–308
Major, John 315
Malcolm, Sir John 119
Malins, William 256–257

Mall, The 316, 325, 336
'man-rider' 25
Manchester-Paris Railway 262
Mandela, Nelson 107, 118
Manners, Captain 119
Manor House Hospital 285
Mansfield Road 35
Mansion House 32
Mansion House station 289
map of the Underground 11–14, 17, 204
Marble Arch station 269–270
Marine Colliery 24
Market Deeping 315
Marsden, William 188
Marsham Street 325
Martello Tower like entrances 270
Martin, Andrew 184–185
Marylebone Road 256–257
Master Carpenter's Court 136, 141
Maundy money 147
Maxwell, Glyn 58
Mayor of London 229, 306, 354
Mecca 337–338
medals corridor 163
Merantum Way 110, 114
Mercury, Freddie 240
Merton 109, 361
Merton Abbey 108–115, 124, 146
Merton Abbey Mills 109–115, 118–119, 226
Methodist Recorder, The 301
Metroland 262
Metropolitan Board of Works 56
Metropolitan Line 38, 257–262, 288–289, 297
Metropolitan Mixture 259
Metropolitan Railway Baker Street Station Buffet, The 289
MI5 56
midden 42
Midland Bank 222
milestones 138
Mill, John Stuart 287
Milton Keynes 244, 247
miners 3, 366–368
Minimal Disease Pig Unit 314
Ministry of Building & Public Works 271
Ministry of Defence 324, 336
Ministry of Defence building 147
Minto of Minto, Baron 120
Mithras 88–89
mobile telephones 10–11

mock battle 91
Model Parliament 167
model railway 325
'moist gamminess' 54
Monmouth, James Duke of 153
Monopoly 13
Monster Soup 46
Monteagle, Lord 169
Monument, The 18, 77
Moorcock, Michael 113
Moore, Henry 268
Moorgate accident 6–7, 287
Moorgate Underground station 6–7, 264, 287
Moriarty, The 289
Morning Star pub 363
Morris, William 109, 113, 115
Morrow, Hamish 19
mosquitoes on the Underground 141–142
Mount Etna 49
Mount Pleasant 33
Mount Pleasant Post Office depot 296, 299–308
Mountbatten, Lord Louis 185
Mountjoy, Christopher 216–217
mourning jewellery 246
Murder in the Cathedral 112
Murdoch, Iris 289
Museum of London 63, 68, 70–72, 90, 187, 298
Mussolini, Benito 339
Muswell Hill 177
My Fair Lady 64
Myddleton, Sir Hugh 139
Mysterious Death on the Underground Railway, The 288

Napoleon III, King of France 209
Napoleon of Notting Hill 203
Nash 56
National Grid 4
National Portrait Gallery 304
National Theatre 64, 166
Neave, Airey 165
Neckinger, River 29
Necropolis 184
Necropolis Railway, The 184–185
Nelson, Horatio 98, 107, 115, 125
Network housing association 334
never opened station on the Underground 285

Neville's Close 335
Neville's Inn 70–71
Neville, George 149
New Oxford Street 304, 354
New Palace Yard 166
New River 139
New River Head 139
Newcastle Close 38
Newgate 68
Newgate Street 191
Newson, Leslie 6–7
Nicholson and Griffin's 73
Night Mail 306
Nightingale, Florence 107
Niven, David 335
no storm in a port 213
Noble Street 70
Nonsuch Park 113, 146
North End station 285
Northern Ireland 100
Northern Line 108, 263, 265, 268, 270, 273–285, 311, 344
northern outfall sewer 41, 43, 45, 52–55, 57, 59, 135
Notting Hill Gate station 288–289

O'Hagan, Andrew 14
Office of Works building 328
Old Bailey 180
Old Palace Yard 168–169
Old Street station 279
Old Trodgon 156
Old York Place 150
Oliver Twist 179–180, 184, 192
Olympic Games 367
'on the floor' 287
'one-under' 287
Operation Foxley 340
Operation Pugwash 98
Oranges and Lemons 91
Orczy, Baroness 288
Orwell, George 51, 87
Our Mutual Friend 258
Oval 270, 345
Oxford Street 90, 299, 307
Oyster Row 189
Oystergate Walk 189
oysters 189
ozoning plants 260

Paddington 90, 299, 304
Paddington Hilton 257

Paddington station 256, 367
'Paddock' 332–335
pagers 10
Painted Chamber 167
Palace of Westminster 46, 161–173, 270, 343
Palace of Whitehall 146–157
Pall Mall 206
Paris 8, 261, 262, 366
Paris Metro 8, 261, 366
Park Lane 361
Parochial School 180
Pat-Mac's Drinking Den 289
patrimony Freedom 108
Patterson, Simon 11
Payne, Sylvia 255
peacocks 99
Pearsall, Phyllis 15
Pearson, Charles 256
Peck River 29
Peckham Rye 362
Peel, Robert 210
pen gun 100
People of the Abyss, The 66
Pepys, Samuel 47, 123, 124, 126, 153, 196–197, 222, 343
Perceval, Spencer 154
Percy, Thomas 168–169
'perpetual chicken' 243
Personality 14
Peter Jones store 30
Petrus restaurant 207–208
Phantom of the Opera, The 119
Piccadilly Circus 129
Piccadilly Circus station 255, 261
Piccadilly Line 142, 267–268, 282, 285, 286, 315, 327–328
Pickwick Papers, The 190
Piece of Cake café 289
pigs 32
Pike, David L. 14, 17
Pimlico 57
Piratin, Phil 269
Pitt the Younger 210
Pitt, William 119
plague 177–178
   664 AD 193
   1248: 193
   1347–1450: 193
   1665, the Great Plague 52, 195
plague pits 21, 177–178, 196
Plaistow station 288

plait of hair 224–225
plommers 140
Pneumatic Despatch Company 297–298
pneumatic railways 296–299
Podola, Gunther 288
Pool of London, The 18, 343
Pope, Alexander 35–36
population boom 49
Port of London Authority 92, 351
port-wine cellars 206
Portcullis House 165
Porter, Roy 56, 66, 106
Portland, 5th Duke of 242
Post Office telephone tunnels 323–326
Post Office Tower 324
Post Office Underground Railway
     295–308
Potter, Harry 332
Poultry 222
Poultry Avenue 290
Poundage 97
PPG16: 90
Pride of London, The 36
Primrose Hill 238
Pritchett, V. S. 86, 230
Privy Palace 145
protected species 99
public conveniences 47
Public Records Office 304
Pudding Mill Lane 40–41
Pudding Mill Lane station 40–41
pump-out shaft 360
Purbeck marble 112, 121–122
Purcell, Daniel 189
Purdy, Det Sgt Raymond 288
Purfleet 346
Putney 57, 346
Pyramid Cemetery for the Metropolis
     238–239

QEII Building 325
quaich 216
Queen Mary's Steps 147
Queenhithe 91
Queensbury, Marquess of 51
Queensway station stairs 364

radar station 313–321, 363
'ragged regiment' 127
ragstone blocks 68
Railtrack 229
Railway Gazette, The 268

rakers 47
Rammell, Thomas Webster 297–299
Ranelagh culvert and sewer 55, 315
Rathbone Place 299
rats 39–40, 50–52, 55–56, 193–194, 361
Ravensbourne, River 30
Ravensbrück concentration camp 288
real tennis 143, 150–153, 155, 206–207,
     315
receipt pinned to clothing 119
red water 33
Redbridge station 311, 313
redemption Freedom 108, 130
reflective wave 351
Regent's Canal 32, 35, 36, 64, 138, 226,
     261
Regent's Park 56, 361
Reigate stone 112
Renaissance 134–135
reservoirs 361–364
retiarius 74
Reynolds, Eric 114, 226, 227
Richard II, King 123
Richard the Raker 40, 47
Richmond 145
rings 23–24
Ripley, Thomas 97
Rochford, Lord 153
'Rogationtide' 91
Rogers of Riverside, Lord 229
rolling old ladies in barrels 192
Roman amphitheatre 74–82
Roman basilica 72–74
Roman ceramics 65–66
Roman fort 70–72, 216
Roman gatehouse 70
Roman London 365
Roman Londinium 66
Roman stockade 68
Roman temple 88–89, 120
Roman times 16
Roman wall 299
Roman wall in underground car park
     66–70
Roman waterfront 90
Rotherhithe station 263
Rowland Hill, Sir 296–297
Royal Albert Hall 361
Royal Chelsea Hospital 55
Royal Court Theatre 30
Royal Fine Art Commission building of
     the year 10

Royal Free Hospital 188
Royal Gallery Power Plant 171
Royal London Hospital 15, 366
Royal Naval Hospital 344
Royal Noor 92–94, 116
Royal Opera House 91
Royal School of Mines 321
royal tennis 143, 150–153, 155,
     206–207, 315
royal warrants 206
Royle, Nicholas 288
Rufus, William 167
Rules for the Conduct of Life 130
Rupert, Prince 31
Russell Square station 21, 366

Sacheverell, Henry 189, 190
Sadler's Wells 38
Sadler's Wells Theatre 139
safety-deposit vaults 218–225, 307
Saffron Hill 192
Sagrada Familia 122
Sainsbury's Savacentre 108, 112, 113
salmon 29
saltpetremen 48
Sanitary Act 1357: 48
SAS 339
Saudi Arabia, King of 338
Savoy Hotel 269
Saxon London 87–88, 90–91
Saxon well 91
scales for weighing people 209–210
Scarlet Pimpernel, The 288
school outings 77
schoolchildren 85, 92–96
Sclater Street 323
Scotland Yard 149
Scott, Ridley 81
'scriptures' 302
Self, Will 55
Selfridges 299, 330
Sellers, Peter 313
Semtex 100
servitude Freedom 107–108
Settle and Carlisle Railway 229
sewage ejectors 170–171, 270
sewer-going wardrobe 43
sewermen 21
sewers 19, 39–59, 133–146, 162
Sexy Beast 222
Shadwell 74, 82
Shaftesbury Avenue 354

Shakespeare, William 216–217
shard 65
Sheen, Martin 36
Sherwood, Ambassador 135
Shivering Sands 344
shooting range 162
Shoreditch High Street 227
Shoreditch station 227, 256
Sigsaly 330
Silent Highwayman, The 46
Silver Barracuda 92–93
Silver Street 216–217
silver vaults 215–218
Sinclair, Iain 16–18, 37, 76, 115, 291
singulares 71
Siren 312
sleepers 277–278
Sloane Square station 30, 289
smallpox innoculation 179
smells of London 42, 46, 53–55, 162,
     169–171, 173, 181–182, 260
smells of the Underground 260–261
Smith, Paul 19
Smith, Winston 51
Smithfield 257
Smithfield Bars 32
Smithfield market 289–291
smoking on Underground 287
Snow Hill 191–192
Snow Hill police station 291
Snow, Dr John 56
Soane, Sir John 37, 241
solitude of the Underground 8–9
Somerset House 29
Soul of London, The 260
South Bank 29, 75
South Kensington station 288
Southall 37
Southampton Row 355
Southampton, Earl of 188
southern outfall sewer 57–58
Southwark 74, 82, 86, 194
Southwark Bridge 91
Southwark station 10
Spark, Muriel 363
Speaker's Court 163
Spitalfields 65, 90, 227
St Albans 67
St Andrew Street 191
St Andrew's church, Holborn 178–200
St Bart's Hospital 290–291
St Bartholomew's church 258

St Bartholomew's Hospital 31
St Chad's Place 38
St Clement Danes church 91, 196
St Dunstan's College 92–96
St Dunstan-in-the-East 92
St George's Hospital 366
St Giles-in-the-Fields 196
St James's 205, 261
St James's church 199
St James's Palace 206, 209
St James's Park 326, 329
St James's Park station 261, 366
St James's Street 206–215
St John's Wood station 280
St Johns Wood 4, 10
St Martin's-in-the-Fields 196
St Martin's-le-Grand 297–298
St Mary Undercroft 164, 172–173
St Mary's Woolnoth church 264,
    269–270
St Pancras Old Church 37
St Pancras station 332, 367
St Pancras Wells 37
St Paul's 77
St Paul's Cathedral 38, 46, 125, 138,
    189, 270, 299, 323
St Peter's Cornhill church 73
St Philip's in the Tower church 91
St Stephen's Chapel 164, 167–168
stagecoach 64
stained-glass windows 128–130, 244
stalactites 246
Stamford Bridge 261
Stamford Brook 29
Standard Conduit 138
Standard, The 203
standards of length 106
Star Chamber Court 150, 162, 163
'Star Lane' 355
Statutes of Merton 112
Stephenson, Robert 257
Stepney 195
Stevenson, Robert Louis 207
Stock Exchange 77, 297
Stocks Market 32
Stockwell deep-level shelter 270
Stockwell station 263, 265
Stoke Newington 234
Stone of Scone 122
Storey Street 74
Storey's Gate 326
'storm charger' 170

Stow, John 31, 138–139, 216
Strand 91, 109, 281, 354
strap-hanging 260
Stratford 57
Stratford station 367
Streatham 255, 361
striations 65
Stuart bric-a-brac 65
submerged interest groups 235
Subterranea Britannica 22, 312–326,
    332–335, 336, 348, 363
Subterranean City 332
subterranean, fascination of 20
Suez crisis 271
Suffolk, Duke of 153
Sugar Quay 94
suicides on the Underground 286–287
Sullivan, Sir Arthur 64
Summer Boiler room 171
Sunk Head 344
Surbiton 361
surge tide 344
Survey of London [1598] 31
Sussex, Duke of 242
Sutton Hoo 321
Swift, Jonathan 35, 192
Swiss Cottage station 269
Swiss Cottager, The 269
Sydney Opera House 350

Tachbrook Street 55
Tacitus 67
tamkins 140
'tap, the' 302
Tate & Lyle depot 351
Tate Gallery 304
tax 67–68, 86, 97
taxi drivers 14, 15
Teesport 100
telephone cables tunnel 323–326
Temple station 366
Ten More Turnips from the Tip? 192
tennis courts 143, 150–153, 155,
    206–207, 315
Tennis Play 151
tenterhooks 78
terrace of Houses of Parliament 163
terrorism 100
terrorist attacks 8, 56
terrorist attacks on the Underground 8
Thames Barrier 46, 343–354
Thames Embankment 57

Thames Flood Act 1879: 345
Thames Flood Control 354–359
Thames Flood Engineering Control 356, 359
Thames Tunnel 263
Thames Water 275, 359–364
Thames Water ring main 359–361
Thames Water's Sewer Week 40–41
Thames, River
    pestilent 57
    power of 343–354
    reconquering London 39
    size 29
    straightened on map 14
    telephone tunnels 324
Thatcher, Margaret 90, 107
Thavie, Alice 180
Thavie, John 180–181, 188
The Times 217, 258
Theobald's Road 354, 355
Theydon Bois station 255
Third Man, The 59
Thomas Crown Affair, The 223
Thorney Island 120
Thrasyllus, Monument of 233
Thunderbirds 76, 241
Tilbury Ferry 351
Time Team 136
Time Vindicated to Himself and his Honours 147
Titanic, SS 210, 247
Told by an Idiot 9
tompions 140
Tooting Broadway station 366
'torpedo room' 170–171
toshers 50–51, 56
Tottenham Court Road 297, 298
Tottenham Court Road station 367
Totteridge and Whetstone station 255
Tourettes 96
Tower Hamlets 86
Tower Hill 68, 87
Tower Hill station 288
Tower of London 20, 146
Tower Ward 92
trade guilds 105–106
Trafalgar Square 317, 324
Trafalgar, Battle of 98
tram subway 354–359
transatlantic telephone 330
Transport for London 12
Treasury 324

Treasury Boardroom 154
Treasury Green 152
Treasury Passage 155–156
Tresham, Francis 168–169
Troughton & Simms 106
'Tube Cuthberts' 268
Tube experience 11–12
Tube see The Underground
Tudor Corridor 155
Tudor Passage 155
Tunnage 97
tunnellers 3, 21–22
Turin Shroud 127
Turnagain Lane 38
turntable 165
Turpin, Dick 363
Tyburn 90
Tyburn sewer 55–56
Tyburn, River 29, 257

Ultra codes 332
underground ballroom 242
underground car parks 66–70, 165
underground fortresses 325
underground London 14–15, 235
Underground Man, The 52, 242–243
underground railways
    Duke of Portland 243
    pneumatic railways 296–299
    Post Office 295–308
underground unhappiness 218
Underground, the 255–291
    accidents 6–7, 287–288
    Aldgate station 288, 366
    Aldwych branch 267–268
    Aldwych station 19–20, 281
    all stations in one day 11
    Amersham station 262
    Angel station 282–285
    Angle station escalators 364
    author as anxious traveller 5–8
    author as happy traveller 255
    Baker Street station 280, 289
    Bakerloo Line 285, 286, 287
    Balham station 269
    Bank station 263, 264, 269–270, 274, 278, 344
    Beck, Harry 11–14, 17, 204
    Belsize Park station 268
    Blackfriars station 366
    Bond Street station 367
    British Museum station 281–282

Underground, the – *cont*
  Bull and Bush station 285
  Central Line 7, 260, 268, 270,
    281–282, 299, 323, 367
  Chancery Lane station 12
  Charing Cross station 260, 285, 366
  Chesham station 262
  Circle Line 9, 243, 262, 288–289, 366
  City and South London Railway
    263–265, 270
  civic works project 11
  Clapham Common station 265
  Coburg Street control room 274
  Colliers Wood station 110, 115
  Covent Garden station 281
  cycle of life 366
  Cyprus station 255
  Death Line 21
  District Line 262, 276, 286, 288–289
  disused stations 13, 76, 189, 263–265,
    281–285, 327–328
  Docklands Light Railway 40–41
  Down Street station 327–328
  dramatic crime 276, 288–289
  East London Line 226, 229, 263
  Edgware Road station 260
  escalator fires 287
  Euston station 261, 274
  Farringdon station 257, 258, 367
  Finchley Road station 281
  first journey 12
  floodgates 275, 283, 344
  fluffers 274–275
  ghosts 280–282
  Gloucester Road station 288
  Golders Green station 285
  Goodge Street station 260, 287
  Green Park station 327–328
  Hampstead station 285
  Hampstead station lifts 364
  Harrow on the Hill station 262
  haven 11
  hidden parts 272–285
  High Court 229–230
  High Street Kensington station
    288–289
  Holborn station 282
  Hyde Park Corner station 327–328
  Isle of Wight 313
  journey to one's own life 366
  Jubilee Line 7, 9, 90, 265, 266, 280
  Kennington station 279
  Kilburn station 11
  King William Street station 263–265,
    276
  King William Street tunnel 267
  King's Cross fire 6, 287–288
  King's Cross station 141–142
  licensed bars 289
  Liverpool Street station 268, 289, 367
  London Bridge station 264–267, 273,
    279, 344
  London Underground Limited 12
  Lots Road power station 286
  Mansion House station 289
  map 11, 12–14, 17
  Marble Arch station 269–270
  Metropolitan Line 38, 257–262,
    288–289, 297
  Moorgate accident 6–7, 287
  Moorgate station 6–7, 264, 287
  mosquitoes 141–142
  Muswell Hill 177
  never opened station 285
  night shift 272–273
  North End station 285
  Northern Line 108, 263, 265, 268,
    270, 273–285, 311, 344
  Notting Hill Gate station 288–289
  Old Street station 279
  ozoning plants 260
  particular features 364
  patrolmen 273
  peaceful place 8
  perfume 261
  Piccadilly Circus station 255, 261
  Piccadilly Line 142, 267–268, 282,
    285, 286, 315, 327–328
  Plaistow station 288
  power switched off 272–273
  Pudding Mill Lane station 40–41
  Queensway station stairs 364
  real reasons for delays 20
  Redbridge station 311, 313
  Rotherhithe station 263
  Russell Square station 21, 366
  security 276–277
  shelters in World War II 13
  sleepers 277–278
  Sloane Square station 30, 289
  smells of 260–261
  solitude 8–9
  South Kensington station 288
  Southwark station 10

St James's Park station 261, 366
St John's Wood station 280
Stockwell station 263, 265
suicides 286–287
Swiss Cottage station 269
Temple station 366
terrorist attacks 8
Theydon Bois station 255
Tooting Broadway station 366
Tottenham Court Road station 367
Totteridge and Whetstone station 255
Tower Hill station 288
train stopped in tunnel 7
travelling singly 8–9
Tube experience 11–12
Victoria Line 315–316
Victoria station 366
violent death 276, 288
wallets 275
Wapping station 263
wartime incidents 269–270
wartime shelterers 265–270
Waterloo and City Line 263
Waterloo station 366
West Ham station 276
Westbourne Park station 11
Westminster station 366
Whitechapel station 366, 367
World War II 265–270
underspill position 347
underwater billiard table 286
underwear 228–229, 248
unimagined interest groups 235
Upper Street 138
Upper Thames Street 109
Uzi pistol 100

Vale of Hampstead 34
Vanity Fair 212
Vatican 167
Vatican City 305–306
Venice 64, 260
'verger-guided tour' 119
Vestiges of Old London 50
Victoria Embankment 58, 147, 262
Victoria Embankment Gardens 262
Victoria Line 315–316
Victoria station 256, 345, 366
Victorian Celebration of Death, The
    239–240
Victorian General Cemetery Company
    241

Victorian Society 41
Victorian voids 163
Vienna 59
Viking raids 91
Vile Bodies 289
Villiers monument 124
violent death on the Underground 276,
    288
viscera chest 251

Walbrook 29, 48, 49, 80, 89
Wallace Collection 304
wallets 275
Walton on Thames 361
Wandle, River 29, 96, 109–110, 114,
    115
Wandsworth 86
Wapping station 263
water closets 48–50
water gate 243–244
water wheel 139
Waterloo 298, 323, 324
Waterloo and City Line 263
Waterloo Bridge 355
Waterloo station 14, 18, 184–185, 256
Waterloo Underground station 366
Watkins, Sir Edward 262
Waugh, Evelyn 289
'we are all in the gutter...' 58
Webb, John 147
weighing people 209–210
Wellington, Duke of 107, 210
Welsby, Jack 11
Wembley 262
Wembley stadium 75, 262
WERHERE 87
West Ham station 276
West Hampstead 4
Westbourne Park station 11
Westbourne, River 29, 30, 257
Westminster 31, 353
Westminster Abbey 118–127, 167, 181
Westminster Abbey undercroft 124–127
Westminster, Abbot of 194
Westminster Bridge Road 185
Westminster Hall 167
Westminster Palace 145
Westminster School 127
Westminster station 366
whispering rushes 35
White Chamber 167
White Conduit Street 138

White Horse pub 363
White House 330
white witches 87
White's Club 261
Whitechapel 195
Whitechapel Road 299
Whitechapel station 366, 367
Whitehall 146–147, 150, 317, 324, 343
Whitehall Palace 146–157
Whitehall telephone exchange 317
Whittington, Dick 38, 51, 103, 105, 118
Who Wants to be a Millionaire? 78
Wick Lane 40, 41, 43, 46, 52, 57–59, 135
Wilde, Oscar 58
William IV, King 242
William the Conqueror, King 109, 120–121, 167
William, King and Queen Mary 144
Willis, Bruce 305
Willson, Thomas 238–239
Wimbledon 115, 345
Winchester 120
windmill power 261
Windsor Castle 151, 242
wine tastings 212–214
wine, expensive 207–208, 211
Winwith, Thomas 168–169
'within the stones' 66
Wittering aerodrome 314
Wizard of Oz, The 308
Wodehouse, P. G. 205
Woking 184–185
Wollstonecraft, Mary 37
Wolmar, Christian 13
Wolsey, Cardinal Thomas 133–146, 149, 361
women of dubious repute 144
Wong, Mr 267

Woolwich 196
Woolwich Ferry 351
Woolwich Reach 346–354
World War I 299, 304, 327
World War II
    air raids 88
    Cabinet War Rooms 326–335
    deep-level shelters 270–271
    enigma machines 300
    Guildhall 77, 128
    Kensal Green Cemetery 241, 244
    King Henry VII effigy 127
    River Effra 114
    St Andrew's Church 178–179, 182–183, 189
    St James's Street 210
    Underground stations as shelters 13, 265–270
Worshipful Company of Carmen 129
Worshipful Company of Fishmongers 94
Worshipful Company of Spectacle-Makers 129
Worshipful Company of Watermen 92–94
Wren, Sir Christopher 31, 49, 56, 96, 97, 180
Wright, John 168–169
Wright, Whitaker 286

X-ray spectacles 15–16
'X-ray' 330

yardsticks 106
Yellow Brick Road 308
Yeomen of the Guard 169
Yerkes, Charles 285–286
York Place 149–150
York, Archbishop of 149